LAURA

Uncovering Gender and Genre in Wyatt,

Donne, and Marvell

Post-Contemporary Interventions

Series Editors: Stanley Fish and Fredric Jameson

LAURA

Uncovering Gender and Genre in

Wyatt, Donne, and Marvell

Barbara L. Estrin

Duke University Press   Durham and London   1994

© 1994 Duke University Press
All rights reserved
Printed in the United States on acid-free paper ∞
Designed by Cherie Holma Westmoreland
Typeset in Pilgrim by Keystone Typesetting, Inc.
Library of Congress Cataloging-in-Publication Data
appear on the last printed page of this book.

Permission to quote from the following

is gratefully acknowledged

John Donne: The Elegies and Songs and Sonnets, ed. Helen Gardner (Oxford: Clarendon Press, 1965). By permission of Clarendon Press.

The Poems and Letters of Andrew Marvell, 3d ed., edited by H. H. Margoliouth, revised by Pierre Legouis and E. E. Duncan-Jones (Oxford: Clarendon Press, 1971). By permission of Clarendon Press.

The Petrarch quotations are reprinted by permission of the publishers from *Petrarch's Lyric Poems* by Robert M. Durling (Cambridge, Mass.: Harvard University Press, 1976). Copyright © by Robert M. Durling.

Sir Thomas Wyatt: The Complete Poems, ed. R. A. Rebholz (New Haven: Yale University Press, 1978). By permission of Penguin Books.

A substantial portion of the chapter on Marvell's "Nymph complaining for the death of Her Faun" was first delivered to the eighth Biennial Renaissance Conference at the University of Michigan–Dearborn and subsequently printed in the selected proceedings of that conference, *On the Celebrated and Neglected Poems of Andrew Marvell*, ed. Claude J. Summers and Ted-Larry Pebworth (Columbia: University of Missouri Press, 1992). Part of the first chapter on Wyatt was read at the MLA Convention in Chicago in 1990 and published in *Rethinking the Henrician Era*, ed. Peter Herman (Urbana: University of Illinois Press, 1994).

A very early version of the second Wyatt chapter appeared as "Becoming the Other / The Other Becoming: Transformation in Wyatt's Poetry," *ELH* 51 (1984): 431–45. Preliminary versions of the Donne chapters were published as "Baring the 'I' and Bearing the 'You': Donne's Elegy, 'Change,' and 'A Valediction of My Name in the Window,'" *Texas Studies in Literature and Language* 30 (1988): 345–62; and "Donne's Injured 'I': Defections from Petrarchan and Spenserian Poetics," *Philological Quarterly* 66 (1987): 175–93.

I am grateful to the editors of those articles for their help at the time of the original printing and for permission to reprint here.

For Mark and Robin

CONTENTS

Acknowledgments   xi

Note on Editions   xiv

Introduction: Gender Performance and Genre Slippage   1

PETRARCH

Inverting the Order: Laura as Eve to Petrarch's Adam   41

"Like a Man Who Thinks and Weeps and Writes": Laura as
Mercury to Petrarch's Battus   61

WYATT

Taking Bread: Wyatt's Revenge in the Lyrics and Sustenance
in the Psalms   93

"Liking This": Telling Wyatt's Feelings   123

DONNE

Small Change: Defections from Petrarchan and Spenserian
Poetics   149

Sylvia Transformed: Returning Donne's Gifts   180

"A Pregnant Bank": Contracting and Abstracting the "You" in
Donne's "A Valediction of My Name in the Window" and
"Elegy: Change"   201

MARVELL

"Busie Companies of Men": Appropriations of Female Power in
"Damon the Mower" and "The Gallery"   227

CONTENTS

"Preparing for Longer Flight": Marvell's Nymph and the Revenge of
Silence   255

A-Mazing and A-Musing: After the Garden in
"Appleton House"   278

Musing Afterward   304

Notes   319
Index   341

ACKNOWLEDGMENTS

As a very small child, my favorite alternative self was the little boy in A. A. Milne's "Halfway Down the Stairs," the one who describes his psychological state in terms of an indeterminate location:

> Halfway down the stairs
> Is a stair
> Where I sit.
> There isn't any
> Other stair
> Quite like
> It.
>
> And all sorts of funny thoughts
> Run round my head:
> It isn't really
> Anywhere
> It's somewhere else
> Instead.

I'm not really sure why my German refugee mother chose the quintessentially British *When We Were Very Young* to read to me as she stuffed one more spoonful of lunch into my mouth. But from then on poetry became what Shakespeare's Leontes calls magic, "an art / Lawful as eating." It presupposed a way of being that included, among its other pleasures, a way of being "someplace else." In college and graduate school, where my childhood escape mechanism became the center of my working life, I was privileged to study with such finely tuned and imaginative readers as Alfred Fisher and Francis Murphy at Smith, Anne Ferry, David Kalstone, and Robert Lowell at Harvard, and Edwin Honig at Brown. I can still hear Murphy reading (with unflinching New England probing) Stevens's "The

Plain Sense of Things," or Lowell (with existential—and oddly Southern—questioning) "They flee from me," or Honig (with simultaneous mythic expansion and self-effacement) from his own *Four Springs*. The reading itself established an indelible link between the exhilaration of first hearing and the much later challenge of articulating my own response.

I was particularly lucky to have been in school at a time when poetry mattered and seemed necessary. It has become increasingly less important as literary criticism has gone the way of cultural studies. At the moment, the great lyric poets are routinely left out of college courses while dramatic or longer forms co-opt what little curricular time there is left for the Renaissance.

Working on this book, I was therefore "elsewhere" in terms of finding a marketable subject. But, more importantly, I was so often unavailing to my other lives. Being someplace else means not being somebody I also want to be. The subject of this book—the displacement of feeling by words—seems to have subjected me too. The anamorphic vision that I describe in *Laura* suggests that, for reader as well as writer, poetry is a competing obsession.

In that sense, I am lucky in, and indebted to, my family. Both my husband, Mark, and (now-grown) daughter, Robin, have tolerated and supported my being elsewhere to a degree far beyond what I deserved. And they have always let me—and on occasion pulled me—back in. I am lucky in my friends, too, particularly in the intelligence of Anne Putzel, with whom I can share my ambivalence about the isolation writing requires and the desire our lives impel to give ourselves more fully to those we love.

At Stonehill, where poetry courses still "go," I am fortunate in having students who always let me try out my ideas and colleagues—especially Chet Raymo and Fr. Robert J. Kruse, C.S.C.—from whom I invariably receive sympathetic encouragement. The Stonehill Dean's Office supported this project more materially: through a sabbatical leave, summer grants and, under Fr. Louis Manzo, C.S.C., a publishing grant which funded the illustrations.

Among those less local, but no less collegial, scholars who have made contributions to this book are an Americanist, Jackson R. Bryer, and, in the Renaissance, Peter Herman and Bill Readings, who introduced me, in very different ways, to the value of theory.

I have been helped in my research by the resources and quiet spaces of the Rockefeller Library of Brown University in Providence and the British

Library in London and by the resourcefulness of the Stonehill librarians, specifically Eden Fergusson and Ed Hynes, who answered my requests for information without ever trivializing them.

I am grateful to Reynolds Smith at Duke for believing in *Laura* from the start and for guiding it through its various stages. I thank him also for finding the two readers whose imaginative engagement and stimulating questions made this a stronger book. The critical acumen of Marie Blanchard and Pam Morrison of the Duke editorial staff provided many creative emendations.

Tess Hoffmann, Anne and Ernst Lieben, and Ella and Fred Scheuer are remembered in these pages. Clara and Abe Estrin, Charles Hoffmann, and Carolyn Sherman are part of this book, too. But mostly present is Mark Estrin, who listened to my early tentative ideas, read through various drafts, and proofed the last version. At all stages, he was there to react from the perspective of his own expertise and to set me thinking anew. First and last, Mark and Robin have given me the kind of enabling love that makes all things possible and that matters most. *Laura* is for them.

B. L. E.

Note on Editions

Quotations are from the following editions:

Petrarch's Lyric Poems
Edited and translated by Robert Durling. Cambridge:
Harvard University Press, 1976.

Sir Thomas Wyatt: The Complete Poems
Edited by R. A. Rebholz. New Haven: Yale University Press, 1978.

John Donne: The Elegies and Songs and Sonnets
Edited by Helen Gardner. Oxford: Clarendon Press, 1965.

The Poems and Letters of Andrew Marvell, 3d ed
Edited by H. H. Margoliouth, revised by Pierre Legouis and
E. E. Duncan-Jones. Oxford: Clarendon Press, 1971.

INTRODUCTION

Gender Performance and Genre Slippage

What need'st thou have more covering than a man?

John Donne, "To his Mistris Going to Bed"

"Ey'd Awry": Reading Backward from the Gesture

The wallcard at the National Gallery in London for the mid-sixteenth-century painting by Paris Bordone called "A Pair of Lovers" reveals some critical uncertainty about its title. The source of that uncertainty is related to a subject this book explores: the multiplicity of gender positions and genre constructs that surface once we stop to think about what the woman—centralized in the painting and in Petrarchan poetry—is doing. What the woman does depends upon which story she's in. Usually connected to the titular heroes of the ancient Greek pastoral romance, *Daphnis and Chloë*, Bordone's painting might as easily be a depiction of "Petrarch and Laura," the central players in the early modern poetic sequence known as the *Rime sparse*. The latter source comes to mind not so much because pairs of lovers immediately bring to mind other pairs, and certainly not because Petrarch and Laura are ever seen on quite such familiar terms with each other, but because of the disruptive presence of Cupid at the viewer's right. Drawing the eye away from the lovers, he troubles the story. Why does the winged boy place a laurel wreath around Daphnis's head, when laurels are the consolation prize for thwarted desire? A pair of lovers signified—as are Daphnis and Chloë—by their determination to love is confounded in the painting by a figuration that instead suggests a plot about a central unwillingness to love—as with Petrarch and Laura. The questions about gender and genre provoked by the Bordone painting (figure 1) anticipate ones that the present volume will later ask about the

Figure 1. "A Pair of Lovers," by Paris Bordone, ca. 1545.
Copyright © 1993, The National Gallery, London.
Reproduced by permission.

several pairs of lovers and different layers of experience implicated in Petrarchan poems.

In adopting for his subject a pronouncedly literary (as opposed to mythological) pair,[1] Bordone presumes a familiarity with conventional forms of written representation. But whose representation? The painting mixes literary genres—confusing the lyric poetry sequence celebrating female unavailability[2] with the narrative of a pastoral romance commemorating female accessibility. It also, thereby, mixes sexual genders, setting the libidinal openness of Longus's story against the restrictive binarisms of the Petrarchan ethos. Longus's romance chronicles a lost child plot. As supposed shepherds, Daphnis and Chloë discover their mutual feelings and only at the end learn that they are royal scions. Though they love, they do not know how to *make* love. Chloë transpires with desire but cannot figure out what to do with her feelings.[3] Laura, on the other hand, is knowledgeable enough but doesn't want to say yes. Her lineage is Petrarch's invention. She acquires her pedigree—angel, saint, goddess—because Petrarch's ardor confers it on her.

The puzzle about the painting suggests not just that Bordone was confused about iconography but that the generic framework upon which he builds isn't as stable as we think it is. While the painting implies that the woman may have two faces (Chloë or Laura), this study maintains that Petrarch's Laura herself may have had three: Laura-Daphne; Laura-Eve; and Laura-Mercury. For each of the women there is a corresponding poet: Petrarch-Apollo; Petrarch-Adam; and Petrarch-Battus. The biblical and mythological names parallel Petrarch's own personae as they surface at different moments in the lyric sequence. *Laura: Uncovering Gender and Genre in Wyatt, Donne, and Marvell* first sketches the tripartite woman and tripartite poet as she appears in the *Rime sparse* and then chronicles her emergence in the work of Renaissance poets who followed in the tradition. The possibilities for new interpretations of gender that arise from such splittings connect to the sense of generic instability the Bordone painting illustrates.

But while the painting shifts *between* two widely different genres, a Petrarchan poem splits its vision *within* the supposedly immutable lyric dyad. Depending on where we stand and how we look, the poem yields different scenarios so that the subject position of the viewer as well as the creator of given cultural signs seems to produce an aporia. A genre is not a fixed construct; rather it generates permeable forms even as the forms provide a focus around which amorphous feeling can be turned into art.

3

Like gender, genre both resists essentializing and comes close to defining an essential nature of experience. *Laura* is a study of Lauras and therefore a study of the consequent—or antecedent—Petrarchs that were formed by—or alternately were the inventors of—her. In the context of this generic aporia, Bordone's painting appears as a psychological perception test, sliding between the rabbit-configuration of Petrarchan denied romance, with Cupid as the child fathering Daphnis-Petrarch, and the duck-configuration of future fulfilled romance, with Chloë as initiator of erotic touching. Either Petrarch will turn inward and concentrate (as Sara Sturm-Maddox and Nancy Vickers claim he does anyway)[4] on shoring up his poetic crown or Daphnis will face Chloë and at last reflect, in mutual gaze, her desire.

The disputed title in the Bordone painting graphically depicts what Jean-François Lyotard calls the anamorphic—or overlapping—space in vision. Since this study relies on an anamorphic reading of auditory signs, and since the Bordone painting provides such a good example of the relation of gender position to literary genre, Lyotard's definition of the imbricated visual space provides a useful starting point for discussing the contradictory images produced by poem and painting: "The play of two imbricated spaces forms the principle of the anamorphic picture: what is recognizable in one space is not recognizable in the other. The good form of representation is deconstructed by bad forms: the skull in Holbein's picture, in the portrait of Charles I."[5] Explaining anamorphism as a psychological (as well as an optical) phenomenon, Lyotard refers to Bushy's attempt to calm the alarmed queen in Shakespeare's *Richard II:*

> For sorrow's eye, glazed with blinding tears
> Divides one thing entire to many objects,
> Like perspectives, which, rightly gaz'd upon,
> Show nothing but confusion; ey'd awry
> Distinguish form. (2.2.17–21)[6]

When he dismisses her premonitions, Bushy maintains that the queen regards events with "false sorrow's eye / which for things true weeps things imaginary" (2.2.26–27). Yet his comfort is itself disquieting. "Right gazing" yields confusion. To witness life with an "awry eye" is to find what, on straight view, isn't visible. To "go wrong" is, then, to "go right" just as the perceptive viewer of the most widely known example of anamorphism, Holbein's *Ambassadors*, understands that death is "structural,"[7] an inescapable part of the scene and an inevitable undoer of the composition.

To read anamorphically is to see the world with a sense that one thing has many parts and multiple layers and that the perceiving subject is itself "multilayered." Anamorphism depends on how the viewer shifts positions. But the anamorphism in the Bordone painting is different from that of the Holbein painting. In *The Ambassadors*, the painter deliberately places a puzzling image—looking something like a windshaft or a painterly mistake—to force the viewer into Holbein's philosophy.

In the Bordone painting, it is not a visual disturbance that draws the mind in; the irregularity is literary. Something about the iconography is off. The characters in the painting seem about to decide their own destiny even as the viewer determines who they are. In its sense of imminence, the Bordone painting suggests another painting, as if the problem will be solved when a different frame comes into view. With respect to the expectations it generates, the Bordone painting is like the first screen or "window" of a postmodern hypertext, where, as Robert Coover writes, "any one text space may be linked to any number of text spaces, the range of choices being created by the author with the choice of which link to take being generally left up to the reader."[8] The lyric poetic sequence might similarly be called a hypertext since the narrative changes as the reader ranges through, and rearranges, the poems, realigning them for different readings. Like that of a single Petrarchan poem, the anamorphism in the Bordone painting suggests a range of choices without actually following through on any of them. Another image would solve the dilemma by making a narrative decision. But, in the configuration of the painting we have, the stories unravel each other. We cannot read both images simultaneously. Conditioned by cultural experience with texts that emerge as mutually exclusive, the viewer brings the divided eye to the Bordone painting as one image pulls at, and detracts from, the other.

Everything depends on how the woman expresses her desire or how the viewer iconographically reads the links. If the scene belongs to Daphnis and Chloë, then the lovers will eventually consummate their love; if it belongs to Petrarch and Laura, their mutuality remains in peril. The "many objects" that confuse the viewer are generated by the "multiplicities of gender position"[9] that a given text can evoke. The effect of anamorphism resembles what Walter Benjamin calls the camera-eye focus: "The enlargement of a snapshot does not simply render more precise what in any case was visible though unclear: it reveals entirely new structural formations of the subject."[10] Like a Petrarchan poem, anamorphic painting consciously uses—and therefore accounts for—the unconscious as part of the field of vision. Alive with the evocative potential for change contained by the unacknowledged subjectivities it represents, the Bordone painting suggests both a fissured subject and multiple objects of desire. The "desired" in one story is the "desirer" in another. The possibility of divided stories, in turn, brings in another dimension—the possibility of a divided desirer and the undercurrent of ambivalence. If *The Ambassadors* refers to death as an external divider, the Bordone painting emphasizes inward division. Whereas in the hypertext "schematic overviews permit the author to see the entire webwork of established links" ("Hyperfiction," p. 8), in the Bordone painting the webwork remains unspecified and the links are held in abeyance. The hypertext builds the picture. The past can usually be retrieved. Anamorphism splits the picture. One reading casts doubts on the other, producing, in Benjamin's terms, "an unconsciously penetrated space" ("The Work of Art," p. 236). Yet the excitement of the Bordone painting stems from the sense that something is about to happen—something that depends on the woman's desire. What the woman does (the story as genre) depends on what the woman wants (the body as gendered). This oscillating visual frame parallels the movable auditory filter *Laura* uses to describe the differences that occur when the signs of the Petrarchan poem are read to suggest that the woman might be the uncoverer who subverts what Lyotard calls "the good form of representation."

The subversion in the Bordone painting—the sense that (like the hypertext) it presumes another painting where the issues it raises might be resolved and the sense that its foregrounded scene suggests other scenarios which take place simultaneously and which might even contradict the apparent one—parallels the imbrication in a Petrarchan poem. Like the painting, the Petrarchan poem reveals both the multiple implications of gesture and the ambiguous sources of inspiration that determine (and sometimes unravel) a generic or gender position thought to be immutable: (1) in each Petrarchan poem is the hypertext possibility—another poem will solve the dilemma the present poem reveals; (2) in each Petrarchan poem is the anamorphic possibility—a given gesture is itself ambiguous and presupposes the erasure of a counter-gesture its generic categories only seem to preclude.

Within the anamorphic frame, even gestures overlap. The eye follows contradictory images as it moves about the Bordone picture—first the circle formed by the lovers' arms, circles repeated again in Chloë's bare breasts, and yet again at their center, culminating in the pivotal curve of the lovers' heads—each about to turn around in another direction. Then the viewer's eye moves toward Cupid's wreath, as the circles tend to erase each other, preparing for the woman's annealment in the Petrarchan poem. The rings around the woman emphasize the loci of her sexual pleasure. The ring around the man accents the sublimation of pleasure—and the annihilation of the woman's body. It's all in the man's head. If the picture becomes Cupid's story, then the lovers are bound to separate. If Chloë prevails, they will turn toward each other and complete the story Longus tells. To define gender in the painting is to read the circles. Cupid's is a noose. It pulls toward closure. Not quite complete, Chloë's circle suggests indeterminacy. The gender of the gesturer is, as Luce Irigaray argues about Freudian dynamics, essential to meaning. Gender theory defines the difference in the rings by setting them against each other. The male patriarchal ring counters the female open form. The painting reveals the same notion of performative gender contained in a Petrarchan poem and uncovered by an analysis of the imbricated meaning of gesture.

As noose, Cupid's gesture is the tail end of the masculine reel Freud describes in the *fort-da* construction for mastering the mother's absence. Freud's little Ernst, as Irigaray describes him, "cannot be a girl. . . . [He] throws the reel away from him, hides it and then draws it back toward him, saying o-o-o-o and da, meaning *fort* and *da*."[11] With the reel he hooks his mother, just as, with the laurel leaves woven into a crown, Petrarch turns the elusive Daphne of the *Rime sparse* into a form he can master and a poem that celebrates his mastery. Through art, Petrarch gives himself the body that life denies him. Little Cupid, signifier of failed love, draws the inescapable circle of Petrarchan form, which, in his story, Petrarch will pursue. But the other circle, the one circumscribed by Chloë, is incomplete. The Bordone painting suggests that the woman determines which story reigns. If the woman's left hand draws Daphnis's body in toward her sexual center, then we read Longus's story. If her hand repels the man, then she is Laura in the Petrarchan ethos.

But what about her right hand? With it, Chloë holds the pipe that Daphnis made for her. Unlike Petrarch, who sought to still Laura's voice, Daphnis taught Chloë to play on it and, correcting her mistakes, "ran his lips over the pipe . . . to get a chance to kiss her by proxy, kissing the flute in places where it had left her mouth," repeating in fact Chloë's very ruse just a bit earlier.[12] In *Daphnis and Chloë*, both lovers express, and then approximate, their desire in music. In the main plot of the *Rime sparse*, only Petrarch is allowed the imaginative consolation of art. The Bordone painting opens up yet another layer of consideration for irregular viewing *Laura* takes up: does the woman have access to the expressive freedom signified by the pipe? Does the usual truism of women's objectification by art need to be rethought? Or is Bordone inventing something that is not part of the original dyad? What is clear from the left hand scenarios is that both Laura and Chloë control the scene of desire. Still to be examined in the right hand perspective is whether the woman's bodily initiative signals a mind leap as well. Does her desire—like the man's—express a need for expressiveness? Does the pipe open up yet another story, one that splits its subjects and subjectivities yet again to open up still other layers of experience?

In bodily terms, the Chloë of the Bordone painting invites Daphnis into the sphere of her erotic pleasure and therefore connects her sense of self to his, just as the excited Chloë in Longus's romance cannot tell the difference between her body and Daphnis's body. Longus describes Chloë's heterosexual awakening as a function of her masturbatory pleasure. She does not yet know what she wants, since the distance between self and other is not measurable: "She washed his back and shoulders and in washing his skin it seemed so fine and soft that more than once, without his perceiving it, she touched herself, for she was in doubt which of the two bodies was the finer" (p. 17). Chloë's uncertainty centers on a subtlety of feeling, on attuning to fine tuning: "she was in doubt which of the two bodies was the finer." Her tentative probings are the woman's gesture, as Irigaray defines it:

> The girl describes a circle both inviting and refusing access to the territory thus inscribed. She plays with this gestural territory and its limits. There, there is no object strictly speaking, nor a necessarily introjected, incorporated other. . . . Graphic examples of the form of such territories are given by Jung. He compares them to Tibetan mandalas. In these drawings, it also seems that the girl or woman does not call the other back, as does Ernst with his reel; rather she calls the other and plays with the frontiers of access to a territory in which she stays.[13]

Representing what the woman wants, the Chloë circle, in Jessica Benjamin's words, "forms a boundary and opens up into endless possibility; it evokes a particular kind of holding, similar to the first bodily holding by the mother."[14] As Daphnis and Chloë, the Bordone lovers cradle each other, enabling the Irigaray circle and presaging the endless possibility

Jessica Benjamin describes as female desire. As Petrarch and Laura, the lovers—prompted by Laura's repulsion of Petrarch's advances—move into the line of Cupid's reel. In both readings, the woman comes first, changing the expected gender dynamics of Petrarchism as, in the Longus romance, Chloë is first to awaken to the permutations of desire and first to find the other as source of sexual pleasure in the self. In both configurations of the Bordone painting, the woman is the problematic agent. If her fore-grounded left hand pulls Daphnis's hand in, then we have the Longus romance. If her controlling hand pushes Petrarch away, then we have the *Rime sparse*. The woman's gesture will determine the genre of the story. And it is with regard to the conflation of narrative and desire that *Laura* will assess the relationship of women to their representations.

What is, perhaps, most interesting about the painting is its positioning of the woman as what Eve Sedgwick calls "a subject of consciousness,"[15] a subjectivity which Sedgwick maintains is denied the woman in Shake-speare's sonnets. Her "hand" will dictate the story the painting tells. In similarly reimagining the position of the woman in the poem, *Laura* views Petrarchism as a series of anamorphic representations imbricated by three principal spaces: the main plot, with Laura as Daphne—or woman who denies sexuality; and the two subplots—with Laura as Eve, or woman who returns sexuality, and Laura as Mercury, or woman who invents her own life by escaping configuration altogether. The process of anamor-phosis, or adjusting the lens, involves redefining the position of the cor-responding Petrarch, as respectively: Apollo, whose sublimated desire becomes the poem; Adam, whose returned desire renders the poem super-fluous; and Battus, who, as victim of Laura-Mercury's rock punishment in *Rime sparse* 23, bears witness to his own ambivalence and the poem's undoing.

The imbricated space in the Bordone painting is turned three dimen-sional through a visual or horizontal reading. Move to the left and it's Longus's story; turn to the right and it's Petrarch's story. In the poetic arena, the disputed space produces an auditory three-dimensionality, overlapping counter-voices that threaten the central plot of Apollo-Daphne. If Laura-Eve seems somehow to be present (as she is in *Rime sparse* 237, 181, 188, and 354), then the poem has no point. Why write a complaint at all, if the woman is sexually willing? If Laura-Mercury surfaces, as she does in *Rime sparse* 23, 125, 126, 127, and 129, then the poem announces its inability to determine anything, largely because the woman in the poem declares her unknowability in the poet's realm of discourse and her ability to determine her own discursive locales. In spatial terms, Laura-Eve and Laura-Mercury threaten the very center of the Petrarchan ethos. Laura-Eve reverses the denial that fuels the poem. Laura-Mercury undoes the appropriations that bolster the poet. Uncovering the woman's resistance, Petrarch releases the uncovering Laura who evades the forms that contain her even as she projects other locations for the imagination. Once the originating poet imagines the imagining woman, she (in turn) proceeds to probe in directions not yet revealed by— but nevertheless implicit in—the original representation. *Laura* describes the difference in the anamorphic frame that occurs as we begin to explore the scenarios brought to the surface by the woman's self-affirming and poem-denying gestures. "Uncovering" that difference in early modern poems requires an interrogation similar to what Lyotard calls the process of "ana" for understanding the "post" in postmodernism: "a procedure of analysis, anamnesis, anagogy and anamorphosis that elaborates an 'initial forgetting.' "[16] With regard to a Petrarchan poem, the process of "ana" involves (as Donne puts it in "To his Mistris Going to Bed") roving "behind, before, above, between, below." Linking memory to desire, *Laura* will touch not only on what is said but on what was left unsaid and what, perhaps, cannot ever be said. If anagogy suggests the abstract—somewhere *above* and in the future—and anamnesis recalls the material— somewhere *below* or *behind* and in the past—there is also the anamorphic space *between* the two that remains radically undefined. In that contested *elsewhere*, we might begin to look for Laura.

Defining Other Lauras

Laura's "forgotten" space subverts the main plot of Petrarchism and accounts for what critics, like Joel Fineman, call its "characteristic nervousness."[17] The main plot of the *Canzoniere* repeats the constant of the lady's unremitting denial and the poet's persistent pursuit figured in the protracted elaboration of the Apollo-Daphne myth, the story of the god who pursued a woman until she turned into a laurel tree. Once he could no longer have Daphne in the flesh, Apollo had her—figuratively—in the songs he sang to mourn her loss. Folded over in that plot is the story of Laura-Eve, who threatens to invalidate the song, and the story of Laura-Mercury, who posits another song altogether even as she wills away the one she is in. In the first two chapters, *Laura* describes both how Petrarch embeds Laura-Eve and Laura-Mercury in the *Canzoniere* and how he struggles to recover himself as Apollo pursuing the original Daphne. The later chapters detail how the three Lauras complicate the Petrarchism of Wyatt, Donne, and Marvell, as they similarly thicken the texture of the main plot.

The main plot assumes as a given Laura's unavailability and the poet's ability to transform her sexual denials into poetic material. Robert Durling summarizes Apollo's impasse: "When the lover catches up with the object of his pursuit, she has turned" into a literal object: the laurel tree of the myth.[18] Durling explains sublimation in terms of that transformation. "Instead of Laura, the lover gets (or becomes, it amounts to the same thing) the laurel of poetic achievement and glory" (p. 27). Of the laurelization complex so persistent in the Petrarchan imitations through and beyond the Renaissance, Gordon Braden writes:

> Petrarch's extraordinary elongation of [his] frustration is echoed in almost all of the *Canzoniere*'s Renaissance descendants, a run of masculine bad luck so insistent that it becomes almost a joke, a sign of Petrarchism's monotonous conventionality. But jokes have their reasons and one may meditate on why the European lyric celebration of the feminine object of desire should begin with several centuries fixated on the unavailability of that object.[19]

And, of the poet's profiting from that unavailability, Nancy Vickers argues:

> At base the speaker's investment in his song reveals itself to be not only—if at all—in winning the lost lady ("Laura") but rather in winning a lost, or as yet unwon glory (the poetic champion's crown of laurel, "lauro") through the exercise of an overpowering stylistic mastery. A battle is indeed fought to victory; Laura may be gone but the manifestations of "lauro" (fame) persist to inform, through conscious and unconscious assimilations, an ongoing discourse of love.[20]

The equation between "romantic failure and poetic success"[21] that Braden, Durling, and Vickers emphasize is less important for this study than its subversion *within* the *Rime sparse* and the consequent variations as they appear in the work of Wyatt, Donne, and Marvell. What seems *new* in Marvell's self-reflecting "I" in "Appleton House" begins with the two Lauras already present in Petrarch's self-doubting Petrarch: Laura-Eve and

Laura-Mercury. If Petrarchism itself questions the conventions it establishes, so subsequent poets, who accept the success of its veneer, inherit the
unease at its core.

And, if Apollo-Daphne is the central myth for the failure-success compact, that compact is bifurcated by the myth of Eve's Genesis 2 appearance
(in *Rime sparse* 237, 181, 188, and 354), which inverts the romantic failure
thought necessary to Petrarchism, and by the myth of Battus-Mercury (in
Rime sparse 23, 105, 125, 126, 127, and 129), which deconstructs the poetic
success figured as its essential by-product. Both myths thicken the texture
of the complex to threaten the eternalizing consolation of poetic laurels.
At various points in the *Rime sparse*, the three women—Laura-Daphne,
Laura-Eve, and Laura-Mercury—counter what most critics see as Petrarch's exclusion of female subjectivity to express the woman's sexual
priorities (in Daphne's denials and Eve's desire) or to voice the woman's
creative capacity (in Mercury's inventiveness). Complicating the sexual
failure in Petrarchism is the presence in some poems of a desiring, albeit
short-lived, Laura-Eve. Casting doubts on the poetic success of laurelization is the interrogation prompted by Laura-Mercury, who turns Petrarch-
Battus to stone. Tensions on both sides of the Petrarchan equation are
inherent to the convention. Romantic success would, after all, cancel the
complaint. Poetic failure nullifies everything.

In four poems in the *Rime sparse*, Petrarch replaces Apollo and Daphne
with Adam and Eve, and reverses the dynamics of the dyad. Instead of
running away as Daphne does, the Eve of these poems faces Petrarch-
Adam, meets his gaze, and responds to his need for an other by being (in
likeness) just that. The run-away Daphne refuses to acknowledge male
desire. The stationary Eve validates it. In 237, Petrarch recasts Adam and
Eve, creating a spiral of libidinal dreamers: dreamers within dreams. A
second Adam, the Endymion figure in the poem, realizes in Selene's desire
for him what Petrarch wants from Laura. The momentary possible counters the perennially impossible of conventional Petrarchism. Its sustaining
power lies in the inversion its consolidation implies. When Petrarch imagines a Laura who returns his gaze, he cancels the frightened Daphne and
the frustrated Apollo. For the brief moments of 181, 188, 237, and 354, he
imagines the sexual imagination of the woman and the possibility that the
construct based on denial might be replaced by a construct celebrating
success.

At the opposite extreme is the totally alienating Laura, the one who
undermines the poetic sublimation most readers assume Petrarchism is

about. This Laura invalidates poetry. If Laura-Eve preempts Adam's gaze, Laura-Mercury exceeds Petrarch's words. Her speaking is itself noteworthy. Apart from warning Petrarch in his sleep about her impending death, or defending him in a fantasy where she describes his helplessness against her beauty, Laura-alive rarely speaks in the *Rime sparse*. Occasionally she sings. Dead, she is more verbose, descending from heaven to give Petrarch a glimpse of the afterlife. Therefore the dramatic moment in *Rime sparse* 23 where she does comment on her laurelization is doubly significant. In the Battus episode, Laura speaks twice. First she forbids Petrarch's poetry; then she belittles his poetic defiance of her. Opening his breast and stealing his heart, she warns: "Di ciò non far parola [Make no word of this]" (l.74). Like the Ovidian Mercury, she tests Petrarch-Battus, assuming "in altro abito sola [in another garment]" (l.75) the role of audience for the confession she initially forbade. When she returns to her accustomed form ("sua figura," l.78) after Petrarch-Battus betrays her to herself in disguise, she turns him into a rock and mocks his poetry: " 'I' non son forse chi tu credi [I am perhaps not who you think I am]' " (l.84). Her rage is double layered: superficially over the betrayal, the mere fact of the confession; retrospectively over the portrayal, the content of the complaint.

Laura competes in Petrarch's arena of expertise and appropriates for herself, with the heart-robbery and critical reaction, both the source of Petrarch's life and the meaning of his discourse. She takes on the poet's role, denies his power to circumscribe her, and asserts her elusiveness in terms of her exclusive control over the field that seemed, until then, the realm where only Petrarch functioned. As reader of the text in which she is central, Laura-Mercury rejects the text, maintaining that Petrarch's failure to recognize her in disguise leads to his entrapment in stone and his failure to recognize her in person leads to her misrepresentation in his poem. He remains unknowing. She remains unknowable. When she defines herself as not being "who Petrarch thinks she is," her evasions annul the cognitive process that brought her into being in the first place. When she provides no rational clues to her being, she clouds herself in a mystery that annihilates all forms of knowing. Triply inscrutable, the Laura who is not *who* Petrarch thinks she is plays no assignable role. The Laura who is not *where* Petrarch thinks she is has no identifiable locus. The Laura who is not *what* Petrarch thinks she is has no tangible substance. As woman she is unreachable; as god she is abstract. Her threefold evasions deny the *who*, *what*, and *where* of poetic materiality. Laura-Mercury remains "airy nothing" while Petrarch-Battus is remanded to stony silence, his shape inscribed by her even as his voice is usurped by her. She has "no local habitation," no "name" (*A Midsummer Night's Dream* 5.1.14–15). Her transmogrifying powers turn Petrarch to stone again in *Rime sparse* 105, 125, 126, 127, and 129. In these poems, his ability to write is contingent on his internalizing—and taking to "heart" as if for the first time—Laura-Mercury's original objections.

The three Lauras Petrarch uncovers make their way into the poetry of Wyatt, Donne, and Marvell as well. For the poet of the English Renaissance, "the past [of Petrarch's *Rime sparse*] was [not] a foreign country,"[22] nor were any of the three Lauras strangers. The fourteenth-century Italian lyric filtered down to Wyatt, Donne, and Marvell as a legacy received through the family of poets. If Petrarch consolidated what he inherited from Ovid and the troubadours, English Renaissance poets, in turn, bequeathed to their cultural heirs the lyric formula Petrarch crystallized and problematized. Along with the construct of the poetically useful main plot, they inherited the subversions that Laura-Eve and Laura-Mercury render inescapable, an inheritance most readers ignore when they argue that this international poetic family was decidedly male and that Petrarchan poems always speak away the woman.

Following the seminal studies of Sheila Fisher, Janet Halley, Nancy Vickers, and Marguerite Waller, feminist critics can continue to show how the woman is fragmented by, and secondary to, the poet's self-formulating pursuit of linguistic power.[23] Or, with Ann Rosalind Jones, Constance Jordan, Barbara Lewalski, Maureen Quilligan, and others,[24] they can turn to those women poets who, like Veronica Franco, Louise Labé, and the Countess of Pembroke, "reassign the [Petrarchan] code to a non-hegemonic group."[25] Finally, they can give up on the love poetry *mythos* altogether, as the current dearth of college courses and books on the Renaissance lyric implies.

Laura assumes that a woman is sometimes the "subject of consciousness" in English Renaissance poems. As the female agent in the Bordone painting encourages us to ask whether the scene is from Longus's or Petrarch's story, so it is possible to ask—within the anamorphic frame of a Petrarchan poem—whether it depicts Laura-Mercury's Battus, Laura-Eve's Adam, or Laura-Daphne's Apollo. The answers to those questions provide a genre and gender framework, a way of organizing the experience of those poems and of reading the female consciousness back into them. Laura-Mercury and Laura-Eve complicate the notion of a univocal Laura-Daphne—as each of the other two Lauras seems somehow to problematize the experience of the one presented in a particular instance. In choosing both to read male-authored texts and to search for the self-conscious woman in the poem, *Laura* follows the double imperative for feminist critics, as Carol Thomas Neely defines it: "to read *over* [male-authored] Renaissance texts from beginning to end as if for the first time . . . [and] to over-read, to read to excess the possibility of human (especially female) gendered subjectivity, identity, and agency, the possibility of woman's resistance or even subversion."[26] In this case the *over*-reading involves going *under*-the-covers, a look beneath the surface of Laura-Daphne's presentation in a poem that reveals—in imbrication—the subversive influence of Laura-Eve and Laura-Mercury.

The three possibilities complicate the Petrarchan dyad in the work of Wyatt, Donne, and Marvell and link Renaissance practice to "performance based" contemporary gender (as defined by Judith Butler) and genre (as defined by Lyotard) theories. If, as Rosalie Colie argues, genre is a shorthand way of expressing a "complex set of ideas," and "a challenge to match an imaginative structure to reality,"[27] then contemporary gender and genre theories ask questions that assume both the provisionality of the "fix"[28] and the groundlessness of the reality it "fixes." Like the Petrarchan poem, those theories depend on what Lyotard identifies as the uniqueness of each "phrase universe."[29] Like the Petrarchan poem, those theories assume that there are as many universes as there are phrases, and as many situations or instances as there are universes. When Butler maintains that "the production of texts can be one way of reconfiguring what will count as the world,"[30] she advocates the flexibility of genre. "Because texts do not reflect the entirety of their authors or their worlds, they enter a field of reading as partial provocations, not only requiring a set of prior texts in order to gain legibility, but—at best—initiating a set of appropriations and criticisms that call into question their fundamental premises" (*Bodies That Matter*, p. 19). The point where Butler and Lyotard intersect is the point that undoes a starting point. Each text requires "a set of prior texts." Each text provokes a set of not yet performed texts. Through anamnesis, Petrarch's successors reopen Petrarch. Through anamorphism, Petrarch anticipates his successor's ambivalence. The present in terms of genre is never perfect. The past in terms of genre is never over.

Because of their insistence on variation and contingency, Butler and Lyotard provide useful mechanisms for reading Petrarchism, critiques that question culturally inscribed forms and immutably essential genders. In maintaining that context is determined by language, that "there is no space or time independent of a phrase" (*The Differend*, p. 70), and that genres are linkages or modes of organization which themselves vary as to the moment of utterance, Lyotard stresses the contingency of genre itself. It is around a similar provisionality that Judith Butler makes a case for performative gender. Her argument that "there need not be a 'doer behind the deed' . . . that the doer is variably constructed in and through the deed"[31] emphasizes both that context is determined by act and that acts are inhibited by their context. Stressing that there "is no such thing" as "choosing a subject" (*Bodies That Matter*, p. 15) and that "performativity is always a reiteration of a norm or set of norms" (*Bodies That Matter*, p. 12), Butler could as well be talking of the paradoxical lyric situation. The poet's variations are part of the reiterative structure but the structure is always implicated in its own subversion. Lyotard and Butler read personality through an oscillating filter. When applied to a text, such a filter opens to a multiplicity of readings, each of which depends on the changing dynamic "uncovering" reveals.

In this context, too, Jonathan Goldberg argues that gender isn't "sutured onto a biological body but is, rather, a term produced by structures of social relationship" (*Sodometries*, p. 58). When Goldberg writes about Book 2 of Puttenham's *Arte* that "this story does not presume that there is only one form of desire" (*Sodometries*, p. 37), he (like Butler) is arguing for contingency. In citing texts such as Butler's *Gender Trouble* and Goldberg's *Sodometries*, *Laura* assumes (with them) that there are no fixed identities and that the lyric poetry sequence, which posits constant transformation within a supposedly solid continuum, is in fact the perfect vehicle for exploring the "undecidabilities" (*Sodometries*, p. 37) that Butler, Goldberg, and Lyotard so provocatively open up. The references are primarily to Butler's work: first, because the emphasis is on the woman's undecidability in the poetic structure; and (then) because Butler provides a more generally theoretical model. But still another anamorphic frame might be used in yet another study, in someone else's book, to describe (as Sedgwick does) relations between men and men or women and women. *Laura* is just one of many approaches to poetry that gender construction theory affords. In asking, with Judith Scherer Herz, "how primary is the idea of a gendered self to a conception of self?" *Laura* follows Herz's suggestion "to extend the argument offered by constructivist historians of homosexuality to heterosexuality."[32] In figuring desire as central to the matrix of imagination, it also assumes, with Denise Riley, that "to speak about the individual temporality of being a woman is really to speak about the movements between temporalities of a designation."³³

Can the temporalities of Lyotard—who sees genre as pliable and contingent—and Butler—who sees gender as performative and variable—be applied to Petrarchan poetry, the very genre that, in its objectification of women, seems most fixed in its use of gender? Further, what is the value of working a theory of incommensurability against—or inside of—a genre that is recognized principally as a vehicle for transforming the uncontainable into the measurable? Does Petrarchism make us aware of the limitations of representation in the way that postmodern texts, as Lyotard argues, "present the unpresentable in presentation itself"?³⁴ To apply contemporary gender and genre theory to early modern texts is to read, as Neely advocates, for the subversive element that has been heretofore overlooked. And it is also to search out what the lyric always opens up: alternative imagined spaces.

Contemporary gender theory often calls that otherness—or the excess that loosens the boundaries of representation—woman's space.³⁵ Most of the theorizing on woman's space has been applied to woman-authored texts or works in which women, as grotesques, "lean too heavily on"³⁶ or break out excessively, as mad-women,³⁷ from the forms confining them. To speak of a female space, an uncovering "that renders the boundaries of discourse permeable"³⁸ *within* male discourse, is to suggest that (1) a man can imagine a woman who imagines back, (2) the poetic imagination can produce imaginings that exceed their imaginer, and (3) spacelessness or absence is sometimes figured as an outcome of the very structures that seem to counter abstraction altogether. To theorize the consequent realignment of genres from such gender unhingings is similarly to suggest that (1) "modes of linkings," as Lyotard defines them (*The Differend*, p. 136), are themselves subject to unlinkings or variations not entirely anticipated by, and yet invariably implicit in, their original use; (2) a mode of organization contains the disorganization its very unity seems to deny. Its coherence reveals its tenuousness; its revelations mark its concealments. In the Petrarchan poem, even a recovery that safely asserts the Apollo-Daphne dyad cannot make up for, or fully cover up, the provisionality Laura-Mercury and Laura-Eve presuppose. Rosalie Colie calls that provisionality, in works that seem to her to cross boundaries in the most interesting way, *genera miste*.³⁹ The project of *Laura* is to situate the Petrarchan lyric in that interesting place, as the site of something both beyond and within the "available order" its genre seems to foreclose and its

genders to preclude. It assumes that Petrarchism offers—within its figurativeness—a sense of what cannot ever be figured and—within its genres—
a sense of what lies beyond the predetermined. If genre is variable, so too is
gender.

Laura asks the kinds of questions constructionist critics have raised
with regard to Renaissance drama and, still more recently, about medieval
romance. Geraldine Heng describes how the lady in the Gawain poem
reinscribes gender roles:

> The lady's oscillation—her sliding—between masculine and feminine
> modes, roles and moments raises, furthermore, the disconcerting spec-
> ter of a secondary turbulence: the prospect of a corresponding slide and
> oscillation in sexual division itself—a fluctuation in the status of that
> separating boundary between feminine and masculine that . . . compli-
> cates the recovery of that boundary in each moment of her perfor-
> mance. Her vacillation between genders necessarily subjects the site of
> gender division to continual displacement and, under the pressure of
> constant revision, the gender-bi-polarity it customarily secures becomes
> precipitously unstable and precarious. As acts and positions in the
> Lady's double masquerade grow interchangeably continuous, reversible
> and slippery, the division of masculinity and femininity into categories
> of mutual exclusion and opposition itself becomes insupportable and
> erodes.[40]

Heng's identification of the slippage enacts on a text precisely the kind of
discontinuity Butler's *Gender Trouble* finds in the body: "The abiding
gendered self will be shown to be structured by repeated acts that seek
to approximate the ideal of a substantial ground of identity but which,
in their occasional *dis*continuity, reveal the temporal and contingent
groundlessness of this 'ground' " (p. 141).

Butler's "groundlessness" applied to the body parallels Heng's "eroding
categories" applied to a text. They both raise questions about gender
bipolarity. *Laura* situates itself in the same margins, in the place between
genre and gender that blurs the edges. Such a space is contentious. Even
critics, like Heng, who argue for gender performance say that it is virtually impossible to find the destabilizing elements in the lyric "which
[arguably] dramatizes the narcissism of a single speaking voice uninter-
rupted by other voices. . . . [In the lyric], the feminine may be constructed
as a mere reflecting surface or speculum for masculine desire."[41] *Laura*

nevertheless maintains that—in certain Petrarchan lyrics—the woman imagined for the poem, like Chloë-Laura in the Bordone painting, recasts the space of her imagining to change the genre of the poem and to challenge the gender binarisms Petrarchism ordinarily demands. If, as Goldberg and others argue, it is possible to read for "multiple desires traversing a poem" (p. 59), then it is possible to assume that the poet can—and must necessarily—imagine multiple desirers within the poem (as is the case with Laura-Eve), even desirers (as is the case with Laura-Mercury) who evade the poem's objectification altogether.

In emphasizing the resignifying moments within the reigning discourse of love, this study acknowledges the tyranny to women that most Petrarchan poems impose. But it also searches out "alternative domains of cultural intelligibility" (*Gender Trouble*, p. 145) in *some* Petrarchan poems to ask why Petrarch, Wyatt, Donne, and Marvell locate their questions about sexuality, society, and poetry in the woman they imagine for the construct. To discover how the signifier "femininity" exceeds the "code of male representation" or how it constitutes itself "in ambiguity" and cites itself in "the uncanny space *between two signs*, between the institutions of masculinity and femininity . . . to threaten the smooth functioning of the very institution of representation,"[42] it will be necessary to reconceive (1) the Petrarchan tradition itself; (2) the poet in the poem; and (3) the woman in the poem. As part of a project that views Petrarchism as a symbolic order which can yield alternative interpretative systems,[43] *Laura* assumes that the construction of gender is invariably linked to the constructedness of the poem and that therefore the destabilizing, parodic, decentering effect of gender performance is central to the construction of the lyric genre as well. Butler's "gender trouble" connects to what might be theorized as Lyotard's "genre trouble." To rethink gender as performative is to rethink the lyric as part of the same inventive act. Contemporary gender and genre theories facilitate such an investigation of the lyric because they posit a self constantly compelled to redefinition even as they recognize the simultaneous insufficiency and impermanence of all categories. Once surfaced in the *Rime sparse*, Laura-Eve and Laura-Mercury don't just fade away. They infiltrate the genre so that even the main plot is anamorphic. Things aren't the same anymore once we read them into the discourse, and that difference is part of the excitement, as well as the trouble, in uncovering the Lauras the Petrarchan plot embeds.[44]

Troubling Genre

As it reveals the multiple layers of the Petrarchan dyad, *Laura* unsettles the divisive categories through which genre organizes experience. If the categories are unstable, the ground might be seen as transformable, and that is the link between genre and politics. Both Lyotard and Butler call the political the very arena where identity is articulated. Both agree that identity therefore is always being rearticulated. As Butler reasons, "if identities were no longer fixed as the premises of a political syllogism and politics no longer understood as a set of practices derived from the alleged interests that belong to a set of ready-made subjects, a new configuration of politics would surely emerge from the ruins of the old. Cultural configurations of sex and gender might then proliferate" (*Gender Trouble*, p. 139). In the same way, Lyotard argues, genre proliferates when no one genre is seen as universal or authoritative. Gayle Ormiston writes of Lyotard that "there is no way, no idiom, no discourse, no genre, no narrative technique for Lyotard that can resolve the crisis of rendering judgment on a case by case basis."[45] The genre and gender theories that seem useful here are those that demand analysis on a case-by-case basis; the variations are what Butler calls proliferations (*Gender Trouble*, p. 144), and Lyotard, "multiplicity" (*The Differend*, p. 138). Analyzing a poem on a case-by-case basis assumes that there is no one poet and no absolutely certain woman. Such an analysis provides a foundation for a poetics open to heterogeneities of all kinds.

Petrarchan poetry seems at first glance about as far removed from political action as one can get. In fact, as Rosalie Colie maintains, Petrarch was fussy about genre,[46] writing his politically prescriptive *Africa* in Latin, his personally confessional lyrics in the vernacular. But in another sense, as Lyotard writes, poetry is politics:

> [Politics] is not a genre, it is the multiplicity of genres, the diversity of ends, and *par excellence*, the question of linkage. It plunges into the emptiness where "it happens that. . . ." It is, if you will, the state of language but it is not *a* language. Politics consists in the fact that language is not a language, but phrases, or that Being is not Being but *There is's*. It's tantamount to Being which is not. It is one of its names. (*The Differend*, p. 138)

Marked by the temporal and signified by temporariness, genre ("each there is") becomes a convenience of expression which nevertheless demands a "poetics of the indescribable."[47] Politics is genre put into practice, but its practice always suggests alternative discursive categories. James Baumlin maintains that "genre never remains static in interpretation; the form itself undergoes a process of restatement as meanings and expectations are sustained, qualified, undermined, revised. And in this way, genre-concepts change not just between but within literary works themselves: that which gives an initial shape to the text is inevitably shaped by the reading experience."[48]

Laura suggests that the unshaping is part of the writing experience as well. When poetry breaks down categories, when its plenitude "plunges into emptiness," it changes the genre expectations that its initial form produces and so becomes political in the sense that Lyotard means. If Laura-Daphne comes close to being describable, Laura-Mercury suggests (as Lyotard would say about the incommensurable) that what "remains to be phrased exceeds what can presently be phrased" (*The Differend*, p. 13). Laura-Mercury's "I am not perhaps who you think I am" puts down both the "existing idiom" (*The Differend*, p. 13) that Petrarch's sublimating laurels perpetuate and the rationale by which such idioms become acceptable. In proposing that "I am" demands both another story (another *there is*) and a different arena of thought (a being which is not), Laura-Mercury questions patriarchal form and hegemonic thinking. Her questions destabilize the "I" so that the poet can bring a "being which is not" into the realm of imagined possibility. "Not being" then becomes an alternative in the way that it does in Hamlet's "to be or not to be" speech if that speech is taken as a tentative probing of an "undiscovered country." To read Hamlet's metaphor literally is to turn temporal categories (the chronological "after") into spatial terms (the directional beyond). To read a poem anamorphically is to expose, transgress, and penetrate the undiscovered—or the as yet uncovered—feelings that hover on the border of known signs, including those of gender positions thought to be culturally codified. "Not being" becomes a viable alternative when "the being which is not" is seen as part of the many layers of experience. That "absent presence" is both anamnetic—someone forgotten—and anagogic—someone not yet formed and possibly unformable.

In presenting what is not presentable "under the rules of formation" (*The Differend*, p. 138), Laura-Mercury heightens the stakes of poetry. Lyotard argues that each new work challenges the rules:

When Cézanne picks up his paint brush, what is at stake in painting is put into question; when Schoenberg sits down at his piano, what is at stake in music; when Joyce grabs hold of his pen, what is at stake in literature. Not only are new strategies for "gaining" tried out, but the nature of the "success" is questioned. A painting will be good (will have realized its ends, have come near them), if it obliges the addressee to ask about what it consists in. (*The Differend*, p. 138)

When the reader "asks about what it consists in," the Petrarchan poem is "successful." Its strategies involve preserving what Laura-Mercury theorizes: the sense of the contingency of self and other; the sense that each poem requires a reinvention of self that covers up "the unpresentable" only temporarily as it leaves room to ask what "recovery" consists in.

Like the genders that compose it, Petrarchism both exceeds the form that contains it and challenges the form itself. Of such incommensurability in the language of dreams, Lyotard writes:

Condensation must be understood as a physical process by means of which one or more objects occupying a given space are reduced to a smaller volume, as is the case when a gas becomes a liquid. . . . Condensation is a change of "state" (a difference in nature). . . . Normally in the linguistic order, a word is transparent: its meaning is immediate, and it is that meaning which is received. . . . The product of condensation as its name implies is, on the contrary, opaque, dense, hiding its other side/s.

Now this immobility which manufactures things out of words is it not desire itself, pursuing its usual course, producing the imaginary? If this is the case, then we should not say that condensation is an exercise by means of which desire disguises itself, but rather that it *is desire working over* the text of dream thoughts.

In the first of these interpretations, the force is located *behind* the manifest content itself assumed to be a disguised text, in the second, and apparently correct one, the force, on the contrary, compresses the primary text, crumpling it up, folding it, scrambling the signs it bears on its surface, fabricating new units which are not linguistic signs or graphic entities. The manifest content is the old text "forced" in this manner; it is not a text. Force occupies the very scenario of the dream as Van Gogh's brush stroke remains recorded in his suns.[49]

Insofar as a poem is also a condensation, words on the page can be folded into other words and other histories, opening to the scenarios "scrambled up" by Laura-Eve and Laura-Mercury even if they have not yet occurred chronologically in the text. The Petrarchan poem conceals as well as reveals its maker. In accounting for the being which is not, it both hides and reveals the other "side/s." Thus condensation involves "a difference in nature," something that "manufactures things out of words" so that—like a robot gone haywire—those "things" acquire agendae of their own and lives which their original inventor could not anticipate. If that is the case, then the force of imbrication played out in the scenario of the subplots is part of the poem—as Van Gogh's brush strokes remain recorded in his suns. The male creator is himself implicated in the disruptive figure of the woman he creates; that woman in turn affects his invention of the next woman, as Petrarch (recovering from the enrockings of *Rime sparse* 105) conjures up the "new angel" of 106 only to discover in 125 that he has advanced no further than he was in 23. He finds himself, once again, face to face with the poem-denying Laura. The force is involved in the thing described, not somewhere behind, or apart from, or opposite to it, but there, in the beginning. The force does not necessarily originate in one man named Petrarch, who invents one woman named Laura. Folded over, the Laura-Mercury of *Rime sparse* 23 is "always already" in *Rime sparse* 1, and "always already" latent in Petrarch even if we at first cannot seem to find her there. Her subversive possibilities hover over all the *Rime sparse*.

In the example of Van Gogh's suns, the inspiration or sun as desired object and informing subject is joined with the brush strokes that produced them so that the end (the sun on the canvas) returns to the beginning (the stroke of the brush). The sun is already part of the stroke because, without the original light of the sun in the sky, the belated and representing stroke that produces the, still later, on-canvas sun would be impossible. Deprived of the force of desire for the sun and its energy, the instrumental and originative stroke would be purposeless. Such fusion also implies that the visual product is connected to the interiorized origin. The sun is the light source that enables the necessary stroke or, as Butler writes, the "self is from the start radically implicated in the other. . . . The other is always from the start already installed in the self."[50] The sun becomes part of the force in the beginning in the same way that the force becomes part of the sun in the end. Through the imbricated presence of Laura-Mercury, the Petrarchan poem suggests what Bill Readings defines as the immemorial in Lyotard's thought: "that which can neither be remembered (represented to consciousness) nor consigned to oblivion."[51]

Even as he describes Laura-Daphne, Petrarch conceptualizes Laura-Eve and Laura-Mercury, folding them over into the poem though they are not specifically re-membered or brought to being in a specific instance. Their presence "works over" the construct to thicken it even as it "works out" the construct to threaten it with extinction. The critical act demands a look beneath the surface, a pentimento that reveals alternative possibilities latent in the event. In that context, uncovering emerges, as undressing does in John Donne's "Elegy: 19," a shift in emphasis, not a change in subject formation.

When it maintains that the disruptive element is implied in the initial construct, *Laura* answers Donne's question to the woman in "To his Mistris Going to Bed," by suggesting that it's an offer the lady cannot refuse: "What need'st thou have more covering than a man?" Throughout the poem, Donne reimburses the woman for each body part she exposes by covering it with a compliment. The more the woman uncovers her body, the more she catches his praise. At the end, Donne asks for some of that covering back. To be covered verbally is to be dressed in the flattering words the poem has already conferred. To be covered physically is to be protected by the armor of clothing the lady still retains. Clothed in words, the woman takes the man's place. To be herself again, to be uncovered, she needs to return the compliment by offering to give back what the man has given, to cover the man with words.[52] Chat for self. With "more covering," she is also twice the man. Through the compliments of the poem, the lady seems to "grow physically" as the poet increases his praise. She emerges as large as America, as broad as India, stretching to the glittering zone of heaven from the glorious meads of the earth. To be downsized again, she needs to equalize desire by conferring a sexual response. The tone of Donne's playful bargaining encourages the fungible: tit for chat, penis for phallus. It also assumes that the woman sees the joke—that behind the exalted compliments lies a measure of mutual cynicism or the baldness the speaker literally reveals at the end. The basic construct theorizes its alternatives to suggest, with Donne, that cover, the confidence engendered by flattery and the desire kindled by exposure, is the marketable province of both sexes. If that's the case, then the binary opposition represented by Apollo and Daphne can be overcome. In posing the question, Donne is asking for a woman he can have (Laura-Eve) and a woman who has words (Laura-Mercury).[53] He maintains that both Lauras are perfectly capable of returning some of that cover (of words and sexuality) back to him. His final question and expectation that the woman will reply are tributes to her sexual and linguistic agency.

When Donne uncovers multiple Lauras, he reveals the woman's capacity to reciprocate sexuality and language, a capacity denied Laura-Daphne. Implicit in the text of "To his Mistris" are the two self-canceling generic contingencies Donne recognizes. (1) The poem has no rhetorically necessary point. Laura-Eve *does* want sexuality. Since they are already familiar enough for the man to be naked *first*, Donne reveals nothing new in the uncovering of the final line. (2) The poem dispels the notion of a linguistically vacuous, and therefore discursively passive, woman. Wearing the speaker's words, "she" is already poetically "he." Laura-Mercury imagines her own subjectivity. That mysterious self awaits its realization elsewhere—beyond the poet's thinking—presumably in the poem she might write when she re-covers the man and makes him her desired object. If, as Lyotard argues, the brush stroke is recorded in the suns, so Petrarch is responsible for the sexual and verbal Lauras. If the suns inspire brush strokes, Laura is implicated in Petrarch—in all his selves.

What happens when Petrarch's famous "celebration of female unavailability" is turned on its heels by the presence of an available woman in the poems, one who seems (like Chloë in the Longus romance) to initiate and return desire? What happens when the poet's "stylistic mastery" is challenged, or undone, by a woman who is perhaps more inventive than the man who presumes to contain her? What happens when the woman in the poems claims to be an inventor herself, one who takes the reed (or caduceus) up in her hands and begins to evoke a music, and to explore a space, of her own? All these "what happens" *do* happen in the poems of Petrarch and his Renaissance imitators Wyatt, Donne, and Marvell, to turn both gender identity and genre normalization around. If such contingencies unhinge genre, they also vex gender.

Troubling Gender

To theorize three women in the *Rime sparse* is to enact a gender theory that moves away from essentialism or "a belief in the real true essence of things, the invariable and fixed properties which define the whatness of a given entity."[54] The approach of *Laura* will therefore be different from the way in which, for example, Laura Claridge and Elizabeth Langland theorize their collection of essays on feminist approaches to male-authored texts (which starts with Milton). Along with Frank Lentricchia and Paul Smith,[55] they argue that men are as obstructed by patriarchy as women, even as they seem nevertheless to return to biological origins to include essentialism: "We construct sophisticated, satisfying explanations of gender identities, but what does it mean to be biologically female or male—to produce more estrogen than testosterone, to have testes rather than ovaries?"[56] In making a case for construction, *Laura* is different, too, from the conciliatory positions of Jonathan Dollimore and Diane Fuss, who see essentialism and its theories of identity as something to be neither "sanctified nor villified" but simultaneously "assumed and questioned."[57]

Laura presumes that no poetic order is automatically gendered. Because we are each the other from the start, as Lyotard and Butler suggest, we cannot separate "wanting to be [from] wanting to have" ("Imitation and Gender Insubordination," p. 26). When Butler insists that "the disruption of the other at the heart of the self is the very condition of that self's possibility" ("Imitation and Gender Insubordination," p. 27), she reasons in terms of life situations what the literary critic might theorize about the poem: the imagined presence of the other is what awakens the poetic self to its selfness. In theorizing the condition of the woman in male-authored texts, *Laura* reads the poem as Butler reads the self—as an arena where there is neither a clearly biological ground nor a necessarily predetermined other.

And, in describing each poem as the performance of a performing self in the way that Butler defines the "I" and Geraldine Heng reads Gawain's lady, *Laura* proceeds retrospectively from the poem. What if the signification itself determines the agency of the signifier? What if the *differend*, that which defies configuration, becomes the subject of analysis? In short, what if the sign—rather than the body—were the premise? *Laura* presupposes recovering Petrarchism as itself a presentation—imagining both imaginer and imagined as constructs. Such reimaginings happen with each poem, as Butler claims the "I" is reimagined for each gendered performance:

> If the "I" is a site of repetition, that is, if the "I" only achieves the semblance of identity through a certain repetition of itself, then the "I" is always displaced by the very repetition that sustains it. In other words, does or can the "I" ever repeat itself, cite itself, faithfully, or is there always a displacement from its former moment that establishes the permanently non-self-identical status of that "I"?
>
> What "performs" does not exhaust the "I"; it does not lay out in visible terms the comprehensive content of that "I," for if the performance is "repeated," there is always the question of what differentiates

from each other the moments of identity that are repeated. And if the "I" is the effect of a certain repetition, one which produces the semblance of a continuity of coherence, then there is no "I" that precedes the gender that it is said to perform; the repetition and the failure to repeat produce a string of performances that constitute and contest the coherence of that "I." ("Imitation and Gender Insubordination," p. 18)

Gender is always a performance that produces the illusion of an inner sex or essence or psychic gender core. ("Imitation and Gender Insubordination," p. 28)

To explain how gender performance mocks the distinction between inner and outer, Butler quotes Esther Newton's definition of drag:

At its most complex [drag] is a double inversion that says, "appearance is an illusion." Drag says [Newton's curious personification] "my 'outside' appearance is feminine, but my essence 'inside' [the body] is masculine." At the same time it symbolizes the opposite inversion; "my appearance 'outside' [my body, my gender] is masculine but my essence 'inside' [myself] is feminine." (*Gender Trouble*, p. 137)

As drag, the Petrarchan poem suggests that the "I" of the poem is at core part of the "you," and that the "you" who appears in the poem bears witness to its capacity also to imagine the "I." More recently, Butler refines her notion of performativity to ensure that it doesn't mean that "one woke in the morning, perused the closet . . . for the gender of choice, donned that gender for the day and then restored the garment to its place at night" (*Bodies That Matter*, p. x). She also redefines performance. "If drag is performative, that does not mean that all performativity is to be understood as drag" (*Bodies That Matter*, 230–231). "Performativity is . . . not a singular 'act,' for it is always a reiteration of a set of norms, and to the extent that it acquires an act-like status in the present, it conceals or dissimulates the conventions of which it is a repetition" (*Bodies That Matter*, p. 12). Regarding the poetic "I" as performative suggests the extent to which the self is always already the other even in those moments when it seems to be most intensively self-assertive.

An example of the way the Renaissance poet plays with such double inversions might be found in the last two lines of "Astrophil and Stella 1": "Biting my trewand pen, beating myself for spite, / 'Fool,' said my Muse to me, 'look in thy heart and write.' "[58] The gender transformations in this sonnet are multiple, as Astrophil passively waits to be impregnated by the wit of other poets and then appears "great with child"—not with the semen of male power but in the helpless throes of labor experienced by the women he imitates. In the context of the "I's" already enacted feminization, biting the trewand pen is redundant. Like castrating the castrato or presenting the absence of absence, the bite toys with the sense of an endlessly self-perpetuating self even as it "ends" its possibility. Biting the true-*end* pen, Astrophil uncovers the self before the apple—the unselfconscious self, which is presumed to be his real beginning. Biting the true-*wand* pen, Astrophil proposes that even beginnings are constructions that presume the magic of transformation. The pen is a wand, Mercury's caduceus. But does Astrophil find his heart or is *his* heart an image of Stella's *self?* To anatomize the heart and still live is to use the mirror that duplicates rather than, as Laura-Mercury does, the knife that penetrates. To look inward, therefore, is to regard reflection or to recognize what is already an imitation. The heart reveals the self—as Butler defines it—in drag. The artificial inner self matches the assumed outer self. The assertion that Astrophil can "look in his heart and write" ends the poem at the point where it might more logically begin. We're never given the poem that comes from Astrophil's inward turning because what he sees there is the problem of textuality itself. Looking inward opens up what might be called a *mise-en-abîme* that keeps turning back to another body of words: "Where there is an 'I' who utters or speaks and thereby produces an effect in discourse, there is first a discourse which precedes and enables that 'I' and forms in language the constraining trajectory of its will" (*Bodies That Matter*, p. 225). Like Herbert's prayer to man's soul, the heart is the word in "paraphrase."[59] Or, as Lyotard puts it, "the textual is already there in the core figure" ("The Dream-Work," p. 51).

Patricia Fumerton writes that "only through con-vention can [the poet] find in-vention,"[60] and that the poet deliberately renders truth finally "unrepresentable."[61] In Fumerton's terms, the poet chooses to frame that incommensurability in the image of Stella. It's a woman who suggests the excessive heart and who therefore knows that language cannot express what—or where—the heart is. Is it in the body exposed on the sleeve or is it the one represented on the page? Is the source of life already constructed by the other whose image is implanted in the self?[62] To call the heart an image is to assume an imitative original. To be reminded that art is embedded in the heart is also to learn that nature is construction and therefore is "always already" covered and that the self is, as Fumerton argues, therefore inevitably secretive.

Sidney's "Astrophil and Stella 1" ends in the self-reflecting and sometimes self-covering moment which constitutes the provisional beginning
of the poems studied in this book. Some poems—like Wyatt's "Whoso
list to hunt"—never get past the ambivalent moment of "Astrophil and
Stella 1." Others, like Donne's "Change," turn the incommensurable into
an openness that overflows the boundaries of self and other. *Laura* presumes that poetic gender is an imitation for which there is no fixed original and that genre is not simply an imagined structure that corresponds
to some immutable reality but an imagined structure that mimics an
imagined structure. All Petrarchism, as Roland Greene suggests, is post-
Petrarchism.[63] As the form of self-perpetuating desire in the Western world,
Petrarchism keeps regenerating itself even as each of the reproductions
deconstructs the original. Sidney's looking and writing commemorate
what cannot be put into words or what can only be signified by someone
who denies the speech occasion, as does Laura-Mercury. If no original
occurs before the poem, then what goes on in any single poem constitutes
a contingent beginning, another version of *a*, rather than *the*, conversionary myth.

Such a momentary reversion resembles what Mieke Bal calls the sexual
origin of Eve in Genesis 2:

> The verb used for Jahweh's forming of the earth creature (ha-a-dam)
> was the specific word for pottery: the verb used in 2:22 refers specifically
> to architecture and the construction of buildings. The action is both
> more difficult, more sophisticated, and requires more differentiated
> material. The difference would indicate a higher level of creation. This
> is consistent with the poetics of the Bible. Just as the creation of human-
> ity in the version of Genesis 1–2:4 is the climax of the creation of the
> world, so the creation of humanity as it is specified in the version under
> consideration is performed in two progressive phases of perfection. . . .
> The material used no longer consists of dust, of clay, but of bone and
> flesh, already enriched with *nepesh* [breath blood]. The result is also
> higher: it is no longer an undifferentiated creature but a sexual being,
> more precisely, a woman:
>> And Jahweh God built the rib which he took from [undifferentiated
>> *ha-a-dam*] into woman [*issa*] (2:22).
> Of the two words, *is* and *issa*, which in this text indicate sexually
> differentiated beings, *issa*, woman, appears first. It is *issa* who changes
> the meaning of ha-a-dam from earth being into earth man. In this
> semiotic sense, the woman was formed first, then the man.[64]

In Bal's reading, it is possible to theorize a woman who is separate from both her representational and biological source: a woman who recovers originary status. Such theorizing produces what Bal calls "the paradox of semiotic creation: Adam was the first to name. . . . But she was the first to be named, hence to be the 'other character' indispensable for him to be a character at all. Thus, they mutually create each other, differently in a different act."[65]

When significations are seen in their transformative capacities, then the poetic construction assumes that no identity abides and no identity precedes the immediate one at hand. If the other character is indispensable for the self to perform the self-defining act, then the other (like Eve in Adam's rib) is implicated—installed—in the self. The self depends on, as well as invents, the other, because in some sense the other is (like Eve in Bal's description) "always already there," installed in the self: Butler's performances = Bal's acts = poetic constructions = Lyotard's dream-work. Such imitative possessiveness is, as Butler writes, central to the erotics of lesbianism and a way of countering the hegemony of heterosexuality ("Imitation and Gender Insubordination," p. 26), but it also can be used as a way of dealing with the erotics of Petrarchism, a system perpetuated in the desire for desire and contingent on perpetual incompleteness. Though Petrarchism generally depends on the denial of desire that keeps the poem alive, it sometimes reproduces a desirer in the poem with a woman who orchestrates sexuality (Laura-Eve) and sometimes reproduces a desire to end the poem in a woman (Laura-Mercury) whose inventive capacities exceed, or seem larger than, those of the "I" presumed to be inventing both poem and woman.

Essential Woman, Essential Self: What Uncovering Isn't

The sexually responsive Laura-Eve and the poetically inventive Laura-Mercury work against contemporary theories for the woman in the poem which dismiss her sexual and poetic imagination by fixing her permanently in the masculine order. *Laura* reads against both the woman's annihilation, as theorized by Thomas Greene, and the poet's inwardness, as theorized by Anne Ferry.[66] Laura-Eve works against Greene, Laura-Mercury, against Ferry.

Thomas Greene's definition of self and other in the lyric is principally a feminist reading. Noting that the woman has no existence apart from the poet's description, he demonstrates how her agency is denied by the poem: "What is crucial is that an emergent self tries to realize itself in relation to a dynamic other constructed and energized by the self's own language" ("The Poetics of Discovery," p. 133). In Greene's reading, the emergent self is an extension of the biological self of the male poet, whose dynamic other must also be related to those biological others the biological self already knows. Within that construct, the woman in the poem is only an extension of the actual experience of the male poet. As desired object in Petrarchan poems, her body seems to preclude her imagination or agency; the mere presence of her anatomy obviates all questions of the woman's autonomy. An emergent male self is limited by the confines of the self's language and by the context of male experience. In Greene's poetic, Echo's voice is silenced by Narcissus's mirror. The "she" of the poem is a product of the "he" of the poem, who is, in turn, a product of—or emerges from— the social situation of a real-life "he," the "historical man whose hand produces the poem" (p. 129). "She" becomes, then, an essentialized other of a constructed self, since her being is determined by the gendered experience of the originary self who, historically positioned, cannot exceed the experience of his essential life.

Thus the woman in Greene's hypothetical poem is a product of a self whose only experience with women is in the context of his personal situation. The poet invents a woman from his circumstances: either as a force who threatens him and therefore must be limited in the poem or as a force whose existence is so negligible that it is logical to deprive her agency in art. Though the "he" of the poem has an imagining life, the "she" has no imagination. Thomas Docherty argues that such deprivations are issued by the male fear of "the female as a consciousness or mode of desire or will which could challenge male authority and domination or masculinist epistemology and ideology. Women feared as incomprehensible subjects in nature are accorded only the status of object in the 'nature' or ideology constructed by masculinism."[67] Read as a version of the extended self, Docherty's incomprehensible subjects become the passive objects of masculinist poems. Even if their historical counterparts are more powerful than the man, their poetic emergence is always reduced: smaller than the man whose image contains her. For Greene and Docherty, the container is always larger than the thing contained. As object, woman is reduced to "thing contained." But if the woman is read, as she is in this study, as "always already" part of the man, then the projected poem can be understood as producing something other than its apparent container, something that exceeds—or overflows—or is impossible to contain at all. As in the dream-work, that new something refolds experience so that it is possible to imagine "a difference in nature" ("Dream-Work," p. 24).

If Greene's theory of the emergent self proves inadequate to account for the sexual imagination of the woman (Laura-Eve), so Anne Ferry's theory of inwardness does not fully take into account the creative imagination of the woman as it is exemplified by Laura-Mercury. In her seminal book *The Inward Language*, Ferry postulates the birth of modern consciousness characterized by the excess of Hamlet's inwardness in the line "I have that within which passes show" to suggest that there is a true self which might be revealed if we could find the words adequately to describe it. "It is a conception which much later vocabularies, clustered around belief in the existence of a real self and an inner language, are used to describe, but which, in the sixteenth and early seventeenth century, was only suggested in the inward language of the sonnets and in *Hamlet*" (p. 250). Her analysis of "Astrophil and Stella 1" concludes that Astrophil's "Muses' prescription of a plain style in place of inventions fine or borrowed does not resolve Astrophil's difficulties because it ignores the distinctions actually troubling him between the lover's inward experience and its presentation in poetry and also because it assumes his inward state to be more simple and single than it is. . . . If Astrophil looks in his heart, he will find there more than Stella's image; he will find a tangled inward state his unsubtle Muse knows not of" (p. 130).[68]

Even though the heart is more complex than the Muse knows, Ferry still cites the disparity between inward and outward in talking about the heart. She argues that a vocabulary of inwardness gradually makes its way into post-Renaissance discourse but that that vocabulary is privileged to expressing the inner being of the imaginer, not of the imagined. In theorizing about Shakespeare's sonnets, Ferry maintains that "both speaker and subjects are portrayed as having a simultaneous inward existence distinct from what they show to the world" (p. 178). But the only exponent for that disparity is the poet, whose disclosures determine what is, and is not, shown.

In downplaying the difference between self and other, Butler and Lyotard don't need to concern themselves with questions of inner and outer. For Lyotard, the outward self is tangled enough. The dream-work creates its own surface complexities. Butler discounts the difference inwardness presumes. In granting that signs are always sufficiently complex and that inwardness is itself a cover, Butler argues that "causal lines [are] retrospectively and performatively produced fabrications [that] reveal every claim to be the origin, the inner, the true and the real, as nothing other than the effects of *drag*" ("Imitation and Gender Insubordination," p. 29). In the same way, Lyotard's contention that the outward show (Van Gogh's sun) itself contains the inward design (Van Gogh's brush strokes) suggests, as well, that the imagined product is inseparable from the imaginer. If that is the case, then inwardness cannot ever be represented by outwardness (Hamlet's dismissal of show and its trappings in Ferry's interpretation) and is always insufficiently represented by outwardness (Lyotard's assumption of incommensurability, Butler's redefinition of drag). In defining the *differend*, Lyotard argues that the unarticulated both testifies to the inadequacy of language and is its absent presence: "In the *differend*, something asks to be put into phrases and suffers from the wrong of not being able to be put into phrases" (*The Differend*, p. 13).

While Ferry contends that post-Renaissance discourse *can* phrase Hamlet's inwardness, that once "the key is discovered, the heart may be unlocked and its contents known by the true names which are engraved in it" (p. 214), Patricia Fumerton maintains that the desire for secrecy expressed in Sidney's sonnets "constitutes the first step or threshold of [a modern] self at a distance from public expression."[69] For Lyotard, language is at best potential. It [always] remains to "institute idioms which do not yet exist" (*The Differend*, p. 13). In a sense, the suffering that Lyotard alludes to when he speaks of deferred expression ("the wrong of not being able to be put into phrases right away") is overcome, in the Petrarchism *Laura* describes, both by the revenge that Laura-Mercury instigates in defining herself as the injured party and the exhilaration poetry expresses (and Lyotard himself finds) in its discovery of "new idioms." Laura-Mercury speaks both her rage at not being accurately represented and her delight at being unrepresentable. If Ferry's Hamlet is self-consciously gloomy and Fumerton's Astrophil deliberately secretive, Laura-Mercury's evasive self is joyful, her defiance a source of the gratification poetry yields when it "performs" her subversions.

Hélène Cixous calls the double feelings, uncovered in Laura-Mercury's simultaneous retribution and escape, blissful. Women "take pleasure," she writes, "in jumbling the order of space, in disorientating it, in changing around the furniture, dislocating things and values, breaking them all up, emptying structures and turning propriety upside down."[70] The happiness Cixous describes involves retaliation. Quoting Borges's story by that name, Julian Pefanis identifies the destructive response as "the revenge of the mirror people" and maintains that "postmodern aesthetics à la Lyotard valorizes the tendency to 'shatter consensus.' When this shattering is done in the name of heterogeneity . . . from the point of view of the mirror people, a subjugated other either internal or external to the consciousness of the west, then it remains a progressive and potentially radical phenomenon."[71] When Laura-Mercury enacts the represented's revenge, she breaks down Petrarch-Battus's projection of the other as a mirror of his desiring self by (in Cixous's terms) "emptying the structure" and forcing "dislocation." Dissolving representational space and the conventions of mimesis that are part of the "consciousness of the west," Laura-Mercury's response—"I am not perhaps who you think I am"— proposes that (1) she exceeds ("I am other") the imagined other the poem proposes—("I am deeper than you imagined."); (2) she denies the cognitive self the poem hypothesizes—("I am not a self you can even think; therefore I am not."); (3) she escapes the grounding process that fixes imagined others—"I am elsewhere." *Laura* plays out its generic variations in the arena of elsewhere, assuming that (1) the same trouble that postulates gender instability presumes genre subversion as well; (2) the Petrarchan original contains the same contradictions as its Renaissance imitations; (3) each of the four writers invents many poets and many women for his poems; (4) when the invented poet challenges the prevailing discourse, he cuts across preconceived notions of gender and periodization to map out previously unimagined spaces or to remap those taken for granted as culturally fixed; (5) such remappings in early modern poems resemble what very contemporary gender and genre theories make explicit. The psychic excess, revealed in the failure of a repeated act fully to express gender in any given presentation, is precisely what impels the performance, in sexual theory of gender, in poetic theory of self.

As poets who span the early, middle, and late stages of the English Renaissance, Wyatt, Donne, and Marvell flesh out the disruptive promise that is part of the conversional premise of Petrarchism. Because each of the studied poems begins where Sidney's "Astrophil and Stella 1" ends, in the confusion between "wanting to be" and "wanting to have"—exemplified by the problematic self, the problematic act of writing, and the problematic woman—they represent in Renaissance terms the genre slippage that is part of Petrarchism itself. Given the current emphasis on locating texts in their contexts and the corollary critical insistence (as Reed Way Dasenbrock argues) that "literature is made up of works not texts, created by individual authors working at specific . . . moments of history,"[72] why persist in reading for multiple poets and multiple women (for undecidabilities) in Renaissance poems?

In assuming more than one locus of desire in the work of a given poet and in examining the multiplicities of desire in a given poem, *Laura* cannot be part of any historicizing project. The univocal John Donne is undone, to use Thomas Docherty's phrase, because there is no one Donne. In presupposing indeterminate poetic selves and problematic poetic others, *Laura* remains outside the arena of biographical history even as it adheres to periodization in the intertexuality of its genre theory. That is, in assuming a chronology of poetic and imagined influence, it downplays the centrality of literal or sociological influence. In supposing that experience is refolded or unfolded in the poem, it suggests the complexity of the imaginative forces that shape it—the way in which what "contest[s] a naturalized effect" (*Bodies That Matter*, p. 8) can, in turn, produce what feels like a "difference in nature" ("Dream-Work," p. 24). Like dreams, poems become states where the imagined force takes off, works its way through, and establishes the terrain of its own reality. What is imagined feels real. In asking, first, with Denise Riley, "Am I that name?" *Laura* seeks to dismantle any idea of a single-layered woman in the poem. In suggesting that the poet also asks "am I even what I myself frame?" it posits the construction of multiple imagining selves for the poem even as it admits that the imagining self is "the effect of a dynamic of power" (*Bodies That Matter*, p. 2). Finally, in terms of genre, when it asks "Am I that poem?" it follows James Baumlin (when he paraphrases Hayden White) to conclude that there is no simple resolution to genre concepts and that discourse involves "a dynamic interplay between received encodations of experience and alternate ways of encoding this reality" (*Donne and the Rhetorics*, p. 299). With Claudio Guillen, it assumes that genre is "an invitation to the matching (dynamically speaking) of matter and form,"[73] an invitation which asks the poetic guest to come to the party even as it expects that he might want to change the rules of the game.

Denise Riley similarly sees gender as an invitation to a mode of being which matches a permeable sense of the body to a varying body of designations. "While it is impossible to thoroughly be a woman, it is also impossible never to be one" ("*Am I That Name?*" p. 114). "Women," Riley writes, "only sometimes live in the flesh distinctively of women, as it were, and this is a function of historical categorizations as well as of an individual daily phenomenology" (p. 105). *Laura* alternates between the historical categorization of poetic influence and the "individual daily phenomenology" of poetic resistance. As an investigation of what Goldberg calls "multiplicities of gender positions" (*Sodometries*, p. 61), it is also an investigation of what Baumlin calls the "concurrent limitation and possibility of genre" (p. 305). "Muddying the content" (*"Am I That Name?"* p. 113) of woman, poet, and poem while presupposing the intertextuality of poetic influence, *Laura* is less concerned with the feminist new historical project of assessing the material reality of women in the early modern period than it is with gauging the ways in which the three problematic Lauras allow us to read female authority and presence in texts where it is thought to be excluded. Assuming with Wallace Stevens that "it is not in the premise that reality / is a solid,"[74] it views a historical time frame as simultaneously necessary for its intertextual approach and secondary to the poetic complications of the anamorphic frame. Chronicling instances of influence and resistance, it understands gender, sexuality, and genre as functions of shifting and deepening planes of imagined possibility.

From Theory to Practice: Renaissance Uncoverings

The first two chapters, "Laura as Eve to Petrarch's Adam" and "Laura as Mercury to Petrarch's Battus," describe in detail how Petrarch evolves the troublesome Laura-Eve and Laura-Mercury in the *Rime sparse* and how they unsettle the ground of Petrarch's own poetic. As the chapter "Taking Bread" will show, Wyatt reveals a similar progression in his translations. First he denies Petrarch in the retaliatory lyrics; then he dismisses Laura in the Psalms. Finally, in the three most anthologized Wyatt poems, "They flee from me," "The long love," and "Whoso list to hunt," poems compelled by Laura-Eve, Laura-Daphne, and Laura-Mercury respectively, he is so absorbed into the woman's incommensurability that he feels compelled to "leave off" poetry. Similarly, Donne bemoans the effects of Petrarchism gone awry by demonstrating how Laura-Daphne inspires a failed poem in "The Broken Heart" and "Of Weeping." In "The Dreame," he argues that, by returning his desire, Laura-Eve inspires her own poem. Speaking as a woman in "Change," Donne voices Laura-Mercury's abstractions, following her into an eternity not yet defined.

Marvell also seems to treat the conventions in three discrete stages, revealing how Petrarchism produces a deadly artist in "Damon the Mower" and "The Gallery" and a disappearing artifact in "Nymph complaining." In "Appleton House," he goes beyond the restrictions of gender and the confines of genre as he experiments with boundlessness in the river and willow sequences of stanzas 80 and 81 respectively. As the chapter on Marvell's "Appleton House" clarifies, the poetic "I" enacts what Monique Wittig calls "an interrogation which involves a process of abstraction where the other, whatever its kind, is included."[75] Abandoning his lazy side, the "I" of "Appleton House" rejoices—giving in to the woman already inside and giving up the restraints that the "cover" of masculinity demands. Releasing himself from the pressure to formulate anything, the poet uncovers a Laura in the self who further frees him from the ties that bind. Identifying the "space between signs"[76] as the realm where he chooses to be, Marvell's poetic "I" abandons himself to the pleasures of being simultaneously elsewhere and nowhere—in being, like Laura-Mercury, unlocatable. That feeling is joyous. It accounts for the pleasure Laura-Mercury experiences when she provokes the gesture "that jams sociality."[77]

Laura delineates the presence in Petrarch of a "you" who renders sexual gratification at least a possible dream and (for certain moments at least) sublimation a vanishing prospect. The doubts about poetic conventions that threaten the smooth surface of the *Canzoniere* are fleshed out by Petrarch's Renaissance imitators as they ironize the line of poetic appropriation through which the male-centered voice in their poems substantiates desire. At some critical point in their work—Petrarch in *Rime sparse* 23, Wyatt in "Whoso list to hunt," Donne in "Change," and Marvell in "Appleton House"—each of the poets writes a poem that undermines Petrarchism. But those moments occur and grow out of what is implicit in Petrarchism itself: the imaginative force of the woman's gendered subjectivity.

Uncovering that subjectivity within the anamorphic frame of the Petrarchan poem, *Laura* "break[s] the very system of representation" (*Gender Trouble*, p. 145) where—in other forums—men imprison women. From the context of those fracturings, it is possible to describe an evolution, in the period from Wyatt to Marvell, of a poetic that expands what Petrarch occasionally defines: the woman's space. If most Petrarchan poems provide models for a culturally determining standard of beauty, the space filled by the bounded and binding entity called Woman, some Petrarchan poems might now be seen as messages from elsewhere, messages that speak for "marginal space, the space of the body, and liquid space."[78] And, if most Petrarchan poems explore what Butler calls a "process of materialization" that reinforces the "naturalized effect" (*Bodies That*

Matter, p. 9) of their own binary systems, some Petrarchan poems might now be seen to open up a *dematerializing* desire, something that loosens the boundaries imposed by established gender and genre norms. The imagined woman who imbricates those other spaces goes beyond the "clear edges" of the poems containing her to reveal—"more than anything . . . the edges that blur."[79]

Petrarch

In this plenty, the poem makes meanings of the rock

Of such mixed motion and such imagery

That its barrenness becomes a thousand things

And so exists no more.

WALLACE STEVENS, "The Rock"

INVERTING THE ORDER

Laura as Eve to Petrarch's Adam

With Laura-Eve, Petrarch recasts the lyric formula, turning from the driven Daphne to a woman who, however fleetingly, returns the poet's gaze and corroborates, by feeling it, the poet's desire. Laura-Eve is Mieke Bal's Genesis 2 woman. As "the 'other character' indispensable for [Adam] to be character at all,"[1] she complicates the dyad and suggests that there is another text—the one in which the woman is the conscious subject of her own imaginative return. When she opens up the realm of the imagined woman's desires, Laura-Eve presents what Goldberg calls an "alternative possibility in the writing of gender" (*Sodometries*, p. 61). A reading of Petrarch and Petrarchism that neither elides gender differences (Petrarch simply turning himself into a Laura who reflects him) nor makes too much of them (Petrarch imagining Laura as another species, a goddess who defeats him) establishes a middle ground with a Laura who seems both like Petrarch and separate. That invention is different from the mirroring Giuseppe Mazzotta writes about where Petrarch "casts himself in the role of Apollo and, in the same breath, casts Laura as the sun."[2] Such comparisons threaten the self because they create parallels that can never meet, an irony Andrew Marvell calls "The Definition of [Petrarchan] Love."

A Laura who shares Petrarch's desire loosens the mold of her monumental idealization and annihilating negativity. Engaged in the same pursuit, Laura-Eve wants what Petrarch wants, returning gaze for gaze and restoring, with that eye, the "I" canceled by static mirroring. Within the parameters of that vision, Petrarch finds a Laura who subverts Petrarchism. Laura is both other and fellow. Like Eve who pulls away from Adam in Genesis 3, this Laura only temporarily suggests the sexual responsiveness that unhinges her conventional representation. But those rare moments complicate Petrarchan dynamics.

The Genesis story that fleshes out these complications inverts that of Aristophanes' twins in *The Symposium*.[3] In Aristophanes' allegory, the once united sexes long for a return to their originating union. In Genesis 2, Adam begins lonely and then has a brief moment, acknowledged in the exultant *now* of his awakening, when his desire is met. The *now* reflects backward to a *then*, a union already realized in his dream, and projects forward to a sequence, a separation predicted by the implied *later*. But for the moment of Genesis 2.23, the *now* fleshes out the *then*, its union, in bone of bone, a substantiated version of the dream. While, as recent critics have shown, Genesis 2 is usually seen as the text that establishes woman's second place,[4] it can also be seen as what Bal calls the text that establishes woman's necessarily identical place. The exhilaration of Adam's exultant *now* expresses his happiness at discovering an external double who knows his internal secrets. Imagining back, the Eve of Genesis 2 gives desire a mutual context. She is, as Bal also argues, the other who makes possible Adam's sexual self. As that other, Laura-Eve counters Laura-Daphne to suggest—in her momentary response—that sublimation is unnecessary. In meeting the poet's desire, she renders the poem excessive. Laura-Eve can be found *in* Petrarch-Adam by a process of anamnesis. She represents what he, earlier, dreamed. Laura-Eve can be seen *apart* from Petrarch-Adam by a process of anamorphosis. Like the implied second woman in the Bordone painting, she revives a latent image and contests the original dyad.

The momentary possible of that latent image subverts the perennially impossible of conventional Petrarchism. As a moment distilled in the course of events, the communion signals a rebuttal against time; as a moment repeated and embedded in poetic discourse, it stands as a bulwark against disintegration. Its sustaining power lies in the inversion its consolidation implies. The once realized union (Petrarch imagining a Laura who wants what he wants) presumes a mutuality of desire and commonality of understanding that makes poetic discourse feasible: it gives it a point.

With a Laura whose existence reflects an implicit understanding, Petrarch shares Adam's excitement at discovering Eve. What he sees is an other whose origin is identical to his own and who understands, because she felt it too, what he wants. Laura-Eve contravenes the exclusivity of what John Freccero calls Petrarch's "self-referentiality."[5] Marianne Shapiro speaks of how such a contravention might work in terms of time: of the presence of "adynata—impossibility—figures," she argues that Petrarch utilizes the "*impossibilia*—a daylight filled with stars, breezes gathered in a net—to affirm the fixity of desire over and above external obstacles (the cruelty of Laura). . . . The end [of the world] will be survived by the stasis of desire and the constancy of the lover. . . . The adynaton invokes the realization of the impossible."[6] If, as Shapiro maintains, the impossibility itself posits its own plausibility, there are thus moments when Laura unlaurelizes herself and naturalizes the sexual possibility. Opposing the disintegration of mere mirroring, Laura-Eve faces the "I" with a simultaneous sameness and difference. As self, Laura-Eve evokes a mutuality of origin, a resemblance represented by her understanding of Petrarch-Adam's desire.[7] As other, Laura-Eve suggests the mystery of creation, a mystery contained in Adam's deep sleep. Adam wakes to claim that he made her, but the fact is that the source of Eve's sleep-induced being, like the origin of her sleep-induced sexuality, is obscure. Petrarch seems overcome by that mystery in the poems where Laura-Eve appears. The unconscious Adam brings forth an Eve whose awakening in fact precedes his. Laura-Eve counters the formulative and confident Petrarch who creates—out of his own resources—the woman he covets. A Laura whose beginning is unexplainable is a Laura who may have a libido of her own. The Laura who undermines Petrarchism also undermines Augustine.

Dreaming Love

When, in *The Secretum*, Petrarch answers St. Augustine's accusation that his love for Laura has "detached [his] mind from the love of heavenly things,"[8] he maintains "the love which I feel for her has most certainly led me to love God" (p. 124); in his answer Petrarch has already arrived at the Augustinian purpose: the depreciation of the earthly. At the end of the *Secretum*, he prays to be led "safe and whole out of so many crooked ways" (p. 192). But it is Augustine's countercharge to Petrarch's defense that is relevant to the *Rime sparse*: "[Your love] has inverted the true order" (p. 124). To *invert the order* is, as Petrarch's Augustine argues, to worship the divine through the earthly and therefore to put the means over the end. But *inverting the order* is also to turn around to the beginning, to get at the place *before* the disintegrating present, which makes discovery possible. It is to arrive at the moment of detachment in which the other both mirrors the self and has a life that is different. It is to invent an Eve whose gaze seems to figure forth and so invent Adam. In *The Secretum*, Augustine turns the other into the self. All await the next stage. In *Rime Sparse* 237, Petrarch changes himself into the other and thereby reimagines beginnings.[9] The poem *does* end by acknowledging an Augustinian afterward (as the *Rime sparse* will in poem 366), but for a brief moment in the sixth stanza it restages a "before" that stops time. In that moment Laura-Eve appears, heralding the double subversion: that of Petrarch and Augustine. The Laura who appears in 237 comes while Petrarch-Adam is asleep.

The subversion begins in stanza two where the "I," speaking of an Augustinian "afterward" in line 1, reverts instantly to a Genesis 2 "before" in line 3: "Di dì in dì spero omai l'ultima sera / che scevri in me dal vivo terren l'onde / et mi lasci dormire in qualche piaggia" [From day to day I hope now for the last evening, / which will separate in me the living earth from the waves / And let me sleep in some meadow]. Petrarch invokes Augustine in the first two lines when he speculates that the separation that created the world in Genesis 1 anticipates the division to be enacted in the self at the end of time. As the firmament was set apart from the waters, so the body will dissolve into its elements. The Augustinian universe is based on differences that fade. It presupposes that the human being, like the earth before God set about to separate it, is chaotic. But when Petrarch inverts the order in the third line, he suspends the ordinary flow of time by praying for sleep. Just as the Genesis 2 Adam moves backward in sleep to await another beginning, so Petrarch moves inward. His desire to sleep in the meadow is a wish to repeat the experience of the dreaming Adam in Eden. In stanza 2, Petrarch prepares the ground he will consolidate in stanza 6. In 2, he is Adam asleep, awaiting Eve, looking forward to the first morning of consolidation. In stanza 6, he doubles the possibility, invoking an Adam-Endymion who stimulates an Eve-Selene. In Selene, he mirrors the desiring Adam. In Endymion, he imagines a successful Adam. As object of Eve-Selene's dream, he represents achieved desire.

Precipitating the end of time partly by incorporating the beginning in the separation of the earth from the waves of Genesis 1,[10] Petrarch leaps to Genesis 2 when he asks to become Adam asleep in the meadow. Petrarch's defense to Augustine "that the Love which I feel for [Laura] has led me to love God" (*Secretum*, p. 124) accounts for the Augustinian process of the poem. Laura prods Petrarch into despising the worldly. Petrarchism dissolves the world in this poem. But the Laura-Eve-Selene of stanza 6 suggests something else: the possibility of circumventing the dissolution. To invent a Laura who is free—one whose autonomous existence is premised on her being both like the poet in pursuit (Laura-Eve) and unlike him in her success (Laura-Selene)—is to subvert *The Secretum's* Augustine and Petrarch. The poem unwinds the way the whole *Rime sparse* ends: in a confirmation of something richer afterward. But in the dream sequences of the sixth stanza, the poem picks up on the third line of stanza 2. When he prays to sleep in the meadow, the "I" seeks an origination that stops the flow of the annihilative future. The pattern of world destruction leads to a sequence of self-consumption until the dreamer remembers the dream that cancels time: Endymion's. The speaker dreams of dreaming, and so becoming, the lover of stanza 6. That dream and its enactment reverse the progress toward dissolution, which is the ostensible story of the poem. The dream's viability approximates the same Genesis 2 euphoria Petrarch alludes to in 181, 188, and 354. The possibility for such joy counterbalances the burden of "cares" which initiates the disintegrating cycle of the sestina. In 181, 188, and 354, the joy fades quickly, as Laura-Eve regresses to the dark moments of Genesis 3. But in 237, it is sustained as dream: Adam doubled into Endymion; Eve consolidated with Selene.

The poem begins by aggrandizing the "caring" self. It is larger than sea, sky, night, woods, or meadows because its suffering contains them. The progress from stanza 1 to stanza 6 includes a recession. The "I," who begins as the larger-than-life generator of the world, ends—smaller than life—diminished by the world he earlier fathered. First he is progenitor; then he is mothered by—nested in—nature's sanctuary. As the sea is filled by waves, so the "I" is engrossed by "cares." In stanza 1, internal "cares" are more capacious than external stars, birds, and grass and the "I" is represented in a figure that renders him the Ur-generator. He is central because he suffers more, his enduring self magnified into a gigantic vessel:

> Non à tanti animali il mar fra l'onde,
> né lassù sopra 'l cerchio de la luna
> vide mai tante stelle alcuna notte,
> né tanti augelli albergan per li boschi,
> né tant' erbe ebbe mai campo né piaggia
> quant' à 'l mio cor pensier ciascuna sera. (p. 395)

> The sea has not so many creatures among its waves,
> nor up there beyond the circle of the moon
> were so many stars ever seen by any night,
> nor do so many birds dwell in the woods,
> nor did any field ever have so much grass, or any meadow,
> as I have cares in my heart every evening. (p. 394)

45

Like God alluding to the children Abraham will father (Genesis 14.14–16; Genesis 15.5), Petrarch numbers the world in terms of infinite fish, stars, birds, and blades of grass, the multiplying vista reduced by what Petrarch fathers: cares. His capacity to contain them makes him larger than the world itself, even as the world is generated by that paternity. His cares emerge as the consciousness through which the expanding universe comes into being. But, if Petrarch is Abraham, he is also Cronos: the father who eats the children he fathers. The desire to reduce cares, and so erase the elements that constitute awareness, leads to a desire to destroy the world. A "careful" self, exploding with world wonders, seeks to make the world less wonderful. The self-reduction that occurs in the course of the poem results in a domino movement. The circular pattern of the sestina— encompassing elements of space (waves, wood, meadow) and time (evening, moon, night)—is self-destructive. The elements are consumed as they circulate. But the "I" whose cares produced the world is also self-reductive. And, in 237, that reductiveness works in his favor. Shrinking himself, he doubles Laura. She is both Eve and Selene.

The bruised "I" bruises the world by caving in. The wished-for world destruction, culminating in the separation of living earth from waves, coincides with the wished-for self-destruction. The only way to stop the process is to stop the "I": "mi lasci dormire in qualche piaggia" (p. 395) [let me sleep in some meadow] (p. 394). A poet who begins with the self as expansive originator of the world finally arrests—by begging for sleep— the self that feels the cares. Once the "I" ceases to think of himself as the father of the world, he creates an aura that brings on the world's separate life. That life unfolds as the "I" wishes away man's makings (the cities he constructs) to be unmade in the pastoralized meadow. Civilization is raised to be razed. The flowers of April lead to the grassy meadows; the sun makes way for the moon; the wet grass evolves into the empty woods and clears the way for the cities. When the thinking "I" subsides, the world returns to its nonhuman origins. Other is other. Another picture surfaces—one where the woman is the founding figure.

The evolution into pastoral that causes division is a nostalgia that leads into the sixth stanza vision. "Cities are hateful to me, friendly the woods." Augustinian division presupposes a future disintegration. Progress within that frame leads to the chaos that destroys it: the tower of Babel. When, in the fifth stanza, Petrarch evokes the idea of *locus amoenus* by personifying cities and woods, he demystifies progress and sets the stage for the dream vision. The cities that he hates are converted into cities that hate him, pushing him into the friendly, more receptive, woods. But the division goes deeper. Earlier in the poem, the thinking "I" contained the woods by virtue of the immensity of his thoughts. Now, by virtue of their friendliness, their compatibility and receptivity to those thoughts, the woods contain him. They become womblike. The father needs a mother and so he sets about inventing one, bringing the sea with him to the woods. The watery afterbirth is sucked back into the wavy origin. To herald the maternity he needs, the "I" imitates the life-giving ocean. His song mimics the murmuring waves now contained by the night. Before he enclosed the world; now the world encloses him. Like Adam in the garden, the "I" befriends the world. Earlier his "eye waves" blew the world down. Here he awaits the orderly departure of the sun. If the world is spatially parceled out into woods and cities, so time is subdivided into day and night. The sun makes way for the moon. Apollo yields to Selene. The "I" who made the world now is made *by* the world. The "I" who pursued the woman now is pursued by her. The creative "I" in this poem decreates himself so that he can, in sleeping, be mothered by nature and loved by Selene. Petrarchism acquires another originary myth.

When the "I" asks for sleep, he lets things happen. His wish emerges as a desire to be Endymion and Adam, dreamers whose women return their desire. With the wish, the "I" inverts the order. Eve-Selene[11] comes to him. Like Endymion, the "I" is granted immortality in sleep. That immortality renders him the eternally entranced Adam: always at the point before the beginning, the night before day. To make Laura into the initiator is to invert the order. Instead of being opposed to Love, she joins "with Him." God and woman act in unison. Laura lulls the "I" into the sleep that imagines her. Held in a moment of arrested time, the "I" finds an end that is a perpetual beginning. As Adam asleep in the meadow, he awaits Eve. As Endymion asleep in the woods, he excites Selene. The doubling myths present two possibilities: first, an Eve who returns Adam's gaze; then a Selene who succeeds in her desire. Coupling biblical expectation with mythic realization, Petrarch's evocation of Endymion in his wish brings on the possible Selene:

> Deh, or foss' io col vago de la luna
> adormentato in qua' che verdi boschi,
> et questa ch' anzi vespro a me fa sera
> con essa et con Amor in quella piaggia
> sola venisse a starsi ivi una notte,
> e 'l dì si stesse e 'l sol sempre ne l'onde! (p. 397)

Ah, would that with the lover of the moon
I had fallen asleep in some green wood,
and that she who before vespers gives me evening
with the moon and with Love to that shore
might come alone to stay there one night,
and that the day might stay, and the sun, forever under the waves! (p. 396)

The "she" who gives him "evening before vespers"—Laura-Eve-Selene—
grants the wish of the fifth stanza: "all day I await evening." Her temporal
gratification is immediate. She brings on the night and moonshine which
turn the sight lines around to focus on the "I" as desired object. Petrarch's transformation from Father-inventor of the world to infant-child
of Mother Earth allows him to imagine the Laura who seeks him. The
"old" Laura, the one who hastens evening, heralds the new Laura, the one
who extends the night of love. Her first mention in the poem is also her
reinvention. It is Laura-Eve who renders Petrarch Adam, thereby making
him the creator of her, the origin of the revision that occurs in the sixth
stanza. Like Bal's Eve, she is the sexual other who discovers—and therefore comes before—man's sexual self. And it is Laura-Selene who renders
Adam Endymion dreaming the dream that posits a moment of sexual
success. As Selene, Laura joins forces with Love to prove her continued
attraction to Endymion. She inverts the order. The chaste woman chases.

Petrarch's dream of Laura actually triples her power. She is all at once
the "she" who started the process of wishing for the end (the "she" who
brings on evening), the moon goddess who hunts the "I" (the "she" who
pursues him), and Love (the woman capable of achieving her wishes). Her
"staying" becomes an eternity. The night perpetuates the stilling day. The
story of Endymion is a non-Ovidian myth and, when Petrarch uses it, he
re-creates an "I" who returns to a pre-Christian beginning. The phrase
"*with* the lover of the moon" suggests that the "I" lives contemporaneously with Endymion and that he doubles for him. In his passivity, he
nevertheless attracts the triplicate Laura who engenders her coming and
staying. Longing for sleep, the "I" becomes Adam, thereby recasting that
moment in Genesis 2 when the shore becomes the shore of the self, the
threshold or interspace that allows for the entrance of the other. Falling
asleep with Endymion, the "I" regresses further into passivity. It is Selene
who determines his being as the object of *her* desire.

When the shore leads to the meadow, the poem returns thematically to
stanza 2 where the Augustinian emergences reverse to a womblike retreat.
Inverting the order in stanza 6 means avoiding the inevitability of disin-

tegration which the poem sets into motion. There are then two shores: the first, the conventional Augustinian end where demarcation succeeds and where the living earth will finally be freed from the waves; the second, a reattachment where meadow and wave hook up, forming the womb that cradles the sleeping "I." There he can evolve a vision prodded by the nay-saying Laura who creates in him the need for an other but fulfilled by the pursuing Laura who comes because of *her* need for him. To invent Laura-Eve is to acknowledge that the woman has the potential to be like him, to be the desirer. To invent Laura-Selene is to imagine a rebirth that engenders a reversal of roles. First the meadow emerges as the womb which makes the man the child of love; then the man grows into the erotic source of the woman's sexual desire.

By referring to a myth whose emphasis is on regeneration, Petrarch's regendering (turning Laura into the pursuer) also turns the sight lines around. As a poetic form, the sestina is anamorphic; the end of one stanza prods another beginning, one that seems totally out of sync with the "good form" of the preceding one. When he appears as Adam, Petrarch envisions Eve; his gaze, on awakening, corroborates her being. When he appears as Endymion, Petrarch becomes the gazed upon rather than gazer, the compelling object that draws the moon to the shore. In the recapitualtion, the "I" is duplicated. In the reversal, Laura comes first. The "good form" becomes a still better form as the myth of Endymion exceeds the "good wishes" of the Petrarchan myth maker. With Selene, Petrarch dispels Daphne (the woman who denies sexuality) to represent a woman who invents sexuality and pursues the sleeping man. Laura-Eve merely repeats what Petrarch-Adam imagines; Laura-Selene achieves what he can never accomplish. Preempting postcoital depression, Laura-Selene keeps coming back for more, compelled, as the moon is by the tides, by a reactivating principle.

The Laura-Selene who prolongs the temporal present of the dream extends the spatial parameters so that they lead not outward to the disintegrating waves but inland to the reintegrating meadow. What she holds at bay is the sun, the original Apollo who conceived the Daphne who evades him. The reversal starts a new cycle. The regendering ends the dynamic of failure figured by the woman's denial. As female song, Endymion's aubade bids the sun stay forever under the waves. When he inspires a woman who, awakened by love, becomes the instrument of perpetuating desire, Endymion stops time. He holds the sun and its conventions at bay. The aubade signals the final gender reversal. When he sings the female wish to prolong the night of love, Petrarch anticipates Donne's "Breake of Day" and Juliet's "nightingale." Even there, Petrarch makes Laura not only his sexual equal but his professional one as well. The poetics of a woman's song govern his. If the sun stays forever under the waves, then the female wish of the aubade is granted and desire is forever reconstituted. Apollo and Daphne are replaced by the moony replicas of Selene-Endymion. The chorus of their regenerating dream is echoed in the vision of their engendered likenesses. Selene is Eve idealized. She returns love without death and reproduces life without the fall.

As Adam dreaming, Petrarch evolves a woman capable of fulfilling the sexual wish. As Eve, she is the dream made flesh. But as Selene, she goes one step further. She is flesh made fleshlier,[12] engendering, in the offspring she mothers, fifty daughters who will (similarly) project fifty lovers to perpetuate the cross-gendered cycle she initiates. She replicates her desire by holding time still. She keeps the sun away and produces daughters who reflect her biological image. When she grants the wish of the aubade and the wish of the family, Selene shatters the semiotic system of conventional Petrarchism. With Apollo out of the picture, she suggests a poetic whose woman inspires a new poem. The aubade promises her poetic success. She displaces the Apollonian sun. The daughters guarantee her procreative success. She engenders the future. Calmly pursuing love with the ease of endlessly fulfilled desire, she outdoes the (at first) frenetic and (then) static Daphne by uprooting the laurel. When the world turns upside down in her song, she stops the sun, canceling Apollo. The female complaint obviates the male lament. Through the sleeping Endymion, Selene initiates a cycle of returned satisfaction. As unconscious object of her gaze, as willing returner of sexuality, Petrarch-Endymion is the instrument of matriarchy.

Glimpsing Love

If, in conventional Petrarchism, Laura-Daphne is the helpless victim of the man's gaze and, in 237, Adam-Endymion is the sleeping stimulus of the woman's gaze, the mutually awakened Petrarch-Adam and Laura-Eve of 181, 188, and 354 are visually equal. Laura-Eve is not only a mutual seer. She is a conscious subject. To the aroused Adam, her look fleshes out the sympathetic other of the deep sleep. In 181, 188, and 354, Adam awakens to see Eve seeing him. The discovery of Eve is a recovery of a self whose consciousness is aroused by her gaze.[13] Though she never reappears in the *Canzoniere*, Laura-Eve signals the responsive possibility. In 181, 188, and 354 the momentary possible is quickly overcome, but its brief presence complicates Petrarchan denial.

In 181, denial becomes a net, holding the "I." In 188, it is called a bane, still another net, foreshadowing Eve's poisonous role. External trap in 181, Laura-Eve is internalized in 188. In 354, she becomes something the poet imagined in the past, the "I" left only with instructions to reconstruct what seems now forever lost. But the reflection remains—opening the possibility for another story. The reconstruction—too late—posits the second story. Unlike the sixth stanza of 237, where time stands still and the dream is repeatedly re-realized, the Genesis 2 poems contain only one realization: the never-to-be-repeated moment of Adam's awakening. Each of the poems quickly dispels that vision. But the mere mention of it (1) undermines Augustine by suggesting the second creation; (2) subverts Petrarchism by incarnating a desiring Laura. In 181 and 188, the movement from Genesis 2 to Genesis 3 comes rather quickly. Laura-Eve emerges as the destructive Daphne and the conventions are restored. But in 354, the perspective changes. Genesis 3 has been usurped by the New Testament regeneration, the original Fall already overcome. In 354, Laura-Eve is neither the blight of 181 nor the poison of 188. Already angelic, she is un-reachable, except in memory. When Love commands Petrarch to "weeping write," he commemorates the possibility for Petrarchan success even as he recognizes the impulse of Petrarchan poetics.

To re-create the momentary possible is to preserve the possibility of the moment. In 354, Love's decree validates the existence of a Laura who, in gazing back, imagines him. That moment gives Petrarch an audience who asks for what the poet wants to give: more poems. In obeying Love, Petrarch anticipates Herbert's commanded "I" in "Love III," an "I" who, following the Christian Love's insistence, gets to do what he has wanted all along. If the expressed answer in "Love III" is "So I did sit and eat,"[14] the implied answer in 354 reflects on Petrarch's accomplishment in the *Rime sparse:* "So I did sit and write." Love's command converts Petrarch's self-indulgent pleasures into divinely sanctified acts—validated (however momentarily) by the Laura-Eve who imagines back. The process of Laura's dissolution from the embodied Eve evoked at the beginning of the poems to disembodied Daphne figured by the shadow of 181, the bane of 188, and the memory of 354 parallels the poet's regression from solid Adam to eclipsed Apollo.

Love begins and ends the Adam sequences in 181. The "I's" focus is not on the dream and its possibility for perpetuation but on the awakening and its potential uniqueness:

> Amor fra l'erbe una leggiadra rete
> d'oro e di perle tese sott' un ramo
> dell'arbor sempre verde chi'i'tant' amo,
> ben che n'abbia ombre più triste che liete.
>
> L'esca fu'l seme ch' egli sparge et miete
> dolce et acerbo, ch'i' pavento et bramo;
> le note non fur mai, dal dì ch' Adamo
> aperse gli occhi, sì soavi et quete;
>
> e'l chiaro lume che sparir fa'l sole
> folgorava dintorno, e 'l fune avolto
> era a la man ch' avorio et neve avanza.
>
> Così caddi a la rete, et qui m'àn colto
> gli atti vaghi et l'angeliche parole
> e 'l piacer e 'l desire et la speranza. (p. 327)

> Love set out amid the grass a gay net of gold and pearls, under a branch of the evergreen tree that I so love, although it has more sad than happy shadows.
>
> The bait was that seed he sows and harvests, sweet and bitter, which I fear and desire; the birdcall was never so soft and quiet since the day when Adam opened his eyes;
>
> and the bright light that makes the sun disappear was lightening all around, and the rope was wrapped around the hand that surpasses ivory and snow.
>
> Thus I fell into the net; and I have been captured here by her sweet bearing, and her angelic words, and pleasure and desire and hope. (p. 326)

The assessment of the "I's" *never* in the second stanza links to Adam's *now* in its recapitulation of the impossible-to-equal day. With the implication that "never" means *never again*, the "I" heightens the exquisiteness of the momentary *now* in Genesis 2. In the "now" of Adam's awakening in

Genesis 2.24, Eve is a physical possibility. In the "never" of Petrarch's awareness here, Laura emerges only a semiotic inevitability. In stanza 1, Love imitates the Genesis moment, casting the net that seems womblike. The seed he sows moves backward in time, luring a bird whose call anticipates a calm: a softness and quiet. The seed that entices the bird in pursuit of nurture equates hunger with sexual appetite. The ungendered bird responds to the seed, which becomes both nutriment, as end, and embryo, as beginning. The bird's song is ambiguous. Is it the call to seduction or the response to seduction? Is the seduction alimentary or sexual? Is the seduced bird the male issuing the mating call or the neutered child responding to the dinner bell? Is Laura-Eve mother or lover? Who sings the song—the beckoning mother or beckoned child, denying beloved or denied lover? In the moment of calm, the nutritional and sexual quest merge.

The desiring lover pursues the desired mother whose presence—as the first to awaken and as gestating parent—precedes his. Lover and child are pacified by the responsive seed-bearer, a Laura who, as mother and beloved, appears as willing to feed Petrarch's sexual and nutritional appetite. But the oedipal union of Laura as mother and lover dissolves when the child, turning toward the light, grows into the man compelled by it. Divorced from nutritional hunger, sexual appetite divides the world. The female privileges the surplus of her nurturing; the male is relegated to the lack represented by his desire. The division heightens the opposition. Similarly, if harmony brings on its opposite, noise, so light evokes its rival, the sun, an incarnation which, in turn, fosters the Apollo-Daphne chase. As mother holding the seed, Laura precedes Petrarch. As beloved refusing the seed, Laura controls Petrarch. In both cases, she determines his status. The seductive invitation and the reductive denial are hers. The beckoning birdcall dissolves into the poet's plaintive voice.

As in 237, the sun disappears. The linear beams from Laura's eyes stretch into the net that encircles the lover. His capture means his rebirth into "pleasure and desire and hope." If, in 237, the sun is vanquished by the enclosing darkness, here it is dissipated, diminished by "the lightening all around." The lightening eventuates into whitening and surpasses ivory and snow as the visible world is blanketed by Laura's overwhelming light. If Cupid's hand sets the net in motion, Laura's hand takes over, so that she assumes the primary position of capturer. As source of light, she replaces Apollo. As source of language, she inspires Petrarch to write. Her "hand" controls the pen of Petrarch's idolatry. Her turning away governs his impulse to project her as his desire. First, he is the bird in pursuit of the seed he wants to absorb. Then he grows into the bird who contains the seed he wants to disperse. The enticing bird flees as the enticed bird follows. She teases with what she will not give. He gives what she refuses to want.

When Laura's hand casts the net, her captivation emerges a trap, the seed no longer something the mother offers but something the woman rejects. Cupid's net now is wound around Laura's hand and that "hand" determines his poetic emergence. A light that fades into whiteness is one that blinds the "I." Overcome by the indistinguishable forms playing into whiteness, the "I" can make out two things only: "sweet bearing" and "angelic words." Ordinary sight is replaced by the elusive "sweet bearing." Ordinary sound is elevated to the heavenly "angelic words." The Laura, who begins by her resemblance to what Adam saw, ends wholly otherwise. Her presence connotes absence. Her being dissipates into impression. She isn't someone to see or hear; she has already been translated into her aura. Clumsily, the "I" falls, his inadequate stance contrasted to her sweet bearing, his faltering words opposed by her angelic ones. Quickly, Laura-Eve becomes her qualities; she is all adjectival (sweetness and angelic)—everything as perfection, nothing as compatriot. What begins as a moment of heightened awareness (a stillness that foster identity) leads to an Eve so different that she turns into the conventionally inaccessible Daphne (a difference that governs unattainability). Her "bearing" and "words" produce the poet's semiotic "pleasure, desire, and hope." They inaugurate the endless Petrarchan chase, which is represented by the disappearing Apollo pursuing the evasive Daphne, each only a shadow of his/her previously embodied self.[15] The Eve who began as distinguishable other who makes sexual distinction possible is reduced to a projection of Petrarch's denied self. Her "sweet bearing" and "angelic words" signify her physical unavailability. As she fades into Daphne, he grows as her originator and the poem comes into being again.

In 188, the disappointment arrives earlier, as the "I" aligns himself with the sun overpowered in 181:

> Almo sol, quella fronde ch'io sola amo
> tu prima amasti, or sola al bel soggiorno
> verdeggia et senza par poi che l'adorno
> suo male et nostro vide in prima Adamo.
>
> Stiamo a mirarla, i'ti pur prego et chiamo,
> o sole; et tu pur fuggi et fai dintorno

ombrare i poggi et te ne porti il giorno,
et fuggendo mi tòi quel chi'i' più bramo.

L'ombra che cade da quell'umil colle
ove favilla il mio soave foco,
ove 'l gran lauro fu picciola verga,

crescendo mentr'io parlo, agli occhi tolle
la dolce vista del beato loco
ove'l mio cor con la sua donna alberga. (p. 335)

Life-giving sun, you first loved that branch which is all I love; now, unique in her sweet dwelling, she flourishes, without an equal since Adam first saw his and our lovely bane.

Let us stay to gaze at her, I beg and call on you, O sun, and you still run away and shadow the hillsides all around and carry off the day and fleeing you take from me what I most desire.

The shadow that falls from that low hill where my gentle fire is sparkling, where the great laurel was a little sapling,

growing as I speak, takes from my eyes the sweet sight of the blessed place where my heart dwells with his lady. (p. 334)

This time, the "I" conflates: Daphne, Eve, and Laura; and Apollo, Adam, Petrarch. The "she," whom Apollo first loved, now flourishes and emerges full fledged into her sublimated being. The initial sighting renders the identical, identifying Eve into the separating, deadly "bane." Her loveliness is momentary, merely an oxymoronic precedent to her poison ("lovely bane"). In its anteriority, however, the loveliness still evokes the joy of waking. The subjective pleasure of first seeing is the result of the objective stasis of having been seen. Eve got there first. She even got there before Daphne, displacing historical chronology and suggesting that the Judaeo-Christian myth imaginatively comes before the Greek one. That anamnesis revives a woman who, folded over into the *Rime sparse*, suggests "a partial provocation that calls into question the fundamental premise" (*Bodies That Matter*, p. 19) of Petrarchism. In fact, Laura-Eve's materiality suggests a "change in nature" ("Dream-Work," p. 24). But the change is only momentary.

Pleading for the unity of that moment in the second stanza, the "I" attempts to still the sun, who in its "running" isolates the "I." If 181 ends in a dazzling whiteness, 188 ends in shadow, the "I" a burnt-out case, separated both from Apollo and Adam. When Apollo pulls away spatially, Adam retreats temporally. As the male gazers disappear, the initial little sapling grows. But, like the whiteness of 181, the darkness of 188 confuses the "eye"/"I." He cannot see the growing laurel because, deprived of the companionship of the other gazers, particularly of that central "eye" (the sun), he is blind. "Eyeless," he is "I"-less. His sight this time is not taken by Laura but by Apollo. She arrests a more important organ: his heart. The "gentle fire" of stanza 2 is Laura, who grows in stanza 3, inflamed by the speaker's praise as well as with his burning heart. Separated from the source of his life (because his heart remains with the lady), the "I" is consumed by a "she" who, having absorbed his energetic center, feeds on its oxygen.

If, in 181, Laura disappears into her aura, in 188 Laura appears as menace. The air of Petrarch's sighs becomes the bellows that aggrandizes her flames. His heart dwindled by the beloved, his body and mind gradually consumed by the fire, the "I" is the Actaeon/Petrarch pursued by his hounds. He is divided from his life, which is absorbed by the lady who consumes it, and divided from Apollo, who refuses to relume himself or gaze on his laurel. If, in 237, the "I" prayed for darkness, here he prays for light, singing of his gradual disintegration and replacement by the flourishing lady. The initiating mirroring lasts only until the loveliness is acknowledged, the unification of Adam, Apollo, and Petrarch overcome by the "bane." The identity between Laura and Petrarch, represented by the allusion to Adam waking, is quickly dissipated in these poems by the allusion to Adam betrayed (in 181 by an Eve who overpowers him, in 188 by an Eve who poisons him). In 181, Petrarch-Adam disintegrates into Petrarch-Apollo pursuing Daphne. In 188, Petrarch-Adam, abandoned by Apollo, is left at the end of the Ovidian myth, with a tree whose phantasmagoric size overwhelms the envisioner and so eradicates his vision. When tainted with the bane of Genesis 3, the sapling of the Ovidian myth becomes the poison tree of Eden.

In 354, the Augustinian separation has already taken effect. Clinging to his "tired frail style," the "I" feels impotent to rise to the heavenly occasion:

> Deh, porgi mano a l'affannato ingegno,
> Amor, et a lo stile stanco et frale

per dir di quella ch'è fatta immortale
et cittadina del celeste regno;

dammi, Signor, che 'l mio dir giunga al segno
de le sue lode, ove per sé non sale,
se vertù, se beltà non ebbe eguale
il mondo che d'aver lei non fu degno.

Responde: "Quanto 'l Ciel et io possiamo,
e i buon consigli e 'l conversar onesto,
tutto fu in lei di che noi Morte à privi;

forma par non fu mai dal dì ch' Adamo
aperse li occhi in prima; et basti or questo,
piangendo il dico, et tu piangendo scrivi." (p. 551)

Ah, reach your hand to my weary mind, Love, and to my tired
frail style to speak of her who has become immortal and a
citizen of the heavenly kingdom;

grant, Lord, that my speech may hit the target of her praises,
where by itself it cannot rise, since virtue and beauty equal to
her were never in the world, which was not worthy to have
her.

He replies "All that Heaven and I can do and good counsel and
virtuous life, all was in her whom Death has taken from us;

there has never been a form equal to hers, not since the day
when Adam first opened his eyes; and let this now suffice:
weeping I say it, and do you weeping write. (p. 550)

If 188 reverts to Eve, the bane who divides Adam from the heart of his
energetic self and the companionship of his sympathetic others, 354 begins
with separation. Eve's birth already anticipates her Augustinian sacrifice.
Equating Eve with Laura, Love laments his impotence and Petrarch's
inadequacy: "there has never been a form equal to hers." In declaring Eve's
superiority to the poetic forms that idealize the woman, Love also proclaims her equality to the dreams that invented her. As woman, she fulfills
the erotic dream. As poetic projection, she dwarfs the eroticized dreamer.
Petrarch cannot, in recollection, reincarnate Eve. Her dreamed-of form
exceeds his poetic form. The "never" in this poem is a nostalgia that leads
only to heavenly realization.

But at the end of the poem, Love himself subverts Augustine. When he says "not since the day when Adam first opened his eyes," he recollects the threshold moment when Eve emerged Adam's sexual equal. Here, she is neither bane nor net. She is still looking backward, standing in front of Adam, the mirror who reflects him, the other who regards him. Here, Love weeps and then commands Petrarch to write. Love's answer recalls the Eve who was Adam's companion even as He anticipates—with the weeping—the fact that she won't come again. Adam's eyes are open, witness to Eve his predecessor. Love's eyes weep, anticipating what has already been described as the hazy separation into the whiteness of Laura's hand (181) and the blackness of Apollo's shadows (188). Petrarch's eyes are mirrors. They duplicate Laura's image. With Love as his spur, Petrarch achieves the companionship 188 denied. The inaccessible Laura eventuates into heaven. But Love's command is commemorative; it inverts the order and returns to that moment, realized in 237, where Laura mirrors Adam-Petrarch and the dream allows him to enfold her. If, as Mazzotta and Vickers argue,[16] Laura is dismembered by conventional Petrarchism, this subversion of Petrarchism re-members her, if only for the initiating moment, sometimes recalled in the course of the *Rime sparse*, that inverts the Augustinian order. To look back at the end to another beginning is to presuppose another story. Genesis 2 is that other story, its momentary discovery premising a *now* where Eve both mirrors Adam—hence shares his desire—and is different from Adam—hence can return his desire. The possibility of such a Laura, the one realized in the dream vision of 237 and remembered in 181, 188, and 354, subverts Petrarchism's main plot.

Love's command to "weeping write" suggests the possibility for a sympathetic other even as it recognizes the inevitability of the withdrawing other. Sexuality involves open eyes—regarding the other regarding the self. Speaking and writing are premised on blurring the eye, partly to re-create, in weeping, the other writing projects, partly to body forth the vision of the awry eye, a being suggesting absence-of-being. The watery vision produces its own vale of tears: the text. And the text is constructed by the poet's imagination. In 237, 181, 188, and 354, Petrarch returns to a poetic origin which momentarily includes external sight, evoking a Laura-Eve, reflective enough to understand his desire as audience, different enough to fulfill his desire as other.

To reanimate the moment of Adam's awakening in poems where Eve slips very quickly into net and bane is to anticipate Love's memory in 354. When Love recalls Adam waking, he unites his weeping self with the weeping Petrarch. Both mourn the lost discovery but both recognize its past existence. Adam opened his eyes to return Eve's gaze and discovered her discovering him. In that moment of discovery, the dream became reality. When Love urges Petrarch to weeping write, he resuscitates a Laura who suggests that the nature of physical attraction is an imaginative return. To privilege Laura-Eve is to kindle the reversal of 237, if only through tears: the loss recovered in what Petrarch perpetually will "weeping" write. In 354, the commanded "I" receives divine approval for what he has been doing all along. Despite tears, the sanction is phrased not in terms of the conventionally denying Laura but in the figure of the accessibly reflective Eve who appears only briefly in the *Rime sparse* as an inversion, promising—however fleetingly—a return that validates poetic dreaming. Taken together, *Rime sparse* 237, 181, 188, and 354 flesh out the subversive possibility that Laura—usually running away from Petrarch— might return the desire she elsewhere evades. That Laura-Eve appears at all gives the *Canzoniere* a focus which the sublimating laurels of other poems diffuse, as they substitute word for woman and Petrarch's invented sight for Laura's reciprocating gaze.

If, in the Laura-Selene of 237, Petrarch imagines a woman who is the agent of her own sexual satisfaction and who uses him to realize her desire, in the Laura-Eve of 181, 188, and 354, Petrarch imagines a woman whose sexual agency temporarily at least precedes his projection. Laura-Eve is a woman whose gaze anticipates—by visually isolating it—and mothers—by visually feeding it—desire. That mutually reflective vision renders sexuality an imaginative return, what Virginia Woolf calls "the collaboration that has to take place in the mind between the woman and the man before the act of creation can take place."[17] The collaboration recasts the lyric myth. Daphne to Petrarch's Apollo, the conventional Laura is first seen by the sun and then subsumed as laurel. The poet's eye and voice are unified in the song that idealizes her form. Eve to Petrarch's Adam, the woman of 237, 181, 188, and 354 first sees the poet and then kindles his sexuality. The poet's eye and voice are preceded by the gaze that objectifies him. As the net of 181 and the poison tree of 188, the woman subsequently reduces him to a dependency which he, in turn and belatedly, calls her inaccessibility. Imaginatively, before Apollo there was Adam, and before Daphne there was Eve, the woman whose presence as sexual mother—holding out the seed—precedes his emergence as poetic father—engendering the forms of male desire. Eve's first look is subsumed in the rest of the *Rime sparse* by a poet who—as blinding sun—renders

Laura incapable of staring back and—as pursuing god—renders her generically resistant to desiring back. But, for the moment of mutual seeing in 237, 181, 188, and 354, Eve contests the fundamental premises of Petrarchism. Those subversions suggest "an alternative domain of cultural intelligibility" (*Gender Trouble*, p. 146) where the woman's sexual imagination kindles the man's sexual awareness.

Such subversions are centralized in Renaissance poems like Wyatt's "They flee from me" and Donne's "The Dreame" where the sexually desiring woman comes before both the sexual and linguistic imagination of the man. Like Chloë in the Bordone painting, Laura-Eve's sexuality prompts the gesture—the out-reaching—which is returned by the circle of endlessly replicated desire. *Rime sparse* 237, 181, 188, and 354 suggest that the form of Petrarchan success—the poem itself—can be upset by a woman whose performance challenges the notion of an originating "I." When the poet presents himself as Petrarch-Adam, he responds to a Laura who wants him.

In *Rime sparse* 23, Laura-Eve's deformations widen to include the knife-wielding Laura-Mercury. Her evasions there are not those of the fleeing Daphne whose laurel the poet invents but those of the abstracting Mercury whose resistance forces the poet to reinvent (by an act of conscious repression at the end of *Rime sparse* 23, or by an art of deliberate conversion in 105, 125, 127, and 129) the forms of his desire. If Laura-Eve posits a moment of fleshly return, Laura-Mercury resists both flesh and poem, alluding to a realm beyond intelligibility, and beyond Adam's image-making and Eve's image-substantiating, capacities. Laura-Eve returns Petrarch-Adam to himself, her sexual enclosures rendering the consoling closure of poetic form unnecessary. Laura-Mercury breaks the form to suggest yet another dimension—that of the incommensurable—opened up by the anamorphic lens.

"LIKE A MAN WHO THINKS AND WEEPS AND WRITES"

Laura as Mercury to Petrarch's Battus

Ending Beginnings: Laura's Evasions

If the Laura-Eve of *Rime sparse* 237 matches the poet's physical desire, the Laura-Mercury of 23 outpaces his poetic ambition. She challenges him: first by claiming to elude his image; and then by proclaiming her own creative capacity, as god who exceeds even his imagination. Why does Petrarch invent a woman to trouble the smooth workings of his invention? Can he get out of the trouble he imagines or is the anamorphic picture Laura-Mercury uncovers too deep? Is she a force Petrarch cannot write out? Does she suggest a "difference in nature" ("Dream-Work," p. 24) which is unalterable? Is her revenge—like that of the mirror people—a takeover? Even critics like Giuseppe Mazzotta[1] and Timothy Bahti,[2] who see a difficult, rather than a complicitous, woman and who describe her problematics in terms of Petrarch's own block, do not account for the full scope of her powers. Their readings (Mazzotta's as representation of Petrarch's failure to believe in the self, Bahti's as representation of Petrarch's success in reconstructing the self) avoid Laura-Mercury's critical and poetic equality to Petrarch.

To overcome the competitive Laura and the nihilism she represents (as Petrarch does in 105, 125, 126, 127, and 129) is both to take her seriously as other and to interrogate the self. Her presence in those poems is not merely an aberration. By imbrication, she works her way through all of the *Rime sparse*. In these five instances, she forces the issue by casting the first stone. As the subjective addressee who asks about "what it consists in" (*The Differend*, p. 139) and as objective reader of the text that contains her, Laura-Mercury indicts Petrarch. The Laura that Petrarch needs to write out if he is to go on writing is the Laura who challenges his writing her in: the Laura of *Rime sparse* 23. The remarkable being she presents there undoes the self Petrarch wrote for her, even though her not being—her refusal to be what he thinks she is—is also authored by Petrarch. Her authority derives from both her alterity and her similarity. If Laura can do what Petrarch does, she can also undo what he does. And if, as Butler reasons, "the materiality of bodies [is] the effect of a dynamic of power" (*Bodies That Matter*, p. 2), part of that dynamic might also be the power to evade prescribed forms altogether: "One of the ambivalent implications of the decentering of the subject is to have one's writing be the site of a necessary and inevitable expropriation" (*Bodies That Matter*, p. 241). Laura-Mercury takes over the writer's domain by proposing de-formation. She thereby hits Petrarch where it hurts most.

In the Battus episode, Laura is not simply the idealized and different "other" to be wooed. She emerges crueller because she exercises her control in the very arena of Petrarch's power: in the field of telling. The sequence begins with Laura's injunction against telling ("di ciò non far parola" [make no word of this]) in line 74, passes to her complaint against the telling ("I' non son forse chi tu credi" [I am not perhaps who you think I am], l. 82), through Petrarch's reduction to watery Byblis and shadowy Echo, and finally climaxes in his deer conversion in 150 through 160. Like Diana who disables Actaeon's telling, Laura-Mercury forbids speech. But unlike Diana, she explains why she resists formulation. In so doing, she undoes Petrarch's words. Her "I am not perhaps who you think I am" is a commentary about his false representation as well as a deconstruction of the vision that leads to the formulation. Her eyes set the stage for her words even as her words define her subjectivity. It's not only that Petrarch can't tell; it's that he can't see. What he can't see is first hidden by Laura's disguise and finally withheld by her revelation. She may look like a woman, but she does a man's work. She may look like a mortal, but she has a god's powers. The nature of her godliness preempts the nature of Petrarch's artfulness as the nature of her elusiveness annuls his prioritizing. She is his mirror as image and his better as god. If poetry casts the poet as the maker of the woman, then *life* renders the gods as the makers of men. As god, Mercury comes before Battus. As human, Laura-Mercury comes before Petrarch-Battus. She is the arch shape-changer, the mercurial thief who steals his energy (by taking his heart) and who sets up a new hegemony (by overtaking his art).

The Battus episode is framed by Laura's gaze ("she who with her glance steals souls" [questa che col mirar gli anima fura], l. 72). It results in the poet's visual split. As the deer in the Actaeon episode, Petrarch first feels himself drawn from his own image and then sees only what Laura sees.

Laura's compulsions tear him from himself. Out of his body, he is out of the mind that projects the images constituting discourse ("chi' i' senti' trarmi de la propria imago" [I felt myself drawn from my own image], l. 157). The disorientation occurs because his idea of himself—his proper image—has assumed the woman's shape. Defining the poet as an image, Petrarch renders the image female. His vision becomes Laura's. His inside is her outside.[3] From the Battus episode through the Actaeon conversion, Laura controls what Barbara Hodgdon calls "the looking relations."[4] But what makes the sequence so crucial is that, in it, Laura's visual control is figured by, and fluctuates between, her linguistic control. She gets all the (sight and poetic) lines. In Ovid, Battus witnesses a crime against others. In Petrarch, the "I" witnesses a crime against the self. If Laura is subject and audience, Petrarch is witness and victim, the doubling redoubled: "questa che col mirar gli animi fura / m'aperse il petto el' cor prese con mano, / dicendo a me: 'Di cio non far parola'" [She who with her glance steals souls, opened my breast and took my heart with her hand, saying to me: 'Make no word of this'] (ll. 72–74). Together with the injunction against telling, the dismemberment at this point in the plot links the Battus story to the Actaeon myth. The incision here prefigures the excision later. Both episodes point toward a reduction, a gradual whittling away of consciousness, a steady disintegration of form: the annihilative vision that Laura's takeover precipitates. With the Actaeon story annulling any recovery from the Battus episode and the Echo story countermanding any recovery from the Byblis attenuation, Petrarch heightens the deterioration of the formulative self. The entire Ovidian episode is terrifying, as if Petrarch invented his undoing by uncovering—at every turn—a Laura who undoes him. Yet that out-doer, as Butler theorizes, is "always already" part of the in-sider. When Laura steals Petrarch's heart, she is, as she claims, only taking back what is hers.

From the very opening of the Battus episode, Laura privileges the world of messages to herself. In *The Metamorphoses*, Mercury fears Battus's words as Diana fears Actaeon's. In the *Rime sparse*, that "panic" is felt by Petrarch:

> Poi la rividi in altro abito sola,
> tal ch' i' non la connobbi, o senso umano!
> anzi le dissi 'l ver pien di paura;
> ed ella ne l'usata sua figura
> tosto tornando fecemi, oimè lasso!
> d'un quasi vivo et sbigottito sasso. (ll. 75–80)

> Later I saw her alone in another garment and that I did not
> know her, oh! human sense! rather I told her the truth, full of
> fear, and she to her accustomed form quickly returning made
> me, alas, an almost living and terrifying stone.

In Ovid, Battus's revelations are teased out; he needs to be bribed. Petrarch's blabbing is instinctual and instantaneous. He tells the truth and
then becomes it, ending as "terrified" as he began. The rhyming of *petra*
and *spetra* in lines 82 and 84 subsequently suggests that the "I's" panic is
externalized. The stone signifies Petrarch's reduction to his psychologically terrified—already ghostly—self. As specter, he is also a spectacle, his
enrocking a permanent engrafting of his fear. Petrarch becomes the vulnerable Actaeon and the circumscribed Battus, the site of their panic rendered in graven images ("chiamando Morte et lei sola per nome" [calling
death and only her by name], l. 140). The more the poet calls to Laura, the
more he announces his own demise. Passing from touchstone, to fountain,
to flint, to deer, the "I" loses all selfhood. Reduced and objectified, he can
neither see as he saw nor be seen as himself. Her looking as Mercury
eventuated into his look as Actaeon. By piercing it, her glance penetrates
his inward being and thereby arrests his formulative self. In the conversion
of the Byblis and Echo stories Petrarch's gender switch is simply a prelude
to his evaporation. In the Actaeon story, the gender switch is the consequence of his self-loss. The poet is "drawn" out of the self and "redrawn" as
the female deer.

In the Ovidian myth, Mercury laughs at Battus's failure to recognize
him. " 'You rogue,' " he said, " 'You would betray me to my face? Actually
betray me to myself?' "[5] In *The Metamorphoses*, Mercury's response
focuses on his triumph, his self-congratulation mingled with his incredu-
lity at Battus's presumption. In the *Rime sparse*, Laura's response is a
critique of Petrarch's representation. In its retrospect, it has more to do
with what he told than with what she did to trick him into confessing.
Ovid's Mercury sets Battus up for a fall. Petrarch's Laura is more concerned
with how *she* has been set up. Her rage turns the anticipatory "be thou
me"[6] of masculine apostrophe into the retaliatory "be thou what you
made me" of feminine revenge. Since Petrarch's story rendered her an
image carved out of his desire—a marble statue of cruelty that resulted in
his weeping—Laura responds artistically, using his form against him. Like
the avalanche in *When We Dead Awaken*, her rock-revenge is an attempt
to strike back in the medium the sculptor distorts. In Ovid, Mercury

confronts Battus and then punishes him, transforming him into a touch-stone, the instrument for revealing the truth. In the *Rime sparse*, Laura transforms Petrarch and then confronts him, her reaction focusing not on Petrarch's inadequacy of character but on his inability as reader. The elusiveness in her "I' non son forse chi tu credi" [I am not perhaps who you think I am] (l. 82) refers not just to the cover of disguise but to the impenetrable self underneath. As woman, Laura-Mercury has many layers. As god, she retains her mystery. He will, she claims, never know the truth because she remains perpetually unknowable, forever Mercury. If Ovid's Mercury is angry at Battus because he attempted to "outrogue" him, then, by implication, Laura's rage is a reaction to Petrarch's efforts to project her.

Petrarch renders the Battus episode semiotic, the tell-tale sign at issue. But the signature is Laura's. She superscribes it by imposing her vision on his. With their emphasis on failed word and failed sight, the Actaeon story and the Battus story return linguistic and specular power to the woman. The Laura who reclaims her gaze—stealing the poet's heart—reclaims her word—privileging her formulations. She takes all. The Petrarch so re-nowned for denying women agency here subverts his own legitimacy. He is the child Laura abuses in retaliation for his abuse of her. She is the parent who criticizes his mimetic behavior. He can never come near enough to know, or to be like, her. In her accusations, Laura speaks both of Petrarch's present failure to recognize, and his past efforts to approximate, her. If Mercury attacks Battus's belief that he could fool the arch-rogue, Laura criticizes Petrarch's art for attempting to know the unknowable subject. In that critique, she turns herself into a text and Petrarch becomes the inadequate reader; like Ovid's Mercury, she pulls slightly ahead, anticipat-ing Petrarch's textualization as the Ovidian god anticipated Battus's blab-bing. Both Laura and Mercury use disguise as a test, temporarily turning themselves into audiences and their victims into tellers in order to pre-serve their initiating primacy.

But the circle of subject emerging as audience who, in turn, emerges as creator makes the episode a paradigm for the reading process, a process Petrarch represents by conflating the battle between the sexes with the struggle for linguistic initiation. The Laura of the dyad is Petrarch's pri-mary text. He "reads" her from his imagination and then figures her forth. She, in turn, argues that he mis-read her, announcing that she writes her own—deeper—story. In the Actaeon myth, she goes one step further, pronouncing herself the determiner of his—attenuated—shape. The Petrarch who invents the Laura he claims to have read is the Petrarch who becomes (as the hounds pursue him) what he invented. The punishment for misreading is to become unreadable: to vanish as linguistic being. Laura's revenge for not portraying her as she is (in the Battus story) is to separate him from what he thinks he is in the Actaeon story. The struggle is textual and sexual. "Citing the law to produce it differently, in order to coopt its power" (*Bodies That Matter*, p. 15), Laura turns Petrarch into objects—the stone immobilized and cast by her, the deer framed and envisaged as her—that signify her vision. In making him feel her victimization by him, she asserts *her* proprietary place toward him. The uncovering Petrarch is, in turn, uncovered by Laura. At the bottom of the imbricated text is a blank space for the man. When he imagines a Laura who frames him, he deconstructs Daphne. When he imagines a Laura who names him, he annuls Eve. Finally, the uncovering Laura-Mercury vanishes from the text. Unnamed, she is unframed. Unseen, she alludes to a totally different vision. Untouchable, she broaches the incommensurable. Nothing is left of poet or woman.

Laura's injunction *before* anticipates Petrarch's subsequent whining poetry even as her critique *afterward* belittles it. In the injunction, she privileges her role as teller. In her critique, she privileges her role as audience. The legitimacy of Laura's voice and the overbearing mastery of her gaze in the Battus episode turn her into the only seer and the only teller. Not only does she disguise her body, transforming herself into someone Petrarch doesn't know—the false listener—she also disembodies her voice, translating herself into an aura whom Petrarch hears only as deconstructor of the text he wrote. As disguised receiver, Laura absorbs Petrarch's plaint. As unveiled critic, she rejects it and pulls herself into the divine position where—like God scolding the guilty Adam and Eve in Genesis 3—her rage renders Petrarch into a quivering projection, unable to see because he doesn't know where to look, unable to speak because he is ashamed of what he has become. Where does Laura come from when she turns Petrarch to stone? She has a perspective, as god, that Petrarch can never return. She has a perspective, as woman, that Petrarch can never penetrate.

As thunder, her tremor has a fallout in his trembling. In fact, her thunder-rage precedes her lightning sight. Her lightning-fire burns out her linguistic form. Petrarch imagines a visual Laura, shaping her in words. Laura-Mercury begins in a voluble sound that only belatedly produces and then dissolves her visual image. "She spoke, so angry to see that she made me tremble within that stone, hearing, 'I am not perhaps who you think I am'" [Ella parlava sì turbata in vista / che tremar mi fea dentro a quella petra, / udendo: 'I non son forse chi tu credi'] (ll. 81–83). First her voice projects her image in anger, his sight a function of her sound. Then her words deny that image, his mind a function of her instability. Her "I am not perhaps who you think I am" unseats the center of his belief. Her being eludes his credibility. First Petrarch sees what he hears; then Laura's voice denies what he hears (and retrospectively) what he sees. In defining herself as not being who he thinks she is, she slips out of any recognizable form. In not issuing a substitute definition for herself, she evades form altogether. His thinking has nothing to do with her being. By not offering a self he can visualize, she denies his specular power. Her unavailing form is beyond Petrarch's range: "I am not perhaps *where* you think I am." In remaining unlocatable as vision, she is also unassignable as object: "I am not perhaps *what* you think I am."

The game of *who*, *where*, and *what* she plays suggests her power to subvert the formulations that engender her. Defying form by leaving Petrarch clueless, she hides whatever it is he seeks in her. Her word determines the intervening vision of her anger, an anger Petrarch reflects in his trembling. But when the words are uttered, they annul the intervening interpolation by denying all interpretation. Her "I am not perhaps who you think I am" suggests Laura's eagerness to slip out of the perceived form, to move on to another place, somewhere apart from the mind and separate from the forms of knowing. In hiding behind what she is *not*, Laura-Mercury posits another creative arena, one that has nothing to do with what Petrarch thinks and that has nothing to do with the formulating impulses of laurelization. In announcing her evasiveness, Laura-Mercury initiates her poetic of abstraction, a poetic based on the openness of her totally different conceptual position. Her argument assumes that she, too, is a writing subject. Her enrocking assumes that Petrarch, too, can be objectified.

That the two empowerment myths of 23 (Battus and Actaeon) turn the "I" into the object seen rather than the seeing subject is not accidental; what the "I" seeks to regain in the rest of the *Rime sparse* is his vision, a vision premised on his initiating primacy. Both Bahti and Mazzotta return to Petrarch's visionary "I," Mazzotta to describe an unrecovered self "caught" in the riddle of language,"[7] Bahti to describe an elated self inspired by what it sees in the mirroring it projects. For both, Laura's being is grounded in the "I." She is what the "I" finds (Mazzotta) or invents

(Bahti) in order to find himself. She is the text. But Laura's separateness in the passages where she speaks renders her neither a mirror of the speaking "I" (as in Bahti), nor a substitute for the desiring "I" (as in Mazzotta). That separateness is different from the conventional representations of Laura as image of a feminine ideal unavailable to the poet. As the Laura-Mercury of this reading, she differs from the poet within the category of sameness: in the sphere of his worldly endeavor. Her power is defined first by her replication of his inventiveness and then by her claim that—as Mercury—she is a better inventor. In 23, she privileges the world of poetry to herself, appearing as author and critic. As competitor, Laura threatens Petrarch and immediately wins. She is Mercury and Diana, always able to turn her victimizer into a victim. As critic, she challenges him and it is the critical challenge Petrarch takes on in the rock poems.

Appearing in 105, 125, 126, and 127, the rock is spit out yet again in 129. The challenge to the male symbolic order, overlooked by evasion in other poems and even in the Olympian figures at the end of 23, is taken up in these five poems until finally, in 129, the punishment speaks of a nature that imitates art, a rock that is "in guisa d'uom che pensi et pianga et scriva" [like a man who thinks and weeps and writes] (*Rime sparse* 129, l. 52). The triumphant poet ends with "his image only" [l'imagine mi sola] (129, l. 72). If Diana pulls his image out of him in 23, in 129 Petrarch consolidates his return to himself. The reversal in 129 obviates the question of priority and substitutes the signifier for the referent. If the rock is Petrarch (his punishment reiterated) and if the rock is "like a man who thinks and weeps and writes," then the Battus story is repeated and temporarily doubled. Petrarch is a rock who is Petrarch. His name and his discourse (thinking, weeping, writing) are reanimated. Laura's injunction as godlike Mercury is outwitted not by Petrarch-Battus but by nature, which repeats (in its eternal coming-to-be) the creativity of the gods and preempts (in its perpetuated recoveries) the possibility of another objectification. A nature that is like man turns the metaphor around. Hence the question of creative primacy, so critical to 23, is subsumed as the rock becomes the man and sculpts itself, the story immersed (like Rodin's statues) in—and therefore inseparable from—the element that shapes it. What Petrarch defines as male artistic acts—thinking, weeping, writing— emerge the generative activities that matter. Female natural acts— seeing, reproducing, mothering—are thereby rendered inconsequential. Fathers come before—and so replace—Mother Earth. Petrarch hardens himself. His consolidation of the rock in 129 hurls itself against the abstractions Laura-Mercury opened up. His defiant selfhood as writer blocks her originating selfhood as procreator. His stone becomes a wall. The sterile earth he imagines stifles all growth but his, and Petrarch can, once again, ignore the ambivalence which produced Laura-Mercury in the first place. Reverting to Apollo, he remands Laura to Daphne.

But the inventing Laura-Mercury continues to imbricate the fabric—to double the trouble—of the text. The solution in 129 is only temporary. In fact, Petrarch's reinventions last only as long as their poems. Laura-Mercury returns even as late as *Rime sparse* 359 to close off his initiative by mocking his "triste onde / del pianto," the sad waves of his weeping (ll. 14–15) and "coll'aura de' sospir," the breeze of his sighs (l. 16). In 105, Petrarch succeeds at staving off the criticism through the creation (prior to the poem) of a second Petrarch who—absorbing the critical Laura—speaks as if he were "she." That absorption, in turn, facilitates the re-creation of the solely sexual Laura of 106. The two Petrarchs (one who, as singing rock, continues to lament and one who, as critical Laura, continues to listen) charge the discourse with Laura's creative challenge. Figured by the reappearing rock in 105, 125, 126, 127, and 129, Laura-Mercury's presence as creative "other" annuls the priorities of Genesis 2. As mirror-creator, Laura-Mercury shares Petrarch's inventive capacity. As aggressive god, Laura-Mercury comes first and thereby anticipates his representational ambition.

Petrarch's recovery in the "rock" poems is two-staged. By regressing to the formulative stasis of Adam's dream in Genesis 2, the "I" gives birth to a separated, and hence secondary, Laura-Eve. That Laura in turn drifts into the conventional sexually unavailable other. When he returns to Laura-Daphne, Petrarch-Apollo regains faith in his expressiveness, a faith necessary to the fiction of the main plot. Petrarch's remarkable reassertion—achieved by bending his language to include Laura-Mercury's voice—is a testimony to her subversive energy, an energy seemingly denied by his subsequently successful attempts to silence her and thereby to reappropriate language. Laura-Mercury starts the cycle which he completes. Her presence in the poems suggests that the sublimation that critics have assumed as part and parcel of Petrarchism is arrived at only *after* the poem-denying Laura is written out. Despite Petrarch's recovery in these poems, some questions remain. (1) Why does the poet locate his abstracting impulses in the woman's unlocatable body? (2) Why does Laura-Mercury prod Petrarch to reinvent Laura-Daphne as a figure who evades the body the poet propagates to represent his desire? (3) Are the reinventions successful? Is the Laura-Daphne who appears after 105, 125, 126, 127, and 129 a secondary—and hence somewhat less satisfying—answer to the incommensurability Laura-Mercury reveals? (4) Is there something in Petrarchism that speaks for evasion? Is that ambivalence picked up—along with the self-confident form—by future Petrarchists?

What we see in 105, 125, 126, 127, and 129 is a Petrarch who "leans too hard"[8] on his own invention. That "leaning" produces some marvelous reincorporations in the violet of 105 and some fantastic reorderings in the self-engendering poet of 129. But those re-presentations are the direct result of Laura-Mercury's enrockings; her initial denial of form prods his belated reformulation of self. It is her defiance that prompts him to question himself. It is her agency that prompts him to reinvent himself. As destabilizing, parodic, decentering force, Laura-Mercury represents Petrarch's ambivalence about the process by which he materializes himself. Her subversions haunt the *Rime sparse* so that none of the reemergences seem totally satisfying. But the poems in which she forces the issue produce some of the most interesting images and some of the densest reworkings in the *Canzoniere*.

"A Single Violet Transplant": Laura Redoubled

In 105, Petrarch answers the questions *Rime sparse* 23 raises and attempts to revive both the old Laura and his earlier poetic. There he (1) uses the opening lines to incorporate Laura's critique so that it becomes his own—from that vantage point describing both the existence of the singing rock and the persistence of an inward voice; (2) invents the metaphors of lines 61 through 75, to amplify that inward voice so that its continuity is assured even in the bleakest moments; (3) reasserts the poetics of loss so that they become the source of the new angel of 106.

To regain the sightlines of an originating "I," Petrarch has to pull Laura-Mercury into his body. In 105 that incorporation consolidates his vision. His heart and her eye function as one. To celebrate that union, the redoubled Petrarch of lines 62 through 75 finds a whole new set of metaphors, images that turn the poem around:

> In silenzio parole   accorte et sagge
> è'l suon che mi sottragge   ogni altra cura,
> et la pregione oscura   ov' è'l bel lume;
> le notturne viole   per le piagge,

> et le fere selvagge   entr'a le mura,
> et la dolce paura,   e'l bel costume,
>   et di duo fonti un fiume   in pace vòlto
> dov' io bramo, et raccolto   ove che sia;
> amor et gelosia   m' ànno il cor tolto,
> e i segni del bel volto
> che mi conducon per più piana via
> a la speranza mia,   al fin degli affanni.
> O riposto mio bene et quel che segue,
> or pace or guerra or triegue,
> mai non m'abbandonate in questi panni. (ll. 62–75)

> In silence, words skillful and wise are the sound that takes
> every other care from me, and the dark prison where there is
> a lovely light;
>   violets at night along the shore, wild beasts within the
> walls, sweet fear and dear custom,
>   and from two fountains one river turned in peace to where
> I desire, and gathered anywhere; love and jealousy have
> taken away my heart and the stars of that lovely face, which
> lead me along the smoothest way to my hope at the end of
> troubles. O my hidden sweetness, and what follows—now
> peace now war now truce—you never abandon me in this
> garment.

What before evoked an *impossibilia* now becomes, instead, an opening
into the plausible: "di duo fonti un fiume" [from two fountains, one river]
(l. 67). In terms of time, the new metaphors form a sequence, an evolution
into something new: "or pace or guerra or triegue" [now peace, now war,
now truce] (l. 74). In terms of space, the new metaphors provide both a
release (the dark prison where there is a light) and containment (wild
beasts within the walls) that is resolved by the tiny unkillable growth—
the violets at night along the shore. With their purple background and
yellow center, the violets emerge (like the walls for the wild beast) the
container of energetic light, another version of night and, at the same
time, futile against the sea. At night, the violets seem to disappear, absorbed by what they parallel (the night sky) and enveloped by what they
border (the waves). They exist and they do not exist. They are the dark
prison with the lovely light; they are the walls that contain the wild
beasts, fragile yet indestructible, invisible yet powerful. The violets simul-

taneously centralize and diffuse Laura. First Petrarch brings her eye into the fold; she is the star in the violet. Then he unfolds the enclosure; she is the star in the sky. Having *violetly* yoked her, Petrarch emerges Laura. He sees through her eyes and then gains the advantage of double vision, pulling her eyes into his heart.

The violence is expanded in the next stanza, where "amor et gelosia m' ànno il cor tolto / e i segni del bel volto" [love and jealousy have taken away my heart and the stars of that lovely face] (ll. 68–69). The annihilating force of the old poetics deprives the "I" of self and beloved (heart and eyes). Both disappear, as the night absorbs the violets and the sea drowns the buds. Yet because both are similarly overcome, they are intertwined— at sea and in space together. The metaphor subtracts the poet's heart and the lover's eyes, exteriorizing them so that they become stars in the sky instead of jewels in the face or propellants of the body. Like the "mark" in Shakespeare's sonnet 116, those stars allow the mariner/poet to achieve an inner strength. When he pulls Laura's eyes into his heart, the redoubled Petrarch finds the way back to an older and more confident being. Like the violets reflecting the sky and the walls containing the wild beasts, the "guide" reconfigures an original relationship so that it becomes something new. The jewels and the heart are transported and connected.

As the "me" here is no longer just the "I" but a configuration of the metaphors, so is the "you" compounded. In fact, the "I" and "you" have changed. Obviating the "he" and "she," the "me" who never is abandoned and the "you" who never abandons become their representations. Since each is figured by the star and the heart, both connect to the heavens. The container and thing contained (the sky and the stars reflected in the violet, mirrored in the heart and eyes) are mutualized. The purple background of the violet with the yellow center is a miniature copy of the night sky filled with stars. The pairing exists (sweetness) and does not exist (hidden). The "hidden sweetness" reiterates the metaphors. They affirm the containment of an unkillable essence (with the wild beasts within the walls) and the preservation of an unquenchable light (with the violets at night along the shore). When the light is exteriorized so that it becomes the guiding star, it simply mirrors what is already a mirror, the violet which contains the same star. The hidden sweetness is energy (beasts in the walls) which inspires and light (stars in the sky) which directs.

But, in the mirroring conversions, the energy "out there" is provided by the initially pumping heart "in here." With the "hidden sweetness," Petrarch ascribes to the "you" ("mai non m'abbandonate in questi panni" [you never abandon me in this garment], l. 75) what he knows is true of the "I" ("I never abandon you"). Only the "you" is no longer Laura and the "I" is no longer Petrarch. It is the situation of their situation which includes both their present state and their past relations ("or pace or guerra or triegue" [now peace, now war, now truce], l. 74). To acknowledge the presence of the past is to accept it. To mutualize their predicament is to join the subject and object of discourse so that the "I" becomes what Butler calls the self in drag. When Petrarch incorporates Laura, he seems to say, "my 'outside' appearance is feminine, but my essence 'inside' [the body] is masculine" even as he implies "my appearance 'outside' [my body, my gender] is masculine but my essence 'inside' [myself] is feminine" (*Gender Trouble*, p. 137). Dragging the feminine inside, the poet acquires Laura's godlike scope. Her inner light is the energy that propels him. Her outer light is the star that guides him. The heart becomes both the container (the place where he writes) and the thing contained (the subject of his discourse) since the process of the poem has mutualized Laura's eyes and the poet's hand. When the new "I" announces that he writes in his heart even more than on paper, he affirms the hidden sweetness as an act, a process that continues *in intensity*. To write more inwardly is both to multiply what already exists (like the propagating violets) and to broaden its dimensions (like the stars in the infinite sky). Writing *in* the heart (which encompasses Laura's eyes and therefore the scrutiny which includes her reaction to him) is to use the inspiring star as the driving force. Writing from the heart, the "I" writes as Laura, projecting a newly energized inward being even as he absorbs her newly idealized heavenly power.

An insignificant love (the violet) achieves the importance of a divinity (the sky) whose investment in the earth (and whose incorporation) the singing heart "measures." He no longer invents rhymes. He merely scans what is already there. When combined with the heart, the eyes which gazed critically become "sweet." Their vision has merged with his desire to justify interiority as the source of the poem. The "hidden" suggests the possibility that the sweetness was there all along but buried (like the star in the violets, the light in the prison, the heart in the body). What inspires Petrarch to continue is not the promise of fame ("I sare' udito / et mostratone a dito" [I would be heard of and pointed out for it], ll. 83–84) but the command to intensity ("non fostu tant' ardito" [you were not bold enough], l. 86). Like Astrophil, he looks in his heart and finds there the writing star and guiding light he sought outside. The Laura Petrarch reinvents is a Laura who encourages the poet by urging him toward the self-realization which first swallows her up as tiny flower and then turns her out as infinite sky. She is the "you" for whom the "I" writes. She is the "you" the "I" joins by planting her in his self. Since that "she" has entered his heart in the complex metaphors of the poem, "she" belongs there and reads that writing uncritically. Guided by her gaze, his writing is hers. Moved by his heart, her reading is his. He will never get her into a sexual bed but he has succeeded in embedding her as the seed of his inventive self. That invention, in turn, renders her the source of his physical arousal even as it renders Petrarch the inventor of her resources.

To answer the unraveling Laura, Petrarch rolls her up. His enclosures contain her. Her light is absorbed. If the Laura-Mercury of 23 eludes form, the Petrarch of 105 includes her in a new form: his. The absorption allows Petrarch to be Adam again. First, Laura is an Eve who seems to crawl back into Adam ("chi m'à 'l fianco ferito . . . et chi 'l risalda" [she who has wounded my side and heals it], l. 87). The original "great refusal," the first "no," leads to a subsequent "yes," an absorption of the woman into the body of the man whose essence this time is described in terms of his craft. To wound his side is to enter him; to heal him would then be to leave him, as Eve emerged from Adam. But in leaving him, she wounds him again and perpetuates the cycle of desire that never stops as the "I" keeps writing in an effort to pull her back in, to be wounded again. Once the "she" is externalized, once "she" is the other, she validates the "I's" existence by returning the gaze as Eve, rather than determining the gaze as Mercury. When he gives birth to the "you" and recalls the oxymoronic wound/balm and fire/ice, the "I" releases his writing as well. It is recharged. As wounding reader, the woman legitimizes his work. To protect his side, she has to leave it; by leaving it, she becomes the other and restores him to sexual life. First she is Laura-Eve. Later, in 106, she will be Laura-Daphne. As critic first and then subject, she makes him "die" and "live" as he becomes first passive Adam dreaming her and then aggressive Adam calling her back. Petrarch has succeeded in reinventing the Laura he internalized as the Laura who rejects his sexuality. But Petrarch's elaborate gyrations are prompted by Laura's rejection of his original representations. He can take control again only after he obscures the boundaries (in the violet overcome by the sea, in the violet mirroring the starry skies) and "reconfigures what will count as the world" (*Bodies That Matter*, 19).

Positing two selves, the sighing heart and the distancing heart, the "I" interiorizes the dialogue he had with Laura, pulling her into himself as she prepares to wound his side. The intensification allows light in the dark prison and admits to a potential opening that might, like violets on the shore, self-propagate. The light prepares for a rejuvenation of faith in the original situation. The new little angel of 106 is really the old Laura— the one before the Laura-Mercury of *Rime sparse* 23—expelled when the second Petrarch is ready to vent the critic he absorbed at the beginning of the poem. The invention of a second Petrarch never denied the first Petrarch who went on lamenting. What it allowed was a reiteration of the old lament as well as an acknowledgment that the lamenter is unkillable. As the Laura-Mercury of 23, the woman objectifies the man; her sight calls attention to his transgression. As Laura-Mercury, the woman shapes the man; her act calls attention to his punishment. Laura-Mercury is her own invention, the menace of her invasive gaze figured by the impenetrable rock. The angel of 106 is Petrarch's invention, a safely human reconstruction of the divine messenger, as the violet is the harmless earthly reproduction of the sky. Laura-Angel in 106, the woman is reformed as the perceived object of the poet's idealization. The Laura-Mercury of 23 undoes poetry. The Laura-Angel of 106 preserves it, her transcendence a product of Petrarch's redoubled energy. The invigorated poet of 105—the "I" who penetrates the stars and breaks down prison walls—answers the demoralized poet of 23, the "I" who, unable to fathom Laura and impotent to rise from the stone, seems locked in the self. His revision sets in motion again the system of reaction and punishment that leads to the recurrence of the rock in 125, 126, 127, and 129.

As the *Rime sparse* progress, the embryonic relationship of Petrarch and Laura ("she" giving birth to a "he" who matches her, "he" giving birth to a "she" who responds to him) is reenacted. In 125 and 129, the "returns" of 105 are reexamined as each poem seems to antedate the last one, preempting the impact of Laura's critical "no" by reversing the mirrors of identity. In 125, the reversals begin and a new sympathetic other, nature, is enlisted. If, in 23, the rock becomes the punishing end of poetry and in 105 it is represented by the annulled poet's singing, in 125 it becomes a figure for rebirth. Poems 125, 126, 127, and 129 work in pairs to continue the initial self-questioning and subsequent regeneration of 105 and 106. Incorporating Laura's criticism, they similarly generate new Lauras. In 126, she emerges as a paradisiacal source to counter the frozen childhood of 125; in 129, she appears as animating spirit of nature, unlocking the confining words of 127. These poems reopen wounds healed in 105. The Laura of 126 and 129 rescues the petrified poet of 125 and 127. *Rime sparse* 127, for example, picks up the violets and stars of 105 only to dismiss the poetry that sought to capture them. But 129 returns to the capturing/scattering "I" and to the writing rock in such a way that it seems possible, once again, to listen and to sing. The rock grounds nature to writing. If 105 places writing at the level of the heart, 129 places it at the heart of the world. But that arrival seems only a temporary stay, like the arrivals in 125, 126, 127, an attempt to return to a redefined beginning.

The new beginning sought from the dead-end of the rock is linked to the temporal zig-zagging in the poems. The progress in 125 and 126 works backward, from infancy to pre-infancy. In 127, the "I" moves forward from childhood to adolescence, to rekindle the sexual desire absent from the purified heaven of 126. In 129, Petrarch appears as fully grown; his inclusion in nature reinscribes his manhood. In all the poems, Petrarch's attempts to challenge Laura's female doubts end in a reassertion of maleness that makes sublimation possible. But it is a second sublimation, one colored by what Laura-Mercury unveils: Petrarch's ambivalence. The progress from infancy to fatherhood involves a passage from Laura-mother in 126, through Laura-rival in 127, to Laura-object in 129. At the end of 129, the image is that of the poet alone. Working through the alternatives to thought—the mindlessness of infancy in 125, the headiness of heaven in 126—the poet submits to Laura. Returning to the poet's thought—via the virility of 127 and the paternity of 129—Petrarch reestablishes the original discourse. Laura submits to Petrarchism.

As he did in 105, the "I" in 125 denounces the singing rock *after* Laura's deconstructive critique and refers with nostalgia to the songs he sang "in the first assault of love." When he names his initial victimization the first assault, the "I" confirms that there has been a second one, the "no" of Laura's critique:

> Dolci rime leggiadre
> che nel primiero assalto
> d'Amor usai quand'io non ebbi altr' arme. (ll. 27–29)

> Come fanciul ch' a pena
> volge la lingua et snoda,
> che dir non sa ma 'l più tacer gli è noia,
>   così 'l desir mi mena
> a dire, et vo' che m'oda
> la dolce mia nemica anzi ch' io moia. (ll. 40–45)

> Sweet graceful rhymes that I used in the first assault of Love, when I had no other arms.

> Like a child who can hardly move and untangle his tongue, who is not able to speak but hates to be silent any longer, thus desire leads me to speak, and I wish my sweet enemy to hear me before I die.

As in 105, there is someone within who always portrays my lady and speaks of her. In 105, the "I" released himself by seducing his keeper, freeing himself temporarily by bringing her into his prison and then claiming he was she. Here both Petrarch and Laura seem permanently enclosed by the stone about the heart, a stone that can't say anything and hence can't bring Laura to poetic life. *Rime sparse* 105 ends with Laura reading the inward heart and then leaving it. In 125, it is the poet who needs to be reborn. Instead of moving outward from the moment of the stoning, the second Petrarch here moves backward to create yet another self. In 105, the second Petrarch was able to hear the first Petrarch. Here the "I" is untuned, out of touch with his past and not yet touched by his song. To come untuned is both to be unskilled (off key) and to be completely without song (silent), to have regressed to a prelinguistic stage.

If the second Petrarch of 105 denounces singing, the second Petrarch of 125 cannot sing. In 105, the initial lament continues even as the "I" stops himself from participating. Here the inward "I" who always "portrays my lady" is trapped. The sweet comfort (both the external lady who leaves the scene and the song that laments her remoteness) is stilled. The second Petrarch of 125 emerges only as the "I" of the poem recognizes his songless-ness. Stripped, the "I" arrives at a new stage. If to be untuned is to be inchoate, to return to a state of childhood is to become also "like a rock." The stage before articulation is a trap. Giuseppe Mazzotta finds this to be an Augustinian metaphor: "The child who cannot speak and cannot be still is the metaphor by which Augustine and Petrarch make desire the foundation of language."[9] Mazzotta argues that the *canzone* ends with delusion; but it is possible to say that it self-consciously paves the way for the new vision of 126. The child can hardly move. His tongue is knotted up. The only hope is to be mothered by the green shore. Rescued as Zeus was by Rhea, Petrarch acquires the same mother Laura had. As she once made herself a home in the green, so he will remain in the woods until he is ready to be thrust into the world. In 125, the rock is incubated and Petrarch becomes Laura's brother, both mothered by a protective nature.

As siblings, Laura and Petrarch share a common origin. Like his, her eye looks backward toward the womby earth. In 125, Petrarch is both a helpless orphan who needs a maternal nature to "rock" the cradle of the self and a voiceless infant who has not yet invented the desirable other. The Laura mothered by nature in 125 becomes a mother herself and it is that Laura who rescues him in 126.

In poem 126, the womb of the world widens from waters to land ("dolci acque" [sweet waters], l. 1; "gentil ramo" [gentle branch], l. 4). When he seeks the same shelter Laura found, Petrarch dies to be reborn with her. If she turned for protection to the womb of the world, so he will now similarly be buried. He expects that, after his death, she will (at last) pity him:

> cercandomi, et—o pieta—
> già terra infra le pietre
> vedendo, Amor l'inspiri
>
> in guisa che sospiri
> sì dolcemente che mercé m'impetre
> et faccia forza al cielo,
> asciugandosi gli occhi col bel velo. (ll. 32–39)

> and oh the pity! seeing me already dust amid the stones, Love will inspire her to sigh so sweetly that she will win mercy for me and force Heaven, drying her eyes with her lovely veil.

To return is to become passive, so small that he can be absorbed: "dust amid stones." If, in 125, the "I" is reduced to the stony silence of childhood, here he is less than the little he was, so much a mote that, in the hypothetical future where both he and Laura are reborn, he poses no threat. By virtue of her earlier arrival, Laura will sing for him. As motherly nature, she will win mercy for him and force heaven to open. As dust, he is either not yet born or already dead. Poem 126 creates yet another beginning, as the "I" thinks he is in heaven, where he achieves a state of "forgetfulness" and thereby obviates the earthly burden. Whereas 105 finds freedom by passing through the critical gates of Laura's complaint, 125 and 126 eliminate the criticism by moving through forgetfulness directly to heaven. In the fantasy of 125 and 126, the "I" as rock child asks first to be mothered by nature and then to be sistered and mothered by Laura, who will sing his praise. In 125, he is locked in the rock of the inarticulate.

In 126, he is further fragmented into dust, so tiny a part of the rock that he is both harmless and ineffectual. Already dead, he cannot threaten Laura. In 126, *she* becomes a poet and forges an opening in heaven which comforts the "I." Rocking him in the cradle of her maternal self, she allows for his unlocking in heaven, totally taking over a role he has vacated. In 126, Petrarch gives Laura the power she asserted in 23. Of course she can win heaven for him. As the angel he rendered her, she has connections there. But in naming her the maternal force, he becomes her child, Oedipus to her Jocasta. In 125, the infant Petrarch, together with his adopted sister Laura, is protected by an outside earth mother. In 126, Laura becomes his mother, his infantilization objectified in the tiny dust he has become and ratified in the maternal interference she runs. Holding the key to language, she opens up the gates of heaven only to return as a vision of her originally inspiriting self. Poem 126 ends in the paradise of the poet's initial feeling, Laura now the angelic self she was at the beginning. Voluntarily giving the reins of language to Laura, Petrarch is absorbed by her. Child to her mother, his identity is hers. Such a "transfiguration" conveys what Mazzotta calls "a lingering consciousness of the wedge that divides the real from the visionary."[10] As a solution to the struggle for power, Petrarch's infantilization recalls a past in which Laura has all the voice and a future in which desire becomes vision. Poems 125 and 126 are fleeting comforts because, for Petrarch, desire is voice. Imagining the Laura who saves him, he also imagines his death as a poet. It is she who sings him into the heaven where, earlier, he placed her. The Petrarch who "wept for joy" in 126 returns, in 127, to the Petrarch who, as Shakespeare puts it in *Much Ado about Nothing*, "joys at weeping" (1.1.26). That joy is the joy of the recovered poet who is pressed into the service of the rejected lover. But his recovery is short-lived.

In 127, the spring begins to remind the "I" not of childhood but of adolescence—of his initiation in love and his past as lamenter of impossible love. If, at the end of 126, the "I" is reborn in death, in 127 he returns to question that beginning:

> In quella parte dove Amor mi sprona
> conven ch'io volga le dogliose rime
> che son seguaci de la mente afflitta:
> quai fien ultime, lasso, et qua' fien prime?
> Collui che del mio mal meco ragiona
> mi lascia in dubbio, sì confuso ditta.

> Toward where Love spurs me I must turn my sorrowful
> rhymes, which follow my afflicted mind which shall be last,
> alas and which first. He who speaks with me about my ills
> leaves me in doubt, so confusedly he dictates. (ll. 1–6)

In 125, the "I" had not yet uttered his sighs. His desire simply leads him to
the threshold of speech. By 127, so much has been spoken that it is hard to
tell which came first, the mind willing the song or the song describing the
mind. If the mind wills the song, the creative Petrarch is all. If the song
describes the mind, then the sexual Petrarch is irrelevant. Similarly, if
Laura is already a song, then imaginatively she is everything.

Yet, if Laura is only a poem, then sexually she is nothing. The poet's
music denies his body even as Laura's musical body overcomes his voice. If
126 ends in spatial disorientation, 127 begins in temporal dislocation.
Since there is only one lady and her lovely face, the repetitions become, as
105 indicated, a source of doubt, here expressed as a confusion about ends
and beginnings. So the "I" speaks of the earliest ending of winter and the
last remains of summer, connecting (as he did in 105) violets and stars. In
127, the ambiguity about endings and beginnings eventuates not to some
past where the "I" can begin again but to a present where the "I" is
consumed—absorbed by his obsession and immobilized by his absorption.
Through anamnesis, the present spring recalls the earlier spring and that
recollection spurs him on to feel the initiating passion. Yet at the very
moment of success, the "I" once again absorbs the criticizing Laura:

> Ad una ad una annoverar le stelle
> e'n picciol vetro chiuder tutte l'acque
> forse credea, quando in sì poca carta
> novo penser di ricontar mi nacque
> in quante parti il fior de l'altre belle
> stando in se stessa à la sua luce sparta. (ll. 85–90)

> Perhaps I thought I could count the stars one by one and enclose
> the sea in a little glass when the strange idea came to me to tell
> in so few pages in how many places the flower of all beauties,
> remaining in herself, has scattered her light.

Encapsulating the three reflective elements of 105, Petrarch reverses them.

In 105, the stars and flowers are hidden, temporarily overcome by the
sea, which, in the waxing and waning of the waves, continually elimi-

nates and reforms itself. What seemed deadening emerged only as a veil, hiding the sweetness underneath. In 105, the sea, stars, and violets suggest each other, affirming an unkillable force. Here the "I" calls the connection he established a containment. The "counting" of his rhyme, the glass of his reflection, and the "few pages" of his tribute elaborate emblems of futility. But they also suggest still another element of Petrarchan incorporation. The implication of Laura's accusation in 23 widens. Condemning the action, the "I" repeats it. If a poem is a container, a glass enclosing the sea, a microcosm of the macrocosm, so Laura is a container, the flower of all beauties. Earthly flower, she radiates heavenly light. But that is the problem. By this definition, Laura is already a poem. As flower of all beauties, she represents them. Her being is a poem, its origin a container—a definition—of her power. In *Rime sparse* 23, Laura evades all containers. Her "I am not perhaps who you think I am" rejects form. Here she initiates containment, her form the quintessence of formality. Once again, like Mercury, Laura seems to have gotten there first. Here, even the discovery of 105 (the heaven on earth represented by the violet) has already been invented by Laura. She holds the figurative in her figure. Petrarch merely imitates a prior configuration.

As a poem, Laura is not a person. She is her own projection, having formed herself as self-determining vision. If Laura is herself already the flower who "scatters" her light, Petrarch's poem emerges at best a redundancy, copying in scattered rhyme what has already been written. In 127 Petrarch discovers what Lyotard says about the dream, that "the textual is already in the core figure" ("Dream-Work," p. 51). Still more dispiriting is the other side of that textuality. If Laura is only a poem, then Petrarch's physical desire is absolutely frustrated. There is no hope. As semiotic vehicle, she has no sexual substance. As poem, she exists without him. As person, he is there alone. Her form both denies his sexuality because she is a different *genus* and preempts his containment because she is her own *genius*. As conscious subject of her own flowering, she is self-sufficient; her being as art expresses an art of the self. Although in 105 Petrarch found a way to fuse the opposites in peace, here there is no such reconciliation. The "I" is all consumed. Trapped by his own enclosures, he can find no release from the scrutiny of Laura's rejecting summation. Reduced to a poem, Laura consumes him as she did in 23, by denouncing his containment. Her revenge for his effort to turn her into a poem is to challenge the reduction. As the second Petrarch of 127, the "I" absorbs Laura's criticism, using the very metaphors of 105 against himself. If, in 125 and 126, he is reborn as Laura's child, in 127 that birth is a stillbirth. The poem ends in Laura's annihilative stroke. The poet is left in the stony silence of self-cancellation. Laura is restored to the verbal energy of self-definition. Remaining in herself, Laura is impenetrable here, as denying Petrarch's self, she is inscrutable in 23. There, having rejected Petrarch's containers, Laura remains elusive. Here, uncovering a Laura who defines herself as fictive, Petrarch is consigned to her fiction.

In 129, he begins by reversing his belatedness, doing to her what she did to him and attempting to return to his original and sexual quest. Enstoning Laura, he wriggles out of her constrictive punishment and turns it into a liberating movement, a movement which stops short in the middle of the poem when the "I" discovers, as he did in 127, that his creation has no substance—that it produces only a shadow self:

> et quanto in più selvaggio
> loco mi trovo e 'n più deserto lido,
> tanto più bella il mio pensier l'adombra.
> Poi quando il vero sgombra
> quel dolce error, pur lì medesmo assido
> me freddo, pietra morta in pietra viva,
> in guisa d'uom che pensi et piana et scriva. (ll. 46–52)

> and in whatever wildest place and most deserted shore I find myself, so much the more beautiful does my thought shadow her forth. Then, when the truth dispels that sweet deception, right there in the same place I sit down, cold, a dead stone on the living rock, like a man who thinks and weeps and writes.

Where Laura goes, the "I" follows. He emerges in pursuit what she was in strength: Apollo. Thus he is involved in a circle of his own making, a sun of his own orbit. Once more Petrarch invents a Laura who assumes his role in the dyad. That becoming ends, however, not in triumph but in doubt. When he confers on Laura what she already has, the redundancy nullifies itself. Becoming Laura means, as it does in 127, assuming her critical perspective.

The manic enterprise brings on the ghosts, the sequence now a procession into death. At the crucial moment of imminence, the "I" begins to incorporate Laura's criticism. His thoughts link to shadows and his inventions prefigure their dissolution. The self-doubting Petrarch enters here, at the height of the clouds, and the "I" descends to earth.[11] With that knowledge ("Poi quando il vero sgombra / quel dolce error" [when truth dispels that sweet deception], ll. 48–49), the "I" is left doubly punished: "pietra morta in pietra viva" [a dead stone on the living rock] (l. 51). In 105, he becomes Laura and that becoming enables him to separate himself from himself so that he can hear the unkillable song that sustains him. Here, using the same process of inverting images so that he moves from earth to heaven, he turns the mirror on himself. At the very moment that he reflects Laura, becoming the Apollonian creator of her, he recognizes that he merely imitates the sun, becoming the dead imitator of her. The shadow is not a mirror. It is a weak copy and it wakens the "I" to the horror of his inventions. Timothy Bahti calls the nothingness "that which is seen or thought when figures are not read (seen) or thought."[12] With the claim that he invented Laura, Petrarch loses both his reader and text. Since both are the same, both disappear. Nothing substantial remains. Everything is a shadow without a body. But the rock reversion has echoes—not only to *Rime sparse* 23 but to the more immediate poems in this group.

When the "I" reverts to the rock, he recalls his various allusions to it. With the dead stone on the living rock, he becomes shadow to his self, like the dust amid stones of 126, evoking an infancy (in the tininess) that prefigures an end ("to dust thou shalt return"). When Petrarch uses it in 126, that end becomes the beginning of Laura's intervention, the one moment that she chooses to become him, pleading for his salvation. In 127, that optimism is deflated, as the "I" uses the violet, stars, and sea of 105 against himself and confronts the futility of poetry. In 129, however, he solves the insoluble dilemma he himself raised. Reversing the reversals, he claims nature is already a *poet*. At bottom, the rock is "in guisa d'uom che pensi et pianga et scriva" [like a man who thinks and weeps and writes] (l. 52)—a Pygmalion who creates yet another Pygmalion, an infinite regression of carvers. The stone chisels itself as chiseler. Not only is the unmoving rock (a figure for an infant locked into silence in 125, a figure whom nature and then Laura rock into comfort in 126) rendered active and sensitive. It is also rendered reactive, moving back, in the allusions to *Rime sparse* 23, to the point where the touchstone becomes its own story. The success of that retrospect is solidified in still another return, to the image of the heart and the "quella che'l m'invola" [she who steals it from me] (l. 71). In line 71, the poem retreats to the moment of Petrarch's initiation into the cycle which caused his petrification.

Petrarch pulls back twice. Each time, he returns to *Rime sparse* 23, first to the punishing rock then to Laura's punishable crime: the touchstone and the theft. But each of the moments is eternalized in a new way. In its presentness, Laura's heart-violation is suspended in time so that Petrarch is caught having-but-about-to-lose, Laura is caught taking-but-not-yet-fully-possessed. Each is locked into a relationship of imminence that binds them together and that annuls the whining poetry of loss and the disdainful critique that follows. To return to such a pristine moment is to be before words (as in 125) but to have them (as here) still in potential. Similarly, the rock which was the result of Petrarch's Battus-like blabbing becomes the cause rather than the effect, catapulted backward in time. Here it represents not a containment of energy but a continuation of it, the reverse of what it was. Instead of the man becoming the rock, the rock becomes a man. Sisyphus is pushed back up the hill. Similarly, in the present tense, the rock thinks and weeps and writes. The mere mention of the rock now produces—by its evocation of history—the movement Petrarch perpetuates. When he evokes Laura in the final stanza, she is at the moment that continues Petrarch's initiation: stealing his heart, beginning the beginning again. But as a frozen image, she is perpetuated, locked in the act that initiates the cycle, as Petrarch is rocked into the shape that continues it. When he collapses the end onto the beginning, Petrarch ends the end and arrives at the shore of a self whose circular discoveries haven't yet happened. Such an encirclement makes the end continuous ("a man who thinks and weeps and writes"), the punishment a contingency, and the beginning a postponement (the robbery is still happening, hence it hasn't quite occurred).

In the *Rime petrose*, Dante mirrors the beloved, becoming in various permutations the rock he accuses the lady of being. But all those reflections are caused by Love, who "me desti come a petra" [turned me to stone].[13] In the *Rime sparse*, Petrarch takes responsibility for the stoning, fixing the blame on his own desire to tell. As he relinquishes the external cause, Petrarch dives beneath the bottom, moving inward and outward in 105 and backward in 129 not to find the vengeance Dante sought but to justify his art. Thus all the poems in the *Rime sparse* are conscious of a self-imposed grief. Nevertheless, they seek an image, in the rock, to represent the aggrieved party. If the rock becomes a weapon against the self, it also emerges, in its permanence, a weapon against self-effacement. For Petrarch, the opposite of pain is nothingness. To return to the condition of unresolved struggle (living death, freezing fire) is to be always at the point of beginning, to be perennially starting over. In 129, Petrarch changes the rock from female punishment to male form. Its shape (in thinking, weeping, writing) reverts the female nature of 125 and 126 into a male origin. Mother nature becomes father Petrarch writing the world. With nature as a man "who thinks and weeps and writes," Petrarch eliminates the ocular event—the fatal flaw of 23—from the creative process. Weeping and writing emerge a function, an appendage really, of thought. Words, like tears, follow thought. In separating the heart-robber Laura from the "she whose glance steals souls," Petrarch separates Laura from her fatal eye. She is defined now only in relation to her potential for stealing his heart, not in her potential for reformulating selves. In that single potential, she emerges not the conversional Mercury but the converted follower. She desires what is already formed, not what she will unshape. The only sight is his compelling insight, represented by his desiring heart: "Here you can see only my image" (l. 72). Laura's being is contingent, once again, on his formulation. Her form is his invention (*my image*). "She" is his again— not as the physical other who satisfies sexual desire but as the invented other who fleshes out his expressive desire. He is Apollo; she is Daphne.

Arresting Beginnings: Laura Retrieved

By definition, Petrarchism avoids the familial future of the plausible and chooses instead the artistic future of the impossible. When Laura says "no" to Petrarch's love, she casts him into the despair of his blabbering. When she says "no" to the depiction of that despair, she causes him to question the describing. In 105, 125, 126, 127, and 129, Petrarch becomes Laura to himself not so much to elide their differences in a gender-neutralizing absorption but to reestablish their differences in a gender-emphasizing separation. Sexual frustration in Petrarch is not always what Gordon Braden calls it, "complicitous with at least a certain kind of poetic success."[14] Petrarch's reaction to his sexual failure (the weeping and wailing of his response to Laura's "no") provokes a Laura who is so much like Petrarch that she usurps his expertise.

The Laura of 23 reappears in the *Rime sparse*, both as the critical voice of 105 and 127 and the punitive spur of 125 and 129. The initiative of her negativity causes the disjunction in 105 and infantilization of 125. If the Laura-Mercury of *Rime sparse* 23 proposes that the woman has a figurative authority which she wrests back from the man who disfigured her, what does she imply about the man who invented her? In one way, her injunction against song voices Petrarch's own inclination *not to write*. Why write if there is neither subject nor audience? In another sense, her activating presence dramatizes the extent to which the lyric moment is ahistorical. "Annihilating all that [Petrarch] made," Laura stops the past and the future. Her signature overwrites his. She erases his creation with the decreative resistance of "I am not perhaps who you think I am." What can Petrarch do after he imagines his own effacement? One thing is to do what his critics and followers assume he does, to ignore it and wallow (just as before) in sublimation. The poet can step out of his story, the way the actor playing Hamlet gets up from his death, leaves the set, has dinner, buys a newspaper, and appears in another play. *Rime sparse* 23 ends as if nothing annihilating happens, as if Petrarch, the poet, were an actor playing another part. The rapid sequence of metamorphoses in 23 forms a narrative of disaster from which the poet-hero always seems to recover. The discovered Battus emerges as the discovering Actaeon. The pursued Actaeon is suddenly the codifying Zeus carrying Laura-Ganymede into the heavens of a laurelization which Petrarch-Apollo assumes is *all that women want anyway.*

But if there is a narrative of recovery, so too is there one that deconstructs the self-satisfied emergences. The ragged troubled edges surface in 105, 125, 126, 127, and 129. Their implications in 105 force Petrarch both to assume Laura's critique and to invent the extraordinary images that bind her vision to his, positing a gaze of equals, she seeing through his heart, he feeling through her eyes. When he drags Laura inside and so becomes her, Petrarch temporarily unites the lovers and disallows priorities; Laura and Petrarch reflect each other and overcome their differences. The violet mirrors the heavens and the waves wash away the shore. But Petrarch's triumph in 105 has a built-in destruction mechanism. The unifying metaphors cancel each other out, as day outfaces the night and the waves uproot the violets. In 125, the critical questions surface again, the returns of 125 and 126 based on a series of quantum leaps backward, in time to infancy in 125, in space to dust in 126. In 126, the poet turns Laura into a mother who becomes his protector. The vision lasts until the specter of sexual desire provokes the negative Laura again, as if her presence as lover fosters her equality as critic. The reincarnations of sexuality challenge the permutations of language.

When he swallows Laura in 127, Petrarch disconnects the comforting metaphors (the violets, ocean, and sky) of 105; 129 picks up where 127 leaves off with a petrification that leads back to the beginning of the Battus episode and the woman who steals the poet's heart. These poems suggest that the sexual denial inherent to Petrarchism results in a self-doubt the conventions are supposed to overcome. Petrarch's paralysis is the locus of his despair. Ironically, the only hope for his art is to return to the situation that produces the anxiety in the first place. With Laura-Mercury, Petrarch faces the stilling effects of failed sexuality on all levels of male inscription. Recovery in the dyad involves returning to the spiral of originating loss. To be reborn as adolescent in 127 is to be reborn as poet, even if the poetry fails. The connection between sexual and poetic failure is circular. The reinvented Laura-Daphne in these poems is stigmatized by her coming after the reinventing Laura-Mercury.

The Laura of 129 is neither the angelic innocent produced through the emanations of 105 and 106 nor the nurturing mother resulting from the temporal and spatial transport of 125 and 126. Instead, her appearance is conjured up by a petrified Petrarch who, evading the evasions of an un-critical beginning or a heavenly end, imagines her about to commit the act that caused his troubling punishment. Here the punishment precedes the crime. The rock represents a creative nature that obviates the rivalry between the "he" and the "she" simultaneously as it validates the man "who thinks and weeps and writes." The acts that identify man (thinking, weeping, and writing) emerge synchronous to the act that perpetuates him (enstoning). In fact, those acts go beyond the span of his life as the rock endures, telling and retelling the forbidden story. What is the crime then? Has any been committed? In continuing the story, the rock turns the past into a future still to be enacted and thereby eliminates its punitive impact. What about the crime of stealing the heart? In the revised image of Laura, she hasn't quite accomplished it. She's menacing but not over-powering yet, her initiating act perpetuated in the constancy of always being about to be performed. In this vision, Laura exists in potential as the rock persists in the possible. Writing is rescued from reading as loving is rescued from loss, each not yet othered.

Petrarch's separation from Laura in 129 is as bizarre as his union in 105 is magnificent. Each of the lovers remains suspended in a moment of arrest that perpetuates his (and her) initiation into the other's consciousness. For the "man who thinks and weeps and writes," there is a woman who cuts and criticizes, and Petrarch's stealing woman, hovering over her potential victim, stands ready to begin the cycle of loss. In the complica-tions of those dynamics, Petrarch covers the abyss and temporarily out-faces the revelations of 23 by co-opting them. If the initiation equivocates between theft and loss, punishment and repeal, Laura about-to-steal but the heart still his, Petrarch enstoned but the stone already humanized, then a new space is invented—the one occupied by the already told story. Folded over, that story tells, by imbrication, its own untelling. At the end of the story, we have what we had at the beginning. Laura-Daphne revives—in 106 as angel, in 129 as avenger. But both incarnations are always already there. The remarkable innocence achieved in 129 is the innocence of imminence where nothing has yet happened and everything has already occurred. The end falls back on a beginning which delays experience. In that space Petrarch maintains an initiating Laura and undercuts his punishment. He cancels prioritization even as he justifies his art. His consolation in 129—the image of the knife-wielding Laura—returns him to the moment of his torment—and the subsequent image of the Mercurially indignant Laura. But the return still places him in the behind/before where, as other, Laura is sexually intent on capturing his heart. She is, despite the knife, still the sexual woman, not the competing man. About to steal his heart, she is returned to the arena of love. When Petrarch masculinizes nature, he reorders the universe. The rock is made in the image of the hierarchically originative poet. As the first stone in 129, he casts the invented world into being and recasts Laura as Daphne.

But because the knife-wielding Laura waits in the wings, the cure simply arrests the crime temporarily and it resurfaces, breaking out again as late as *Rime sparse* 359, whose Laura-Mercury descends from heaven to belittle the whittled away self:

> "Le triste onde
> del pianto di che mai tu non se' sazio,
> "coll'aura de' sospir', per tanto spazio
> passano al Cielo et turban la mia pace." (ll. 14–17)

> "The sad waves of weeping with which you are never sated, with the breeze of your sighs, through so much distance pass to Heaven and disturb my peace."

In *Rime sparse* 23, Laura denies the content of his verse because she is unknowable; in 359, she denies his form: it's unpleasant enough to disturb her heavenly peace. Mercutio to Petrarch's Romeo, she cuts through his "groaning" and "driveling" (*Romeo and Juliet* 2.4.88, 90) even after her death. With a Laura who is both determiner of language and arbiter of taste, Petrarch continues to elaborate reconstructions, despite the fact that his solutions lead him back to the cancellations he sought to avoid.

Such reconstructions produce the imaginative configurations of 105 and 129, empowering the woman who causes them. A present that precedes the past also makes its reenactment possible. By connecting the poet's energy to write to the woman's enervating capacity, Petrarch revitalizes the potential of female figurative power and links it to the inspiration of female sexual attractiveness. The vision posits the lyric moment, a moment of identification based not on the oedipal model of 125 and 126 where the male finds his infantile voice realized in the maternal song but on the Genesis model where, like Adam creating an Eve who answers back, the poet discovers in the fully grown woman what she is about to take from him: the vital center. Laura-Mercury recalls Laura-Eve in her reaffirmation of sexuality. But she cancels Laura-Eve in her denial of poetry. Her reification of desire situates the centralizing energy of art in the heart; but her animus against Petrarch's desire prompts her to relocate the heart—where it originally was—in her body.

The Petrarch everyone knows is the recovered word-maker who reanimates the forms of his desire in Laura. The Petrarch that Laura-Mercury uncovers is the poet whose ambivalence—whose inclination not to say—is represented by her injunction to "make no word." The remarkable openings Laura-Mercury forges in her "I am not perhaps who you think I am" establish, within the *Rime sparse* themselves, an arena where namelessness suggests a region apart from the forms of knowing (thinking, weeping, writing) by which poetry materializes the woman. Petrarch's Laura-Mercury is impenetrable. She goes beyond male "thinking" to provoke the identity crisis that subverts the origin and forms of Petrarchan invention to make the poet appear as her invention. Her disruptions cause Petrarch to founder. The ground of his invention seems "groundless" when nothing is what he thinks it is. Laura-Mercury's striptease in 23 regenders thought to unseat the conventional Laura-Daphne whose presence in the *Rime sparse* is in fact a reinvention. That Laura-Daphne needs to be reinvented—in 105, 125, 126, 127, and 129—is a testimony to Laura-Mercury's disturbing mirror.

Laura-Mercury's abstractions—her subversions of gender, place, and metaphor—suggest Petrarch's own reluctance to father the fixed, male-centered, confident poetic legacy he names and bequeathes to his cultural imitators. Speaking herself as diffusion and breaking out from the fixed system that imprisons her, Laura-Mercury seems the subject of another discourse. Petrarch never develops the other discourse or the discourse of the other. But in 105, 125, 126, 127, and 129, Laura-Mercury penetrates the rock to suggest that, even for Petrarch, there are moments when the objectifying practice seems unable to contain the speaking subject it invents. There are even moments when it seems as if Laura-Mercury invents him, pressing beyond the forms to uncover the heart and to re-possess it. Arguing that it was hers to begin with, she seems to say "my outside appearance is feminine but my inside is masculine." If Astrophil looks into the heart and claims it is Stella, Laura-Mercury looks into Petrarch's heart and reclaims it as her own. If he wants it back, Petrarch will have to find a way to say: "I am 'always already' this woman." At the very least he will have to reveal, as he does in 23, 105, 126, 127, and 129, his doubt about both the gender through which he envisions himself and the genre through which he materializes the woman. Working his way through those mixed feelings in 129, Petrarch recovers with a renewed faith in "thinking, weeping, and writing." His faith is a kind of emphatic counterpart to Laura-Mercury's cognition-defying "I am not perhaps who you think I am." It requires a "change in nature" whereby Petrarch emerges not only the father-creator of Laura but the generator of the world. Even the rock is made in his image since his word is clearly shown to be the ground of all being. But the weight of that ponderous reemergence is an acknowledgment of the seriousness of Laura-Mercury's indictment. Only through such triply reinforced masculinist activities can Petrarch return to the discourse she threatens. Only with such triply reinforced covers can he overcome the impulse to uncover and confess at last, without disguise, his own ambivalence.

Wyatt

There have been poets who would go to any lengths to slip something by at odds with tradition—men capable of loving love and hence capable of loving others and of wanting them, of imagining the woman who would hold out against oppression and constitute herself as a superb, equal, hence "impossible" subject, untenable in a real social framework. Such a woman the poet could desire only by breaking the codes that negate her. But only the poets—not the novelists, allies of representationalism. Because poetry involves gaining strength through the unconscious and because the unconscious, that other limitless country, is the place where the repressed manage to survive: woman or as Hoffman would say, fairies.

. . .

It's no accident voler *has a double meaning, that it plays on each of them and thus throws off the agents of sense. It's no accident: women take after birds and robbers just as robbers take after women and birds. They (*illes*) go by, fly the coop, take pleasure in jumbling the order of space, in disorientating it, in changing around the furniture, dislocating things and values, breaking them all up, emptying structures, and turning propriety upside down. What woman hasn't flown and stolen? Who hasn't felt, dreamt, performed the gesture that jams sociality?*

HÉLÈNE CIXOUS,
"The Laugh of the Medusa"

TAKING BREAD

Wyatt's Revenge in the Lyrics and

Sustenance in the Psalms

Critics tend to read Wyatt's distortions of the Italian sources he Englishes as functions of his cranky personality or reflections of his Henrician sensibility. Alexandra Halasz maintains that Wyatt's conflictedness is apparent from the very opening lines of the *Penitential Psalms*, which she calls Petrarchan rather than Aretinean.[1] Reed Way Dasenbrock argues that Wyatt's transformations of the *Canzoniere* into laments which deny both "Love's presence as a mediating form" (*Imitating the Italians*, p. 26) and the lady as an idealized object are expressions of his sixteenth-century self-absorption. Dasenbrock's Wyatt "finds his own identity through his struggle with his [Petrarchan] model" (p. 30). Halasz's Wyatt distances himself from David as a way of questioning the value of all poetic expression. Thus he creates a "tension in his poem between the narrator and David, or, put alternately, between narrative, which works to dislodge David, and the Psalm sequence, which works to redeem David" ("Wyatt's David," p. 342). With Dasenbrock, one can account for the discrepancy between Wyatt and his Italian models by describing how he changes poetic conventions, or, with Halasz, one can attribute it to a more serious reservation about the regenerative possibility of poetry itself. But it can also be explained (as it will be here) by reading backward from Wyatt's most original poem—"They flee from me"—where the poet locates his anomie in the difficult woman he imagines for the construct, a woman who in many ways—and certainly in the ambivalence she inspires—resembles Laura-Mercury. This reading, then, assumes that Wyatt's often-noted acerbity is a retaliative response to a woman whose being undermines both self and poem.

With the sexually aggressive and verbally threatening woman of "They flee from me," Wyatt amplifies the "characteristic nervousness"[2] that critics have noted about Petrarch into the serious angst of impasse. The poem presents anamorphic Petrarchism at its most dangerous. The poet is teased by the Laura-Eve of the first picture and then mocked by the Laura-Mercury of the second. In the first encounter, as the initiating Laura-Eve, the woman seems anxious to please, her "how like you this" a question directed at finding the source of the man's sexual pleasure. As the Laura-Mercury of the second reading, she speaks of her verbal accomplishment, her "how like you this" calling attention to her mirror of the man's semiotic powers. Petrarch's Laura-Mercury mocks his representation of her: "I am not perhaps who you think I am." She's more mysterious than he knows. In "They flee from me," Wyatt invents a woman who carries Laura-Mercury's subversions even further. She implies, "you are (both sexually and verbally) who you think I am" and thereby suggests that he's more obvious than he imagines. Her sexual comparisons unravel the lover's confidence in his ability to inspire and retain the physical excitement that sustains relationships. Her linguistic powers unseat the poet's confidence in his ability to make the comparisons that engender poetry. If readers know one Wyatt poem, they know this one. If readers remember one Henrician woman, they continue to be both titillated and repelled by this one. Her effect on Wyatt himself is devastating. Armed with the "bread" she takes from his "hand," the woman of "They flee from me" seems licensed to overtake the self she takes in her arms. Her "trouble" within the poem parodies the poetic process and destabilizes the self Wyatt invents for the poem. Inside his private and poetic "chamber," she completely depletes his sexual and verbal energy. She attacks. He withdraws. She is articulate. He babbles. The poem ends in a bullying and vague threat figured by the poet's inability to find the words to say or the form to express his rage: "I would fain know what she doth deserve."

The "trouble" she causes inside the poem will be analyzed more fully in the next chapter. Here, the difficult woman will be followed as she emerges outside "They flee from me" in poems where she serves as catalytic agent who prods Wyatt's self-sufficiency and consequent distancing from the Petrarchan original. If the Laura-Mercury of *Rime sparse* 23 energizes the recovery of Petrarchism even as, by imbrication, she undermines it, so the woman of "They flee from me" seems to subvert Wyatt's translations by impelling him to strain the discourse. In his translations, Wyatt knows exactly what to do—giving Laura less than she "deserves" by withholding Petrarchan idealization or by withdrawing from Petrarchan poetics altogether. Either he doesn't translate enough of the dyad and thereby denies Laura, or he makes too much of the poet and so outdoes Petrarch in the acquisitive self he creates. In the *Psalms*, he betters what he does in the translations: he simply borrows the idealized Bathsheba and the generous Mary he imagines and appends them, rendering his Petrarch-David androgynously creative. If the woman's aggression in "They flee from me" stems from her desire to be the Petrarch who shapes the "other" in her own image, Wyatt's reaction, in other poems, is to reshape Petrarch, to bend him beyond recognition and so to cast out the woman. If Laura-Mercury retaliates against Petrarch's misrepresentations first, by turning Petrarch to stone and then by triumphantly refusing all definition, Wyatt second-guesses the woman's evasiveness by withholding the traditional paean the woman has come to expect. His evasions reflect a desire not to desire. In the *Psalms*, the woman emerges simply ancillary to David, his annunciation an expression of his desire not to bother with the flesh at all.

When he issues a series of indictments against the threatening woman, as he does in the dark future of "My lute awake," or the eviscerated past of "When first mine eyes" and "Process of time," Wyatt sets the idealized Laura into a body that might feel some of the poet's pain. When he projects a sequence of appropriations that write the woman out of the poem, as he does in the involuted craft and art of "Go, burning sighs," the self-sufficient answer of "What word is that," and the self-induced reproductivity of "Will ye see what wonders," Wyatt internalizes poetic energy and invents a mythology that renders creation exclusively male. In the first set of poems, Wyatt attempts to manipulate the lady into malleability, offering the hope that if she modifies the behavior he identifies, she might still be laurelized. In the second, he positions himself independently so that he can function without her entirely. If Wyatt denaturalizes the woman in the retaliatory lyrics, he supernaturalizes her in the *Psalms*. The process of deconstruction begins in the translations, proceeds through the poems where he demands a "no," and evolves into the vision of "Will ye see what wonders." The phoenix image of "Will ye see what wonders" masculinizes the inspirational flame[3] and mythologizes the body. It frees the "I," as it will Milton's Samson, from the burden of the woman who, in the doubling of likeness, knows too much.[4] In the self-sufficiency of the phoenix, Wyatt fashions himself as the woman without paying homage to her resources. If drag seems to take *on* the other gender as a nod in the direction of sympathy, Wyatt's take*over* in these poems is hostile. Halasz sees David's expansionism and womanizing in the *Psalms* as a critical commentary on kingship, specifically on the reign of Henry VIII ("Wyatt's David," p. 335). But it also can be seen as a form of retribution against the woman who inspires David's repentance. In the lyrics, Wyatt rebels against the woman more directly. The retaliatory circle in Wyatt is more complicated than it is in Petrarch. Despite the fact that, in *Rime sparse* 23, Laura-Mercury challenges the fundamental premise of his poetic, Petrarch's answer is, more often than not, to go on writing as if her subversions had never taken place. Wyatt deals with the destabilizing woman by appearing to perform the Petrarchan regime badly or by sending back yet another round of revenge.

Withdrawing Petrarch in the Lyrics

In "My lute awake," his hostility propels him to withhold the signification through which the idealized "you" is materialized in the first place. When he urges the lute to be *still* at the end of the first and last stanzas, he points in the direction of his intention, once again, to cut short the supply of Petrarchan praise. His "stilling" command enjoins the instrument both to continue a previously held position and to remain silent. Jonathan Crewe defines the poem's deliberately self-defeating syntax: "The poem not only keeps on repeating its own wish to end, but the desire to end is paradoxically what causes the poem to start in the first place."[5] The poem perpetuates its own negations. With the lute's distilled image, Wyatt represents not only the death of love but the death of the poetic impulse in himself. The condition of stillness depends on the meaning of "I have done." In the first stanza, the speaker urges the lute to retain its past resonances and repeat all that he has "done" (experienced) in the name of love. At the conclusion of the poem, he urges it to be quiet because he has "done" (outlived) the name of lover. There is a third dimension to the equation between stillness and experience that transfers the burden to the woman, who will herself both bear the sting of the poet's refrain and sing the "burden" of her own misery. The poet refrains from singing at the very moment the woman sings the refrain, the "stillness" of his silence instilled by her lapsing into imagined song.

If the plaint is the instrument for registering the absence in desire (the wish and want of Petrarchan stasis), to end the complaint is to proclaim the absence of desire (the quieting of the Petrarchan lover). The "stillness" suggests a remembered vacant past and an anticipated future silence. At the very moment the woman becomes the man, the "I" ceases to be the self who sings the song. His revenge is to make her what he was so that he can be something else. In stanza 6, the lady will inherit the man's emptiness:

> May chance thee lie withered and old
> The winter nights that are so cold,
> Plaining in vain unto the moon.
> Thy wishes then dare not be told.
> Care then who list for I have done.
> (*Complete Poems*, p. 145)

Her future will repeat his history as it relates to her unavailability. When she lives his past, she will, like the lute to the "I," reflect the state of absence the "I" already hollowed out (wishing and wanting) and feel the effects of rejection she had previously issued forth (lost and spent). When she reaches into the hollow, she enters the abyss. The "I" multiplies her punishment by making her future his past. She sees her past for what it was and lives his past as what he suffered. Her punishment is both to repent her past and to become her own victim.

If, in the future, she feels what he is feeling now, then she will understand the unrequited desire (wish and want) that provokes swooning songs and the knowledge that the songs come to nothing (are in "vain"). In the premature old age the "I" has invented for her, she is robbed of her spoils (denied his songs because he has stopped singing) and despoiled (denied the self he defined for her). She is left with both the barrenness of her unsung self and the nothingness of his philosophical awareness. No longer the idealized and fully formed beloved of the song, she instead acquires the deprived and always hollowed out psyche of the lover. As the "you" is personalized in his rhetoric, she is literally de-personalized in her selfhood, transplanted into the dying body of the "I" and therefore denied both the exalted prominence of his idealization and the comforting music of his expressiveness. Spoiled, she is besmirched by his reality.

Her third emergence, however, provides yet another torture. When the "I" announces, as he does in the three last words of each stanza, "I have done," he speaks both to his past experience and his present escape. "Done," he is dead to the self she must continue to live. Finally, his lute can be "still" in both senses. As *his* lute, it is silent; now that "she" is "he," it becomes hers, playing out the past as a sepulchral chorus and endlessly repeating the "wishing and wanting" the speaker has transferred to the lady. Even in "stillness" (quiet), the lute represents the love situation; it is the abandoned instrument of love, from which the lover, having conferred his identity on the lady and hers on the instrument, is released. *His* lute can rest, since her lute will remain—still—as a reminder of the lady's cruelty.[6] In "Ma Jolie," and in the endless Petrarchan collages Picasso and

Braque invented for cubism, the lady appears as Wyatt's lute. The male instrument emerges the woman's "still" life, her being represented as the projection of lapsed male desire. Her image contracted to the form she enables the "I" to manipulate, the woman assumes his phallus, at the moment when it remains—in stillness—a representation of lost desire. In "My lute awake," as in "She sat and sewed" (another poem where Wyatt projects his poetic and sexual ambivalence onto the woman), the lady is meant to feel "if pricking were so good in deed" (p. 92). Through the male tool she acquires, she repeats (in stilling song) the history of male pain. Like the colorless modernist cubes, her grey, aged image reflects—in its physical attenuation—the poet's presently depressed emptiness. In its stillness, the lute is sterile, the lady's reproductive potential remanded to the instrument's wooden immobility. Wyatt triply spoils the woman: first, he effaces her idealized self; then he cancels her reproductive self; finally, in stillness, he dries up her desiring self. The lute's repetitions are hollow, its song having no future potential. Rendering the woman's future as the dead end of Petrarchism, the Wyatt of "My lute awake" perpetuates the death wish of his own distillations.

If "My lute awake" cancels the future, "When first mine eyes" annihilates the past and thereby reverses Petrarch's revitalization of history. As Petrarch celebrates the feelings of love's first assault by retracing the steps of the beloved and transplanting Laura's body everywhere, Wyatt's "I" begins by wishing away the body, sucking the earless other of "My lute awake" into the deaf self, decorporealizing where Petrarch *in*corporates. The body that felt the pain washes away:

> And when in mind I did consent
> To follow this my fancy's will
> And when my heart did first relent
> To taste such bait my life to spill,
> I would my heart had been as thine
> Or else thy heart had been as mine. (p. 140)

The heart exchange that the "I" proposes decomposes the self to create a scenario that perpetuates the original love situation. Such a transposition repeats, without changing it, the nothing that was. "My lute awake" is about the demise of the Petrarchan lover. When the "I" stops singing, his complex of feelings is sustained by the woman who, in becoming him, retains his desperation. "When first mine eyes" is about the beginning of love viewed from that sour end; when the "I" stops singing here, all feeling disappears. In following fancy, he tastes the bait that "spills" his life. In Shakespeare's sonnet 129, the swallowed bait of sexual consummation drives the taster mad. Here, the bait is tasted but never consumed. It consumes the speaker. The stillness of "my lute's" immobility—stasis perpetuated—reverts here to a spilling—form overrun. "My lute awake" turns the woman into an instrument that records pain in *still life*. "When first mine eyes" creates a vacuum that is numb to pain and therefore speaks of *no life*. As he opens his body to love, the poet actually ejects his inner self, a loss which, in the process of the poem, he attempts to finalize by wishing away the organs (eyes and ears) that perceived the beloved and recorded the love (lips and tongue):

> I would as then I had been free
> From ears to hear and eyes to see.
>
> I would my lips and tongue also
> Had then been dumb, no deal to go. (p. 140)

The "I" does to himself what he wishes for the beloved in the vindictive future of "My lute awake." First, he presides over his own dismemberment. He commands his dissolution and so does away with the body. Then he transfers the pain he felt to the lady, testifying to the waste that was by calling its initiation a spilling, an outpouring that cannot be returned in the clarity of metaphor.

"My lute awake" turns the instrument of love into a reminder of death. "When first mine eyes" turns organs of love (the senses) into origins of absence (senselessness). "My lute awake" retains feelings and so perpetuates pain. "When first mine eyes" dispels feeling and celebrates nothingness:

> And when my hands have handled aught
> That thee hath kept in memory
> And when my feet have gone and sought
> To find and get thy company,
> I would each hand a foot had been
> And I each foot a hand had seen. (p. 140)

Wishing away the instrument of poetry (the imagistic *hand* of invention, the musical *foot* of meter), Wyatt washes away the song which immortalized ("kept in memory") the lady. If foot becomes hand, the poem is all music. If hand becomes foot, the poem eliminates words altogether. All feet, the excess robs the poem of its body. It ceases to be plastic. All hand, the poem remains static. It ceases to commemorate because, without the rhythmic element, it goes nowhere in memory. What for Petrarch is a change from one solid form to another—a metamorphosis—becomes in Wyatt simply a return to formlessness—an annihilation. The spoiling of "My lute awake" cancels future songs. The spilling of "When first mine eyes" repudiates songs already sung. They dissolve, having neither form to record them nor body to receive them. What is articulated in the sublimated Laura of Petrarchan memory vanishes in the hazy past of Wyatt's undifferentiated waste.

In these poems, Wyatt cancels the idealized Laura of the Petrarchan dyad and replaces her with (1) his instrument in "My lute awake" and (2) his vacant history in "When first mine eyes." In other poems, Wyatt sets to work on Petrarch. First he turns him into the ferocious and therefore unpoetic woman in "Process of time." Then he silences him in the new poetic of "Go, burning sighs." In "They flee from me" the physical violence of the woman's takeover mimics male aggression even as it anticipates male pleasure. When Wyatt imitates the woman in "Process of time," the pleasure is in breaking bounds not in encircling them, the imitation an excess of violence not a containment or return of it. The "scant" help of the lady's denial revokes the "scanning" life of the poem. Wyatt begins "Process of time" where Petrarch concludes in *Rime sparse* 265:

> I live only on hope, remembering that I have seen a little water by always trying finally wear away marble and solid rock:
>
> there is no heart so hard that by weeping, praying, loving, it may not sometime be moved, no will so cold that it cannot be warmed. (p. 434)

Working within contraries, Petrarch posits a process that lends him hope. If nature can change art (rain soften marble), then art (weeping, praying, loving) can soften nature (move hard hearts, warm cold wills). Like the steady stream of rain, the steady flow of the Petrarchan arsenal (weeping, praying, loving) will work. Petrarchan hope is based here on the continued violation of Laura's injunction in *Rime sparse* 23. By softening the love-denying Laura, Petrarch hopes to efface the poem-denying Laura.

Wyatt's imagined "you" is different. She expects poems. Wyatt's revenge in "Process of time" is to cease being the poet she expects. When he establishes a philosophical equivalent to her psychological ferocity, he gives the woman a self she would rather not be. The revenge follows two stages. In stanza 2, he accuses her of upsetting the Petrarchan balance in her pretense. In stanza 6, he moves with her out of the Petrarchan arena and pits his exaggerated vindictiveness against her excessive bestiality. Outside the frame of Petrarchan gentility and gentleness, "he" becomes "she." Beginning with a Petrarchan premise, the "I" undermines the purpose of Petrarchan persuasion on which it is based. In stanza 2, the lady seems too persuaded (already where Petrarch would have Laura, already tender); in stanza 6, she is unpersuadable, so monstrous and unnatural that art is pointless. "Process of time" violates the Petrarchan patience it seems (in the opening imitation of Petrarch and subsequent allusions to Isaiah) to be rigorously following. In his "seeming," Wyatt matches the lady's pretense. In his abandonment of art, he avenges her unnaturalness. In both sections of the poem, he undermines her expectations and thereby retracts the spoils his opening pretends to deliver.

Starting with the Petrarchan assumption, Wyatt heightens its sexuality. He stiffens the soft water into the phallus that pierces the marble:

> Process of time worketh such wonder
> That water which is of kind so soft
> Doth pierce the marble stone asunder
> By little drops falling from aloft. (p. 136)

Like *Canterbury*-Chaucer's gentle showers and *Merchant*-Portia's forgiving cloudbursts, Wyatt's rain starts the natural growth cycle that depends on making different qualities similar (water softening marble) and similar qualities multiple (water inseminating the earth). Poetic power is thereby linked to procreative power, as rain prepares the earth for what Chaucer calls "engenderings." To render likenesses is to be engaged in the poetic process, a process Wyatt seems to enter in the act of translation. Moreover, in speaking of working wonders, the "I" situates the poetic act in the natural order of the universe, which will evolve into the supernatural era of biblical revelation. In its repetitious invocations, his rhetoric alludes to the Christian millennium and further heightens the imagined lady's expectations. The persuasion of the poetic word anticipates the realization of the biblical promise where opposites merge in a union of understanding: "And it shall come to pass that before they call, I will answer; And while they are yet speaking, I will hear" (Isaiah 65.24). The constant repetition of "it shall come to pass" in the biblical sequence parallels the "process of time" in Wyatt's poem. In Isaiah, the softening of the world proves the mercy of the divine word; in Petrarch, the future yielding of the woman in the millennium of love will prove the ultimate power of the persuasive

plaint. Both the biblical passage and the Petrarchan complaint are premised on an initial hardness that melts. Time works not only to soften the
hard nature of things but also to allow a realization of the complete
nature of things: marble is not fully marble until it is battered by rain; a
heart is not fully a heart until it is sounded by love; a woman is not fully a
woman until she responds to a man.

In the second stanza, Wyatt short-circuits the biblical and Petrarchan
imperative by demonstrating how his woman violates the construct of
process:

> And yet an heart that seems so tender
> Receiveth no drop of the stilling tears
> That always still cause me to render
> The vain plaint that sounds not in her ears. (p. 136)

In Isaiah, all things evolve into a compression where speech is answered
even before it is articulated and eventuality becomes simultaneity ("while
they are yet speaking, I will hear"). But in her seeming tenderness, Wyatt's
"she" has condensed the eventuality. She renders the tears vain. They
cannot sound in her ears because their work has already been done. His
"she" is a "he." She plays his part. She seems "tender"; she hides "under so
humble a face"; she pretends to be what he already is. The idealized Laura
of *Rime sparse* 265 permits the Petrarchan opposites to occur by resisting.
The biblical lion begins in opposition to the lamb. But Wyatt's woman
disrupts the formula by an initial pliancy that inverts the order, both of
poetry and of miracle. Already tender, this Laura threatens the lyric dyad
by being too like the Petrarch who pursues her. In "They flee from me," the
woman's resemblance to the poet causes him to question the metaphoric
process through which she mirrors him. Here the "process" of rhyming—
dependent on the progression of timing—is undermined: first by the lady's
seeming tenderness in stanza 2; and, then, by her actual excessiveness in
stanza 3: "So cruel, alas, is naught alive, / So fierce so froward, so out of
frame." Her pretense makes the persuasive process seem unnecessary. She is
already persuaded. Her violence breaks the order of idealizing progress. She
is already inflamed. In her initial "seeming," she erodes the difference that
structures metaphor. In her subsequent extreme, she escapes the metaphor
that contains desire.

Following Petrarch, the "I" sculpts a marble statue of entreating poet
and denying mistress, a configuration which the "she" undermines. If she
is what she seems, then she isn't Laura. She is Petrarch to the poet's

Petrarch. She renders the plaint pointless because, in her pretense, she has already been mollified. The marble of the original statue corrodes into the miasma of her pliability. The subversion of her seeming tenderness leads to the perversion of the third stanza. Wyatt's "she" exceeds Laura and puts his Petrarchism "out of frame." If the woman of "They flee from me" invades the chambers of poetic origination by entering the poet, the woman of "Process" shatters the boundaries of poetic discourse by emerging incomparable. She is like "naught alive." That perversion explodes, rather than forms, metaphor. Her fierceness here is too "froward" to be contained. If the lady's likeness in "They flee from me" embodies the concision of male metaphor, the lady's excessive behavior in "Process" removes her from the frame of the poem. No longer Petrarch, she is Laura-Mercury with a vengeance. But Wyatt meets her, retaliating in inverse ratio to her behavior. If she is out of bounds in her excessiveness, he is out of words in his withdrawal. With the third stanza, Wyatt changes the mode of discourse. Since he cannot negotiate with the troubling woman, his revenge is to become her.

What begins as a definition of poetry ends as a deconstruction of its premises:

> Each fierce thing, lo, how thou dost exceed
> And hides it under so humble a face.
> And yet the humble to help at need—
> Naught helpeth time, humbleness, nor place. (p. 136)

When the "I" defines the "you's" bestiality, he links the falsity of her initial pose to the fierceness of her ultimate deformations. Her monstrosity lies in her seeming lowness and consequential short-circuiting of the natural cycle. But when he pulls her out of the range of the possible, the poet kills off the lover who lives in the "process"; instead he develops an acrimonious self who comes into being as the "beseecher" ends his plaint. In the identification of the lady's monstrosity, he assumes it and emerges as menacing in his estimation of her as the special "she" of "They flee from me" was disquieting in her imitation of him. Initially used, the Petrarchan frame is dismantled, first by the lady's playing Petrarch to his Petrarch and equaling his tenderness, then by the poet's playing tiger to her tiger, matching her extremes.

The contagion of her ferocity transfers her violence to him. Petrarchism is undermined in the first half of the poem because there seems to be no reluctant Laura. In the second half, the persuasive Petrarch disappears.

The "you" spreads her influence, like fire, to the "I." Masked by humbleness, her fierceness breaks the frame of metaphor. The conflagration of her "process" renders "time" and "place" (the loci of poetic likenesses) unrecognizable. She has effaced the materials. As a consequence, he materializes her effacement. In "When first mine eyes," the poet pulls out the bottom of the poem, undoing the boundaries of metaphoric identity; the past is vacant. In "Process of time," the lady breaks the frame, shattering the construct of patient formulation; the present is savage. Language has no form to hinge a metaphor on in "When first mine eyes." In "Process," language tears the form, its containing utterances collapsed by the ferocious things contained. The final contrast between fierceness—an excess of self—and humbleness—a denial of self—derides Petrarchan modesty. The "I" wears the lady's mask. His refusal to be the meek lamb leaves room only for the poem-eating tiger. Petrarch retaliates against Laura-Mercury's excess by pretending to ignore her deconstructions. He continues to contain her body in the poem. Wyatt reacts by retracting the body of the poem. But it is the lady who starts the cycle the poet cancels. She instigates the "excess" that provokes the poet's recess from the idealizing process.

In "Go, burning sighs," the poet seems wiser. He himself stifles the art the lady has come to expect. As it burns itself out, some other art is born. In "Process of time," the poet is reduced by the lady's indifference to naming and so assuming her monstrosity; in "Go, burning sighs," he is similarly at first motivated by her coldness to calling her icy and heartless.[7] But in the course of pointing to her villainy, he finds another source for his poem. He splits from the Petrarchan model:

> Go, burning sighs.
> I must go work, I see, by craft and art
> For truth and faith in her is laid apart,
> Alas I cannot therefore assail her
> With pitiful plaint and scalding fire
> That out of my breath doth strainably start.
> Go, burning sighs. (p. 72)

Wyatt turns the optimistic Petrarch of *Rime sparse* 153, one who believes cruel fortune may end, into one who sees no end to his end. Whereas Petrarch contrasts his anxiety and darkness to Laura's peace and light, Wyatt questions the lady's "truth and faith." If, in "Process of time," the "I" defines how the woman breaks the frame of Petrarchan discourse, here the "I" defines a new art.

When he commands the "burning sighs" to "go" in the refrain, he no longer sends them back to the lady who inflamed him. He asks them to wither away. Having no fuel to fan them, they become extinct. Since neither pitiful plaint nor scalding fire can get the lady to yield, the speaker must use other means. Once more, she is out of range. Truth and faith (pitiful plaints and burning sighs) are useless with her. When the speaker dismisses the burning sighs as ineffectual and abandons his spontaneous songs, he finds inspiration from a source that "worketh" independently of the Petrarchan dyad. That artifice depends on something in the self which the speaker calls craft. Allowing the "burning sighs" to extinguish themselves, he acknowledges the powerful center of his art. At the end of "Process of time," he names both her unnaturalness and his acrimony. Here he defines a new kind of unnaturalness—one based neither on an inversion of the love situation nor on a distortion of the human anatomy—having discovered that the first leads to the pretense of the lady's humbleness, the second to the excessiveness of her monstrosity. Aimed at a Laura who one day will be accessible, Petrarch's flaming sighs are fueled by expectancy. Wyatt's flames die with the resting "I" of stanza 1 and burn out with the absent "I" of stanza 2. Canceling the Petrarchan lover, the "I" negates the Petrarchan "you." She is neither a Laura who might eventually succumb nor a lady whose ego may be inflamed by his ardency. This time she goes with the sighs, banished from his art.

When he detaches himself from Petrarch and announces his intention to write in a different vein, Wyatt heralds a self-contained doubling. He uses his anger at the imagined woman to justify his dismissal of her as source of his poem. He will work with "craft and art." The practiced accomplishment of craft suggests Mercury. The elusive mystery of art premises privacy. Wyatt's new art is self-sustaining. In "Go, burning sighs," it comes into being against the futility of Petrarchism, the tears of the Petrarchan plaint dried by the annihilative fire of the Petrarchan flame. The poem goes, banished by a poet whose muse has been pushed away. But the inward turning suggests the possibility of a doubleness in the self which counters the woman's indifference and is independent of it. Petrarchan sighs have their origin in the single-minded obsessiveness of the lover, but an "I" who begins in doubleness, in craft and art, speaks to ambiguity and mystery. His art implies the craftiness of a secret expertise which he will ply not in the flame of the beloved's eye but in the darkness of something personally fostered. Mirroring Petrarch's Laura-Mercury, Wyatt's "I" denies the lady a self she can feel confident about and a poem she can recognize.

Wyatt annexes the doubleness of the lady's duplicity and turns it into the complexity of his many-layered (and hence partly secretive) self. Jonathan Crewe emphasizes the various meanings of "craft" in Wyatt as a combination of technical skill and ethical doubleness. From that premise, Crewe argues that the discovery of the woman's duplicity "makes no difference in the end since the movement of the poem culminates in an anticlimactic repetition of 'Go, burning sighs.' "[8] But it is possible to see the difference Wyatt insists on by reading the sighs not as emissaries to the woman but as poetic swan songs. "Go, burning sighs" heralds the end of Petrarchan negotiations. As self-immolative commands, the burning sighs stop the discourse before it starts. If the "I" of "Process of time" is outward bound, the "I" of "Go, burning sighs" is inward bound. He seeks an art whose origin lies in his privileged arena. That exclusivity becomes clear in the "no" poems—like "What word is that" and "Madam, Withouten many words"—where the "I" launches a non-Petrarchan assault on the "you." He turns Laura's refusal into something other than a poetics centering on the woman. In some ways, Wyatt's overt recognition of the value of sexual denial to the poetic art signals his distance from the very poetic he ostensibly uses. Seeking the lady's "no" is a way of licensing the independent "I," a way of saying "yes" to the selfhood Petrarch only found through the woman. When Wyatt engenders this semiotic "I," he negotiates a different dynamic of power, expressing his love of language directly. The woman's body is irrelevant to poetic being. The poet loves the word itself.

In "What word," Wyatt calls the lady's refusal "mine answer," identifying her "no" as his initiative. No longer a sign of the woman's leverage, the "no" empowers him. Anthony Low suggests that the answer is not, as most critics agree, the elusive "Ann, sir" (Anne Boleyn) but the exclusionary "an na" ("a no" in the Renaissance spelling).[9]

> What word is that that changeth not
> Though it be turned and made in twain?
> It is mine answer, God it wot,
> And eke the causer of my pain.
> It love rewardeth with disdain,
> Yet is it loved. What would ye more?
> It is my health eke and my sore. (p. 96)

The lady's "no" becomes an expression of the poet's negativity. Wyatt assimilates the lady's denial. He calls Laura-Daphne's "no" the poet's "own" answer and therefore dismisses the woman as necessary other. If the sexual or external rebuff rewards desire with pain, the internal answer dissolves desire and so obviates disdain. The question is intentionally worded to suggest an enigma; in that light the answer lies not in the exposed "other" but in the hidden self. A "no" may be the lady's response. But in making it "mine answer," the "I" posits a resistance in the self, a private resource merely matched by the lady's refusal, "loved" because it ascribes to the other a reluctance already existing in the self. The double possessive of the "no" establishes in the self the resources Petrarchan poetics locate in the other. Laura-Daphne is unnecessary to the poet who successfully incorporates Laura-Mercury. Her evasions become his health as, assimilated, the soreness of her denial emerges the source of his acerbity. The humbled Petrarch keeps petitioning the disdainful Laura, finding the life of the poem in the death of love. The sharpened Wyatt ends the petition, honing his strength through his own craft. Word, not woman, sparks the poem.

In "Will ye see what wonders," the woman's absorbed energy is transmuted into a mythological—and hence altogether semiotic—status. If Laura-Daphne's sexual denials become the poet's resource in the "no" poems, Laura-Eve's biological reproductivity abets his strength here:

> Will ye see what wonders love hath wrought?
> Then come and look at me.
> There need nowhere else to be sought,
> In me ye may them see.
>
> A bird there flieth, and that but one;
> Of her this thing ensueth:
> That when her days be spent and gone,
> With fire she reneweth.
>
> And I with her may well compare
> My love that is alone,
> The flame whereof doth ay repair
> My life when it is gone. (p. 234)

In *Rime sparse* 135, Petrarch begins with the phoenix, uses the magnet metaphor, and then proceeds with transformation myths that continue the magnet effect: the catablepa, the African springs that annihilate the self, the Epirean springs which burn the self, the Fortune Island springs which torture the self, until he returns to the spring near Sorgue which started the process of his misery. In Petrarch, the self is always extracted.

The lady becomes the powerful magnet who slights the ever-slighted and abject lover. Wyatt reverses the journey so that he rests not with unending Petrarchan depletion but with a continued vision of growth. The "I" begins as "the most monstrous thing of kind," having become what, in "Process of time," he accused the woman of being. If, in the first stanza, the "I" combines with the most monstrous "she" that the lady often was elsewhere, he also emerges the hermaphrodite. He assumes the bisexuality, the monstrosity of kind, implied in the figure he evokes.

But while Petrarch survives that annihilation only to resurface as the continuously unmanned self, Wyatt returns to remasculinize the hermaphrodite as he becomes the self-engendering phoenix of the last metaphor. Petrarch begins his poem with a desire that keeps fueling itself. Wyatt ends his with the doubling of "mine own," now tripled in its insularity. When he speaks of "My love that is alone," he refers to "repairing" as an energy independent of desire. To "re-pair" the self is to find the other in the self, that "most monstrous thing of kind" whose being in the regendered private arena contains the flame of its own regenerating resources.[10] To "re-pair" the self is, then, to pull Laura back inside: to double by retracting. Finally, to compare himself with the "she" that is the phoenix is to find in the monstrosity of the hermaphrodite all the othering one needs. Anticipating Marvell's variously plumed bird in "The Garden," Wyatt's self is mother and lover to the poem. When the flame becomes a light guiding the self onward instead of a cinder returning the self to the other, the concentrated and concentric "I" kindles in himself the inspiration Petrarch claimed came only from Laura's eternal spark.

Wyatt's "love that is alone"—a withdrawal that defies the woman— answers her challenge to the male privileging of the figurative by annexing her territory. It patterns its creativity on her enclosures and locates its mystery in her evasiveness. In firing the woman out of his poems (matching her ferocity in "Process of time" and extinguishing his own embers in "Go, burning sighs"), Wyatt immolates the Petrarch who idealized the lady. But in "Will ye see what wonders," Wyatt internalizes the womanly flame. Sexually neutral, he wipes out Petrarch. Absorbing her reproductivity, he annuls Laura. Attaching himself to the Ovidian bird, he circumvents the dangers of the physical woman, his muse now exclusively his own. Yet the self-sufficiency of Wyatt's reparation imitates the encircling powers of the woman he sought to escape. The signification of his phoenix (and restored phallus) is partly hers, the revitalization of his visual space with her duplicated image synchronous to the autoeroticism of his linguistic self-homage. If "They flee from me" invents a woman whose sexuality threatens Wyatt's textuality, in "Will ye see what wonders" Wyatt textualizes the woman—retreating behind a figure that reproduces the forms of its own history. Duplicating his alone-ness, he privileges agency, his poetic outlook a reconfiguration of his lonely—and only—life. Dressed in her feathers, the poet reveals himself in a sort of defiant drag. He can be as monstrous as the woman he internalizes. In the "no" poems, Wyatt obviates the woman by making her denial an answer that liberates him sexually to turn elsewhere for satisfaction and poetically to look inward for inspiration. In "Will ye see what wonders," Wyatt disempowers the threatening woman by rendering her affirmations his premise. The "yes" of Laura-Eve's reproductive courage becomes the source of his metaphysical renewal.

Absorbing Laura in the Psalms

The recovered poet of "Will ye see what wonders" appends the female body and then extends *his* redoubled self into the poem. Appropriating the phoenix's reproductivity, his deliberate simile ("I with her may well compare") calls attention to the poetic device that turns him into what he describes—just as the woman in "They flee from me" refers self-consciously to poetic representation in her "how *like* you this." When he emerges the phoenix, Wyatt redirects the woman's climactic fire into his inspirational flame. Her end is his beginning. In "A Paraphrase of the *Penitential Psalms*," Wyatt similarly uses the Petrarchan destiny as an assumed prologue. By-passing the woman altogether, he widens the lyric experience to include the holy trinity; then he narrows the trinity to the lyric dyad. First he takes in Mary, as he "mothers" the child of his verses; then he takes in Christ, substituting the words he gives *to* the world for the suffering that Christ endured *for* the world. He renders the poetic art (a world he fabricates) parallel to the divine act (a world God fathers).

While Petrarch's songs are challenged by the critical Laura-Mercury, those of Wyatt-David are accepted by a receptive God whose mercy vouchsafes the poet as not only a receiver but a giver of grace. Armed with the female reproductive powers he appropriates in the hermaphrodite, the "I" of "Will ye see what wonders" identifies his poetic potential. In the *Psalms*, David enacts his poetic realization, as he emerges first author to, and then reader of, his own productivity. The *Psalms* write out the woman both in their incorporation of maternally generative organs of creation and in their assimilation of maternally nurturing functions of growth. The child produced by the song and protected by its engenderings is Wyatt-David himself. Most critics read the *Psalms* as serious examples of Wyatt's faith in God rather than as a *construction* of the God that David craves to become. Stephen Greenblatt argues that the audience for the *Psalms* is "God as ultimate reader" and that the creator is God as penultimate writer.[11] Shormishtha Panja doesn't go quite so far but she does read the *Psalms* as a "gradual submission of [David's] will to God's."[12] Only Alexandra Halasz problematizes the victory. She terms the poet finally "unregenerate" ("Wyatt's David," p. 343).

Greenblatt's theory that the *Psalms* are governed by a belief that "power over sexuality produces inwardness"[13] and that the power comes from God fails fully to acknowledge the degree to which Wyatt's inwardness is pronouncedly self-made and the degree to which Wyatt's faith is constructed on a desire that appears as Petrarchan. The *Psalms* continue Wyatt's struggle with Petrarchism by casting Petrarch's abjection—a petrification that comes from Laura's sexual and linguistic denial—into an accepted fact which David eventually subsumes. In the course of the *Psalms*, David becomes the child of the God he imagines. That emergence, however, is simply a prelude to his becoming God himself. Though love is eschewed (very rapidly dissolved at the opening), the lover (as a desiring figure) is embraced and very nearly deified at the end of the sequence. Wyatt-David doesn't deny the desiring "I"; he recasts him into a "craver" (l. 719), one whose desire is realized as he feeds his own appetite. The transformation of desire (a wish) into craving (an act) constitutes Wyatt's reemphasis; no longer the pining Petrarch seeking what he *can't* have and begging another who won't respond, he emerges the rewarded craver who gets what he *can* have from a responsive other—God himself. He makes Petrarch's impossible end a "sured" (l. 725) goal which he will, in time, realize. As singer, David reads his own text. He asks for what he has already gotten: the word. His word becomes, in turn, the source of his "assurance" (l. 710). His utterance is a song he will repeat, the repetition both a reaffirmation of his originating power and a preparation for the word's immortality. David builds a reinforcing ladder to his own apotheosis. The *Psalms* end in a prefiguration of Christ's birth and ascension that renders David's reformulations invincible.

If, as Marguerite Waller writes, Wyatt's habits of self-realization assure the "non-identity"[14] of the woman he effaces, nowhere is that habit more evident than in the *Psalms*, which begin with a successful Petrarch who, appropriating the Godhead, renders the maid of the trinity as someone he made. Barsabe (Bathsheba) is obviously irrelevant; Mary becomes the Petrarchan other that David elides in the end. In the conception of the *Psalms*, he writes as father to the self he is to become. In the singing of the *Psalms*, he maternally cradles the words which define his potential. The repetition feeds his growing confidence in the godhead he will assume. Fathering his conception and mothering his birth and growth, he formulates his regeneration in the fictional family.[15] The powerful women of the *Psalms* are dwarfed by the poet and ignored by the narrator. Halasz sees a split between narrator and Psalmist on the subject of spirituality. The reading here, however, posits their similarity. Their mutual use of Petrarchism (its presence in *Psalms* and narrative) unites them in a woman-denying ethos.

The *Psalms* open with David as the typically Petrarchan abject lover. He begins subject, the slave of Barsabe, and then proceeds to free himself of Urie, the one obstacle obscuring his unfettered enjoyment:

> Love, to give law unto his subject hearts,
> Stood in the eyes of Barsabe the bright,
> And in a look anon himself converts
> Cruelly pleasant before King David sight;
> First dazed his eyes, and further forth he starts
> With venomed breath, as softly as he might
> Touched his senses, and overruns his bones
> With creeping fire sparpled for the nonce. (ll. 1–8)

Love becomes the snake in the garden of Barsabe, changing his shape so that David, like Barsabe, will be "sparpled"—divided and so conquered. The visual space (the bright eyes of the woman) merges with the linguistic space (the venomed breath of the serpent) to produce the creeping fire of Petrarchan subjection, what Roland Greene calls a "sparple" for Petrarch's "sparse."[16] Having insinuated himself into Barsabe, Love crushes her resistance and renders her (in turn) the snaky poisoner of David. In the submerged image of the snake, the woman becomes the determiner of male shape (overriding his bones) and cause of male division (demolishing his opposition). The creeping fire of the serpent renders David spineless, inflaming him and crushing the backbone of his resistance. For the "nonce" of the first eight lines, David is Petrarch to Barsabe's Laura. Once successful in love, David is free to forget God's precepts, kill Urie, and enjoy Barsabe. Love emerges as overrunner of his bones and liberator of his flesh.

The freedom David finds is the power to do for himself what Love did to him: "to frame" (ll. 13 and 711). At the opening he is shaped by love; in the end he shapes his song. As lover, David is a figure for all men. But, as singer, David is a figure for the poet who triumphs in him and prepares for that triumph in the final commentary. The narrative describes the transformation of a twice divided David, first overcome by love, then by remorse. "Carved in the rock" (l. 308), converted by God's craft (l. 309), the early David seems like the Petrarch of *Rime sparse* 23: frozen in a shape he didn't contrive.

Yet, from the marble image of singular reverence in line 307, David rises in the second half of the *Psalms* and appears as the "statuas moving" of romance who, with the power derived from his singular assimilation, emerges the framer of his own life. In line 719, the David carved in the rock of 308 transforms himself into the metaphysical craver reshaping his own destiny, the anagrammatic folding over (carve/crave) emblematic of the visual power of his linguistic control. With a doubled self, he annexes the female inspiration and silences the female critic of the Petrarchan complex. David finds in his own words an echo of the divine word and thereby emerges the redeemer of his divided self. If Petrarch freed himself of the rock by incorporating the critical and self-assertive Laura in *Rime sparse* 105, 125, 126, 127, and 129, David frees himself from the rock by incorporating the giving and self-denying woman. The *Psalms* themselves, particularly 32 and 102, resemble Wyatt's Petrarchan transformations. The self-redemption in the second half of the *Psalms* follows the consolidating pattern established in the lyrics, countermanding both Wyatt's Petrarch and the Italian original. In their images and assumptions, the *Psalms* allude to the *Rime sparse*. In lines 262–80, Wyatt departs from the biblical original and returns to it with a complicated reversal that allows God to speak in the poem. The poet becomes horse to God's rider and vessel for God's vision. His internalization of the womanly burden (with God "on top") and scopic power (with God inside) prefigures his assumption of the divine "bearing" of Christ and the majestic vision of God at the end of the sequence.

The poetic inversion, from external star in the sky to internal eye of the soul, reworks the Petrarchan image of *Rime sparse* 189 and Wyatt's own "My galley charg'd with forgetfulness":

Such joy, my joy, thou hast to me prepared;
That as the seaman in his jeopardy
By sudden light perceived hath the port,
So by thy great merciful property
Within thy look thus read I my comfort:
'I shall thee teach and give understanding
And point to thee that way thou shalt resort
For thy address, to keep thee from wand'ring.
Mine eye shall take the charge to be thy guide.
I ask of thee alone this thing:
Be not like horse or mule that man doth ride
That not alone doth not his master know
But, for the good thou dost him, must be tied
And bridled lest his guide he bite or throw.' (ll. 266–77)

In "My galley," the "I" remains despairing of the port. Here, David perceives and enters it. The guide becomes both the beacon in the sky (275), pulling despairing man toward him and the inward restraint, keeping rebellious man from wandering. When he adds the starry image of a guiding light to the biblical original, Wyatt reverses his revision of Petrarch's *Rime sparse* 189 where Love "steereth" the speaker into the despair of an unreachable destiny. Here God is approachable. In both the Wyatt and Petrarch sonnets, Love turns the speaker's spatial loss, his sea-sickness, into a psychological loss, his immense confusion. In the sonnet, Wyatt's galley is charged with forgetfulness. The oblivion renders physical displacement mental and mental incapacitation physical. Wyatt is lost at sea and out of his mind. Burdened by Wyatt's infirmity, the world bears the weight ("charge") of Wyatt's loss. In the Petrarch and Wyatt sonnets, the speaker's mental state is caused by the lady's physical disappearance and figured in the hidden stars. As Anne Ferry observes, Petrarch begins to despair at the end of the poem; Wyatt's despair began before it opened. The speaker "remain[s] at the end in the same disquieting seas he found himself in at the beginning" (*The Inward Language*, p. 178).

But, in the *Psalms*, the jeopardy of the sonnets appears as a "sudden light." Converting God into the female port he enters, Wyatt-David assimilates a female bounty. With that entrance, God's eye guides the poet. David internalizes Laura. He pulls the elusive star-eye of the sonnets into his own socket. The heavenly body is an animal he becomes. First God enters David, as man to his woman—giving him divine insight. Then God rides David, as man to his beast, lending him divine control. With each approximation, David assumes the gender and *genus* he dominates. Not only has he reached the goal (converting the aim into a memory), he has redefined the goal (converting himself into the female horse or mule God rides). In the rapid assimilation of the woman, David acquires her wisdom and strength. He turns the end into a beginning which, as the sequence progresses, he will stretch still further. In carrying God, David acquires a female endurance. In seeing as a woman, David internalizes divine insight. The appropriated past becomes a prologue, as Wyatt-David retracts the biblical present into a narrative assumption. At both ends, he is the hermaphroditic God whose controlling power mitigates against the wandering spirit of the sonnets. The process doubles David's capacity. He sees with the woman's visionary eye and supports with her animalistic strength. As eye and mule, David contains divine inspiration and womanly perseverance, his energy an insight and vehicle he absorbs by the proximity of metonymy. The figure of despair in the sonnets (the hidden eye of the lady) becomes the configuration of success in the *Psalms* as Wyatt's David sees (with the incorporated eye) what Wyatt's Petrarch couldn't reach. First, David becomes a woman in drag, pulling her inside him and wearing her power. Then he forgets the woman he incorporated, claiming her power as his own.

If, in Psalm 32, he works his way out of an intensified spatial loss of Petrarch's *Rime sparse* 189, in Psalm 102 he escapes the temporal misery of his version of *Rime sparse* 19. In both sonnets Wyatt heightens the tragic division in the Petrarch he translates, even as he subsequently uses Petrarchan images in the *Psalms* to describe the triumph of David's consolidation. In the Psalm revision of "My galley," Wyatt-David incorporates the female eye he follows. In his Psalm revision of "Some fowls," Wyatt incorporates the female eye that follows him. The stumbling block of "Some fowls"—that the poet invents the woman whose critical gaze he can't escape—becomes the enabling image of the *Psalms*, where the poet reduces the woman's critical eye into a maternal glance he incorporates. In the sonnet, the woman gazes at the poet and thereby undoes him. In the Psalm, the poet sees through her eyes and thereby strengthens himself. In the sonnet, the woman is invented by the poet, partly to suggest, in her look, his own decreative ambivalence. In the *Psalms*, the woman is incorporated by David, mostly to represent, in her inclusiveness, his own self-aggrandizing desire. In "Some fowls," Wyatt complicates Petrarch. He turns Petrarch's destiny into his memory. If the Wyatt of "Some fowls" recognizes his own culpability and therefore distorts the Petrarchan original to match his own poetic doubts, the Wyatt of the *Psalms* affirms his own innocence. He rewrites Petrarch to suit his own poetic confidence. Exaggerating Petrarch's despair, he creates a Laura who defeats him and a self who recognizes the self-destruction of his own inventiveness.

The unshielded Petrarch of *Rime sparse* 19 follows what sucks him up. Like a snake with his tail in his mouth, Petrarch is caught in the unending circle of desire: "Therefore my destiny leads me with tearful and weak eyes to see her: and I know well I am pursuing what burns me." Apollo to Daphne and Daphne to Apollo, Petrarch cannot free himself from the conversionary misery that makes him like what he pursues and pursued by what he likes. He is fired out by his own burning fire. In "Some fowls there be," Wyatt picks up on what is a hint in Petrarch. He converts Petrarch's present misery into a historical fact:

> Some fowls there be that have so perfect sight
> Again the sun their eyes for to defend,
> And some because the light doth them offend
> Do never 'pear but in the dark or night.
> Other rejoice that see the fire bright
> And ween to play in it, as they do pretend,
> And find the contrary of it that they intend.
> Alas, of that sort I may be by right,
> For to withstand her look I am not able
> And yet can I not hide me in no dark place,
> Remembrance so followeth me of that face.
> So that with teary eyen, swollen and unstable,
> My destiny to behold her doth me lead,
> Yet do I know I run into the gleed. (p. 79)

If the Petrarch of the *Rime sparse* is bound to Laura by the destiny of his personality, the translating Wyatt is followed by the destiny of his invention, his past experience rendered a future he created, the "face" he follows a "fate" he designed. Pygmalion to his own Galatea, he shapes his desire for self into a face he can't face. Wyatt describes the present in terms of a past that he himself rekindles. His hell is a consciousness that he can never escape, the light of the pursued flame fused with the heat of his pursuing passion. While Petrarch makes the poem out of what he covets, Wyatt is haunted by the poem he has already made, his "remembrance" his own. While Petrarch forgets that he invented Laura, Wyatt is reminded of his inventing self: "that face." While Petrarch claims that he is "not strong enough to look on the light of this lady," Wyatt claims that he cannot withstand *her* look. His Laura has agency. She looks at him. Yet he is the sculptor who determined her look. Both as configuration and criticism, that "look" is his invention. He can neither escape nor resist it. The double burden—the woman as source of the critical gaze, the self as propagator of the woman's eyes—renders the poet victim and origin of his own unmaker. The imaginative guilt of the Petrarch who invents Laura-Mercury in the *Rime sparse* becomes, in the Wyatt sonnet, a confessed "remembrance."

The "teary eyen" and swollen cheeks he describes are the minute particulars of his own instability. He acknowledges what Petrarch sublimates. The face that follows him is not that of the beautiful lady but an extension of his "unstable" self. His image objectifies the weeping Petrarchan poet. Petrarch sees the "other" face and the image of the beautiful Laura he projects. Wyatt sees, in "that face," the image of his own undoing, an undoing he invented. No longer pretending that the woman is the other, Wyatt sees himself. While Laura's beautiful face swells Petrarch's tribute, Wyatt's swollen face mars his words. Petrarch is miserable because he knows he will always run toward his pain. The Wyatt of the sonnet is miserable because he himself will always run toward his memory. His pain increases as his past catches up with him and algebraically multiplies the misery. He follows what burns him and is followed by his burning self: Petrarch reheated. Petrarch is trapped by desire. Wyatt is trapped by his desire for desire, "*remembr*ance" an anagramatic container of the *ember* implied in gleed. Like flies in winter, the image comes to haunt as well as to inspire him. His plight is heightened by a consciousness that he is the inventor of the instability he calls hers and of the feeling he calls Petrarch's. The gleed is the fire he rekindles as he retraces Petrarch's steps in the embers. Unable to withstand her gaze or to resist fabricating it, he is caught refiring and refining the look he covets. Wyatt cannot avoid the norms he follows because he is produced by them.

In the *Psalms*, the "I" converts the guilty past into a prologue for an absolved future. If the failed light of "My galley" surfaces in Psalm 32 as a saving grace, the self-canceling birds of Wyatt's "Some fowls" and Petrarch's 19 emerge, in Psalm 102, as the self-sacrificing parents of David's rebirth. In the *Psalms*, Wyatt erases the woman's critical gaze by absorbing the woman's protective eyes. He eliminates his responsibility for her

divisiveness by stressing instead his appropriation of her nurturing function. In specifying the specific birds he will become, David transforms the
hopeless "fowls" that describe Petrarchan stasis into the winged creatures
he can imp:

> So made I me the solein pelican
> And like the owl that fleeth by proper kind
> Light of the day and hath herself beta'en
> To ruin life out of all company.
> With waker care that with this woe began,
> Like the sparrow was I solitary
> That sits alone under the house's eaves.
> This while my foes conspired continually
> And did provoke the harm of my disease. (ll. 560–68)

If the biblical David simply compares his present loneliness to the solitary
pelican, owl, and sparrow, Wyatt regenders the experience, the loneliness
defeated in the *maternal* pelican, *female* owl, and *domesticated* sparrow
he self-consciously becomes. Incorporating the womanly functions, the
single birds he fashions in the *solein* image emerge the singular birds he
envisions in his metamorphosis. Each sacrifices himself for the good of
others. As the "solein pelican," he eats away at himself in order to provide
the life he can give to others. Reducing himself in *genus*, he also enlarges
himself in *genius* so that he can become the ideal:

> So made I me the solein pelican
> And like the owl that fleeth by proper kind
> Light of the day and hath herself beta'en
> To ruin life out of all company. (ll. 560–63)

The pelican and owl make less of the little they have, the pelican by
feeding her brood with her own blood, the owl by deliberately denying
herself and thereby giving vocal light to those in darkness. David is his
own daemon. He fashions his external and internal selves into the maternal (female pelican and owl) protector of others. In that moment, he
surfaces as both Mary and Christ, anticipating the child he can nurture
with his blood and then becoming the nurtured and reborn child with his
sacrifice. He turns the self-denying renderings of memory in "some fowls
there be" into the self-aggrandizing sacrifice that precedes his flight. In
their sacrifice and flight, the birds anticipate the Christ he will emulate.

In the sonnets, the unavailable woman leads to poetic impasse; in the psalms, the available woman produces poetic reincarnation.

Sacrificed and sacrificer merge in David, as the narrator recalls in triumph the process of redemption David initiated:

> This word 'redeem' that in his mouth did sound
> Did put David, it seemeth unto me,
> As in a trance to stare upon the ground
> And with his thought the height of heaven to see,
> Where he beholds the Word that should confound
> The sword of death, by humble ear to be
> In mortal maid, in mortal habit made,
> Eternal life in mortal veil to shade. (ll. 695–700)

The word *redeem*, which suggests at once the exchange of sacrifice (presaging Christ's death for man), the quality of restoration (predicting the effect of that sacrifice on man), and the possibility for reorientation (preparing a changed thought for man) constitutes David's comfort. The narrator enjoys that comfort as well. He renders David's experience, in the "it seemeth me," his own. In his triumph, David regresses chronologically from nurturing parent to pregnant maid, each backward glance a look ahead. As redeemer, he will return (with redoubled grace) the potential and nutriment he appropriated. If the pelican is the maternal end, the mortal maid is the maternal beginning. The pelican protects. The maid begets. But David's own word reactivates the vision. He puts himself into a trance, just as Adam was in when he brought forth Eve, incorporating the female power even as he penetrates it. The pun on *maid* and *made* suggests how David links male and female creativity and bridges the gap between eternal life and mortal habit. Like Adam, he invents the new Eve he needs, engendering his poetic "maid." His thought is what enables him to see heaven. His art becomes the mediating daemon, allowing him both to remake himself in the image of God, the word-as-idea, and in the image of woman, the bearer-bringer of the idea.

In the three times repeated "veil" which follows this passage, David gradually reveals the power of his own gaze, each time removing a layer of difference between himself and God. In the first veil, he predicts the insemination of Christ, embedded in the mortal veil of Mary. In the second, he sees the unstripping of the veil, the body of Christ returned to its heavenly father. But in the third veil he redefines mortality in terms of David's confidence. With that circle, he recapitulates his own power:

Eternal life in mortal veil to shade.

He seeth that Word, when full ripe time should come,
Do way that veil by fervent affection,
Torn off with death (for death should have her doom),
And leapeth lighter from such corruption
Than glint of light in the air doth lome.
Man redeemed, death hath her destruction,
That mortal veil hath immortality,
David assurance of his iniquity. (ll. 702–10)

The birth of Christ, predicted by the word and then enacted in the ripe-ness, prefigures the rebirth of Christ, transacted by his death and then guaranteed by his ascension. The second birth of death is a leap into another life. The third veil then becomes its potential. In the "assurance," it presumes forgiveness. The circular pattern of the veil, where the pre-dicted end (the veil of Mary's body) becomes the predicated beginning (the veil of Christ's body), returns (in the third "mortal" veil) to the sense of possibility inherent in the word. If Petrarch frees himself temporarily from the rock by acknowledging the woman's desire in 105, 125, 126, 127, and 129, Wyatt-David frees himself from the entrenched carving of line 308 by his own inversion in lines 719 and 726. His cravings are his will. All three veils suggest the sublimation of metaphor (the word substituting for thing) and the consolations of faith (the thing corroborating word). But the circle is complicated because of its self-reflexivity; it is the word "redeem" (l. 695) that puts David into the trance where he "stare[s] upon the ground / And with his thought [sees] the height of heaven" (ll. 697–98). David penetrates the veil of the body and, as he stretches to the heavens, prefigures bodilessness. His words acquire vatic authority. His gaze presumes divine insight. The figure of David imitates the descend-ing/ascending pattern of Christ, the trance, like the deep sleep of Genesis 2, the place where the poet invents the woman (Mary as second Eve) whom he can assimilate. David's act—the grounding that precedes levita-tion—is David's word—the metaphor that describes his ascension.

If, in the female birds of lines 560–65, David nurtures the nurturing child he will become, here he creates the pregnant mother he needs. He emerges writer-inventor, reader-interpreter of the text. The veiled power of the word is unveiled, the Wyatt-David beneath the three layers suffi-cient unto himself. The David of the final sequence turns the carving of his enrocking in line 308 into the craving of 726 and transforms the stillness of the marble image into an activating potential still to be realized: "Then will I crave with sured confidence. / And thus begins the suit of his pretence" (ll. 726–27). To crave is both to desire and request. Turning the need into a demand, absorbing the image of the other, and shaping a self who (remade in the image of his maker) can bring suit to God, David finds a new confidence. He transcends the confines of his human-hood by enlarging the frame of his man-hood. Then in the "hood" of the womanly "veil," he appropriates the kindly maid who gives birth to the redeeming god. His word calls the vision into being and so produces a poetics based not, as in the lyrics, on a divided self always separated from the ideal but on a unified self who has already become, in the potential of language he shapes, what he craves. His desire is his word and for the word.

If David finds a way out of the past sin with Barsabe, the narrator of the interlude predicts his escape from the future sin with Absalom. A David whose word predicts future life discovers that his desire becomes his act:

> 'He granteth most to them that most do crave
> And he delights in suit without respect.
> Alas, my son pursues me to the grave,
> Suffered by God my sin for to correct.
> But of my sin since I my pardon have,
> My son's pursuit shall shortly be reject.
> Then will I crave with sured confidence.' (ll. 719–26)

As his assurance from iniquity presupposes his knowledge of Christ's birth and foreknowledge of Christ's resurrection, so his knowledge of Absalom's jealousy becomes (through the same means) his prediction of Absalom's defeat. In both cases, David follows the Psalmist's pattern of swallowing the future to make it a prologue to his present capacity, the emphasis, as in the "solein pelican," on turning—almost by mastication—the creative energy of poetry into a realized fact whose figure prefigures something well beyond the present. Wyatt's David uses the assurance his past activity confers as an excuse to go on creating. When he invents his audience, Wyatt-David envisions an eternally receptive God, eager to grant mercy to those who continually ask for it. The response validates the *Psalms*, the remission a promise that the audience will continue to respond. God's secure mercy (assurance for iniquity) emboldens David and allows him to speak with "sured confidence" (l. 725). Because God gives more of his mercy to those who give more of themselves, David justifies the continued composition of his verse, even as he ratifies his double role in the construct. His imitation of God as producer fosters his reproduction of God as listener. With God as the sympathetic "other" Petrarch sought, David grants himself the auto-redemption he needs.

In "Will ye see what wonders," Wyatt enlarges his potential. His multi-gendered being anticipates a repairing of the injured Petrarchan "I." In the *Psalms*, David spreads himself out in time. First he experiences a multi-generational realization of potential and fashions himself as the solein pelican parent who nurtures his growth. Then, as nurtured child whose offering becomes the word that transacts his reincarnation, he turns bread into body. His desire feeds his satisfaction. If Petrarch sacrifices what he wants (Laura) for the expression of desire (the poem), David fashions the poem (as craving) into what he wants. That condensation obviates the woman and makes the poetic act itself the object of desire.

In this context, Wyatt alters the Latin version of Psalm 102, "qui cineram tanquam panem manducabem" (usually translated "for I eat ashes like bread"). He fashions the ashes the biblical David ate instead of bread into the bread that resembles ashes ("wherefore like ashes my bread did me savour," l. 569). That transformation of the Psalmist's literal ashes into metaphoric likenesses prefigures the poetic imagination that subsequently turns poetic likenesses into usable facts. Wyatt's David eats bread that may taste *like* ashes, but it's still bread, a bread which in turn expands into the eucharistic body of Christ David enters. Rendering the biblical experience palatable, Wyatt's David eats and becomes the oppositional other. His craving (asking for what he wants) satisfies his craving (defining what he likes) as the act itself becomes the source of an assurance—a confidence—that turns Petrarchan ends into divine beginnings. Expression in Petrarch substitutes for possession. Speaking desire in the *Psalms*, David doesn't have to resort to sublimation. He gets exactly what he wants: divine power. As rapist-murderer, David literalizes Petrarch's imaginative violation of the woman. Then he turns the literal into the figurative, as he does with the bread, removing himself from the psychic pain of loss and the nagging voice of guilt.

As David, Wyatt describes the endless possibilities of his own invention, an appetite that escapes both the confines of Petrarchan inspiration and the indebtedness of Petrarchan sublimation. With the craving of the psalmist's prayer, he exalts in the freedom of poetic license and thereby consolidates the vision of his self-creative enterprise into the chorus of his self-satisfied voice. Wyatt's psalms incorporate the open body of the woman into the satisfied body of the poem. He feeds the hungry self with the regenerative bread Petrarch found only in loss. He nurtures the poetic self with the assimilated woman Petrarch sought only in absence. In the *Psalms*, her agency isn't even a question. Enclosed within the boundaries of the male poem, absorbed by the totalizing power of the male body, the woman's gendered identity—like that of the dismissed Bathsheba and transcended Mary—is appropriated as a stage in David's self-apotheosizing song.

Halasz sees a split between the spiritual David and the critical narrator. But the Petrarchism of both narrator and David illustrates that Wyatt's biblical transformations—like his lyric ones—are permeated by appropriations of earthly (Bathsheba) and divine (Mary) women. The narrator is part of the conspiracy. In turning the Psalmist's ashes into burnt toast he can nevertheless swallow, and in internalizing the literal Bathsheba and the divine Mary so that they become parts of his own body, David eats the evidence of anything that exists outside the self. Like the revisionist historians who deny Auschwitz,[17] David makes sure there are no Lauras around to testify to his annexations. Without Laura, there is no Petrarch. God songs are not love songs. Without the *differend* to testify to the unspeakable—without the woman—there is only the sanctimonious testimony of ritualized faith. The anamorphic frame of the lyrics is flattened to the one-dimensional image of David. Though the *Psalms* begin with a *sparple* for Petrarch's *sparse*, they end up with only a self-infatuated—and unambivalent—singer.

"LIKING THIS"

Telling Wyatt's Feelings

Several recent critics—Jonathan Crewe, Alexandra Halasz, Pamela Roy-ston Macfie, and Marguerite Waller[1]—have challenged the origins of the confidence Wyatt derives from his Petrarchan reformulations in the lyrics and his Petrarchan appropriations in the *Psalms*. Their questions[2] about what constitutes poetic origination reopen the canon in ways that ironize the line of poetic self-aggrandizement through which Wyatt's male-centered voice materializes. Their caveats from *without* (Waller's about the absence of female vision in the text, context, and contextualizers of "Whoso list to hunt," Macfie's about the presence of female art in the sampler of "She sat and sewed," Halasz's about the value of poetic plea-bargaining in the *Psalms*, Crewe's about the ambiguity of craft in Wyatt's poetic) rephrase in contemporary critical terms the anxieties the Henrician Wyatt faces from *within* his three most anthologized poems— "They flee from me," "The long love," and "Whoso list to hunt." Wyatt renegotiates Petrarch in the lyrics and so gets even with the woman. He gives up Laura in the *Psalms* and so writes out the woman. But, in these three poems, he cannot sufficiently deal with the questions that the woman he invents raises. Laura reigns; the anxieties she provokes prove unanswerable.

In all three poems, a confrontation with the woman results in a poetic impasse registered through Wyatt's unique application of the Actaeon myth to his own poetry. In all, Actaeon's question about fate implied in Ovid and the commentators—"Why do I have to see?"[3]—surfaces as yet another question—"Why do I need to tell about it?" The identification of the woman's feelings in these poems challenges the equation Wyatt so easily makes elsewhere between maleness and poetry. The implications of that subversion are broad enough to shake the foundations of the self-enabling poetic that Wyatt assumes in his Petrarchan translations and the self-transforming stance he approximates in the *Psalms*. Wyatt's original use of the Actaeon myth links his doubts about seeing to his doubts about saying and casts poetic revisioning as the thrall of an invasive and appropriative vision. The woman in the three poems disarms the hunter even as she decenters the man.

The habit of questioning maleness is, as Macfie argues,[4] implicit in "She sat and sewed" where Wyatt confers his hesitation about male pursuits onto the woman. In his question about "pricking," the poet transposes the pain of failed sexuality onto the sublimating pleasure of representation. The "feeling" prompts the question that challenges the semiotic status of the inscribing instrument:

> She sat and sewed that hath done me the wrong
> Whereof I plain and have done many a day,
> And whilst she heard my plaint in piteous song
> Wished my heart the sampler as it lay.
> The blind master whom I have served so long,
> Grudging to hear that he did hear her say,
> Made her own weapon do her finger bleed
> To feel if pricking were so good indeed. (p. 92)

When she reverses the gender of Petrarchan appropriation, the woman annexes the man. As her sampler, her heart represents both the original which she imitates and the organ she incorporates. By sampling, she feels what he feels, laying his heart on the table. By pricking, she isolates the feeling and exposes his instrument to her probing. When she wonders "if pricking were so good indeed," she guesses what it is to be "he" with a "she" who doesn't respond even as she presses the instrument into the art that records her indifference. If his heart is her sampler, an extension of her, then (when she bleeds) she feels both the pain of his sexual entrance (which would be what all women feel) and the pain of her denial (which is what the rejected man endures). She turns the physical experience of a woman (the broken hymen) into the psychological feeling of a man (the broken heart). While the "weapon" is the instrument with which she inscribes her power and the cloth sampler is the vehicle that records it, the seemingly passive finger which receives the prick plays both roles. It emerges a corporeal counterpart of the needle (the masturbatory instrument) and the sampler (the pried-open body). Aligning cloth and needle, she folds his experience into hers, the instrument of penetration attached to the penetrated flesh. As inscriber and text, she feels the impulse to revenge the other and the impulse to question the self.[5] Folding sampler into heart, she prepares to "scramble the signs," as Lyotard might say. The force of her vehemence extends to the phallic agent of her own undoing. "Pricking" becomes gender neutral as the woman's questions about art simultaneously impede sexuality. Whose question is this? Is it that of the lady feeling the pain now or the man who has always felt it? Is the speaker's assumption of the woman's point of view a form of retribution: "Let her feel what I've always felt"? Or is it a mutual complaint about Cupid, the blind god who interferes with, and so stymies, human endeavor?

Such questions about manly assertion merge with doubts about artistic insemination. They surface from an exploration of the double role of the finger which, as receiving vessel, feels the pain and, as transcribing vehicle, remembers it. Serving as both inscriber and artifact, masturbatory instrument and erotized object, the finger is the locus of self-examination. If, through the imaginary ashes of David's bread in the *Psalms*, Wyatt realizes the power of art to eliminate feeling altogether, in the stabbed and then stubbed finger of the lady's hand, Wyatt questions the adequacy of art to mask (at once to conceal and protect against) the feeling it records. The pain is larger than the inscriber. The feeling overrides the form that expresses it. As emotions swell, art unravels. The shrinking pattern of the canvas and the shirking evasions of the finger are variations on the dismembering consequence of inarticulation in Ovid's Actaeon story. The experiential pattern of "She sat and sewed"—the remembered pain censuring future action—becomes the prevailing mode of "They flee from me," "The long love," and "Whoso list to hunt." In the accusatory fingering of "She sat and sewed," the female is maled. She experiences male inscription as trap.

In the three major poems, the male poet voices the woman's detaching impulses, his immersion in the woman's body expressed as a hesitation to form the poem's body. Because they separate vision from narrative, the poems present versions of the Actaeon myth. In all three poems, Ovidian memory—the recollected image of shattered enclave in "The long love," the transferred fear in "They flee from me" and "Whoso list to hunt"— operates to foreclose confidence. In all three poems, female excess cancels male form. The second sight of poetic impasse is a consequence of the initial sighting figured by the violations in the Actaeon story. The telling silence Diana imposes on Actaeon emerges as the feeling silence the poet chooses as he recognizes the representational bind. If "She sat and sewed" phrases artistic hesitation in male terms, the three most anthologized poems voice the woman's doubts. In each poem, it is a woman who begins the questioning cycle that ends in male self-denial. Laura-Eve sets "They flee from me" into motion only to unleash Laura-Mercury as the anamorphic portrait uncovers a double threat; Laura-Daphne instigates "The long love" and Laura-Mercury pervades all of "Whoso list to hunt."

If the central myth for Petrarch's ambivalence is the Battus story, the essential myth for Wyatt's impasse is the Actaeon punishment—particularly two parts of it omitted in Petrarch's references to it in *Rime sparse* 23, 51, and 190: (1) the identification of Diana's bower as the locus of what emerges—with female hindsight—a threatening enclave; and (2) the dramatization of Actaeon's transformation as he experiences—with male "endeerment"—an acquired anxiety. In Ovid, Actaeon painfully learns that he cannot tell. His inability to speak as a man leads to his dismemberment as a deer. His tongue-tied silence is Diana's revenge. The speaker in "Whoso list to hunt" exempts *himself* from telling. If hunting leads to Actaeon's inability to speak—in the process of turning ends to beginnings which is part of the early modern retelling of Ovid—so does hunting come to be another metaphor for poetry.[6] In all three of these poems the variously compressed stages of the Actaeon story lead to a questioning of the speech Diana nullifies in the original. In "The long love," the "I" substitutes inarticulate blind faith for Petrarch's formulative—and therefore poetically expressive—"loving well"; in "They flee from me," the speaker's pleasure resolves itself in the unformulated "this" of the second stanza and dissolves in the vague forsaking of the third stanza; in "Whoso list to hunt," the "I" renounces the poetic pursuit figured by the "hunt." Leonard Barkan writes about Orsino's Actaeon conversion in *Twelfth Night* that "the lady disappears from the hunt the moment she has been seen; from then onwards the lover is engaged in a chase of himself."[7] In "Whoso list to hunt," Wyatt brings the lady back into the myth. Wyatt's "endeerment" is an engagement in the violation and apprehension originally felt by the goddess.

Reducing Olivia to the occasion for his own self-searching, Orsino in *Twelfth Night* makes her over into an object he can then dismiss. At the other extreme is Giordano Bruno who operates by a kind of takeover. He turns "the apprehended object into himself,"[8] and acquires Diana's divinity by osmosis. Wyatt's treatment of the woman is therefore unique in the early modern history of the Actaeon myth. His use of Ovid separates him from both the retaliations of Petrarch's Ovid and the appropriations of

Bruno's Ovid. The difference in Wyatt's Actaeon is implemented by an extension of those moments in Ovid where the woman's feeling—in the gradual progression of the endeerment—becomes more than an apprehended reality. It is a transferred reality. "Whoso list to hunt" is an expansion of the psychological space that Petrarch precipitates in *Rime sparse* 23 and that Orsino assumes in *Twelfth Night*—the time between the sighting of Diana and the presence of the hounds. In those versions of the myth that emphasize the dogs, there is often a deus ex machina, an escape through majesty that remasculinizes the myth. Petrarch surfaces at the end of *Rime sparse* 23 as a Zeus who carries Ganymede-Laura to fame; Bruno's frenzied hunter arrives at the godhead; Orsino's calamity is resolved in Viola's sublimating love. Wyatt's versions of the myth prolong the dismemberment. The breakdown of identification in "The long love," the dissolution into inexpressiveness in "They flee from me," and the impasse of fatigue in "Whoso list to hunt" operate to question male configuration. For Wyatt, the deer-conversion lasts. More than a temporary cover, it is inescapable.

Examining two Greek sources for Ovidian metamorphosis, Gregory Nagy writes that, in Pausanias, Artemis "flung the hide of a stag around Actaeon" and, in Aeschylus, the gods "flung a feather wearing body" around Philomela.[9] Transformation becomes a kind of adding on or adding over the original. The superimposition layers on another surface, but an identical self is maintained. The double bind—wearing another skin but perpetuating the original psyche—is part of Petrarchan metamorphosis as well. Petrarch is buffeted from Battus to Actaeon to Zeus in *Rime sparse* 23 but remains fundamentally himself. In Titian's "Death of Actaeon," the hunter, pursued both by hounds and Diana, wears the head of a stag but is still two-legged. With a deer skin over his body but nevertheless at least half-man, Titian's dying hunter retains some of his former self. In Wyatt's "Whoso list to hunt," the manly "I" ceases to exist. His mind has become all woman: "He may by no means [with]draw [it] from the deer." Her being is more than skin deep in him. Her inside is his too. Wyatt's entrance into the "excluded and abjected realm" (*Bodies That Matter*, p. 6) of the woman results in his hesitation vigorously to pursue poetic materialization. In "They flee from me," he emerges inarticulate. In "The long love," he remains "in the field," indifferent to life or death. In "Whoso list to hunt," he follows the woman's deforming impulses but seems—as she is—overwhelmed by a power-complex that reforms him—as it does her—into something wholly otherwise.

Crossing Over

In "They flee from me," Laura-Eve's invitational "how do you like you this" and Laura-Mercury's imitational "how like you this is" rephrase the self-inflicted pain of "if pricking were so good indeed" in terms of a self-canceling pleasure. The lady's "how like you this" is both a congratulatory salute lauding her accomplished duplication of male entrapment and a promissory note testifying to her imminent delivery of exactly the release the "I" wants. In the salute, she mirrors male behavior. In the promise, she demonstrates her understanding of where the seat of male pleasure lies. Since she is like him, she knows what he likes. "She sat and sewed" suggests that any future inclination to sew stitches (sow seeds) will be deflected by the woman's painful experience as victim of male insinuation. In "They flee from me," a similar one-time "special" encounter results in an undoing that involves an unsaying, the "forsaking" of the third stanza: dire heart (language art). Only it is the poet—not the woman—who hesitates. The pun in the first half of the question suggests the overlapping of gender: "Dear heart, how like you this?" As female deer and male hart, the "I" is both the passive recipient of what the lady is about to give and the active model for her knowledge. She is identical to him in assault. The "this" of what she has done renders her, like Laura-Mercury, a fellow talker. She is, like him, a dire heart. She is also cognizant of him in her sexuality. She knows where his pleasure lies. The "this" of what she proffers renders her—like Laura-Eve—a companion in love. When she calls the man both an intensifier in the romantic "dear" and a talker in the Italianate "dire," the woman links sexual release to linguistic excess.

Verbal and physical ejaculations dissolve the formulations that bring them about:

> Thanked be fortune, it hath been otherwise
> Twenty times better, but once in special,
> In thin array after a pleasant guise,
> When her loose gown from her shoulders did fall
> And she me caught in her arms long and small,
> Therewithal sweetly did me kiss
> And softly said, 'Dear heart how like you this?'
>
> It was no dream: I lay broad waking.
> But all is turned thorough my gentleness

Into a strange fashion of forsaking.
And I have leave to go of her goodness
And she also to use newfangleness.
But since that I so kindly am served
I would fain know what she hath deserved. (p. 117)

The redoubled flesh of the stanza-two experience becomes the vanishing tissue of the stanza-three dissolution, as the woman anticipates the telling which is the substance of the poem. If the question of "She sat and sewed" frames pain in terms of art and masculinity, the question of "They flee from me" frames pleasure within those confines, only the borders are crossed this time so that, in her articulation, the woman mirrors the "he" she becomes. Her question renders her the inseminator; she penetrates and controls. Her knowledge about physical pleasure (liking) relates to her experience in linguistic identity (likeness). She acts and then talks like the man. Labeling her actions similes, she calls attention to the mirror she holds and is. The question in "She sat and sewed" focuses on an already performed act, the deed as opposed to the idea of it. The question in "They flee from me" comes in the midst of the action. The lady assumes the man's stalking attitude and promises to deliver a pleasure she knows (from the identity she has already assumed) he will enjoy. The ramifications of the woman's knowledge locate the site of his pleasure even as the replication of her mimicry identifies the source of his shame. He is compelled to look and afraid to see. But, in crossing over, she also emphasizes that the visual space corroborated by what must be his enlarged member in the second stanza bears an inverse relationship to the vanishing voice of the third; the actualized "now" of the second stanza marks her assertiveness in naming him. The retrospective "later" of the third stanza records his recessiveness in the game of name calling she initiated.

As "dire heart," he would like to equal the formulations of her poetic powers. As flattered listener—endeared hearer—he would like to believe that language has an effect, that what she says and what he *hears* are the same: dear/*hear*[t]. He would like to believe that she values him. But her verbal prowess in the stanza-two invasion prefigures only his prophetic vagueness in the stanza-three retreat. She is indifferent to his feelings. As "deer hart," his expanding lower extremity in the second stanza anticipates his tormented head in the third. Penis now, horns later. As "dear heart," he is her possession; she shapes the form of his body and the measure of his language. Her domineering initiative now, his self-canceling revenge later. In fact, the third stanza proves his impotence, his dilation there an evisceration of his expressive powers, her departure there a comment on his sexual failure. Adam "dreams" of an Eve who "cleaves" to him. Her antecedent unreality anticipates his subsequent solidity. Wyatt's "I" experiences a woman who leaves him. "It was no dream." Her anterior reality dictates his later loss. When she departs, he founders in inarticulation. He cannot hold the woman. He cannot shape the words of his expressiveness. She is the Laura-Eve who names him: "dear heart." He is the inexpressive Petrarch-Battus who "would fain know" what to name her.

In a speech that describes a similar crossover, Cleopatra becomes Antony in drag. But, in Shakespeare's play, the recollected pleasure encourages Cleopatra to believe that she will, one way or another, repeat the joy she tells. In Wyatt, telling and enjoyment are separate functions. The "I's" revelations in the second stanza anticipate the untelling and undoing of the third. For Cleopatra, the story is the means by which she manages to sustain her belief in Antony during the absence which (in 1.1.3) she called her oblivion. Cleopatra fills the vacancy with sensual language that turns sensuality into a language. Her way of being is identical to her way of saying. As she describes her past, she comes to believe in her future. The relaxing patience of release *then* flashes forward into the supportive patience of anticipation *now*:

> That time? O times!—
> I laughed him out of patience; and that night
> I laughed him into patience and next morn,
> Ere the ninth hour, I drunk him to his bed
> Then put my tires and mantles on him, whilst
> I wore his sword Phillipan. (2.5.18–23)

With the "times," Cleopatra recalls the many occasions when (like Wyatt's stalking woman) she "laughed [Antony] out of patience," and encouraged him to pursue and tame her. But when she recalls "that time" when she laughed him into the patience (of a woman), she relives the one moment when she became him, wearing his sword Philippan and flaunting the dominating power of penetration. The special time that she speaks of involves a transference that defines the sexual act as an artistic interchange. She becomes Antony by appropriating his signs. Her outside is his inside. She wields the phallic instrument simultaneously as she receives his sexual member. Her inside is his outside. Laughing Antony into patience, she quiets him because he must endure her sword, but she also makes him calm, composed, pacified, satisfied. The regendered experience simply reassigns roles and thereby leads to a redistribution of patience. Her stilling patience *then* becomes the distillation of memory *now*. The moment of quiet there inspires her discourse here. Playfully, Cleopatra remembers the completed act. Both lovers experience as the other what they felt as themselves.

Wyatt's "I" similarly crosses a border into the other, as he must in acknowledging his resemblance to the "she" that has become, in "likeness," "he." But the transition in Wyatt hardly seems a game. His lady separates sign from signifier. She dangles the real body even as she withholds the imagined one. Memory and anticipation remain inexorably separated. Just as Cleopatra remembers "that time . . . that night . . . next morn . . . ere the ninth hour . . . then," so Wyatt describes a chronological progression in time: "once . . . in special . . . after . . . when . . . therewithall . . . and," a sequence of evocative actions. But whereas Cleopatra's series leads to a climax of composure that is disclosed with what she calls patience, Wyatt's series leads to a climax of eroticism that remains unresolved. Confronted with a lady who matches the baldness of her physical initiative with the boldness of her verbal gestures, the "I" finds himself frustrated, not patient. If Cleopatra pursues Antony to enjoy him, Wyatt's woman pursues the speaker to tease him, her "this" a sample of what she might (or might not) give, her likeness a reminder of how she came to give it. Her power is expressed both in what she offers to do and what she declines to tell. Cleopatra uses her past encounter with Antony to stimulate herself into believing that she will have another one. The repetition unites fact and imagination. The reversal of gender in the past renders Cleopatra the articulator (with her sword/pen) of the future. Wyatt's "she" crosses genders to threaten the future, her power derived from withholding pleasures she might not give, words she might tell. Does the speaker want her to tell or to give? Is telling a way of not giving? Does the specificity of language reduce the excitement of sexuality? Cleopatra's bedroom stories promise deliverances. The fluidity of reversal opens the possibility of recurrence. Wyatt's details are cautionary. The permissiveness of reversal premises the certainty of infidelity. Cleopatra's telling anticipates return. Wyatt's telling merely precedes betrayal.

In calling the speaker a deer/heart and a dire/heart, the woman refers both to Actaeon's transformation (naming the man the animal she controls) and to Diana's interdictions (alluding to the telling the goddess forbids). When she combines seeing and telling, she reverses the gaze and the discourse and transfers the surprise through which Actaeon overtakes the naked Diana to the surprise through which this naked Diana overtakes the man. Wyatt's speaker is both a spectator who sees himself in the woman and a spectacle whose objectification is determined by her. She dictates his act and catches his word. Cleopatra's cross-dressing renders objects signs of a fluidity that anticipates sexual relaxation: patience as confident power. Wyatt's uncovering Laura renders objects signs of a rigidity that anticipates sexual disappearance: impatience as prelude to impotence.

In the multiple layers of "She sat and sewed," art and masculinity are conflated. The present pain thwarts the desire to prick again. Here the anticipated pleasure stimulates a desire to repeat what has never been realized. When he recollects the "once in special," the "I" is acutely aware that he hasn't got it anymore. In the question, the woman anticipates the fiction of poetry and its basis in denial. She gave "then" what her actions now deny. The "I's" insistence in the "it was no dreame" underlines what he corroborates: the encounter seems (in the likeness of metaphor) only a wish; the mirrors of identity emerge (as they were for Narcissus) the medium of annihilation. Dreaming at least perpetuates a hope. Wyatt's real encounter annuls expectation. In the *Psalms*, language determines reality, as the "I" appropriates the woman and turns her energy into his. Here all is lost in the indeterminacy of language, the "this" at once everything the "I" desires to achieve and the promise (in its vagueness) that it vanishes. The proof of having becomes the woe of wanting. Physical expansiveness and verbal expressiveness cancel each other out. The "I's" intensity in the "dire" compresses the distance through which Petrarch invents the terms of his endeerment. As the deer-animal—all flesh—the man is unable to form words. As the dire-talker—all words—the man is unable to sustain physical experience. In either case, the man is in extreme (dire) distress. And the woman who speaks calls all the shots. In the concision of "dear heart," the woman's likeness enacts metaphor. In the expansiveness of "dire heart," the woman's indictment undoes metaphor. Sexual release reduces the man. Narrative dilation dissolves poetry. The poem ends in unspecified speculation, the speaker at a loss for words. He can neither have nor tell. If Ovid's Diana says "tell if you can," the "she" of this poem anticipates the verbal impotence concomitant to specular gratification. The Petrarchan lover *can* tell what he can't have, his desire sublimated by his telling. Here the lover is left in vagueness, his telling belied by an evasive subject. What he tells in the third stanza is the story of his abandonment. "She" forsakes the man she became. He loses hold of the language that would preserve the becoming. The physical withdrawal in forsaking is also a verbal denial.

In "They flee from me," the woman challenges the masculine desire for form by assuming the form of the pursuer. She appropriates the penis as instrument of pleasure to tease the sexual self. She appends the phallus as exponent of desire and deconstructs the linguistic self. Infidelity and sexual license prefigure a linguistic hesitation that leads to total inarticulation. Her representation of him cancels both his sexual powers and his semiotic imagination. There are no dreams. In *Rime sparse* 237 and 23, Petrarch similarly invents a woman who could be (the former sexually, the latter poetically) he. But in the *Rime sparse* he silences those women by returning them to a realm where their being is either (1) rendered by him (never realizable because consistently a projection); or (2) critical only of his sexuality (incessantly denying and hence never approachable). There are always dreams. In Petrarch's "Amor, che nel penser" (*Rime sparse* 140), the poem-denying "she" reigns; in "Un candida cerva" (*Rime sparse* 190), the sexually inaccessible woman presides. But in Wyatt's versions of these poems, the intensification of feeling seems almost psychologically to result from the identification of intensity in "They flee from me," an intensity which works against Petrarchan poetic confidence. The "I" of "The long love," overtaken by his feeling, is mastered and enmeshed in its pain; the "I" of "Whoso list to hunt," overtaken by the woman, can imagine no pleasure.

Longing Unmanned

In *Rime sparse* 140, the Petrarchan "I" retains his identity, fortified, rather than overcome by, feeling. The "good" in Petrarch reaffirms masculinist values:

> Love who lives and reigns in my thought and keeps his principal seat in my heart, sometimes comes forth all in armor into my forehead, and there sets up his banner.

> She who teaches us to love and to be patient, and wishes my great desire, my kindled hope, to be reined in by reason, shame and reverence, at our boldness is angry within herself.

Wherefore love flees terrified to my heart, abandoning his every enterprise, and weeps and trembles; there he hides and no more appears
outside.

What can I do, when my lord is afraid, except stay with him until the
last hour? For he makes a good end who dies loving well. (p. 284)

In Petrarch, the psychological drama, between the speaker with his un-
vocalized love and the lady with her unverbalized anger, operates by
innuendo. Love is the cowardly general whose inward pressure forces the
"I" to take up his cause. The inarticulate Love (weeping and trembling)
bequeaths to the subsequently articulate speaker what the poet wanted in
the first place, the unequivocal task of expressing desire: "For he makes a
good end who dies loving well."[10] Love commands Petrarch to do what he
has been doing all along. His free will coincides with the god's will. Poetry
becomes a sacred task, necessary for the defense of the state. Loving well is
equivalent to speaking well. The undoable act is sublimated by the say-
able word. The good "end" is recorded in Petrarch's self-congratulatory
rhetoric. Having found that mere innuendo (the man's blushing brow)
reinforces disinclination (the lady's inward anger), the "I" confines himself to the discourse of love. Within the frame of masculinist, militarist
enterprise, the "armor" of his metaphor provides at least some shape (and
hence some containment) for desire.

In "The long love," Wyatt intensifies the feelings and dislocates the "I."
He renders Petrarch's consoling last line a matter of faith which—like the
indefinable "this" of "They flee from me"—remains unarticulated:

> The long love that in my thought doth harbour
> And in mine heart doth keep his residence
> Into my face presseth with bold pretence
> And therein campeth, spreading his banner.
> She that me learneth to love and suffer
> And will that my trust and lust's negligence
> Be reined by reason, shame, and reverence,
> With his hardiness taketh displeasure.
> Wherewithal into the heart's forest he fleeth,
> Leaving his enterprise with pain and cry,
> And there him hideth and not appeareth.
> What may I do when my master feareth,
> But in the field with him to live and die?
> For good is the life ending faithfully. (pp. 76–77)

The "long love" is first a prolonged love, having harbored extendedly in the speaker's thought; then it is a longing love, having extensively created a residence of desire in his heart; finally, when it presses itself out in the open, it surfaces as an elongated love, stretching its limits and forcing the speaker to wage its war. From the very beginning, the protracted duration of love anticipates its endlessness: its failure to satisfy or shorten the desire that instigates it. The paralysis is figured in the similarity between the repressed and expressive self. "Longing" is perennially unsatisfied. Speaking is continually silenced. While Petrarch's "loving well" is deliberately semiotic, Wyatt's "longing" remains more explicitly physical. The heart changes in the course of the poem from harbor to forest (from seashore to borderland and from refuge to wilderness). Since feeling breaks the confines of secrecy, the shift renders distinctions meaningless. The forest where Love hides in his retreat and the field where the speaker fights in his loyalty are the same. Both are fraught with danger. Both represent a wilderness where reason has been abandoned and war rages. If Petrarch's lady remains quietly "angry within herself," Wyatt's "she" more menacingly "taketh displeasure." The speaker's excess of *love* is the surplus the lady seeks to restrain when she urges him to withdraw. The speaker's excess of *body* is the "hardiness" the lady seeks to castrate when she denies male enterprise. Once having presented himself to the dreaded "she," Love flees. But the speaker is exposed, first sentenced to reveal on the outside what before he harbored inside, now having to cope on the inside with "the excess" the lady urged him to withdraw.

Absorbed by the motion that spurred him on, the "I" is marooned with his attachment. Faithfully, he appends himself to the now cowering master. In Petrarch, the "I" is fortified in his masculinity, prepared somehow to continue his pursuit of love. In Wyatt, the "I's" "good" is less certain. With the "longing" of love, the "I" acquires a feeling whose intensity increases his inarticulation. The heart becomes a forest fraught with beasts. Like the snake whose head is wrapped and choked by its tail, his end is defined by a beginning mired in "pain and cry." Petrarch is spurred toward articulation to say for his master what the master cannot say. Wyatt is spurred toward identification. His master's fears become his own. Love's distension reveals the sameness of field and forest and identifies the consequential impotence of language in terms of a spatial haziness. Unable to define difference, the "I" of "The long love" is unable to tell. The blurred borders undo the distinctions upon which metaphors ride. The mute exertion of Love in the opening press strangles the "I," who in the rush of retreat loses his voice.

Redoubled by the complaining love, Petrarch will continue to sing. Conscripted by his fidelity, Wyatt's "I" is bound to the feeling that initially pricked him out of, but now restrains him in, the forest. The tentacles of love may be long but they form encirclements of strangling intensity. Inundated by Love's released emotions and threatened by Love's repressed feelings, the harbor of the opening and the bower of the forest are equally fraught with danger.

With the wildness of "They flee from me" and the wilderness here, Wyatt's "I," like Ovid's Actaeon, seems spurred by a force beyond his control,[11] a force whose appearance is coincidental to an intensified feeling. If Diana is surprised in the place where she feels free to be herself, so the besieged lover experiences the invasiveness of the outside world even in the retreat of his inward heart. If, in "They flee from me," the woman penetrates the man's chamber, here the lover, having violated the woman's reserve by showing himself, discovers that he has no place to hide. The broken barriers in the Actaeon myth impinge on the breaker as well, as the lover discovers what Diana did—that there is no escape from bestiality. The implosion of harbor and forest, violator and violated, telescopes Ovid in such a way that telling (an art based on differentiation) becomes impossible. Unspecified by the Petrarchan formulations of "loving well," the protracted desire in "long love" remains unresolved. Feeling dissolves form. Its expression increases, rather than assuages, pain. Its "excess" provokes, rather than contains, fear. Laura-Daphne's denial of sexuality does not inspire, as it does in Petrarch, the substitute laurel of a poem. Instead, it suggests that the "I's" expressiveness—his desire to demonstrate passion—chokes on its own excessiveness.

The Last Helas

In "They flee from me," the breakdown of gender distinctions results in the abandonment of language; in "The long love," the breakdown of spatial distinctions instills similar doubts about poetic effectiveness. But nowhere is the questioning habit, elaborated from a telescoping of Ovidian transformation, more dramatic than in "Whoso list to hunt," where the mere mention of the lover's sigh—the "helas" of the second line—effects the Ovidian conclusion: "I may no more." Diana's interdiction is understood by an "I" who has absorbed her teachings. Ovid's Actaeon tries to express his misery. Wyatt's Actaeon understands that he doesn't even need to try:

he is already banished from the world of "alasing"—the Petrarchan sighing—that violates Diana's interdiction. And he is banished because he
sides with the deer, feeling the frustration of her violation. In Ovid, the
Actaeon deer is torn between his former thoughts and his deerlike feeling:
his "mind remained the same as before"; in Wyatt, the "I" "can by no
means [his] mind draw from the deer." In Ovid, Actaeon vacillates between his desire to "return home to the royal palace" and his need to "hide
in the woods." Wyatt's deer/hart "leaves off" and resigns himself to the
deer's fate. If, as Nancy Vickers maintains, "subsequent imitation, no
matter how creative or how wooden, bears witness to the reader's awareness of and the writer's engagement [defying Diana's injunction] in the
practice of 'speaking' in Actaeon's voice,"[12] Wyatt's "Whoso list to hunt"
silences Actaeon's voice because his speaker is totally immersed in Diana's
plight. He has absorbed it. Ovid's Actaeon-deer is in an impasse resulting
from his inability even to articulate *his* feeling, his "miserum." Left to
womanly tears and subject to fear, he is skittish, not knowing which way
to turn. Wyatt's Actaeon-deer turns *away*; his paralysis reflects the woman's anomie.

Most critics define the impasse in "Whoso list to hunt" as a male
problem,[13] dependent on the speaker's seeing the woman as an object he
cannot restrain himself from desiring. Stephen Greenblatt calls it "the
impression that, despite the poet's attempt at decisiveness, he never quite
'leaves off,' that he is incapable of fully drawing his mind from the 'deer':
the poem itself bears witness to his continued obsession even as it records
his attempt to disengage himself from it."[14] For Marguerite Waller, "the
Wyatt persona is therefore dependent for its very existence upon what
Greenblatt terms the poem's 'impasse.' This kind of self can emerge at all
only by neither succeeding nor leaving off the pursuit. Furthermore, this
self depends upon *maintaining* the power structure of absolutism. Relative positions within the structure may be at stake, but never the structure
itself. 'Caesar' may be superficially ironized but never done away with."[15]
Jonathan Crewe maintains that the deer bears the man's marking, that
"Wyatt's feminized hind (female subject) emerges as a crafty rather than
idyllic figure."[16] In Greenblatt's view, Caesar is the cause of Wyatt's undoing. He blocks the appropriation of the object. Waller and Crewe see Wyatt
as complicitous in the blockage that keeps "the political economy of male
sovereign selfhood [and the subsequent reduction of woman to the status
of an object]" going.[17] Regardless of their differences, all three critics
define Wyatt's impasse in the hunter's terms. He may have a female skin

flung over him, but he is still a man. The reading here suggests, instead, that the impasse is the deer's. Because his immersion in the woman is more than skin deep, the speaker corroborates the deer's double bind: her linguistic impotence as visual object unable to speak in her own voice and her linguistic servitude as ventriloquistic originator who gives the man voice. She is silenced but she inspires. Ovid's Diana forbids poetry because it affords her no chance to answer back, to counter the poet's *use* of her, a use which keeps her earthbound (an object of male obsession) and inarticulate (an object of poetic revision). Wyatt voices Diana's injunction himself. He is silenced and alienated.

In Petrarch's poem, Caesar is god and the deer is freed from male formulation because of her connection to the divine. In Wyatt, the deer's quote is ambiguous. Muir and Thomson, Rebholz, and Waller suggest that it has something to do with "rendering unto Caesar the things that are Caesar's."[18] As earthly creature confined by the mere fact of the collaring, the deer receives her identity from the tag, the naming device that impedes tagging (the future pursuit, or tagging-along, of poetic reformulation). The poem defines poetry in terms of the man's desire to hold—to confine in words—what the woman seeks to withhold—to reduce to abstraction. As wind, she is invisible; as sighted object, she is untouchable. In terms of chronological sequence, Wyatt's poem works backward. The octet describes how Wyatt feels; the sestet depicts what he saw that made him feel that way. The octet is a result of the sestet. The poem suspends act in punishment. Jonathan Crewe maintains that the poem turns the tables on itself in the final couplet—that its meaning only becomes clear at the end.[19] The argument here is that the poem doubles back from the beginning. Its description of the deer at the end is a flashback. Its subject is the consequence of seeing expressed as a sequence of feelings, feelings that involve what Lyotard calls "the suffering of being unable to signify" (*The Differend*, p. 13).

If Wyatt interferes with chronology and reverses the order of memory (what Wyatt saw) and desire (what the deer feels) within the course of the poem, Petrarch moves backwards between two poems. The events of *Rime sparse* 23 occur later in the day than the events of 190. In Ovid's version of the Actaeon story, much is made of the time of day—the noontime heat which forces Actaeon to cancel the hunt and Diana to bathe. The time of day forms the narrative focus of the tale, a narrative Petrarch follows in *Rime sparse* 23, where he alludes to his confrontation "with the lovely wild creature [who] was in a spring naked when the sun burned most strongly," and encircles in *Rime sparse* 190. The sun rises as the vision begins in 190 and reaches noon in 23. Several hours transpire between the time of the initial sighting and the disappearance at the end but all the re-visions occur before the events of 23. Petrarch's fall into watery dissolution in 190 precedes his forest dismemberment in 23:

> A white doe on the green grass appeared to me, with two golden horns, between two rivers, in the shade of a laurel, when the sun was rising in the unripe season.
>
> Her look was so sweet and proud that to follow her I left every task, like the miser who as he seeks treasure sweetens his trouble with delight.
>
> "Let no one touch me," she bore written with diamonds and topazes around her lovely neck. "It has pleased my Caesar to make me free."
>
> And the sun had already turned at midday; my eyes were tired by looking but not sated, when I fell into the water, and she disappeared. (p. 336)

In terms of actual time, 190 is a preamble to 23; in terms of psychological space, it amplifies the first story and turns it into, as Waller writes, "clearly a Narcissistic projection."[20] In 23, Petrarch feels himself drawn *from* his own image. Here he is drawn *to* the lady's reflection between two rivers. His initial attraction to her as "other" precipitates his fatal attraction to himself as Narcissus. When he falls into the river and suffers Narcissus's fate, the deer he sees in the vision merges with the self he seeks to define. In 23, Petrarch becomes the deer he sees and then is pursued by what he wants—the hounds of his desire. In 190 what he wants is, as Waller also suggests, "what he cannot have, not because of some circumstantial prohibition but because it does not exist in the form in which he conceives it."[21] Petrarch is caught in the image-making process. In 23, it looks like the image maker is Diana. In 190, the maker is Petrarch who antedates his withdrawal in 23 to redraw Laura in his image. Conflating Diana with the deer/hart that had become sacred to her, Petrarch recasts his victimization in 23 into yet another triumph for his vision-making capacity.

In 190, Petrarch sees at dawn the self he will become in 23 at noon. Taken together, the Petrarch poems double the mirror. He becomes "she" in 23. She becomes "he" in 190. Both images reflect the poet's visionary capacities. In 23, Petrarch recovers from the hounds pursuing him by flying as the eagle carrying Ganymede-Laura to her fame. In the later sequence, he postpones his recovery, holding off until 191, where he surfaces from his 190 immersion. There, Petrarch calls Laura the "life-giving" sight he lives on. He turns the object that he sees into the sustenance he imbibes, the way chameleons feed on fire: "Some live only on odors and the fame of it is believed, and some on water or on fire, satisfying their taste and touch with things that lack all sweetness, why should I not live on the live-giving sight of you?" (p. 336). In making her one of the absorbable elements in 191, Petrarch turns Laura into the bread of his life.

The self-dissolving water of 190 is transformed into the self-sustaining bread of 191. In the later poem, Laura revives Petrarch's phallic being as salamander-chameleon. He lives on the fire of her inspiration. Once he absorbs the Laura he invents, he can turn the deadly water of 190 into his self-reviving spirit. In 23, Petrarch overcomes Diana's punishment by moving out of the Actaeon myth and transforming himself into the vehicle for Laura's apotheosis. In 191, she feeds his imagination, her fire and bread the source of *his* apotheosis. In both poems, the poet recovers from the fall of his endeerment to retain Diana's vision and power. That process continues in Petrarch. His doubts about writing—expressed as problematic in 190—emerge surmountable in 191. The reflection in the later poem turns the generative Laura into a regenerative fiction the poet can work out, even if he seems temporarily to be "drawn" by her shaping fantasy in 23.

In the complicated revisioning of *Rime sparse* 23, 190, and 191, Petrarch loses but then reinforces his faith in telling. His perception of the object always returns to an affirmation of the subject of poetry and the subjectivity of the poet. In the opening lines of "Whoso list to hunt," the deer filters back to the hunter. Her indeterminate status mediates between origin and denier of desire (the elusive scopic object) and origin and denier of text (the forbidding verbal subject):

> Whoso list to hunt, I know where is an hind,
> But as for me, helas, I may no more.
> The vain travail hath wearied me so sore,
> I am of them that farthest cometh behind.
> Yet may I by no means my wearied mind
> Draw from the deer, but as she fleeth afore
> Fainting I follow. I leave off therefore
> Sithens in a net I seek to hold the wind.
> Who list her hunt, I put him out of doubt,
> As well as I may spend his time in vain.

And graven with diamonds in letters plain
There is written her fair neck round about:
'*Noli me tangere* for Caesar's I am,
And wild for to hold though I seem tame.' (p. 77)

As wind, the woman is felt but unseen; as deer she is seen but untouchable ("*noli me tangere*"). The physical deer of the sestet is the metaphysical inspiration of the octet, but the transference works to undermine the sublime sublimation. The holding of the hunt in the sestet results in the withholding of the image in the octet. The deer's visually distinctive characteristics are not described until the last two lines when they are transformed into linguistic markers that explicitly render her the untouchable force that opens the poem.

In the opening lines she is invisible. She is the wind even as he becomes "winded," his exhaustion determined by the hind. He "may no more"; he is "wearied so sore." He faints. He cannot hold her. He emerges the spectacle she is in the sestet, his exhaustion an objective correlative for her anomie. If Petrarchism idealizes the woman in the image of the man as idolator, here the "I" decorporealizes the self as the imitator of the lady's evasiveness. The rhyme of "hind," "behind," "mind," and "wind" suggests that, as wind, she determines his thoughts. "He" is a belated "she," exhausted and pushed into shapelessness by her. The hind is both first cause and ultimate end. It leads and he "cometh from behind." The speaker's mind is absorbed by what pursues him and pursued by what absorbs him: the wind. Usually seen as the inspiration that propels language, the wind here cuts off discourse. The speaker is "winded," stopped by what should move him. The other rhymed words "more," "sore," "afore," and "therefore" trace the history of act and consequence even as they indicate that consequence—the stasis of desire figured in the excessive "more"—is a condition of arousal—the state of apprehending expressed in the catapulting "afore." Both sets of rhymed words connect an Ovidian sequence to Wyatt's telescoping. The distance between "afore" (an anticipation) and "more" (an epilogue) is collapsed, as the "I" becomes trapped in the represented deer. Mired in her egress, his excess—the "more" of his fatal pursuit—is conflated with the "afore" of her fatalistic—and evasive—lead. The escape of her "at last" is the trap of his "helas."

The gradual change in Ovid emerges Wyatt's already premised fact. Hunting (endangering pursuit) becomes poetry (the forbidden words). Petrarch recovers from his endeerment to render Laura the endearing object of his laurelization. Wyatt becomes the deer and recognizes that, in hunting, he traps himself. Petrarch begins in *Rime sparse* 1 by invoking a reader who might be a fellow poet ("anyone who understands love through experience"). Wyatt begins also by soliciting fellow writers from whose amorous pursuits (alasings) he desists. If, in Petrarch, Caesar is God, and the woman therefore free from earthly preoccupation, in Wyatt, she is Caesar's (in the sense of "render unto Caesar") and therefore preoccupied by earthly things. Thus both are possessed (he by her, she by Caesar) by the power that makes them sought. That circle links memory to desire as the impression of the deer dissolves to feeling in the octet and the vision of the deer resists feeling in the sestet. Petrarch's dismembered Actaeon ("I felt myself drawn from my own image") surfaces as Wyatt's dismembering deer.

Withdrawing from feeling in the exhaustion of the octet, redrawing what can't be felt in the evasions of the sestet, Wyatt extends the woman's elusivity. The deer is "wild for to hold," her being described by her resistance to taming and naming, the forms by which men define women as their own. Unlike Actaeon, who longs to return to his former self, Wyatt's speaker "leave[s] off," giving his former quests to others, calling them to the hunt, as he already had been called, his invitation an expression of his disinclination: "Whoso list to hunt." In soliciting a vague "whoever," Wyatt clearly separates himself from those who still are engaged in male pursuits. Wyatt follows fainting, having lost his own strength. Through the chase, he becomes wearied, feeble, no longer capable of desiring desire. The "I" that hunted "may no more." The old self is discarded as he emerges the deer and feels for the first time what the woman feels: a resistance to formulation. In "Whoso list to hunt," the Ovidian telescoping technique is complicated still further as two opposites are doubly paired, the self-cancellation of Petrarchan *impossibilia*—"since in a net I seek to hold the wind"—and the self-division of poetic oxymoron—"and wild for to hold though I seem tame." In the octet, the act of holding emerges futile. The wind is invisible as scopic object but tangible as provocative feeling. The "I" cannot retain in voluble sound what is elusive as evocative sight. When the woman announces that she is "wild for to hold though [she] seem[s] tame," she loosely echoes Laura-Mercury's "I may not be perhaps who you think I am." Her resistance to what she *seems* parallels Laura's insistence on naming only *what she is not*. In attempting to hold the wind, the "I" seeks—as Petrarch does—to fix inspiration and to fuse intangible feeling with the tangible object he invents. But while Petrarch persists, Wyatt desists. His feeling remains uncontainable. The

"I" shares the woman's deconstructive impulses. The disinclination of her un-winding produces the exhaustion of the poet's winded-ness. While Petrarch temporarily wears the deer skin, Wyatt's feeling goes deeper. He is the deer. If there is a certain exhilaration in *Rime sparse* 23, found in Laura-Mercury's "I may not be perhaps who you think I am," it is the exhilaration of a language not yet formed. Her resistance suggests that there are vocabularies that might still be discovered, languages wherein she might still name herself. Wyatt's *differend* is different. Lyotard writes of linguistic despair: "It is that of someone who thought he could use language as an instrument of communication and who learns through the feeling of pain which accompanies silence to recognize that what remains to be phrased exceeds what can presently be phrased" (*The Differend*, p. 13). Wyatt, similarly, is collared by Caesar, by the restriction that the male power complex imposes on feeling.

In the sestet, the beheld victim turns on her victimizers, explaining her elusiveness in terms of a wildness they acknowledge in the fetters that name her. Caesar's taming exposes *his* bestiality. The deer may seem tame but she is "wild for to hold." She is unnameable: the wind. Unaccountable to the forms that would describe her, she first projects herself as projection and then calls all definitions illusions. She only *seems* tame: "Caesar's I am."[22] In attaching herself to Caesar's taming, she detaches herself from others. But in figuring herself as Caesar's projection, she separates herself from *reality*. Using the strongest of men—Caesar—to break free of all men, she also calls herself "dangerous"—in the sense that her being is an illusion that renders her namers also "groundless." To pursue an illusion is to emerge similarly illusory. The threat at the end suggests that the "I" of the opening is a shadow seeker. Attempting to hold the uncontainable, he shadows himself and becomes a shadow of himself. The deer's detaching impulses are expressed by an "I" who "leaves off." A hunter who no longer hunts, the "I" merges with his former target and wilts as she withdraws. When Wyatt's deer casts herself as Caesar's possession—and hence as bodiless—she means that she exists only as the effect of Caesar's "dynamic of power." For Caesar, possession is naming; for the poet, desire is naming. Caesar's power equates having with being. Poetic power is about not having. But what Wyatt discovers here is that both forms of naming constrain the subjectivity, and therefore deny the materiality, of the other they appropriate. The deer's evasions repudiate Caesar's tag; the deer's body eclipses the poet's naming. The temporal sequence of Wyatt's poem reverses Ovid. The inability to tell concomitant to the endeerment precedes the visual entrapment that causes the endeerment. Wyatt's Actaeon knows Ovid, his victimization already present from the outset. It is the attempt to hold (to retain vision *in* the more permanent form of language) that promotes wildness, as it was the attempt to behold (to acquire vision *of* a more permanent form of being) in Ovid that unleashes the wild dogs. Wyatt's telescoping is an abyss of returns. The sighted object merges with the objectifying seers. Her victimization becomes theirs.

Leaving Hunting

In "She sat and sewed," an anticipated memory (the scarred finger) invites speculation about a prospective poetic hesitancy. In "Whoso list to hunt," the poetic doubts are enacted as the holding—the retention of form necessary for poetry—emerges a consequence of beholding—the initiation to the form that sets into motion the desire to tell. All Caesars, all men, turn the objects of their desire into the subjects that turn on them, rendering unto Caesar the wildness he names. The opposites—wild and tame—become identical to the *impossibilia*—net and wind. The "seek[ing] to hold" of the eighth line and the "for to hold" of the fourteenth both suggest the elusiveness of the inspiring wind and the futility of the poetic forms that seek to tame her. What Wyatt sees in the octet is what he has already seen. The second sight reads back to the as-yet-not-sighted, coloring innocence with the experience of the woman's vision. The hind Wyatt reveals to the reader in the last lines is the self to which he alludes in the opening. The narrative flow of the sequence is guided by the second sight (hindsight) of the already premised transformation. If Petrarch manages to recover from his endeerment to make other poems, Wyatt remains locked in the impasse of be[ing] the hind. His memory of victimization blocks his will to formulate. To leave off hunting is to side with the deer.

If in "She sat and sewed" and "They flee from me" the pain and pleasure of male "pricking" problematize poetry, in "Whoso list to hunt" the feeling that stops the poem is the woman's experience. And what is the woman's experience for Wyatt but the desire to resist formulation and move into abstraction? To stop hunting—sighting the pursued object—is to stop citing the acquired subject. It is to understand the desire to resist the shapes through which maleness and poetry materialize. In "She sat and sewed" the woman experiences the danger of poetic probing, of crossing the borders the poem uncovers. She opens up a world of feeling (a lesion widened in "The long love," tested in "They flee from me," and finally assumed in "Whoso list to hunt") that results in a reluctance to pursue the form that produces the poem's body. The woman's insistence on the un-containable body undermines the representational impulses that produce the poem. Wyatt's sensationalism, with its opening of the self to feeling, emerges antipoetic. The pain in all three poems challenges the maleness (in "The long love" the martial loyalty of the soldier, in "They flee from me" the amorous initiation of the lover, in "Whoso list to hunt" the dominating pursuit of the hunter) that results in poetic emblematizing. Abstraction—the movement represented by the wind—works against in-scription—the containment figured by the poem. Petrarch falls into the waters of his own self-love in 190 to arise in 191 with an image of Laura-Venus that extends his originality. The Caesar-God that frees his vision of the deer enables him to envision his own apotheosis as her creator. He may drown in 190 but in 191 he surfaces to form another love out of his severed—and severally scattered—parts.

In resisting holding and affirming wildness, Wyatt's woman sucks the "I" into a vortex he can't escape. Petrarch reassembles himself as ener-gized poet. Wyatt ends with throbbing instrument in "She sat and sewed," dissolving image in "They flee from me," unspecified faith in "The long love," and empty net in "Whoso list to hunt." His artistic uncertainty is represented by the respectively shrinking, forsaking, forbidding, and van-ishing woman. The coupling of the woman's reluctance with the man's doubts in these poems works against the program of what Waller calls a male lust for power and what Crewe calls the poet's power in craft to voice Wyatt's aversion to the form through which his Petrarch generally pre-vails. In the cross gendering of "She sat and sewed" and "They flee from me," the woman articulates the man's hesitation about form—his fear of betrayal canceling his art, his fear of dissolution annulling his sexuality. In "Whoso list to hunt" he voices the woman's evasions. His poetic results from her detaching impulse. The feelings generated in these poems are somehow larger than the selves transcribed by them. They lead the "I" into territories staked out by the "you" (Diana's forest in "The long love," Diana's retaliations in "They flee from me," Actaeon's transformation in "Whoso list to hunt") that erase the hierarchy of gender distinctions through which the confident speakers of Wyatt's other incarnations mar-ginalize the woman. These poems exist in the margins. The feelings spill out of the forms and the genders transgress the boundaries that formalize

Petrarchan discourse. In "Process of time" and "Go, burning sighs" Wyatt dismantles Petrarch and the poem the woman expects. In "Whoso list to hunt" he revitalizes a Laura whose abstraction fingers his ambivalence.

When the woman of "They flee from me" (1) imitates in likeness what the man does; (2) presents in likeable acts what the man wants; (3) alludes in vagueness to what the man says; and (4) eludes, by mystifying it, what language specifies, she seems to provoke the retaliatory and the exhausted Wyatt respectively. Her reality stops Wyatt from dreaming of an idealized Laura even as he ceases (in "Whoso lists to hunt") to "joy in [the] sighing" of Petrarch's consoling sublimations. Hunting (poetic revisioning) and "helasing" (poetic lamenting) provide pleasures which the reluctant poet of "Whoso list to hunt" pursues "no more." Eliot's enervated Prufrock blames his ineffectuality on the woman's aura, reducing her to a vague, disembodied essence. ("Is it perfume from a dress that makes me so digress?") But his irresolution simply reverses Petrarchan revenge: scattered woman; scatter-brained poet. The elusive woman of "Whoso list to hunt" takes the lead. As the unsettling and unsettled wind, she prompts the poet to distrust the nets of form that Petrarch uses to idealize Laura as his influence, an idealization Eliot's Prufrock later diffuses when he blames her perfume for his impotence. Petrarch exalts the lady. Prufrock atomizes her. But both end up denying her material body. In admitting his inability to materialize anything, Wyatt dissociates himself from the male power complex.

Pushed beyond the confines of totalizing structure in his obsession with the woman's abstracting impulses, sympathy with her incommensurability, and assumption of her elusiveness, Wyatt transforms the Ovidian and Petrarchan Actaeon story into a vehicle for poetic doubt. His "windedness" ends the discourse that entraps him simultaneously as it breaks through the discourse that previously (as hunter of woman and maker of words) empowered him. Her exploding feelings—breaking through the confines imposed by Caesar—become his frustrated feelings, unable to find a form large enough to contain the suffering he absorbs. Laura-Mercury's joyous evasions are "plunged into [the] emptiness[es]" (*The Differend*, p. 138) of Wyatt's troubling immersions.

Donne

Who is Silvia? What is she

That all swains commend her?

Holy, fair, and wise is she,

The heaven such grace did lend her,

   That she might admired be.

Is she kind as she is fair?

For beauty lives with kindness.

Love doth to her eyes repair,

To help him of his blindness;

   And, being help'd, inhabits there.

Then to Silvia let us sing,

That Silvia is excelling;

She excels each mortal thing

Upon the dull earth dwelling.

   To her let us garlands bring.

TWO GENTLEMEN OF VERONA,

4.2.36–52

SMALL CHANGE

Defections from Petrarchan and Spenserian Poetics

What [Jacqueline] Rose [*The Art of Sylvia Plath*] leaves out of account (and what her colleagues in the academy left out of account in their anxious and contorted writings about another hideous divorce case, that of Paul de Man and his wartime journalism) is the psychological impossibility of a writer's not taking sides. The writer, like the murderer, needs a motive.

Janet Malcolm, "The Annals of Biography," *The New Yorker*, August 23–30, 1993

[Sylvia Plath's] *Letters Home*, I found pretty distasteful, but I could understand at least their tone—I found myself writing pretty artificial letters, about the children, to Aurelia.

Olwyn Hughes, on Sylvia Plath's letters to Aurelia Plath, as quoted by Janet Malcolm in "The Annals of Biography"

Perhaps more than that of any other poet in this study, the work of John Donne has been critically regarded as misogynistic: "written by a man whose central theme is his own intense personal mood and whose poetry is composed exclusively, even domineeringly, from the viewpoint of a man."[1] Accordingly, Donne becomes a poet who (in Janel Mueller's terms) "perpetuates the prevailing asymmetry of outlook and sexual role that casts the male as persuader and possessor, the female as persuaded and possessed."[2] His poems and letters thus provide an almost perfect laboratory for feminist critics to explore gender "asymmetry" as it emerges in the early modern period. But a brief look at the maps of two learned feminist critics, Janet Halley and Ilona Bell, indicates the inherent difficulty of clearly charting the histories of women's lives. Each critic produces a different story, partly because each theorizes a very different Donne and a very different woman from the same textual evidence: the poems and letters. The theoretical apparatus of one is canceled by the historical position of the other, as each attempts to locate the "real" woman in the "real sphere" of Donne's life.

On the one hand, Janet Halley maintains that "the representations of Ann Donne that we have inherited from her husband function no differently in the context of Donne's representations than those of that quintessentially fictional female, the Muse."[3] In poems and letters, Donne "gathered to himself a power he shared whenever he circulated female figures: the masculine power to control the meaning of the feminine" (p. 202). For Halley, there is a single-layered poet who, imposing what Ann Rosalind Jones calls "the violent hierarchies that shore up masculine identity,"[4] invents the women he writes about, even his real-life wife. In Halley's view, the life Ann Donne lived can be found "not only by her presence in history but also by acknowledging her absence to us in her husband's discourse" (p. 191).

For Ilona Bell, who on the other hand advocates (in Jones's terms) "the non-victim status of women" (p. 76), Donne himself is multivalent, spinning out speakers who vary from "lusty braggadocio, to efficacious rhetorician, to cold avenger, to empathetic understander."[5] Bell's lady, however, is a composite one whose point of view Donne is "never able to disregard" (p. 116). "Unlike his Petrarchan predecessors, Donne writes not of imagined love or exalted beauty but of loving and being loved . . . not of ladies seen and admired but of a lady who is highly present, loving and criticizing, judging as well as admiring" (p. 129). When, in a later article, Bell turns from the poems to the historical evidence of the letters and concludes that three were written by John Donne to Ann More over a year before their elopement, she also concludes that "if, as these letters suggest, Donne's love affair with Ann entailed a much wider range of feelings than we thought, it may well have inspired a broader, more various group of poems than we have considered."[6] According to Bell's logic, the lady listening to the poems must have been Ann.

Bell's "woman" is independent. Above all she is present in her feelings to poet and man. Created by poet and man, Halley's women are "absent" in the text and in the life (p. 191). While Bell assumes that Ann More could read the letters she speculates Donne wrote to her, Halley conversely reasons that since no documentary evidence remains "statistical studies suggest that it is highly unlikely that she was [literate]" (p. 187). Historical argument often proceeds from what Janet Malcolm calls "the psychological impossibility of a writer's not taking sides" and what Marguerite Waller calls the disinclination of the critic "to contextualize and relativize—to consider as an ideological construct—the critical ground from which [s]he is arguing."[7] In this context, the discrepancy between the historical evidence of Bell and Halley can be read as part of their particular "projects" even if their conclusions "resist creating presence where none is."[8]

Halley nevertheless argues cogently that "if we admit that women in their historical actuality remain the constituency of feminist criticism, we oblige ourselves to keep in mind that the subjective experience and authority of women are, perforce, absent from the representations of them" (p. 191). Halley is right when she says that the subjective experience of women is missing from male representation, if the biographical life is what is meant by subjective experience. But the corollary to that axiom is another question. Can we know the man Ann Donne married from the poetry of John Donne or even from John Donne's letters? Letters, too, can be subject to the conventions of their circulation and to the need, and sometimes even unconscious motivation, for the cover of personae.[9]

But when she speaks of the *authority* of women, Halley enters into yet another sphere—the realm where women might have power—power in the sense of how they materialize in the imagination, either their own or that of the inventing poet. And it is within the realm of multiple identifications that Donne imagines an imagining other with an authority that might make her author of the very representation in which she appears. In such configurations, it is very easy for author and authority to get confused even by the inventing poet who is produced by the original man named John Donne. As "something imagined, not recalled,"[10] a poem suggests that the scales of Halley and Bell are ballasted by ideological projects based on mutually exclusive asymmetries. Neither theory accounts for the "force" of Lyotard's "dream-work," or the way in which it refolds and changes experience. When he speaks of condensation as "a change of state . . . or a difference in nature" ("Dream-Work," p. 24), Lyotard describes the mysterious process of "producing the imaginary" ("Dream-Work," p. 24). That process also produces the authority—or the force—in the "scenario" of the poem. "Hiding its other sides" ("Dream-Work," p. 24), the condensation refigures desire in ways that are not always definable by the biographical self or apparent to the historian. Like the dream-work, the poem presents yet another layer of experience, an opacity that makes it possible to imagine the shifting subjectivities that constitute an anamorphic vision.

If Halley's position results in a feeling that we can never know for certain the "materiality of women's lives," and Bell's in a feeling that we can never know for certain the "materiality of poets' lives," then it might be possible to introduce a theory of "undecidabilities" which functions apart from what Jonathan Goldberg calls "the single-minded story that some New Historicists have been telling, but also from the ways in which its feminist critics have replied" (*Sodometries*, p. 61). To read Donne with Denise Riley's understanding that individual temporalities are modified by "the many temporalities of a designation" (*Am I That Name?*, p. 98) is to emphasize the complex negotiations between self and other that emerge from an understanding of the many "alternative possibilities in the writing of gender" (*Sodometries*, p. 61).

The anamorphic frame of *this* "project" suggests that multiplicities of sexualities and gender produce more than one poet who might imagine more than one other who in turn can respond to—or prod—the originary imagining and imagined self. The following chapters begin with the possibility that Donne's Petrarchan experiments might involve the woman as a "subject of consciousness," a possibility that allows him to question the constructs he uses. The first chapter chronicles Donne's relationship to Laura-Daphne in "The Broken Heart" and "Of Weeping" where the imagined listening woman, who is herself aware of the way women are conventionally idealized, shapes the poem she is in and future poems the poet might write. The second chapter turns to "Jeat Ring Sent," "The Funerall," and "The Dreame" where Laura-Eve's gestures determine the discourse. Finally, chronicling Donne's difficulties with Petrarchan assumptions in "A Valediction of My Name in the Window," the last Donne chapter turns to "Elegy: Change" where Laura-Mercury breaks down all barriers so that the poet speaks her ideas and so relinquishes all ties to the idea of a biologically gendered self. The woman Donne imagines in "Change" unhinges the notion of "boundary, fixity, and surface we call matter" (*Bodies That Matter*, p. 9) to suggest matterlessness as another imagined possibility. While the Wyatt of "Whoso list to hunt" remains mired in deformation and depressed by the woman's resistance, the Donne of "Change" is exhilarated by the potential of letting go. Donne's desire to "recast the symbolic as capable of resignification" (*Bodies That Matter*, p. 22) gives poems like "The Broken Heart" and "Of Weeping" the feeling of futurity, the sense that the next poem might instill a different power structure, one which will complete the task of rethinking Donne only begins in those poems.

In the Petrarchan experiment of "Whoso list to hunt," Wyatt internalizes the lady's reluctance and thereby accounts for his own artistic impotence. Avoiding a similar impasse, the Donne of "The Broken Heart" and "A Valediction: Of Weeping" argues his way out of the denial that customarily energizes the lyric. His aim is to convince the imagined lady that she can get a better poem if she says "yes" to the poet. From the start, he appeals to a lady who wants the poet to praise her and who therefore believes in poetic constructions. With the knife-wielding Laura of *Rime sparse* 129, Petrarch returns to the initiating moment of his expectation in *Rime sparse* 23, his excitement fraught with danger, his beginning threatened with an ending. Preferring sex to death, Donne seeks to go beyond the resistant other. When he argues that her active complicity as muse must be brought into the poetry-making complex, Donne preempts the lady's obduracy.

In assuming that the man is always already the woman he convinces, Donne also assumes that the woman can be seen as sympathetic to—and therefore always already—the man who does the convincing. Writing against the grain of Petrarchan sublimation, he reasons, in "The Broken Heart," that the denied lover produces only a hollow poem and, in "A Valediction: Of Weeping," that the absented lover drowns out—with his tears—even a remnant of a poem. "Broken Heart" and "Of Weeping" involve the Petrarchan litany of denial, absence, pain, and adoration. But when Donne invokes the tradition, he renders the distinctions between *self* and *other* indeterminate and the distinctions between *then* and *now* inconsequential. Sexual and temporal divisions are overcome in the mutualized continuity of experience. Donne's aim is to turn Apollo's Daphne into Adam's Eve. He does that by inviting Laura-Mercury into the poetic complex.

The belief that he can postpone endings through the sexuality of Laura-Eve stems from a belief that he can take the risk out of initiation by asking Laura-Mercury to put down her knife. Christopher Ricks maintains that Donne's poems record "a dislike of having come."[11] But what William Kerrigan calls Donne's "bedrock insistence on answered love"[12] allows him to write out the disappointment of the experiential *after* by rethinking the anticipatory *before* and envisioning an *at last* that annuls an *at first*. That reversal challenges the poetic benefits of denial. In arguing that "yes" might produce a better poem, Donne presumes a circle of connectedness: (1) the woman's imagined responsiveness encourages language; (2) the woman's imagined consent nourishes imagination. When he dismisses Laura-Daphne from the poetic cast of characters by saying she produces shadow poems, Donne uncovers the imbricated layers of the Petrarchan subplots. He reasons that Laura-Mercury's potential as artist might produce a different poem and that Laura-Eve's generosity as a woman might encourage a better man. When he shifts poetic initiation and ethical responsibility to the imagined woman, Donne attributes the poet's imagination and the imagined poet to her. In the spiral of the newly gendered dyad, an alternative to Petrarchism begins to take hold: with selves not yet formulated but now poetically licensed; with poems not yet written but now imaginatively possible. If the Bordone painting asks the viewer to imagine the next painting in a hypothetical series, so "The Broken Heart" and "Of Weeping" suggest—by testing and end-running the confines of their own structures—the next poem in yet another narrative sequence. Yielding to the woman, Wyatt's winded "I" of "Whoso list to hunt" sees only the oppressiveness of the old Petrarchism. Similarly opening to the woman, Donne's poems offer a new poetic, one where Petrarchan denial is suspended in the affirmation of feeling in phrases which "are in principle possible" (*The Differend*, p. 13). Is the next poem that "The Broken Heart" and "Of Weeping" presuppose discoverable the way the next screen is in the hypertext, or is it necessary for the reader to find that poem somewhere in the works by reading backward, beyond, or behind the text? Or does the reader need, as Neely suggests, to over-read? With Donne, over-reading might involve moving retrospectively from the sermons to see where mercy (as the "yes" the poetic Donne wants) fits into the scheme of the ministerial Donne's efforts to eliminate the gender structures—and therefore the sexual asymmetries—that come from Genesis 2.

In *The Secretum*, Petrarch speaks of an inversion of order that enables him, in the *Rime sparse*, to invent an Eve for his Genesis 2 Adam. In his theology, Donne returns to a Genesis 1 that eliminates human hierarchies. The Christmas Day sermon of 1624 preaches against the prioritization which is at the center of Petrarchism:

> When we fixe ourselves upon the meditation and modulation of the mercy of God, even his judgements cannot put us out of tune, but we shall sing, and be chearefull, even in them. As God made grasse for beasts, before he made beasts, and beasts for man, before he made man: As in that first generation, the Creation, so in the regeneration, our re-

creating, he begins with that which was necessary for that which fol-
lowes, Mercy before Judgement. Nay, to say that mercy was first is but to
post-date mercy; to preferre mercy but so, is to diminish mercy; The
names of first or last derogate from it, for first and last are but ragges of
time and his mercy has no relation to time, it is not first, nor last, but
eternall, ever lasting.[13]

Arguing that "mercy has no relation to time," Donne gives a postmodern
interpretation to the meaning of assent. Through anamnesis and anamorphosis, mercy is always in the picture: first and last are immaterial for
his anagogic—"eternal"—vision. In its insistence on Genesis 1, the Christmas Day sermon yields the self Petrarchism withholds. Donne's logic is
based on a preparative and dependent relation. As grass exists for the
beasts it feeds, so creation anticipates re-creation and so mercy predates
justice, not because it comes first but because it is necessary for the other:
its being derives from its purpose. In the logic of the sermon, all relationships feed on dependency, as beasts eat grass, men eat beasts, and re-
creation overtakes creation in a vision that cuts out firstness. The end
brings the original into focus. "First and last are but the ragges of time"
because the eternal, the everlasting, eats (like moths) the "stuff" that
constitutes the form that eventuates into it. In "The Extasie," Donne
concludes:

> And if some lover, such as wee,
> Have heard this dialogue of one,
> Let him still marke us, he shall see
> Small change when we'are to bodies gone. (p. 61)

At the heart of the movement from eternal to temporal is a relaxation that
implies "small change" instead of cataclysmic event, a "dialogue of one"
because the rupture—so essential to Petrarchan creation—has been cir-
cumvented by a sense of interdependence. Like the Christmas Day sermon, "The Extasie" proposes a sequence that stipulates a reversible contingency. Souls need bodies and bodies need souls, a turning around that is
fluid. Where Petrarch attempts to overcome need by appropriating the
other, Donne answers need with mercy, each so close—the one anticipating, the other realizing—that they are irreducible. The logic of Donne's
theology is already apparent in the rhetoric of his lyric experiments. In
"The Extasie," he enacts the connection. In the retaliative lyrics, he
demonstrates to the imagined Laura-lady what happens when connec-

tions are severed or when they are stretched too thin. Dealing in "The Broken Heart" with the consequences of severance and in "A Valediction: Of Weeping" with the reality of separation, Donne demonstrates how "no" cancels the poem Petrarchism engenders. Denial for Donne doesn't just threaten sexuality. It endangers the poem.

In examining the consequences of denial and distance, Donne literalizes Petrarch's self-effacement to show the vacancy of poetic sublimation and the pointlessness of poetic idealization. In "The Broken Heart," denial fails to produce a poem. In "Of Weeping," idolatry fails to produce a poet. In "The Broken Heart," Donne presents a sequence of substitutions which is irreversible: "but us Love draws, / Hee swallows us and never chawes" (p. 51). Unlike Jonah, the entrapped lover cannot be expelled. There is no release. In "Of Weeping," he argues that the breach of separation cannot be bridged. The Humpty Dumpty world he envisages is irreparable: "This world by waters sent from thee my heaven dissolved so" (p. 69). Through the annihilative swallowing of "The Broken Heart" and the self-canceling flood of "Of Weeping," Donne graphically depicts the results of Petrarchan rupture. In "The Broken Heart," he questions the value of Petrarchan consolation and challenges its habit of replacing the one love with many poems; in "Of Weeping," he subverts the comfort of Petrarchan idolatry when he argues that the idealization of the beloved, concomitant to the poet's deification of self, results in a god who can be smashed. Both poems deal with the aftermath of shattered relationships, the first with the wound of denial, the second with the rupture of separation. "The Broken Heart" literalizes a figurative disfiguration. "Of Weeping" converts a literal absence into a spiritual bankruptcy. Donne's critiques of Petrarchism argue for the lady's authority: she disrupts the poetic process. But the new configurations Donne proposes are the result of his defection from the Petrarchism the imagined lady expects. In refusing to vouchsafe automatic replacement or to grant poetic idealization, Donne's "I" insists on a capable "you." Though she comes to "The Broken Heart" and "Of Weeping" with expectations fostered by her familiarity with the conventions, Donne's lady is asked to inform a new poem. In this revisionist poetic, the persuasive act is a tribute to the woman's—rather than the man's— shaping powers. Donne enlists her agency (as Mercury) to shape the course of his life and hence the art of his future poems.

Where the Petrarch of *Rime sparse* 129 obviates punishment and crime to preempt the events that caused his poetic and amorous misery, the Donne of "Of Weeping" moves backward, not to the moment before a failure that seems irreparable but to the moment of a success that warrants prolongation. If the Petrarch of the *Rime sparse* offers more than anything a desire to keep offering himself, the Donne of "The Broken Heart" instead presents a vision of the wounded self-sacrificer. Whereas Petrarch tries to recover, the Donne of "The Broken Heart" gives into his injuries. The failure in "The Broken Heart" stems from the inadequacy of Petrarchan healing, best illustrated by the sublimated Rosalynde of *The Faerie Queene* 6.10.10–28. The failure in "Of Weeping" involves a rejection of Petrarchan recovery best represented by the triumphant laurelization at the end of *Rime sparse* 23. In the Petrarchan and Spenserian ethos, the poet finds himself through a process of physical distancing which results in a psychological separation from the fact of the rejection. Discontent with distance, Donne denies himself the consolation, and the lady the fame, that the conventions have conditioned them to expect. Donne's rhetoric assumes what Bell would identify as a literate lady. He argues with the lady reading—to change her role in the writing of—her image. While the Petrarch of *Rime sparse* 1 and the Colin Clout of the Acidale sequence enlist male sympathizers, Donne speaks to the woman. While Petrarch and Spenser continue to sing of their beloveds despite the woman's physical absence from the scene of creation, Donne first puts the lady inside his head and then threatens to crack his skull; his threat cancels the eternalizing cycle through which Laura and Rosalynde are immortalized. The Donne of "The Broken Heart" shatters it by claiming he can love no more. Broken, he cannot gather enough energy to formulate the rhetoric of desire. The Donne of "Of Weeping" stops the complaint. Separated, he cannot remember the image that articulates his despair. In the half-hearted recovery of "The Broken Heart" and excessive gestures of "Of Weeping," Donne illustrates how Petrarchan sublimation extends, rather than overcomes, the amatory denial at its base. Both poems assume that the reading woman is nearby and that she has, some time in the recent past, demanded for herself what the denied Colin gave Rosalynde and the rejected Petrarch gave Laura. Predicating the lady's presence, Donne emphasizes her necessity to the creative process. Her belated reality as listener reflects her antecedent importance as determiner of poetic shape.

In "The Broken Heart," she stands somewhere behind the poet, reprimanding him with something like a Spenserian model of endless replication. In "Of Weeping," as his direct audience, she stands before the poet, somehow asking for the Petrarchan admiration his impending departure should inspire. Like the woman who overhears Shakespeare's sonnet 130,

Donne's ladies greet him with standards fostered by other similarly suffering poets. Though he denigrates other poets, the Shakespeare of 130 nevertheless compliments his lady; similarly demonstrating the limitations of the poetic compliment, Donne concentrates instead on the injured poet. In "The Broken Heart," he focuses on the wound of rejection, in "Of Weeping," on the wound of separation. In either instance, the Petrarchanly idealized woman cannot assuage his real pain. Each poem therefore questions the poetics of substitution. "The Broken Heart" challenges the solace of Spenserian nature; "Of Weeping" undoes the consolation of Petrarchan art. In its subscription to the Apollo-Daphne dyad, poetic sublimation pays lip-service to the woman as *anima* but finally endorses the animating poet. In its assertion of the woman's superiority, Petrarchan idealization seems to undo the dyad. When it renders the woman the god of the poet's idolatry, it makes her the inventor of his being. But Donne argues that the appropriation inherent to both processes simply substitutes one form of emptiness for another. In his rejection of the Spenserian replication that precedes sublimation and dismissal of the Petrarchan distance that facilitates laurelization, Donne pits the antihierarchical principles of the Christmas Day sermon against the hegemonical empires of sixteenth-century biblical commentaries. His mercy obviates the denials of Genesis 2 and 3 and so challenges the Petrarchan Ur-myth and its Renaissance incarnations. The commentaries present Eve not as equal who can return, gaze for gaze, Adam's present yearning but as a nascent Mary who anticipates, sequence by sequence, Adam's future incarnation. In that context, Adam's sleep in Genesis is simply a prelude to his New Testament awakening.

Typical of the commentators is Miles Coverdale, who asks about, but does not accept, Adam's passivity:

> Here now ought we to consider the occasion why God made the woman out of the sleeping man and not while he was awake: of the rib and not as well of the earth as he had made man before.
>
> First in the sleep of Adam did he set forth the death of Christ, out of the which unto the same Lord Christ there is prepared a pure and holy soul in the fountain of water through the word, as Paul says to the Ephesians in the fifth chapter. The woman was taken from and out of the side of man and not from the earth, lest any man should think that he had gotten his wife out of the mire: but to consider that the wife is the husband's flesh and bone and therefore to love her: yet was she not made of the head. For the husband is the head in the matter of the wife.

As soon now as the woman was set before Adam, he acknowledged immediately that she was for his purpose: that he liked her well and that he could find in his heart to love her, as one that was of his own kind, of his own blood, flesh of his flesh and bone. For though he slept when the woman was created out of his rib yet he saw well that she was like him as such one as he hitherto had not found among all other living creatures. God also had planted in them the kind, the love, the heart, the inclination and natural affection that it beseems them one to have toward the other.[14]

Coverdale's analysis renders the dream a lapse—like Christ's temporary death—which affirms, as Patricia Parker emphasizes,[15] Adam's hierarchical firstness. But unlike the commentators who see the sleeping man as half a man (semi-virile),[16] Coverdale views the sleep as anticipatory of a double man: Christ. When paralleled to Christ's death, the dream becomes gestative, a prelude to birth that is part of the creative process. The swoon leads to an awakening and man emerges both the ruler (the head as chief) and originator (the head as inventor) of his own estate. His seminal powers earn him his authoritative dominion. Coverdale's rationale stresses Adam's acknowledgment of Eve in terms of his self-knowledge. Through her, he sees his future likeness in Christ. In Coverdale's Genesis, Adam's recognition of the woman's strength makes him likewise the creator of it. Adam sees himself, not the mire, as Eve's source. His afterlife, not his earthly life, is the future he dreams.

When Petrarch uproots himself from Laura and when the Petrarchan Spenser rises from the low-louting caused by Rosalynde, each re-creates the woman, as Coverdale's Adam does, out of himself. All three assert man's invention of the woman he idealizes. And all idealize the man who created her. Adam is, according to Coverdale, a pre-Christ whose formation of Eve signals his re-formation as God. His awakening on earth is a prelude to his awakening in heaven. In Coverdale's view, Adam's sleep is explained away by calling *all life* a sleep, a momentary respite until the next waking in heaven. In the Christmas Day sermon, Donne focuses on the steps of this life and its necessary contingencies. Coverdale anticipates instead the arrival at the next life, a promise based not on acts (like eating) or processes (like nurturing) but on words. By linking the word to Adam and Christ, Coverdale asserts the verbal primacy of man. Woman comes in the afterbirth after words. "For though he slept when the woman was created out of his rib yet he saw well that she was like him." As Christ's identity is promised by the word that he will be a permanent second Adam, woman's identity lies in man's word that she will be a temporary second Adam. Corroborating his imagination, she appears almost as a result of his language.

Eve is Adam's word made flesh. He came first; she reflects him even as she anticipates his second (and more important) coming in the afterlife where she ceases to be. Hers is a likeness that prefigures his divine Otherness. The sequence Donne describes in the Christmas Day sermon obviates mirroring and necessitates contingency. Beasts need grass and man needs beasts. Each flows into, and falls back on, the other. Eliminating primacy and insisting on the nurturing nature of mercy, Donne does away with hierarchy; men and women feed and need each other, their coming-to-be established in a supportive *difference* which subsequently establishes identity, a mutual need. For Donne, the "yes" of mercy, the immediacy of its response, avoids separation: the flow is all. For Coverdale, separation is the means of recognition that endorses the visionary capacity: the "no" is all. Even if it takes until the millennium, separation is antecedent to divine ascendancy. For the Donne of the Christmas Day sermon, connection is necessary, the giving of the self to the other, the means by which giver and taker are validated.

When he chooses Genesis 1 as his version of creation, Donne renders Adam and Eve mutual. The union of their re-creation is shared. In Coverdale, Adam is the creator of Eve and the re-creator of the self. When he turns to Genesis 1, Donne pronounces charity, not appropriation, as the source of re-creation. When he denies firstness, Donne overcomes lastness. His obviation of chronology outdoes hierarchy. When he says the woman was "taken" from man, Coverdale speaks of her in poetic terms. The woman is "like" man. Petrarch begins with those likenesses and ends with the idealized other who represents his earthly ambition. Coverdale similarly begins with reflection. But he ends in real difference; his Eve replicates Adam but is ultimately ancillary to him. The heavenly ascension is all that matters. Petrarch creates from himself the goddess Laura he admires. Coverdale's Adam creates from himself the servant-Eve he uses. But, in both instances, the self is the inventor of the necessary other.

A Hundred Lesser Faces: Spenserian Replication

When, in the Petrarchan tradition, Spenser's Colin Clout of *The Faerie Queene*, book 6, invents Rosalynde, he transforms the resemblances of

Genesis into the satisfying—and self-reflective—substitutes that his music provides. His pleasure in the song he *can* make erases his sadness over the woman he *can't* have. If death is what happens to man after the fall, then the artist must deal with it even in his prelapsarian fantasies. The sublimated Rosalyndes he creates from himself replace an experienced loss and perpetuate an established vision. One hundred naked ladies dance to his music. Just as Adam uses the temporary absence of his sleep to formulate the presence of his "likeness," so Colin turns the "low-louting" denial of Rosalynde's rejection into a preliminary for his vision; similarly, Petrarch calls the transformation, caused by his obsession with Laura, merely a stage in his evocation of her. Like Adam's trance, the state of physical loss becomes the base of revived intellectual confidence. And, like Adam's exhilaration after the trance (compared by Coverdale to Christ's recovery of Adam's life), Spenserian denial and Petrarchan obsessiveness are converted into thresholds for a reconfirmed self. The confidence in both instances results from the poet's calling himself the self-contained parent of the woman. Like Coverdale's sleeping Adam, Colin produces replicas from the void:

> But that faire one,
> That in the midst was placed parauaunt,
> Was she to whom that shepheard pypt alone,
> That made him pipe so merrily, as neuer none.
>
> She was to weete that iolly Shepheards lasse,
> Which piped there vnto that merry rout,
> That iolly shepheard, which there piped, was
> Poore Colin Clout (who knowes not Colin Clout?)
> He pypt apace, whilest they him daunst about.
> Pype iolly shepheard, pype thou now apace
> Vnto thy loue, that made thee low to lout:
> Thy loue is present there with thee in place,
> Thy loue is there aduaunst to be another Grace.[17]

Colin Clout re-creates Rosalynde from the vacancy fostered by denial. "Low-louting" in the flesh fosters his high ambition in the music. In the Spenserian myth, art imitates nature. The artist produces copies in the same way as nature grows leaves on trees. The pain of the initial loss is a necessary antecedent for the joy of continual recovery as Colin repeats, in his endless piping, the vision of the deified Rosalynde who will continue to deny him. Where the Christmas Day sermon depends on continuity, Spenserian re-creation depends on rupture. The lady's denial is the poet's health.

Contrastingly, the Donne of "The Broken Heart" begins—and re-mains—in sickness, the irreparable split created by denial. While Colin produces one hundred beautiful maidens out of his unhappiness, the Donne of "The Broken Heart" ekes out one hundred lesser selves. While the Spenser of the Mount Acidale sequence uncritically multiplies, the Donne of "The Broken Heart"—similarly speaking of numbers—subverts quantification. Spenser spins maidens out of his creative self. Broken by the single lady of his imagination, Donne replicates only shattered selves. He presents first a sequence of unfolding volume (the increase of hours, days, years) and, then, its consequential inverse: progressive diminution (the decrease caused by gunshot wounds, plague, decay). Spenser finds consolation in replication. Donne finds replication hollow, its impetus merely an approximation, not an amplification, of feeling. He illustrates the futility of replication by multiplying parts of his self. While Spenser invents whole bodies, Donne presents fractured feelings. If Colin fills the vacuum of his love's denial with images of Rosalynde, making her physical absence the emotional presence of his vision, Donne, writing a poem about the creation of a vacuum, fails to fill it with his beloved. Instead of praising the woman's parts, he multiplies parts of himself. In his reproduction of Rosalynde, Spenser's Colin imitates the creative power of Venus and Genius by remaining isolated and disconnected. His self-sufficiency allows him to function like the goddess of love: "Syre and mother . . . her selfe alone, Begets and eke conceiues, ne needeth other none" (*TFQ* 4.10.41). To be like Venus, "alone," Colin must be denied. If Venus is a woman who incorporates the man, Colin (alone) is the man who incorporates the woman. "Beget[ing] and eke conceiu[ing]" the sequential vision of unfolding Rosalyndes, Colin—like Adam in Coverdale's description—"needeth other none." In contrast, "The Broken Heart" explores the extended loneliness of the denied self. Donne's poem is about need and what happens when needs are not met. Like his Venus, Spenser's Colin endlessly replaces the nature he avoids. Donne's "I" denies the poetry that makes an art of the self in the first two stanzas and satirizes the poetry that reveals the self in art in the last two. Where Rosalynde's rejection encourages Colin to create the other as he pipes merrily alone, Donne's losses result in a self who sings—gloomily—of his fractured heart. Alone, Colin invents his unique song of the woman. Injured, Donne hollows out only the song of the self. The poetry

Donne denies in the first two stanzas is trivial; it cannot imitate nature. The poetry of the last two stanzas is egocentric; it cannot produce a lady.

Like the Petrarch of *Rime sparse* 105, Donne incorporates the critical other and belittles the persistent lover, the one who—wounded by love—continues loving:

> He is starke mad, who ever sayes,
> That he hath beene in love an houre,
> Yet not that love so soone decayes,
> But that it can tenne in lesse space devour;
> Who will beleeve mee, if I sweare
> That I have had the plague a yeare?
> Who would not laugh at mee, if I should say,
> I saw a flaske of *powder burne a day?*
>
> Ah, what a trifle is a heart,
> If once into loves hands it come!
> All other griefes allow a part
> To other griefes, and aske themselves but some;
> They come to us, but us Love draws,
> Hee swallows us, and never chawes:
> By him, as by chain-shot, whole rankes doe dye,
> He is the tyran Pike, our hearts the Frye. (p. 51)

There are two links between the first and second stanzas: the first, the image of love the devourer (completed in the tyrant pike of the second stanza); the second, the image of poets devoured (resolved in the "our hearts" of the second stanza). The stanzas are alike in their representation of massive suffering (the eaten ten of the first stanza, the several "fry" of the second). When he compares himself to other poets in a "school" that seems Spenserian, the speaker explains why all such poets are prey to mockery. The intricate series of containers he sets up places his poetry—and that of other Spenserians—in the center. Contained by the rhyming "hour" and "devour" is the little "our" of the first stanza; contained by the rhyming "heart" and "part" of the second stanza is the tiny "art." "Our art" is immediately absorbed by the larger truth that love destroys the poet totally. As his swearing is out-shouted, his art is overcome, trivialized by the larger power of love.

As the remover, Love allows no partial discourse. In the realm of Love, in the belly of the whale, art (human endeavor and measure) is defeated.

The lover who claims that his passion lasts into hours, days, and years is enveloped by decay, the plague, or gunshot. All undermine the prolongation he extols. The poet is outwardly pressured by voluminous Time and inwardly emptied by devouring decay. The increasing numbers of time weaken the poet. The increasing numbers of poets (the ten of stanza one, the whole ranks of stanza two) deny his originality. In the Spenserian ethos, the artist allies himself, as self-sufficient creator, with the strength of the androgynous Venus. The "I" of "The Broken Heart" is overcome in the first two stanzas by the increasing avalanche of decay and the reductive impact of numbers that Spenser (through Colin in book 6) escapes. Like Venus, Colin guarantees his immunity from the pull of love by replacing the fleshly Rosalynde with successive musical imitations. But the "I" of "The Broken Heart" cannot prevent his absorption into the "tyrant" Time. Surrounded by the feeling h*eart*, his *art* is absorbed by the larger forces Spenser escapes. Donne's "I" lives in the long aftermath of denial. Capitalizing on its immediate impact, Spenser's Colin protects himself by a ring of naked ladies. The encircling Rosalyndes of his imagination sequester, feed, and so strengthen his pipe. But the circle depends on his initiative. Its movement reflects his energy even as its dependency encourages him to keep on piping. Surrounded by the destructive critics in stanza one, joined by other poets in stanza two, the "I" of "The Broken Heart" is finally devoured by the crippling pike. His instrument is sterilized. It brings forth no life.

If the strategy of the first two stanzas is to reduce the "I" as the world enlarges, the strategy of the last two is to make more of less. In the first two stanzas, the "I" is the size of a heart, small enough for the pike to swallow it, as the whale engulfed Jonah and Cronos—the father—ate his children. In the last two stanzas, the heart is replicated and enlarged. In response to the fact that Rosalynde made him low to lout, Colin produces many Rosalyndes. But Donne subtly questions the replication of the Spenserian solution. Instead of reproducing many fully formed ladies, he projects many hollowed-out selves. Reliving his initial confrontation with the "thee," the "I" calls her (as he did the pike in stanza 2) a devourer of men. Taking the lady's theft seriously, the "I" investigates heartlessness; unlike Petrarch's, his heart-robbed Battus doesn't automatically go on singing. Where Petrarch survives his robbery and Spenser rises from his low louting to reinvent music, Donne cannot continue writing: "I brought a heart into the roome, / But from the roome, I carried none with mee" (p. 51). If the first two stanzas present Love as Cronos-the-father eating his children by drawing them back into the self, the last two, going back further in chronology, depict Love, as Cronos-the-child, shivering his parent's member, and rendering him (as he says at the end) unable to love. In answer to the woman's objection to the initial disclaimer that the "I" lacks a believable self, the poet counters with yet another disclaimer: broken in pieces, the "I" contains too many selves. Diffuse, he loses his potency.

Cronos's dismemberment of his father produced the goddess Aphrodite, who, as in Spenser, contains syre and dame in one. But whatever happened to the dismembered father? Donne takes the mutilation literally. No member, no remembrance. Castrated, the "I" reproduces versions of his castrated self, weak remnants of his scattered parts. In the revisionist history of stanza 3, Donne places the blame for his impotence on the woman's initial failure to accept his love:

> If it had gone to thee, I know
> Mine would have taught thy heart to show
> More pitty unto mee: but Love, alas,
> At one first blow did shiver it as glasse. (p. 51)

Piping merrily alone, Spenser produces the sequential vision of Colin's dancing ladies. Donne's shivered "I" reproduces many shivering selves. The shivered heart is, by implication, a cold heart and that coldness, Donne also implies, is the true source of Spenserian replication.

The glassy selves Donne proliferates reflect the icy self of the lady. Instead of assembling a complete body out of his broken self, Donne multiplies the broken pieces. The shivered heart thus enables the "I" both to revenge the lady and to defend his silence. If, as Rosalie Colie argues, postulating a vacuum was sinful,[18] Donne's woman is the sinner. The postulation is hers. After he confronts her, his *one* heart is *none* and *gone*. She is the source of his cancellation even if Love at the end delivers the fatal blow. In stanza 3 he says of his heart: "I carried none with mee." The "I" speaks of himself as empty, the *vide* of the vacuum Pascal was later philosophically to corroborate.[19] He has no heart. It is gone. But, in stanza 4, he quickly retracts that statement:

> Yet nothing can to nothing fall,
> Nor any place be empty quite,
> Therefore I thinke my breast hath all
> Those peeces still, though they be not unite. (p. 51)

165

When he denies the heterodoxy of the previous stanza, Donne substitutes an emotional for a physical emptiness.[20] Like Adam and Eve expelled from Eden, his heart continues to function after the fall, albeit in a diminished state.[21]

Stanza 3 speaks of three forms of simplicity, the zero of emptiness, the oneness of initiation, and the first blow. Stanza 4 speaks of multiplicity and multiplication, a heart replicated endlessly:

> And now as broken glasses show
> A hundred lesser faces, so
> My ragges of heart can like, wish, and adore,
> But after one such love, can love no more. (p. 52)

As the broken glass "shows" (both displays and reveals) a hundred copies of the same originating image, so the broken heart performs the hundred lesser acts of the unsatisfied "I." All three verbs—liking, wishing, adoring—turn backward to the self rather than forward to the other. The "lesser faces" reflected in the multiplying glasses are the poet's diminished selves not the lady's idealized likenesses. They stem from the poet, are his *littler* emotions. All three verbs suggest—in the comparison of metaphor (liking), the expression of desire (wishing), and the act of worship (adoring)—variations on nothingness. The source of this distorted replication is the injured and uncreative self, giving off an afterglow of energy—liking, wishing, adoring—that reflects his emptiness. Manifold variations on a theme without a center, the remnants of a heart, like the shards of broken glass, produce fractions of what once was but now is disembodied. The liked, wished for, and adored "you" doesn't exist in her own right. She is simply carved out of the "I's" inadequacy. Donne refuses to make from himself the Spenserian other. Denied, he offers instead one hundred sequential versions—liking, wishing, adoring—of his injured "I."

When, in *The Winter's Tale*, Florizel tells Perdita that "all [her] acts are queens," he describes her in a social context, "speak[ing], sing[ing], buy[ing], sell[ing], pray[ing], ord'ring, danc[ing]" (4.4.30), of a diurnal, even a mundane, existence. In its cataloging technique, his list is similar to Donne's "liking, wishing, adoring," but Florizel describes communal acts, Donne private feelings. Florizel's community of action leads to a communion with nature. With the oxymoron "move still, still so" (4.4.42), Florizel seeks to make Perdita a wave of the sea, part of an eternally recurring cycle. As the wave is defined by the shore, so the image of Perdita depends on contact. The sequential acts Donne describes (liking, wishing, adoring) result from the remoteness, the insularity, of separation. Like Colin to the Spenserian maidens dancing in a ring, Donne remains at a distance. But that position is unsatisfying to him and, he implies, unrewarding to the lady. Unlike Perdita who lives through her function in the world, the "liked," "wished-for," and "adored" lady of Donne's broken self exists apart from the world. She is a product of his lack. The injured "I" can hobble through with the poetics of absence—liking, wishing, and adoring—but the poetics of fullness, the re-creation of regeneration, demand a partner, a fleshly other. Like Florizel's wave coming back to the shore, Donne's ideal vision of love, exemplified by the Christmas Day sermon, includes the fertility of procreation, rather than the androgyny of succession. For a brief moment in *Rime sparse* 129, Petrarch admits that his "thought shadows [Laura] forth," that his attempts at re-creation produce imitations that are self-deceiving. In "The Broken Heart," Donne elaborates the shadow. His ragged heart is the remnant of a vacant body, his evaporation into ineffectuality an extension of Petrarch's depressed moments in *Rime sparse* 129.

Liking, wishing, and adoring are the linguistic manifestations of the shadow self, voices that echo (as the images look like) what they mirror. Love produces poems. Liking produces shadow poems. The voice is empty, the image vacant. Unlike Colin Clout, the injured "I" of "The Broken Heart" cannot substitute a lesser feeling for the initial impact of love. While Colin pipes merrily alone, the speaker of "The Broken Heart" is joyless. Out of an "I" who can "love no more," Donne cannot re-create (as Spenser does) more lovely "yous." Deprived of the energetic instigation of love, Donne is unable to generate consequentially idealized versions of the beloved. Unmanned by Love, Donne produces only shrinking replicas of the shivered self. No Venus arises, like Colin's Rosalynde, from the broken member. Castration does not augur the phallic reemergence of the sublimating poem. A lessened self produces lesser versions of its own image rather than progressive images of the idealized lady.

On Divers Shores: Petrarchan Separation

The "Of Weeping" speaker is similarly unable to recover from the blow of denial. But if, in "The Broken Heart," the poet-lover makes himself into the many-faceted singer of emptiness, here the poet-lover turns the lady into the multiply originating man. That conversion comments on the

Petrarchan model. Petrarch uses the woman to create an art where the man is at the center. In "Of Weeping," the speaker creates a world where the woman emerges as the potential poet presiding over a dismembered world. Rendering to the woman the power which Petrarch only *claims* to give her and spreading to the world a disorientation in the self, Donne questions the healing power of sublimation. For the Donne of "The Broken Heart," no alternative feeling can substitute for love. For the Donne of "Of Weeping," no other presence can replace the beloved.[22]

In "The Broken Heart," Donne refers to a past failure to praise the denying beloved; here he anticipates his future silence. In "The Broken Heart," it is her remembered refusal (whatever happened in that room); in "Of Weeping," it is her imminent excess (whatever will happen after she sighs). In both poems, *she* becomes the deadening, rather than inspiring, force. If "The Broken Heart" reappraises the origins of Spenser's Petrarchan replication, "Of Weeping" questions the sources of Petrarch's reflex deification. "Of Weeping" begins where *Rime sparse* 23 ends: in separation. Petrarch recovers from the devastating Lauras of 23 (who first as Mercury paralyze, then as Diana dismember, him). He reinvents a moving (even a flying) and a remembering (even an apotheosizing) "I." Such an emergence into eminence can only come from the divergence into difference Petrarch forges in the remarkable last stanza of *Rime sparse* 23 where all the previous annihilations seem miraculously not to have happened. In the light of such a second reading, Petrarch's initial laurelization (his conversion into a womanly shape) leads ultimately into a reaffirmation of his manliness.

At the end of *Rime sparse* 23, Petrarch defines the process whereby he achieves the separation essential to poetic articulation:

> Song, I was never the cloud of gold that once descended in a precious rain so that it partly quenched the fire of Jove; but I have certainly been a flame lit by a lovely glance and I have been the bird that rises highest in the air raising her whom in my words I honor; nor for any new shape could I leave the first laurel, for still its sweet shade turns away from my heart any less beautiful pleasure. (p. 68)

In the final telling he details the stages of the process: his history before he met Laura (he never was a cloud of gold); what he became when he met her (the first laurel); and what that becoming enabled him to be (a flame and an eagle). Petrarch alters the chronology of his encounter with Laura to describe those states. There are three stages in the Petrarchan transformation: first, the poet's absorption by the woman; second, the poet's separation from her; third, the poet's deification of her. At the end of *Rime sparse* 23, Petrarch catalogues what he never could have been, what he did become, and *then* the laurel that facilitated the second stage. The laurelization should come second not third. But it is told last because it suggests his final resting place—the sweet shade of an eternal laurel *under* which Petrarch presently composes. In that shade, the laurel emerges at last the poetic crown he sought before Laura's injunction in the Battus episode. The recovery Petrarch describes has something to do with his separation from the branches that seemed in the first transformation to have been intrinsic. Hoping to gain the laurel as crown *then*, Petrarch received instead the ignominy of the laurel as hindrance to his achievement: "What I became, when I first grew aware of my person being transformed and saw my hairs turning into those leaves which I had formerly hoped would be my crown" (p. 62). Early in the poem, when the leaves started growing, he mourned the loss of his former pursuits: he complained that—because of Love—he became *like* what he pursued—a trapped Daphne.

When he refers at the end of the poem to the laurel of his first metamorphosis, Petrarch acknowledges that the manliness of the implied second laurel is rooted in Laura's feminine trappings. The first conversion put her into his mind (lit him up) so that he subsequently was able to become the eagle leading Laura into the place where she could be turned into a goddess.[23] Though he "never was a god" descending, he is now, with her in his mind, a god ascending, carrying her physically (like the eagle who transported Ganymede) to her apotheosis.[24] Though the roots need to be established, they are subsequently severed as (spurred by the woman inside him) he pulls away from the earth to convey her to the heavens. The fire of her presence in him simultaneously enables him to separate himself from his roots (to fly) and to distance himself from the leaves (to be reborn). Since she is his invention, she was in him all along. In attachment, he made her what she was, as now, in separation, he renders her what she is. To be rootless (unattached) is to be wordy (detached). The separation enables him both to rise (like the bird) and to push Laura away. She must be higher so that she can cast the "sweet shade" at the end. The upwardly mobile progress in the final section (from flame, through phoenix, to Jupiter) reverses the downgrading spatial rigidity of the opening sequence (from poet, to laurel, through roots), as the "I" acquires heights never before dreamed. The laurel protecting him becomes both an eternal haven and the crown of human achievement. But that emergence is facilitated only by the separation which occurs through the conflagration of Petrarch's now internalized inspirational fire. Though the familiar shapes of Ovidian metamorphosis form the flora and fauna of *Rime sparse* 23, the final figure is that of the incontrovertible poetic "I." Separate from the woman he absorbed, Petrarch defines her renewed otherness and—like Adam recovered from his trance—his consolidated originality. As crown, Laura is the culminating adornment, rather than the rooting fixture, of the poet's identity. She is what he projects. His energy renders her divine. But it is only *within* his discourse that she reigns.

That self-conscious "I" is what Donne stands to lose in "Of Weeping." Whereas Petrarch remains in coolness, protected by the shade of the laurel, Donne (all emotion) emerges vulnerable to the forces of nature he sought to control. When he emphasizes his victimization, Donne also adumbrates the limits of Petrarchan consolidation. Petrarch creates Laura in the gap between imminence and distance. He is reborn when he pushes her out of himself and into the heavens while he remains autonomous in the cooling distance of shade. In Laura's physical absence, Petrarch celebrates her presence as artifact. It is the absence Donne fears. At the end of "Of Weeping," Donne's "you" is painfully earthbound, blasted with the sighs and tears of conventional poetry. Petrarch's Laura inspires even in her remoteness. Donne's "I" argues that his "you" can only inspire in the temporal present of his physical presence. Through his woman poet, the "I" of Donne's "Of Weeping" demonstrates the deadening impact of Petrarchan separation. It kills in its excessiveness.[25] If the Coverdale Adam rejoices in his doubly creative capacity as inventor (through the mind) and parent (through the rib) of Eve, Donne tosses that creative and procreative doubleness to and from the woman of the poem. In the first stanza, he builds her up by making her into the artist-man. In the second stanza, he retracts her power and attempts (by his own force) to restore his world. When that fails, he makes her an artist-god again in the third stanza where, totally dependent on her sighs, he anticipates the death of the reduced self he initially had. Twice through the lady and once through himself, Donne rejects prioritization, the "derogation" of firstness. Through his woman-artist, Donne argues that loving connection, not separation, is necessary to art. Through his woman-coiner, Donne demonstrates that hierarchy has little to do with poetry.

The first and second stanzas ridicule the separation and the third stanza undermines the deification that Petrarch effects at the end of *Rime sparse* 23. The reduction is apparent from the outset:

> Let me powre forth
> My teares before thy face, whil'st I stay here,
> For thy face coines them, and thy stampe they beare,
> And by this Mintage they are something worth,
>> For thus they bee
>> Pregnant of thee;
> Fruits of much griefe they are, emblems of more,
> When a tear falls, that thou falls which it bore,
> So thou and I are nothing then, when on a divers shore. (p. 69)

Like Juliet, who calls parting a "sweet sorrow," Donne attempts both to stay, to remain in place as long as possible, and to create a stay, a prop against the ensuing annihilation: he will say "good night till it be morrow" (*Romeo and Juliet* 2.2.186). As long as he is able to pour forth in her presence the tears which re-create her image, so long can he ward off the nothingness of separation. If Colin re-created Rosalynde in the absence of low-louting, so Donne re-creates his woman in the presence of equality. The tears must be at the level of her face. They depend upon her presence. Like the Petrarch who returns to the moment before Laura's heart-robbery in *Rime sparse* 129, Donne sets up a peculiar set of antecedents where the tears both precede her face and her face in turn produces more. Nothing has happened; all will still happen. The speaker has not yet wept, but his tears are ready to fall. He has not yet left, but he is about to leave. They are not yet nothing, yet they will soon be undone. By creating an anterior present and by putting off the act which can only take place before departure, Donne further postpones that departure and relegates it to the future. The more actively he weeps, the richer life he will conceive in the first half of stanza 1; the more tears she inspires, the better able he is to postpone death in the second part of stanza 1.

In order for the mirror of his tears to become her, she must be "before" him. Her chronological place as originator of his being is tied to her physical space as origin of his reflection. He must give her an antecedent rationale as well as a formulating presence. He establishes her prior existence and creative potential by pulling her into first place. As originator, she coins and stamps the tears so that they emerge, by this mintage and through the present stamping, round. Without her stamp, the tears are empty. With it, they both contain her (are pregnant *with* her) and are instigated by her (are pregnant *of* her). Without the mirrors of identity, there is no artistic recognition. She emerges, like Petrarch, the substance and originator of the poem and, like Adam in Coverdale's Genesis, the inventor and parent of her partner. But the reflection is dependent for its substance on constant presence. In order to be, she needs the tears that contain her. Though she is the originator of the poet, he provides the cylindrical mirror that proves her materiality. Without his reflection, she doesn't exist. Like Mieke Bal's Eve, Donne is the "other character indispensable for [her] to be a character at all."[26] Her material body is crucial to the body of his idealization. If she moves away and rejects him, then he must cancel the terms of her idealization.

Petrarch brings Laura to her apotheosis through the separation of birth; in this poem, the "diversity" of separation signifies death. Once the tear falls beneath his face, the lady falls too. The poet must continually weep in her presence in order to produce a new supply of vessels to contain her. In diversity, he cannot continue to create vehicles that signify her value. She is nothing without the vehicle; he is nothing when he cannot contain her. As mirror-producer, he needs the emotion to create the mirror. As mirrored originator, she needs him to feel the emotion. Closeness produces the stimulation that feeds desire. Desire produces the void that necessitates closeness. The circles encircle each other. Petrarch finds his strength by separating himself from the being—the laurel—that possessed him. Once separated, he can make more of her. In "Of Weeping," Donne refuses to accept the consolation of separation. He argues instead that even a moment of sadness together is worth more than something recollected in the shade of distance.[27] Separated from Laura, Petrarch rests comfortably beneath her. Donne denies the inspiration of absence.

In the second stanza, Donne renders himself the artist, the woman the artifact. But the result is the same. As Bal writes about Eve: "they mutually create each other, differently in a different act" ("Sexuality, Sin, and the Emergence of Female Character," p. 336). In the first stanza, as coiner, she is the maker of him. In the second, as workman, he is the maker of her. Without her frame of containment and without the difference of her difference, his art dissolves. As she needed the mirror to contain her in the first stanza, he needs her frame to support his art in the second. Without her sustaining wrapper, the globe falls apart. Without his originating presence, there is no initial circle which will subsequently grow. That reversal back of roles (he as impresser in stanza 2, she as coiner in stanza 1) illustrates the necessity of physical presence and the futility of poetic substitution. The validity of impression results not from an identity where each is the same but from a sharing where each retains the original and joins with the other. Yet if diversity causes the nothingness in the first stanza, mixing causes the dissolution in the second. If, like him, the lady becomes all tears, then the result is a flood. In both stanzas Donne stipulates that the first two Petrarchan stages—the originally inspiring woman and the powerfully re-creative man—can exist only in a state of physical equality. Whereas Petrarch recognizes the first stage through the lady's denial and the second through his absorption into her, Donne demonstrates how both stages undercut the poetic impetus. His first stanza ends in the nothingness of difference, the second in the vagueness of similarity. If she pulls apart from him, then there is too much distance. If she becomes totally like him, then there is too much of the same. Poems depend, he argues, on the demarcation of formal boundaries her nearness and difference provide. Absence yields nothing for both sexes. To remain the creative generator in stanza 1, she needs the mirror he holds. To fulfill the creative mandate of stanza 2, he needs the wrapping she lends. In the first two stanzas Donne subverts the productivity of Petrarchan separation.

In the last stanza, he undercuts the piety of Petrarchan apotheosis. There the recovered "I" invents the woman's godliness, her superiority to nature:

> O more then Moone,
> Draw not up seas to drowne me in thy spheare,
> Weepe me not dead, in thine armes, but forbeare
> To teach the sea, what it may doe too soone;
> Let not the winde
> Example finde,
> To doe me more harme, then it purposeth;
> Since thou and I sigh one anothers breath,
> Who e'r sighes most, is cruellest, and hasts the others death.
> (pp. 70–71)

Donne's moon and waters are dependent upon each other for their cyclical and recurrent being. To be more than the moon is to be greater than nature, to have both the power (as magnet) to pull the man to her and the force (as wind) to push him totally away. When she pulls him to her, he becomes the dead baby, smothered in her arms. When she pushes him away, he becomes the dead man, lost at sea. By destroying the balance, she creates either the diversity of the first stanza (as wind) or the dissolution of the second (as water). To be more than moon is to be more than full—no longer the pregnant woman of the first stanza. But her "more" makes less of him. As larger container, she exceeds the potential of fullness (realizing

Petrarchan separation). As greater power, she presses beyond the dimensions of nature (achieving Petrarchan deification). The full moon (the more than moon) causes his annihilation. For him to be her child cradled in her arms is for her to be physically overwhelming. For her to be his child and made a goddess by his design is for her to become creatively overbearing: the ruler of the sea, the example for the wind, and the cause of his end.

If the first stanza begins by asking for permission—"Let me," which operates to preserve the balance of wholeness—the last stanza ends by imposing an injunction—"Let not," which attempts to avoid the pitfalls of idolatry. If the first stanza begins with waters, the last ends with the wind upon the waters, the spirit of inspiration. As tears are the microcosm of amorphous waters, sighs are the microcosm of potential winds, winds humanized. Winds cause separation. They push the sails of the ship. In the first stanza, equal tears preserve their union. In the last stanza, equal sighs preserve their lives. The preserving quality is equality not distance: "Since thou and I sigh one another's breath." The interanimation, sighing each other's breath, is both a plea for balance ("don't be more than the moon") and a plea for union. ("If you blow too hard, you will blow me away, into the fall of stanza 1.") He asks her just to breathe enough to maintain the parity of mutual goodwill and the proximity of mutual support. "If you sigh too much you become (like Petrarch) the annihilator of my earthly being. You become the Petrarchan poet who hastens my death." When he casts the woman as the sighing poet in the end, Donne places the onus of separation on her. If she sighs too much, she will push him away. In the distance, he will emerge the absent beloved, and she, the sad suitor, of the poetry of separation. Too much sighing—too much Petrarchism—leads to too much dying: the end of the poem. He leaves her where he found her, in the "coining," or originating, position. While Petrarch recoups an energetic self through psychic distance, Donne underlines the speciousness of such a spaciousness.

In "The Broken Heart," Donne demonstrates the limits of Spenserian duplication via the empty mirror of his replicated self. In "Of Weeping," he denies Petrarchan distance through the destructive potential of the deified beloved. "The Broken Heart" reproduces only a broken poet. "Of Weeping" turns the woman into another version of an empty self. By refusing to write a Petrarchan tribute in these two poems, Donne challenges the poet's kinship to the biblically inherited Adam who, finding Eve in his own likeness, claimed her for his own. His poems move away from Acidale and Eden and into the long aftermath of the initial confrontation. Still injured, his "I" refuses the recovery his poetic models found. Through that refusal, he must deal with the world beyond Adam's "now." In terms of time, that means remembering the difficulty of the long year after in "The Broken Heart," and anticipating the perils of the imminent separation in "Of Weeping." In terms of the psyche, it means more than Shakespeare's saying "granted I never saw a goddess go" when he refuses to deify his lady. It means dealing with her expectation that he would do so and his own feeling that perhaps he should do so. Donne turns his rejection of the Petrarchan and Spenserian models, so culturally available, into a disquisition about the futility of denial in "The Broken Heart" and the anguish of separation in "A Valediction: Of Weeping." His refusal to accept the solace of art and insistence on maximizing his injuries are, in their ways, homages to the woman's power. Each poem is a rhetorical argument, saying "see what an actual broken heart yields and a literal physical separation means," in order presumably to find a way to avert the denial and postpone the departure Petrarch and Spenser celebrate.

What Is Silvia?

The Wyatt of the vindictive translations throws out the lady with his Petrarch and, in the privacy of his rejected self, finds a newly energized resourcefulness. The Donne of these retaliatory poems deals with the reality of rejection and demands a new—or a modified—inspiration. "The Broken Heart" is a rasping configuration of a poem that insists on its own hollowness. When he writes "Therefore I thinke my breast hast all / Those peeces still though they be not unite," Donne's scratchy rhetoric reflects neither a Spenserian multiplication nor a Petrarchan sublimation but the discord of his discordances: an imperfect replica of his brokenness. If the broken "I" can neither love nor produce "more" images of his love, what choice does the "thee" of stanza 3 have but to make the "I" whole again? In denying the poetics of loss, Donne tests the imagined lady. His restoration depends not so much on her kindness as on her intelligence. A right reading of what was "brought into the room" of stanza 3 would demand the setting right of sympathetic understanding. If Laura rejects Petrarch because he misread her, the rejected Donne accuses his Laura of having misread him. Stanza 4 is the result of misreading. Like "Las Meninas," the mirrored Velázquez painting in the Prado, the shards of the broken mirror reflect not just the poet's broken self but the breaking lady whose presence in the poem is refracted and internalized. In *Rime sparse* 23, Laura takes back what was originally appropriated. In "The Broken Heart," Donne retracts what was originally proferred.

The ideal reader must return what was given. The circle of exchange shifts as Donne implies a new role for the woman, one based on the mercy that feeds, like the grass for the beasts or beasts for man, in a circle that posits an intelligent giver as the originator of the poem. Such a connection renders the woman the nurturing source of the poet's healing. In "The Broken Heart," Donne suggests to the lady that she become the maternal feeder of his poem. In "Of Weeping," he goes one step further and rejects the motherly because it stifles the man ("weep me not dead in thine arms") and kills the mother. To be "more than moon" is both to reap the aftereffect of afterbirth (the more than moon is nothingness) and to pretend to be the sun: the originator of the poem. As she is in the mirroring shards of "The Broken Heart," the lady is brought, through the pictorially flowing tears and the auditorially voluminous sighs, into the poetic scene. Promoting her active complicity in the poetry-making complex, Donne assumes her active participation in the poetry-reading spiral. Her reaction is crucial. It dictates future poems. Such an incorporation into the life of the poem forces the lady to choose between the annihilative wave of separation and the self-canceling void of absence: "So thou and I are nothing when on divers shore."

The permutations of the poem are connected to the changes in life: first the diurnal rise and fall of the waves, then the monthly waxing and waning of the moon. The nest of relationships—an inversion of the lost connections in "The Broken Heart"—emphasizes the lady's necessity to the poem even as it manifests the art of life. If Petrarch's rock in *Rime sparse* 129 is "like a man who thinks and weeps and writes," Donne's woman in "Of Weeping" is like the man who is like the world. Her control of his life governs her place in the poem. When he urges her to get out of the race to the sun, presses her to accept her mortal place as less than the moon, and challenges her to find an end to the dead end of competition, Donne forges a new beginning for the poem. If "The Broken Heart" suggests maternal healing as poetic origin, "Of Weeping" posits collegial support, an equality of compassion and inspiration: "sighing one another's breath."

In the *Rime sparse*, Laura's idealized presence corroborates Petrarch's sexual defeat. Sublimation is a form of self-denial. Donne's rhetorical strategy connects the woman's poetic eternalization to his sexual restoration. In such an arena, the mercy of her "yes" obviates both the prioritization and appropriations of Petrarchism. With the alternative selves presented to the imagined woman—she healing him in "The Broken Heart," he joining her in "Of Weeping"—Donne discharges an end to ascendancy and invites the woman into the regenerative complex of the poem. Her rescue of him, the denial of her denial in "The Broken Heart," the retraction of the distance in "Of Weeping," would make another poem possible. If in "Whoso list to hunt" and "They flee from me" Wyatt becomes as elusive as the woman, in "The Broken Heart" and "Of Weeping" Donne brooks no evasions. Instead, the mirrors he holds up for the lady—the shards of the self in "The Broken Heart" and the cycle of tears in "Of Weeping"—multiply the argument of his cause. His raspiness in "The Broken Heart" and breathlessness in "Of Weeping" are the products of the woman's divisive cruelty and destructive separation respectively. She determines his weakness as she might, in future poems, mother his strength. The reappraisal of maternal resources turns the burden of origination back to the woman.

Through the unraveled disguise of *Rime sparse* 23, Laura-Mercury demonstrates that the audience Petrarch has in mind is not necessarily the woman. It may be anyone who extends the sympathetic pity of empathy or the poetic laurel of fame. Petrarch's bonding is fraternal. He appeals to those who understand the man's experience. Laura-Mercury's outrage is directed at Petrarch's having rendered her the specular pin-up girl other men ogle. Her punishment is for the misrepresentation such tellings incur. For Donne, the primary audience is the imagined lady. In "The Broken Heart" and "Of Weeping" he suggests that she has control of future tellings. Her reflection, in the broken glass of the former and production of the cylindrical mirror in the latter, depends on the image she commands. To render the anamorphic vision whole, the lady must intervene with something that will inspire a better picture. That "device" is nothing less (or more) than her assent to the wholeness Donne withholds. To round out the picture, she need only say "yes." Petrarch's Laura is a projection of the poet. Donne's lady in the next poem has the opportunity to project herself in an image she is persuaded to choose. Her reinvention of herself will produce another poet. By reasserting her importance to the productions of her life and by implying that she can change the poem she hears, Donne acknowledges the woman's formulative capacity and her real difference. She is the only reader that matters. In such a configuration—the woman feeding his love, he feeding her words—inspiration emerges a continuous revitalization that triumphs over the first and last of Petrarchan hierarchy and the false mothers and fathers of male poetic dominance. Love and words mutually nourish.

Who is the Silvia-Laura of these poems? Is she a biographical woman or is she (as Proteus suggests in *Two Gentlemen of Verona*) a thing "all swains commend," her beauty validated only within the coterie of the "swains'" imagination? The distinction between the biographical and poetic woman is made in the opening line of the play's most famous song: "Who is Silvia? What is she . . ." In the play, everyone knows *who* Silvia is. She is the daughter of the duke who, in the Folio dramatis personae, is listed as "Father to Silvia." But *what* is Silvia? In the song, she is the daughter of her wooer, Proteus, who engenders her idealization so that she becomes the common property of what Eve Sedgwick calls the homosocial group.[28] She is the "swains' creation," a construction evolved by, and then circulated among, male image-makers. The transference from earthly body to heavenly orbit is the result of a song which self-consciously proclaims its parenthood:

> Then to Silvia let us sing
> That Silvia is excelling.
> She excels each mortal thing
> Upon the dull earth dwelling
> To her let us garlands bring. (4.2.48–52)

When the audience observes the idealizing process through the eyes and ears of the betrayed Julia, it retreats with her from swain to Proteus. (She quickly shifts from song to singer. "The music likes you not." "You mistake: the musician likes me not," 4.2.54–55.) Julia reads beyond the excellent Silvia of the song. She sees the musician who betrayed her. In the drama, art is framed by life. There is always a listening *who*. In the song, life is generated by art. There is always an invented *what*. Like Colin's exalted Rosalynde, the excelling Silvia is assembled out of denial.

In "The Broken Heart" and "Of Weeping" Donne suggests that the rejected and absent self can neither invent a song out of his brokenness nor fabricate an ideal out of the lady's absence. Though the lady in the Petrarchan dyad is always a constructed "what" and the man in the Petrarchan dyad is always an invented "swain," Donne's contribution to the lyric form changes the poetic power structure. As the next chapter will show, his *whats* have more agency, an agency he fleshes out in the poems where the lady's gesture initiates the poetry-making cycle. There is no univocal reading woman for Donne existing somewhere outside the poem. Inside the poem, she is what the poet is, an imagined creation who—with the poet—might experience yet another incarnation inside yet another poem. The overhearing Julia of *Two Gentlemen* suggests that there is, even for the confident swain, a sense in which the woman's reaction to a poem may change its impact, may in fact reveal how little authority poets have in shaping their world. Sometimes even a controlling swain can become an object lesson. When Donne brings the imagined woman into the poetry-making complex, he assumes a still more complex reading woman. Consequently, his swains have less agency and emerge less artful. His empty self in "The Broken Heart" spits out a likeness of poems. His submerged self in "Of Weeping" pours out an excess of lines.

When he shifts poetic initiation to the imagined woman, Donne makes her responsible for the poet's imagination and the imagined poet. He becomes her *what*—a self produced by the construct she determines. Imagining the woman's agency, Donne begins to see her (as he will absolutely in "The Dreame") as a writing subject. In "The Broken Heart" and "Of Weeping," Donne takes literally the idea that the force of the woman is implicated in the representing man. If she chooses to be destructive or excessive, the result is a broken or inundated poem. The cracked mirror and the flooding poem are the result of her flawed or overbearing brush stroke. In this vision, poet and woman are products of the dream-work, where experience is unfolded and refolded to provoke a "change in nature." Within yet another spiral the scrambled signs might, in some future poem, produce a change in art. Donne invents that future poem in "The Dreame" where the woman's originary and shining light inspires his belatedly reflective glorification. Rekindling Laura-Eve's generosity as the origin of the poem, Donne calls the woman the source of his giftedness.

SYLVIA TRANSFORMED

Returning Donne's Gifts

If Donne alters the relationship between garlandizing swain and garlanded lady in his poems, he also confers on the lady the "gift" of poetic imagination which initiates the cycle. And he does so in those poems where he plays with gifts and giftedness to alter another Elizabethan convention: the gesture poem. Of the sociology of gifts, Patricia Fumerton writes that the Elizabethan "ring of exchange" engenders "the social body of literal and poetic children: instead of war or competition, there arises trust and its greatest source, the spirit of generosity. And instead of death—of which war is the collective perpetuation—there arises life."[1] The gift asserts the power of the giver and pressures the taker into returning what was given. A symbol of union, it nevertheless establishes hierarchy. The gift represents a noblesse that forms the central bind of social obligation.

When Donne questions gifts in "A Jeat Ring Sent" and "The Funerall," he subverts the gestures that use partial offerings as representations of total control. He refuses to return—with his poem—the tribute that would include him in the circle of gratefulness the gift demands. His indictment of the gift in "Jeat Ring" and revenge against the giver in "The Funerall" challenge Petrarchan prioritization. But in "The Dreame" he recasts his reservations and explores a psychology of giving that reveals the possibilities for exchange. With "The Dreame," Donne renders foreknowledge dependent on after-knowledge, anticipation part of realization. Corinna's daylight interruption of Ovid's nap in the second *Amores*, Laura's nocturnal visit in *Rime sparse* 359, and the Wyatt lady's "once in special" intrusion are responses in the bedroom to what Ovid calls his "inviting ambuscade."[2] Laura denigrates such lures as the "sad waves of [Petrarch's manipulative] weeping."[3] Wyatt's poet identifies them as the "bread"[4] of a male gesture that invites the lady's aggressive return. However awkward, all of the lady's gestures in these poems are responses to something the man does to provoke the attention given.[5] But in "The Dreame," the lady's gesture—her entrance into the poet's life—is occasioned by her shaping fantasy, not his. If in "The Broken Heart" and "Of Weeping" Donne renders the semiotic assent and presence of the woman "indispensable"—as Mieke Bal argues—to his idea of poetic creation, in "The Dreame" he makes her into a god who understands him and invents herself.

Despite their initiating woman, most of Donne's gesture poems, like "Jeat Ring" and "The Funerall," continue to put the man back on top.[6] "The Dreame" does something different and it is that difference that casts aside what Janel Mueller calls "the monopoly on discourse enjoyed and exercised by male speakers."[7] In prompting the dream and then finishing it, the lady retains the creative ascendancy Petrarch seized from Laura as he sought, in the tribute of his idealization, to advance the mystery of difference between them. In "The Dreame," the woman corrects the wrongs of absence and separation the lady of "The Broken Heart" and "Of Weeping" commits. She is the bridge Donne asks for in those poems. When he portrays the "Dreame" woman as someone who knows what he wants and who becomes what he wants, Donne heightens the possibility for an exchange that cancels hierarchies. In "The Broken Heart" and "Of Weeping," the woman is merely invited into the inspirational network. In "The Dreame," she designs it. When he renders intelligence the key to her attractiveness and attractiveness the key to her intelligence, Donne equates sexuality and poetry. He collapses the Laura-Eve who mirrors his desire into the Laura-Mercury who preempts his creativity. Then he calls the condensation the source of both his manly strength and poetic realization.

In naming the woman the omniscient seer, Donne casts her as the acknowledged bearer of what Christopher Ricks calls "postcoital sadness."[8] But in giving her that burden, he also reopens the possibility of an angelic intelligence that ranges beyond "before" and "after." He thereby eliminates the divisive power struggle of Petrarchan idealization and the disappointing aftermath of libertine realization. When he identifies knowledge as a gift that precludes return, that is itself a return, Donne revitalizes gestures which are self-defeating in "Jeat Ring" and destructive of others in "The Funerall." When she takes on the risk of loss implicit in love, the "Dreame" woman presupposes a return to sexuality, a second coming that renders her son to the divine father of her first incarnation. In "The Dreame," Donne gives the lady all the firstness Genesis 2 gives Adam. And he goes one step further. If, like most Petrarchan women, she is the "god of his idolatry," the image of perfection he worships, in this poem she is both a statue that moves and the Pygmalion that wills the movement.

In "A Jeat Ring Sent," "The Funerall," and "The Dreame," Donne expands the vehicle of the gesture poem. He complicates its terms by challenging the gesturing woman and her gift. If a gesture anticipates some sort of reciprocal response, Donne responds to the gesture by reciprocating *in kind*. He neither retracts the original praise by calling the poet the true origin of what was given, nor awaits a subsequent cycle of exchange by raising the ante of the terms of commitment. Donne changes the genre: first, when he admits to the lady's power to stimulate the poet's response; second, when he concedes that the cycle may stop, as in "Jeat Ring" and "The Funerall," or be averted, as in "The Dreame." The lady in Donne's gesture poems is equal to the man in her ability to bring him to the full force of the retaliative powers implicit in them. Donne's woman becomes not merely something for the poet to work off. She is more than the "other." She is also like him, a force he understands.[9] Each of the poems subverts the obligation the gift confers. "Jeat Ring" publicizes through imitation and "The Funerall" silences through burial the questionable motives of the lady's initiative.

In "The Dreame," Donne allows the lady to choose between the fame of publicity and the censure of criticism. He offers her renown as his resource if she remains in place as lover and promises her ignominy as his shadow if she leaves him unsatisfied in love. Faced with a Laura-Mercury who establishes her generative primacy in *Rime sparse* 23, Petrarch attempts to reclaim the origin of creativity by writing that Laura out. The Donne of "The Dreame" encourages his woman to know and to supersede him. He thereby obviates the theft implicit in the Petrarchan exchange, rendering the initial gift a recognition. In the song of *Two Gentlemen*, the male "I" is absorbed into the inventing swain and the poetic "you" is assimilated onto the invented "what." In "The Dreame," the "what" invents the swain. She determines both the thought of sexuality and the idealized language of the tribute. "Jeat Ring" and "The Funerall" are retaliations for the *what's* initiation. The "I" names and then mimics the lady's cruelty. "The Dreame" is an imitation of the lady's generous imagination. As the "I" emerges Adam to her God, he corroborates her divinity, as knowing resource, and her power, as writing subject, of the poem.

What She Meant

Donne demonstrates his understanding of the woman in "Jeat Ring" by promising to become her. Instead of continuing the cycle by returning a tribute in exchange for her gift, Donne returns exactly what she offers: an "I" to match her "you." That return is all the more remarkable because, throughout the poem, the speaker stresses the gap between himself and the lady. The "she" in "Jeat Ring" is originally so unlike the poet that her gift represents their differences. When he refuses to be the "he" that evoked the gesture, Donne threatens the woman by reflecting accurately, and in his own person, what her gesture means. Though it starts with the lady's gesture placating the man, the poem ends by becoming a gesture implicating the woman. The gift in "Jeat Ring"—which was initially the woman's way of getting the man off her back (by sending something of herself to the man in order to retain some things of her own)—emerges in the end the vehicle that frees him from the obligation she initially felt.

In "A Jeat Ring Sent," the poet doesn't utter the threat himself. He has the ring do it. James Baumlin similarly reads the ring as the lady's signifier: "In asking the ring what 'wouldst thou say?' the poet admits his inability to control its meaning, at the same time lamenting love's instability as a semiotic system."[10] But Baumlin stops short of having the ring speak differently in each stanza and therefore of acknowledging the ring as a *shifting* signifier. The argument here is that, in stanza 1, the ring speaks retroactively to describe the couple's situation; in 2, it represents what the lady meant; in 3, it prognosticates the future, reflecting—in its warning—the mirrored behavior the gesture invites. In the dialogue between speaker and symbol, the symbol converts the speaker into it. In that way, the speaker becomes the woman just as, in a conventionally Petrarchan poem, the woman becomes the man. In the third stanza, he is ringed by her, a victim of the lady's broken promises. In retaliation, he will become like her: a heart breaker. The poem presents a dialogue where the "I" speaks the first three lines of each stanza and the ring, in response, answers in the last line of the respective three. In the first stanza, the ring represents both the speaker and the lady in its response. In the second, it speaks as the lady's representative and, in the third, as an instrument of prophecy. Meanwhile, in the first three lines of each stanza, the "I" becomes simultaneously more self-assertive and more self-delusionary. In the first stanza, he sees the ring as an emblem of his present situation. The speaker casts himself as the mournful Petrarchist and the lady as the cruel resister. In the second, he evokes an idealized love, something like the "true love" of Shakespeare's sonnet 116, while the lady (whom he there addresses) presents the impediment of her infidelity. In stanza 1 she is the Petrarchan heart breaker, in stanza 2, the libertine heart-obscurer. Finally, when in the last stanza he turns the ring into the female sexual organ he would like it to be, the ring answers that such a regendering will have its consequences. If the man becomes the woman in fantasy, he will become her in fact: he will emerge her equal libertine. The more wishful the speaker becomes, the more wrathful the ring becomes. As the "I" moves into fantasy, the ring returns to reality. The "I" attempts to move clockwise; the ring pushes back the clock, making the woman the precursor of the man. In the last three lines of each stanza, the ring announces the woman's agency. She controls. The man merely fantasizes his power.

In the first stanza, the ring inadequately represents what the poet calls the nature of each of them; at the opening it is in little what they are in large: "Thou art not so black, as my heart, / Nor half so brittle, as her heart, thou art" (p. 38). The quality describing him (blackness) relates to a state already established—a fact; the quality describing her (brittleness) relates to a state still to be achieved—a potential. He is already black; she is not yet broken. The ring is not yet what he is nor half of what she might become. His realized blackness contrasts to her still to be proved brittleness. When he addresses the ring, the "I" announces his pessimism in terms of a bottomless bottom, his blackness a lens that determines a prescribed barrenness. The black vision assigns the lady to the brittle role in the Petrarchan dyad. He precedes her in the first part of the stanza, having already felt the darkness. She has not yet broken. He is eminent; she is imminent. But when the ring answers, it is clear that she predates him. The ring describes itself as "nothing more endless, nothing sooner broke." The ring's response changes the balance. It sides with the sender. It speaks as the container and defines the thing contained. The woman is the first cause of the man's pessimism. According to its logic, the speaker is boring (endless) in his plaintiveness; the lady is restless (sooner broken) in her infidelity. Since she arrived at her position "sooner," he is an accessory to her. His desolation produces the dark vision. Her initial restlessness determines his resultant inquietude. As denier, she names the terms of his demise. As initiator, she retains her hierarchical ascendancy.

The "I" responds in the second stanza by reversing the clock again. He proposes a different world, one of priceless durability—nothing less precious, nothing less tough. He answers the lady with a ring (like Vaughan's eternity) of endless light in contrast to her container of endless night. Unsatisfied with his lady's gesture, he suggests what might have been another—a better—lady's gesture and accuses her of sending a ring that represents the worst of womankind. The ring's answer anticipates his insult: "I 'am cheap and nought but fashion, fling me' away." The jeat ring becomes a jet ring—a sender of senders. The message is now neither precious nor eternal. It is cheap and "fashion," meant to be jetted, thrown out. The ring represents only her. It speaks in her voice and at her bidding, to undercut both the nihilistic vision of the first stanza and the golden light the speaker attempts to project early in the second stanza. As mere fashion, it is part of a throwaway culture. If the "I" proposes a public marriage in the first three lines, the "you" counters with a public divorce. Again, the lady sets the terms of the discourse. The "I" who began by evoking the ring of eternity ends by being defined in the artifact that determines his exclusion. Instead of an eternal ring, he is a temporary fling. He sought centralization and emerges, in the ring's answer, marginal.

In the third stanza, the "I" evades the ring's message by burying himself in the imaginary harbor of sexual union:

> Yet stay with mee since thou art come,
> Circle this fingers top, which did'st her thombe.
> Be justly proud, and gladly safe, that thou doest dwell with me,
> She that, Oh, broke her faith, would soon breake thee.

Whereas in the first stanza the "I" is already black and still to become endless, in the last stanza he speaks of extensions rather than anticipations. Pulling the ring over his finger, he stretches the earthly abode (top) into a paradise—figured by a circle (hers) on top of a circle (his). The proposal describes the sexual act as one of equality (justly proud and gladly safe) where the male stay and the female circle are interchangeable. He makes the return of the single ring ceremony (male offering the circle / woman becoming the firm stay) into a double ring ceremony (woman encircling / man remaining). The ring first circled her initiating thumb; now it shields his erect finger. With the last command to circle him, he hopes to bring the lady into the arena of his sexuality. As his encircler, she would take him into herself. If her thumb is her erect phallus and his thumb mirrors hers, then in this vision he simply extends her original gesture. There is no preexisting gender. As in Butler's sexual performances, the gesture determines gender. But the hope for an opening into the other which obviates a predetermined "he" and "she" is closed off in the last line by the ring's interruption. As it repeats the pattern of the first three stanzas, the ring challenges the equality the "I" proposes. It claims it will transform, rather than comfort, him. In becoming the woman, the man will assume her brittleness as his fate.

The warning, which is usually read as the speaker's protection of the ring,[11] is here read as the ring's prediction for the speaker. Her brittleness, not his blackness, comes first. In the ring's final retort, the lady emerges the antecedent who will soon make him into an extension of her. It is her quality that dominates and antedates. She is the source of the symbol which will finally define him in her terms. It is her brittleness, her broken faith, that instigates his faithlessness and prompts the broken words of a libertine poetic. With the ring's last word, Donne alters the gesture poem by rendering explicit the contagious destructiveness of the gesturing woman and by ending the gesturing cycle. If the "I" will "soon be broken," then he will be what she initially was: "nothing sooner broke." His performance will mimic hers. He will be her equal libertine instead of, as he was at the opening, her Petrarchan laurelizer. The ring transcribes his end onto the lady's beginning. Returning the lady's gesture in kind, the poem identifies the lady as the destroyer of true love and faithful lovers. When the man breaks with his past in the imminent "soon," he will emerge an image of her. The ring's prognostication will become his behavior. Like De Flores flaunting the ring and the finger of Joanna's dead betrothed in *The Changeling*, this gesture represents, in the crudity of its accusatory "fingering," the death of a self that once believed in an ideal beloved. The broken "I" will no longer speculate about alternative "meanings." He knows the lady's intention because, as her representation, he mirrors her thoughts.

At the end of "Jeat Ring," the "I" learns that the lady's potential brittleness has become, perhaps always was, an actual break. And it is that transition from hypothesis to thesis that lends the ring's voice an air of vatic authority. Surfacing so soon after the beatific vision of circle upon circle, the speaker's transformation into the lady constitutes the poet's revenge. In the game of catch-up Donne plays with the lady—he anticipating her unreliability in the blackness of his loss, she emerging his model in the brittleness of her infidelity—the poet becomes what the ring now is: the mirror of her instability. "Soon" is overtaken by "now" as "now" will become "then." He will substantiate in actuality what she was in potential. The ring's brittleness here reflects their mutual divisiveness. The belated poem is a retaliative "return," a record of the man's emergence as the woman; its history is his transformation into her divisive self. The ring anticipates the collapse of poetic idealization. It reflects the end result of the woman's agency to record the broken voice of her destructiveness. The speaker will *soon* become what she was: broken.

In "The Funerall," the revenge takes the form of a demotion rather than a substitution. The speaker reduces the lady's gift from heavenly crown in stanza 1, through earthly manacle of stanza 2, to insignificant "what'er" in stanza 3. If the ring of "Jeat Ring" urges the "I" to retaliate against the lady by imitating her brittleness, here the "I" is prepared to retract his vulnerability and to reflect her strength. The imposing and superimposing ring of "Jeat Ring" ends as an insignificant and buried "ringlet" here. When the "I" breaks at the end of "Jeat Ring" he will, by implication, also cease to sing of the "she" who breaks him. Similarly, when the " 'I' . . . bur[ies] some of you" in "The Funerall," he consigns the woman to obscurity. Though the speaker begins by providing for his own funeral, he ends by burying the woman. If the "I" gradually understands the meaning of the ring in "Jeat Ring," in "The Funerall" the "I" has already done the interpretation. In fact he offers two, one for the future (of stanza 1 and half of stanza 2), one for the present (from line fifteen on). Read retroactively, the second interpretation will overwrite the first, just as in "Jeat Ring" the truth of the ring's warnings will render the conventions of the opening stanza obsolete.

In "Jeat Ring" the beatific vision of unimpeded love is marred by the realistic injunction, "except" in stanza 2. The heavenly demesne of "The Funerall" is also disrupted with an "except" at the end of its second stanza. In both poems, the "except" turns the poem around to announce a dark truth about the lady's intent. And that dark truth signals the poet's reversal from memorializer to burier. When the "I" becomes the lady in "Jeat Ring," he ceases to be the "endless" singer of praises he presumably was at the beginning. By becoming her, he no longer is the poet. The end of his poetic career is a by-product of the revenge in "Jeat Ring." But in "The Funerall," the silencing of the poet's voice constitutes the main point of his revenge. He begins by addressing a future audience even though he talks about his present state of attachment to the lady. He ends, contrarily, by speaking to the present lady about his future indifference to her. The Petrarchan poet eternalizes the lady in fame. The "I" of "The Funerall" buries her in obscurity. In "Jeat Ring," the "I" deprives the "you" of a mournfully faithful Petrarchan follower. As mirror of her emptiness, he has no self left to offer. In "The Funerall," he deprives her of a duly reverential Petrarchan following: she has no audience left to confirm her laurelization. As the poet narrows the spectrum of listeners to the single lady, he restricts the arena of her power. When he buries her, he loses the audience that signifies his poetic career and she loses the audience that witnesses her controlling status. "Jeat Ring" depicts the end result of the woman's poem-destroying agency. There is no Petrarch to kick around. "The Funerall" chronicles the collapse of the woman's self-aggrandizing agency. There is no Laura to exalt.

"The Funerall" begins with a hierarchy that resembles Petrarch's in *Rime sparse* 359. Petrarch pays homage to Laura's hair as his strength and inspiration, the source of whatever light he has: "Is this the blond hair and the golden knot . . . that still binds me, and those beautiful eyes that were my sun?" (p. 558). Laura's hair holds the poet together "still." It rules him from heaven through his life on earth. He is restrained by the golden knot of her hair as he is blinded by the golden sun of her eyes. She guides from on top as Apollo to his Daphne and pulls from up front as Daphne to his Apollo. Laura's eyes direct his gaze. As source of light, she teaches him and, as desired object, she leads him, to recognize her divinity. Her knot governs his obsession. Similarly, the "I" of "The Funerall" begins by raising (from wreath, to crown, to mystery, through sign) the bit of hair his lady sent to a knot that controls and ties him. The ringlet directs his gaze upward to her apotheosis. In "The Relique," the bracelet is different from this wreath.[12] There, it is a mutual "device" (89), planned by both lovers to ensure a future equality. In "The Funerall," it is the lady's gift—meant to show her superiority. As the "I" deifies the [ring]let's status, giving it the divine aura of a marvel, so he elevates its source, raising her, in the hypothetical future of the first fourteen lines, to a controlling goddess. And, as Laura continues to govern Petrarch, so Donne's future lady of the first 14 lines controls the poet's body, keeping him from dissolution. Her brains are given a history which becomes the presumed present of the poem: "These haires which upward grew and strength and art / Have from a better braine" (p. 91). Not only does he make the lady his future governor after death, he makes her into his present superior in life. In the future past that is his present, she has a better brain, whose strength and art dominate him now. That Petrarchan tribute makes the lady his once and future superior. Determining his confines, she is Mercury to his Petrarch, her manacle a stone, his idolatry a laurel.

The gravedigger audience is both witness to his destiny and memorializer of her centrality. That audience represents the future readers who will learn of the lady's apotheosis. In the first half of the poem, the speaker is controlled by the lady, a control which defines the Petrarchan process. Through the power acquired from her control, he can in turn dominate the buriers. The lady emerges the conventional muse, the gravediggers, the conventional audience, of the poet's praise. That chain of command is first cut short when the imposing "I" of the third stanza asks the shrouders to "bury it with me" and finally is severed in the conclusion when, no longer addressing the gravediggers, the "I" speaks directly to the lady. When the "I" turns to the "you," he intends for there to be no future readers. In the burial, he already denounces what Petrarch calls the lady's "fame."

All the reversals begin in line 15, when the poet questions, with the except, the lady's intentions: "Except she meant that I / By this should know my pain, / As prisoners are manacled, when they'are condemn'd to die" (p. 91). The exception here initiates a totally different scenario, one where the lady is tyrant and he, prisoner. In the first section she is preserved in heaven; in the second, she disappears totally. In the first, there is a sense of oneness deriving from a great chain of being with her at the helm; in the second, there is a multiplicity implied by the "breeding" of idolatry. Principally, at the end, it is the "I" who rules the multitude. He is alone without a "she." When, in the verse structure, he separates his self from her control, he redesigns the future by reassessing the past. Using *since* as a preposition, he stresses his strength in terms of a past sacrifice that renders him presently (like Christ) godlike. Using *since* as an adverb, he speaks of what follows immediately after her now understood meaning. With the "I am," he asserts his own being:

> For since I am
> Loves martyr, it might breed idolatrie,
> If into others hands these Reliques came;
> As 'twas humility
> To'afford to it all that a Soule can doe,
> So, 'tis some bravery,
> That since you would save none of mee, I bury some of you. (p. 91)

He is both divine father ("I am" as paternal Yahweh) and divine son ("I am" as sacrificed martyr). Whereas the opening of the poem allows the hypothetical reader retroactively to see the lady's greatness, the conclusion has a series of pasts in which the lady is obscured and the "I" is advanced. He asserts himself: first, in his command to the shrouders; second, in his identification of an independent self; and, third, in his burial of her. All three acts involve an extended present, a filling out into a state that sustains the man's totalizing command.

When he reinterprets her meaning, he makes her act of denial the cause of his separation from her. She pushes him into the bravery of "being" not by keeping him (as in the first scenario) but by her refusal to "save." The poet plays with enclosures similar to those in "The Broken Heart." For the "one" and "all" of the Petrarchan first stanza, there is the "none" of the last. If he is nothing to her, then he will make less of the little she now is. Since the symbol represents her, then "some of [her]" punningly becomes the "sum of [her]." If the "subtile wreath" of the opening extended upward toward heaven and inward through every part of him, so the little wreath (the some at the end) contracts as he pushes it away. And if his "humility" (a retraction of self to make her prominent) facilitated her expansion at the beginning, so now his "bravery" (a promulgation of self to emphasize her insignificance) brings on the reversal at the end. Placed in juxtaposition, the words "humility" and "bravery" summarize the poet's sense of self in both parts of the poem.[13] At the opening, her gesture encouraged him to think of himself as dependent on her disposition. Early on, she "keeps" him from dissolution in order to regulate the strains (like the puppeteer Urania in Sidney's "double sestina" whose "parts maintaind a perfect musique")[14] of the poets' song. Similarly, he safeguards her in the poem which records her "better braine."

When, in the second half of the poem, he switches from humility to bravery, he also announces a change from passive solemnizer to active warrior. As manacled prisoner, he seeks freedom, and his final "bravery" is the means by which he releases himself from her. In the first half of the poem he is headed toward disintegration as she comes in to "tye" him up; in the second half he points toward the reintegration that signifies his liberation from those manacles. As he shifts from lover to warrior, he writes out amorous discourse and chronicles instead the history of his ascension. Here the hair receives its identity from its association not as remains of her but as emblem of his martyrdom. The process of the first half of the poem is to bring her into him. As "braine," she governs his province. Every part of his territory becomes her domain. In the end, her refusal to save him becomes a refusal to savor him. It is the sexual refusal that instigates the metaphysical rebuttal.

Her spiritual denial in the poet's future heaven equals her earthly spurning in his physical present. Since she rejects even the smallest part of him (the semen he might have sent her), he will save only the smallest part—some—of her. Like the Laura of *Rime sparse* 359, this "she" is already in heaven. Like Petrarch, this "I" is still earthbound. But there the similarity to the *Rime sparse* ends. She may go on denying him, but he will end the laurelization. That burial will consign her to the sole oblivion he (as writer) has the power to impose. He will send her to the obscurity of his silence. His revenge is (first) to swallow—and (then) to think like—her. Including her thoughts (what she *meant*), as earlier she had tied his brain, brings her into him—instead of him into her. He matches her refusal to save with his espousal of burial and thereby equates her meanness with his ending. When he speculates about what she "meant," he turns her past gesture into a future portent. The meaning of "meant" as he uses it carries a sense of design, the configuration that renders her the gothic support of his being. When he buries the purport and removes from view her intention of herself, the "I" undermines the Petrarchan idealizer and the deified goddess of part one. He silences whatever she "meant," and so obviates the significance of her being.

He begins the third stanza by belittling the intention he had earlier magnified ("what ere shee meant by it") and prepares himself to take final command. In the end, he no longer addresses the anonymous shrouders. Using "since" about her in the same retrospective and projective way he had used it about himself, he can now talk directly to her. Through the bravery of his martyrdom, he has catapulted himself into the superior position. When he scatters them to obscurity, the poet dissolves the eternal ring[lets] of her resolve. Even her denial is denied in the burial. In the silence of his refusal to be, the poet renders the lady obscure. If she intends to deny his being and if her gesture was a way of tying him to her denial, then his return refutes her staying power. Her initial withholding of mercy to him justifies his future refusal of grace to her. His burial guarantees her oblivion. As he undercuts her superiority, the "I" severs her origination, his bravery now an assertion of self that denies her. The burial renders her anonymous. The unnamed locks represent the unraveling of her renown. Burying her signifier, the "I" denies her materiality. She never mattered. In "Jeat Ring," the "I" first poses as a mournful Petrarch who finds himself in the blackness of the lady's denial, and then as an uncaring imitator who mirrors her libertine unfaithfulness. In "The Funerall," he first crowns his lady as idealized Laura and then denies her any fame at all. In both poems, he refuses to return the lady's gesture with the gift of his Petrarchan tribute. He writes out its Petrarch in "Jeat Ring" and its Laura in "The Funerall."

What She Understood

The woman's preeminence, which in "Jeat Ring Sent" ends the Petrarchan cycle, in "The Dreame" instigates it. Idealized God, she achieves the deification "The Funerall" withholds. Controlling woman, she dictates the tribute "Jeat Ring" retracts. In her divinity, the woman emerges poet and poem. She is both the God who imagines the construct and the construct she imagines. In either instance, she invents herself. With the confirmation of the first two stanzas, the poet renders her the Laura-Mercury and the Laura-Eve of his poem. As God and woman, she undoes the hierarchies of male priority. Donne gives her the poetic and sexual initiative Petrarch recognized in, but struggled to wrest back from, Laura. Only in the third stanza does he demonstrate what will happen to her representation if she withdraws the gift she so amply bestows in the first two stanzas. In "The Funerall," she loses her memorializer. In "The Dreame," she might lose her desirer.

The rhetorical aim of "Jeat Ring" and "The Funerall" is to demonstrate to the Petrarchanly breaking woman that the "I" has persuasive means of self-preservation. In "Jeat Ring," much is made of arriving at the true past revealed in the gesture. In "The Funerall," much is made of understanding the anticipated future revealed in the manacle. Both poems evade the present by delving either into the past reason for the gesture or its future promise. And, in both poems, what could have been a sign of eternal continuity (pictured in the circling ring of marriage and mysterious crown of heaven) becomes instead (the more the "I" enters into the thought of the "you") a sign of temporal rupture. Each poem undermines its vision of perfection ("true love" and the "heavenly desmesne") with the intrusion of the lady's meaning, expressed in "Jeat Ring" by the ring's prophecy, in "The Funerall," by the speaker's interpretation. Like the speaker in "Jeat Ring" and "The Funerall," the "I" of "The Dreame's" third stanza threatens to turn the poem into a disquisition about the gesture gone awry. But when he gives the lady a choice, Donne demonstrates how the disaster of self-defeating obligation can be averted. The lady can change her role in the poem. She can either become the imitated "she" of "Jeat Ring" and the disfigured "she" of "The Funerall" or she can join with the "I" in recasting beginnings so those endings are averted.

The convention of the dream poem allows the woman to enter the man's thought. As Sidney writes in "Astrophil and Stella 38," the dream's "closed up sense" arrests what in "open sense flies away." In the conventional dream poem, the lady vanishes with the dream. Her physical presence in the dream merely corroborates what her emotional denial in life suggests: she is always unavailable to the waking poet. Donne attempts to abstract the lady during the dream (rendering her the God who knows him) and then to contract her after the dream (rendering her sexuality the product of her own divination).[15] He makes her reality simply an extension of her own dream. When he calls the woman the sympathetic God who fosters Adam's sleep and the man the recipient of that grace, Donne reverses Petrarch's Genesis 2. Where Petrarch sees man as the dreamer of woman, Donne goes one step further back and attributes to the woman the prescience of God's Genesis 2 *knowledge*. In that retrospect, Donne's Eve presents herself as the object of Adam's desire because she wants what he wants. She is the God who invents herself, her Adam merely the vessel for her reincarnation and the expression of *her* desire. The woman in Wyatt's "They flee from me" seems similarly to take the sexual initiative, but, in giving, she mocks—and so threatens—the man. Donne's "she" in "The Dreame" creates herself without losing the difference that completes desire. "They flee from me" renders the man's secrets the source of his downfall. "The Dreame" renders the man's secrets the beginning of a mutual triumph. Donne's exultation in the second stanza is in the imagined woman's intelligence, a knowledge which names her as the source of his energy and the proper author of his tribute. But whereas the gesture genre stipulates that the poem reciprocate the lady's initiative (a return Donne withholds in "Jeat Ring" by denying the poet, in "The Funerall" by denying the lady), in the first two stanzas of "The Dreame" the gap between giver and taker is closed.

In the redefinition, Donne works out of two traditions—one rhetorical (getting the lady to stay), one metaphysical (acknowledging how she came). In the rhetorical tradition, his source is Adam's reaction to Eve in Genesis. In the metaphysical, his source is God's knowledge in Genesis that Adam needs Eve. ("It is not good that the man should be alone; I will make him an help meet for him." Genesis 2.18.) The rhetorical frame operates to govern the future. The metaphysical theme accounts for the present. In Genesis, when Adam is awakened (presumably by the formed Eve), his joy is that she is "now bone of [his] bones, flesh of [his] flesh" (Genesis 2.23). Adam's possessive *now* (echoed by Donne in the *now* of Donne's persuasive third stanza) is the means by which he hopes to keep Eve to himself. When Adam speaks, he emphasizes a future (now and henceforth) that stems from his present illusion of power. The biblical narrator stresses the process of God's past understanding. Adam sees his power in terms of specific acts. The biblical narrator defines God in terms of a constant intelligence. In "The Dreame," Donne alludes to that understanding with the many times repeated "knowing" and "seeing," and that process is the explanation for the lady's intrusion. Donne's strategy in "The Dreame" is to arrive at a "deep sleep" similar to Adam's trance. He wants to retreat to that moment when he, unknowing, was known and God was his protective originator. Adam's rhetoric operates in the third stanza; God's knowledge controls the first two. In stanza 1, the woman enters at the moment "before" in the speaker's dream. In stanza 2, the speaker retreats to the "before/before" to define the process of her arrival. In stanza 3, when she rises, the speaker attempts, through a rhetoric resembling Adam's *now*, to get her to be "before" once more. His "thou . . . goest to come" is a ploy to start the process over again.

Like the Eve of Milton's *Paradise Lost* who postpones completion to avoid disappointment,[16] the Eve of Donne's "The Dreame" fulfills expectation, partly because the fulfillment promotes more expectation: "I will dream that hope again." Donne's Eve invents the self she becomes, and that becoming fosters the mutuality of desire. In "They flee from me" there was "no dream[ing]" because life undid ideality. Here life enacts the ideal. In the first stanza, "The Dreame" retraces the process of knowing whereby God understood Adam's need in Genesis. The awakened "I" begins by persuading the woman to fulfill in act what the dream promised as ideal:

> Deare love, for nothing lesse then thee
> Would I have broke this happy dreame,
> > It was a theame
> For reason, much too strong for phantasie,
> Therefore thou wakd'st me wisely; yet
> My Dreame thou brok'st not, but continued'st it,
> Thou art so true, that thoughts of thee suffice,
> To make dreames truth; and fables histories;
> Enter these armes, for since thou thoughtst it best,
> Not to dreame all my dreame, let's do the rest. (pp. 79–80)

In the space now opened between dreamer and dreamed, her knowledge of what the speaker wants becomes his knowledge of what she wants. In "Jeat Ring," the woman is "sooner broke." Here, the woman doesn't "breake." She sustains. If Eve creates herself in the image Adam dreams, then mutual sexual desire asserts the woman's imagination. The oxymoron "do[ing] the rest" involves completing the vision of sleep by extending it and canceling the passivity of sleep by exercising in it. The playful punning in Donne's suggestion "let's do the rest" represents his argument for realized love, as if having many meanings might itself substantiate the multiple desires—and the desire to multiply the "doing"—the dream proposes. When it enacts desire, the dream "undoes the rest[fulness]" of sleep. But in realizing desire, the dream completes the quest it inspires. It "does" what remains by finishing the "rest" (the remainder) of the story the lady dreams. The poem reifies the lady's divinity because it implies that the woman is more than the static goddess who, in Petrarch, *does not*. Donne's "she" does. When she says "yes" to the poet's dream, she writes the poem. When she says "yes" to the poet's desire, she rewrites their lives. "Doing the rest" involves moving into the arena of the as-yet-unarticulated "rest," the arena of excess. "Doing the rest" means undoing completion by outdoing or exceeding ends and achieving completion by realizing (in act) the remainder of the dream. It means believing in surplus (the rest) and composure (the resting place) in the repeated arousal and climax of sexuality. "The rest" is the excess Laura-Mercury defines. "Doing" the rest is the response Laura-Eve gives. In its excess, the "rest" is the woman's space as feminist critics define it: the arena that renders the "boundaries of discourse permeable."[17] But here it is a space that men and women mutually "enter." To "enter these arms" is both to emerge the "he" that sees "her" (to assume the point of view of his vision) and to embrace the "he" that wants "her" (to return his vision by responding to—rather than postponing—desire). By becoming him (entering his arms) the lady will achieve repose (the quest of the dream) and completion (the rest of the dream). She will relax and she will compose the dream she imagines. Her entrance into him will "enter" their love in the chronicles of poetic fame. With that return, "enter" acquires a linguistic meaning. To "enter" is to record. To "enter these arms" is to extend the anticipated dream into the reality corroborated by the phallic hand: both to write the poem the woman dictates and to enact the plot she invents. Reversing sexual roles, she is the enter*er*, the recorder or poet, who writes the story. In the linguistic role, he is the enter*ed*, the body whose life she inspires. In the corporeal role, he is the interred, the dead (or sleeping) "he" she brings to life. His hand follows and extends her commanding presence. She constructs him as the object of her desire and starts the process of materialization which renders her the object of his desire. Their sexuality becomes part of what Butler would call "the phantasmatic field that constitutes the very terrain of cultural intelligibility" (*Bodies That Matter*, p. 6).

When he calls the lady wise, the speaker argues that she protects him both from "dream[ing] all [his] dreame" and from descending into fantasy. Breaking the isolation of a wet dream,[18] she continues it in the physical realm by allowing him to remain aroused with her rather than about her. "Entering these arms" is a way of both moving into his life and pulling him into hers, as (in Genesis) God shared and empathized with Adam's desire. The next stanza should move forward into the Genesis sequence of "cleaving."[19] Instead, it moves backward, to describe the Genesis process of understanding. When he returns to the moment of imminence, the "I" emphasizes their interchangeability. She is most "she" when she is most "he." And he is most "he" when he anticipates her. The dream represents the best of both of them:

> But when I saw thou saw'st my heart,
> And knew'st my thoughts, beyond an Angels art,
> When thou knew'st what I dreamt, when thou knew'st when
> Excesse of joy would wake me, and cam'st then,
> I doe confesse, I could not chuse but bee
> Prophane, to thinke thee any thing but thee. (p. 80)

The three times repeated knowledge is the experience of the Genesis understanding as the "I" portrays the lady as God and himself as Adam. She is the Laura-Mercury who outdoes the man. He is now secondary to her production. The "I" sees his lady seeing the desiring heart which is visible and the imagining head which is knowable. She reads him in the arena before language, in the "behind/before" the Word, and then creates the language which becomes his text. When he moves backward to instinctual knowing, she invents him as Laura-Mercury. When he moves forward to practical "doing," she becomes Laura-Eve. Seeing and knowing, the woman projects herself into his heart and his thought even if what the heart and mind see is *she*. Her sight is fore-sight and her knowledge is fore-knowledge, an infinite regression of mirrors that centralizes the woman as writer of the text the man fleshes out and embodiment in the text of the self she invents.

The lady moves inward so she can look out with him. The dreamer asks her to share his vision as well as his bed. He wants her to be the nascent Eve: first, to crawl back into him through her identification with Adam; and, then, to be the prescient God, and to present herself as his desire. Seeing and knowing are identical. When he *sees* her knowledge, he gives her the controlling gaze, as her vision of him becomes his desire for her. When he deifies her, he returns to her the creative primacy Petrarch stole from Laura and Laura wrested back from Petrarch in the heart-robbery of *Rime sparse* 23. She ratifies his heart by seeing it, first as the knowing God looking ahead to a sexuality she invents and then as the desiring Eve who responds to a sexuality he imagines. His "inside" becomes her "outside." As God, she creates desire. As Eve, she fulfills it. But as Eve not yet born, she is still anticipated, always imminent. His seeing her seeing—his return of the gaze—becomes his feeling her feeling—his response to desire. The poem extends the lady's generating and originating primacy. The expression of sexuality continues their doubly understood—and mutually experienced—quest.

The third stanza threatens to disavow the first two, by eliminating (with the "thou art not thou") the knowledgeable "thou" of the second, and by obviating (with the threat of "else will die") the dreaming "I" of the first. If the strategy of "The Funerall" is to weaken the lady as the man grows, the strategy of "The Dreame" is to make man and woman less. As she is not herself, so he will die. Both poem and poet are thereby "undone." The first two stanzas make her most fully herself when she is most completely responsive to him. In order to be the "she" that is "she," she has to be where he is—at the apogee of potential: the moment before "excesse of joy." When he argues that separation renders her less than what she is, the "I" retracts the masculinity (spirit, purity, and bravery) he bestowed on her as she entered his arms in stanza 1. Left with only a feminine mixture of "feare, shame, and honor," she is bereft of strength: "Thou art not thou." When he annuls her capacity as Yahweh (her "thou art not thou" a second person inverse of "I am that I am"), he refuses to be both her equal as God and her partner as Adam. In the third stanza, his "arms" become the source of his militant and masculinist strength. If she leaves, she loses what she gained by entering him. The prelapsarian oneness is gone, as he is left to die without the "she" that, deprived of his arms, is no longer "he." Donne's reversion to the "he" and "she" in this stanza voices the conventional gender dynamics that the stanza 2 dream obliterates. As it does in Petrarch's appropriation of Laura-Daphne, his movement into a hierarchically superior male mentality—spirit, purity, and bravery—relegates the woman to a petty order of female materiality—fear, shame, and honor. If the idealization of stanzas 1 and 2 consists totally of imagined selves, the reality of stanza 3 returns to essentialized selves and preconceived notions of male and femaleness.

Once having established the necessity of each to the other, the "I" attempts the rhetoric of Adam's "now." With the "perchance" of the torch image, he argues that the lady's flame is kindled by his desire. If his dream is a hope, then its being is constituted by expectation. The "she" that

"saw" and "knew" is the woman who understood that the source of both
their lives is identical. His final plea (or else would die) is not just a ploy to
get her (as brave and valiant) to save his life but an insistence that she
retain her own identity as maker of the poem. Like Eve, she exists as his
quest. Like Adam, he exists as her source. As dreamer who feels desire, as
lover who needs her being, he is critical to her life. She exists (like God) as
his imaginer. He exists (like Adam) as her imagination. As God who
inspires his desire and as woman who fulfills it, she is critical to his life.
The union of Donne's Genesis episode is twofold. God knows man and
therefore creates Eve as Adam's complement. Eve becomes both a companion for man and a sign of God's knowledge. Insofar as she understands
Adam's needs, she is like God. Insofar as she feels with Adam, and insofar
as she came from him, she is like man. She is most heavenly and most like
God when she is most earthly and most like Eve.

If she goes, and the poet dies as a consequence, then she loses the
connection represented by his dream and the being identified by his desire.
The poet must continue to dream in order that she can reenter his arms
and find her present identity in the companionship of his "now" and her
retroactive deification in the "before" of the poet's hope. His last threat
("or else would die") is a vow to stop desiring, to end the process of
expectation through which she can find and recognize herself as the object
of his dreams and the inventor of the poem. To "dreame the hope again" is
to believe that sexuality breeds sexuality. Her appearance in the poem is
contingent on her behavior in life. To become the poet's inspiriting soul,
she must repeatedly re-create herself as desiring woman. The poet's threat
to die becomes a threat to stop beginning again the process which arouses
the lady to be the "she" she was. When the poet dies, he ceases to dream
the vision that leads to the lady's incarnation as an Eve who recognizes,
the lady's deification as God who anticipates, and the lady's extension as
poet who memorializes, desire.

In "Jeat Ring," Donne threatens to become the denying woman. He returns her off-putting gesture with his put-out self; in "The Funerall,"
Donne threatens to undermine the laurelization that the Petrarchan ties
promise. He retaliates against the lady's obscurational tactics with a future oblivion. In both poems, Donne turns the life-giving, socially sustaining gift into the vehicle for denying the giver and society. If the lady in
these poems uses her figurative authority to cancel his life, Donne annuls
the tribute that would sustain her ascendancy. The promised silence in

both poems deprives her of the future immortality Petrarch conferred. In the first two poems, his knowledge of the lady's motives determines his refusal to deify her; in "The Dreame," his exultation in the lady's knowledge determines the end of Petrarchan rivalry. The lady is the acknowledged initiator of sexuality and creativity.

When Donne transforms the poetic situation from an impasse that never knows completion (Laura always elusive, Petrarch always in pursuit) to a relationship that already knows completion (the excess of joy in which both will participate), he also changes the cycle of the gift (the poet returning in tribute what the lady gave in inspiration) into a mutually reciprocated, rather than deferred, knowledge. The sex in "The Dreame" keeps happening and that recurrence is what generates the eternalizing conceit. The lady's continued presence is an active annunciation of her divinely originating capacity. In "The Dreame" Donne argues that poetic immortality, the deification implicit in the eternalizing conceit, corroborates a literal immortality, the divinity explicit in psychological understanding. The "she" who enters "these arms" enters Adam's mind. She pierces the walls of his flesh and bone to emerge her flesh and bone: the Eve he desires. Sexuality is her idea. Entering his arms, she controls the poem she inspires.

In "The Dreame" the knowledge of physical experience emerges as the excitement of mutual rediscovery. The lady generates both an Adam who wants her and an Eve who wants him. She fulfills a dream she inspired; he experiences what she imagined in the dream imagining her. Her gaze is enough to wake him because her vision contains and anticipates action. "She" is dependent on a "he" who responds. She is responsive to a "he" she imagines. When the lady "enters these arms," she emerges the writer. When full knowledge of completion dictates the sexual choice ("and cam'st then"), then the comings and goings of life are included in the representation of an art that is "beyond an Angels."

In the arena of that angelic beyond—a space that first precedes and then exceeds conventional representation—"The Dreame" envisions a sexuality and an art that overcomes Petrarchan denial and libertine disappointment. Yielding to "excess of joy" and moving beyond the Petrarchan angel's codified "no" involves yielding up the culturally inscribed body and imagining an Eve who frees both herself and the poet to "do" the undefined "rest." When he imagines a poetic of satisfaction, the Donne of "The Dreame" reinvents the dynamic of desire.

If Petrarchism calls absence and denial the engendering source of the poet's invention, the poetic of "The Dreame" posits presence and affirma-tion as the regendering source of the woman's inventiveness. Spilling over the forms of desire into the possibilities of "excess of joy," finding success in surplus rather than containment, and dream rather than precision, Donne's "Dreame" transforms the gesture cycle to name poetic gifted-ness—and the gift of the poem—the woman's. By feeling his feeling, the woman redefines divinity. The language of the generated poem is different, though the terms of idealization and the deification of the woman seem like conventional Petrarchism. What's new about the poetry of praise that comes from "The Dreame's" gift is that the man begins to imagine "excess of joy" as if he understood that boundaries—the difference between "he" and "she"—can be suspended. Instead of the clarity of Petrarchan meta-phor, the arena of the dream is permeable. It is an excess to which the woman lends access. Her knowledge sustains sexuality and its language and so re-creates the garden of earthly delights. In "Change," Donne moves away from mortal "joy" into an eternity the woman anticipates. The "eternity" he speaks there is the undiscovered country beyond the borders of the known or remembered. It becomes the woman's space and so bespeaks fluidity and diffusion. But *it is*.

"A PREGNANT BANK"

Contracting and Abstracting the "You" in Donne's

"A Valediction of My Name in the Window" and

"Elegy: Change"

When he renders her the god of his Petrarchan idolatry, "The Dreame" speaker returns to the woman the generating primacy Petrarch took from Laura-Mercury. Through her restored imaginative and physical dominion, she directs the pen and sexuality which he, in turn, devotes to her. But in "Elegy: Change," the poet exceeds "The Dreame's" interchange to imagine a nonphallocentric art, one that goes beyond retracing earthly happiness. "The Dreame" repeats the history of a self-enclosing desire. The "I" imagines a "you" who enters him. "Change" enacts an open-ended desire. The "I" enters the "you." In that reversal, "Change" breaks down all enclosures, its expansiveness different even from the reversals of "The Extasie." There, Donne alternatingly locks in vision, by calling the fortress of the spiritual selves he invents a prison, and frees it, by arbitrarily denying all walls. The "small change" of "The Extasie" reverts to a dominantly male form; the "great prince" is released from prison through his own cleverness. The revisioning in "Change" involves the larger dynamic of "never looking back." The princess kisses herself into life. While in "The Extasie" the dialogue of one calls for a single voice and in "The Dreame" the mutual reverie renders the woman the man, in "Change" the "I" speaks as a woman. The art of "Change" is no longer based on the remnants of Petrarchan control (where fulfillment reinstills the memory of origination). Instead, a different art is envisioned (where departure brings on what has never been imagined). That new poetic reverses the dynamic of the chase. The woman turns not (as Daphne does) into a static tree but into the spirit of movement itself. Her force carves an opening into the light.

When he speaks as a woman, the narrator of "Change" effects what Barbara Johnson calls a "critique of logocentrism [which] opens up a space for a critique of phallocentrism as well."[1] In conventional Petrarchism, the woman is a pretext for the text, her being ancillary to her representation. In "Change," the woman dictates the text. The man is puppet to her ventriloquist. "Change" eliminates the interspace of mirroring and the distance of reflection, the operative physical dimensions of Donne's Petrarchan experiments where an image repeats an aspect of the original and so fills the void of denial. Here there is only the prospect of the immaterial. In "Change," the vision is too large to be held by the frame of an image, its parts too connected to be informed by the stamp of individuation. Petrarchism involves finding the self in the conceit. "Change" dissolves the self in formlessness. If, in Petrarchism, as William Kerrigan argues, "metaphor is the clearest thing around,"[2] in "Change," eternity makes *things* seem less important. In opening the dyad, the woman no longer shapes the man's desire. She unhinges its expression. The "musicke, joy, life, and eternity" produced in the nursery of "Change" suggest surges forward that involve no returns, surges outward that break all boundaries. Abstraction replaces Petrarchan formalism. Connection obviates the need for sublimation. Voicing the woman's vision, the "I" slips into the "you." In "The Dreame," the woman enters the man's arms and guides the hand that figures her idealization. In "Change," the lovers no longer look back to each other; instead they look ahead in the woman's direction to a prospect that carries them both along. The man's entrance into the woman is assumed, not announced. His doubling is totally opposite in its quiet impact to that of the professed union of "A Valediction: Of My Name in the Window's" "I am you." In its emphasis on effusion and escape, "Change" represents Donne's rejection—as the frame and enclosures of "Window" suggest his disparagement—of Petrarchan conventions.

"Window" is a poem about the vitrification of too much thinking. "Change" is about melting, the elimination of reflection. When Donne writes in the third stanza of "The Dreame" that "staying show'd thee, thee," he argues both that the eternalizing power of the poem is the show-and-tell of the woman's divinity and that the staying power of the woman is the reason for her continued representation in the poem that worships her. When he invites the lady into the poem, Donne's strategy in "The Dreame" is to make her its inseminator. In his Petrarchan remonstrances, Donne's argument is: "imagine what poems you'll get if you reconcile your desire to mine; imagine what you won't hear if you insist on breaking me." With the poem as mirror, Donne represents its images in terms of the present situation he either wants to eliminate (as in "Window") or perpetuate (as in "The Dreame").

In these poems, the Donne persona emerges as what William Kerrigan calls the "master rhetorician, doing little things with big words, exhorting, commanding, seducing, threatening, mounting winkingly fallacious arguments in order, over and over again, to have his way."[3] In "Change," where the "way" is the woman's, the "I" abandons argument entirely. In "Window," Donne returns to the bare bones of the self. Having scratched his argument out so that it reflects finally the dead end of rhetoric, his "way" emerges hardly audible and barely visible, the ghost writings of a ghostly writer. "Window" splits its speaker into two multidimensional personae: the expansive self-aggrandizer of the opening (who insists on the initiating primacy of his intent) and the judgmental self-deprecator of the conclusion, whose dwindling voice compacts Narcissus in Echo and contracts the mirroring extravagance of the manic opening to the depressive reductiveness of a failed rhetoric.

Dying Talk

Recent critics concur that the "I am you" of "Window" is serious and that Donne, elsewhere accused of being only concerned with self-reflection, has committed himself to the woman's wishes.[4] His self is hers, they say, reasoning that the "I" of the poem not only writes about the woman but thinks like her. The mirror of the glass suggests that the lady is the "fairest of them all," both as the poet's origin, on departure, and his destiny, on return. Elaine Scarry argues that the inclusiveness of the "word-image-object triad in the poem is not subverted by the fact that there are two persons present since, within the fiction of the poem, man and woman are one."[5] But it is possible to see the fiction of that oneness as a rhetorical device. As persuasive strategy, the "I am you" of the second stanza is an attempt to make the "you" into an "I" and thereby to undermine the achieved love celebrated. In "Window," Donne practices and comments on Petrarchan revision. He calls the first stanza lady the mercurial engraver of his vision but then he denies that tribute through actions that centralize only his controlling art. The process attempts both to cover up his fear of the lady's resistance (by overwriting her hardness with his intensity) and to control it in his insistence that she position herself as reader of his text. When he pays lip service to the lady's initiative in a Petrarchan homage to her gaze, the "I" directs her eye to his reformulations.

Inventing the future not out of a benevolent confidence but out of a genuine uncertainty caused by an initial insecurity, Donne uses the instrument and subjects of one medium—the diamond of glazing and pose of portraiture—as the vehicle for another—the pen of poetry and auto-biography of self. "Window" is both an attempt to impose the "I" onto the "you" and an admission that the attempt fails. The imposition is voiced by the presiding "I" of the poem, the admission by the separated poet, the one who sees the limits of Petrarchism. That second self surfaces only at the end to announce the death of love, lovers, self, and other; the hollow vision is reflected in his empty talk. In "Window," Donne formulates an aesthetic ostensibly based on picturing the woman but actually premised on a deconstruction of the Petrarchan mentality. By distancing the poet from the "I," Donne presents a portrait of the artist in love that eventually shatters. In "The Broken Heart," Donne fixes the blame for fragmentation on the "you." In "Window," the "I" bears the self-critical brunt of the indictment.

The poem plays with the three functions of glass, defined by Albert Cook as: the window, "which tends to open up on a world beyond the frame of the organized scene foregrounded in the painting," the engraving, which "segments the world into separate ordered scenes," and the mirror, which "presents an assumed self-referentiality."[6] Aware of those three dimensions,[7] Donne's speaker incorporates them to ensure that his image is engraved (as Stella's is in Astrophil) as securely in the lady's bosom as it is in the window. When the "I" invites the woman to enter into his name, he asks her to be vitrified in his life as she is etched in his wishes, perma-nently his.[8] When the "I" says, "I am you," he means: "I want you to think I am you—and I want to make myself think you are I—so that I can be confident that your fidelity and love are what I propose them to be: unfoundering." But his "I am you" really is a way of saying "you are I." The lady is urged to give up her identity for his. Donne uses the trifold glass so that he can explore the implications of the lover's framing device. As "A Valediction: Forbidding Mourning" dissects and attempts to dissolve the fear of the "you" who must stay behind, this "Valediction" reveals and seeks to resolve the fear of the "I" who leaves. The "I" of "Window" hinges the woman's "hardness"—her Petrarchan resistance—to his "firmness"—his creative insistence. In retrospect and prospect, he wants to create a secure love. The manic structure of the poem—where the "I" binds the woman to him by imposing himself on her—is a response to that fear.[9] The depressive substructure of the poem—where the poet, distanced from the imposing "I," reveals the destructive limits of imposition—surfaces in the "dying talk" at the end.

In order for the manic strategy of his poem to work, the woman must remain psychologically and physically where the "I" wants her. The closed casement contains the multiple glasses of the poem, the glass as mirror and the glass as window, a picture in words of the "I's" longing to be crystallized in art and love. And there are five versions of those glasses: the eye and diamond of stanza 1; the stars and tears of stanza 4; and, finally, the poem as all of them. The eye and diamond (as seer and recorder) are instruments of art. The stars and tears (as foreseers and reactors) are versions of nature. Throughout, the "I" attempts to control the "you" of the poem, in stanzas 1 and 2 by overtly calling himself a reflection of her, in stanzas 6 and 7 by commanding her to reflect him. The first and second stanzas outline the manifold functions of the glass as the "I" (assuming the lady will remain both in place as reader of his name and in her place as lover of his self) calls attention to his engraving. The glass is a mirror reflecting her to herself and a window revealing him to her. That duality is used when it suits the "I's" purposes. In stanza 3, it is called an "intireness" which the woman can fulfill. In stanza 5, it is called a "paradise" in which the man can grow. The "I" speaks of spatial and temporal expansion (the mirror as physical doubling, the entireness as enlarged enclosure, the paradise as eternal source) even as he seeks (in the "through-shine" glass of 2, the pattern of 3, the house of 5) to limit—by contraction—the woman's vision. His aesthetics are based on his desire to extend his possession into the past and the future. First, he extols the triple nature of the glass; then he seeks to impose a single vision on it. That single vision always works retroactively to assure the "I's" imposition. His vision controls. Her picture is his. The "I" never really leaves the self that inaugurates the poem.

He attempts to project himself onto the "you" by a process which allows him to superimpose the mirror vision on the window vision and the etched impression on both. He thereby reproduces one all-encompassing self. In order for that enlarged self to survive the present departure, it has to have existed from the very beginning. Dismissing and applying Petrarchism as it suits him, the "I" seeks to have the best of all possible poetics. When he asserts the all-encompassing "I," he escapes Petrarchism and the annihilation of its denials. When he contradicts with the divisive "you," he retains Petrarchism and the empowerment of its inspiration. In the first stanza, the "I" reconstructs his amorous origin and claims that everything stems from the woman. Then in stanza 2 (lines 5–6) he denies that claim to assert that everything stemmed from him. When he says, "I am you," he really means to deprive the lady of any selfhood apart from his. Though he says that they are clearly two people, finally he denies doubleness. The manic enterprise of his reconstruction allows for the contradiction. He can call his love both a unity (one self) and a combination (two selves) as long as all the selves are his. In stanza 1, he unites the lovers. Her eyes are the original source of his engraving. In stanza 2, he separates them and calls attention to the dual function of the mirror-window and to the individual selves displayed there. But (with yet another reversal) in 2 he denies separateness through what he calls "love's magic." Retroactively, both stanzas revert to him. The deconstruction cements his security.

Emphasizing separation in stanza 2, the "I" refers to the manifold possibilities of the glass as its "rules." Denying separation, he calls its extensive function, in 1 and 2 respectively, a "charme" or "magique." That "charme" occurs because of the poet's imposition of yet another function. His etching triples the use of the glass and describes his quest in the poem. The quest is triggered by a depressive fact appearing somewhat harmlessly in the first stanza: a reference to hardness. When the "I" makes the lady's "hard" piercing the source of his engraving, he refers, however unwittingly, to the Petrarchan convention where the unyielding woman wounds the man who, in turn, creates the art eternalizing his agony. The "I" attempts to evade that future by making her hardness the equivalent of his firmness. Such an evasion would undo Petrarch by rendering the man's insistence rather than the woman's resistance the origin of the poem. The evasion also undoes libertinism, whose hardness is linked almost directly to Petrarchism. The woman who initially resists him in stubborn denial is the woman who subsequently betrays him in callous indifference. The poet's doubts about the initial stages of his love lead directly to the concluding dissipation of it. He fears what he idealizes in the woman: the resistance that links her to the denying Laura-Daphne who undermines his sexual firmness; and the evasiveness that connects her to the scornful Laura-Mercury who challenges his artistic dominance.

The process of extension begins in the first stanza when the "I" describes a compounded firmness equal to his:

> My name engrav'd herein,
> Doth contribute my firmnesse to this glasse,
> Which, ever since that charme, hath beene
> As hard, as that which grav'd it, was;

> Thine eyes will give it price enough to mock
> The diamonds of either rock. (p. 64)

His psychological certainty adds to the physical stability of the window which becomes as solid as he was when he engraved it. The diamond needle penetrates the glass to make it equal to him. In its firmness, the needle is an extension of the lover; in its shining, it is an extension of the glass. The connecting needle is a link and a parallel for the things connected—window and lover. Since the glass has been acted upon by the needle, it becomes the lover. He has given his phallic firmness to the glass. But that extension forward from man to glass is shattered in the last lines of the first stanza with the conventionally poetic assumption that the woman's eyebeams are the real source of artistic identity. The eye is seen neither as absorber nor as reflector but as piercer, superior to the diamond instrument that engraved the lover's name into the glass. Her eye surpasses the needle and the lover's pen in its ability to grave. It imitates (mocks) the artifacts and at the same time laughs at (mocks) their artistic enterprise by preempting them. Their engravement deadens; hers inspires. The woman of this vision is at once Laura-Daphne, the poet's denier, and Laura-Mercury, the poem's denier. If he engraves the glass, she engraves the "I"; her "hardness" precedes his firmness, rendering the glass an extension of the eyebeams that initially pierced him. Skewered by her projections, the impressed "I" is hers. In that construct, she writes on him, becoming Laura-Mercury to his Battus. Her inscription dictates his description. Calling the woman's eyes the source of the poem, Donne establishes the lady as the poet's double Laura and so adds the substructure of Petrarchan denial to the poem. His fears of the lady's sexual unattainability and his concession to the lady's generating primacy render his foundation uncertain. The self-doubt fostered by the lady's sexual and poetic resistance mandates the contradictory aggressiveness of the second stanza expansion.

The method of the first stanza extension (from woman, through lover, to glass) is denied in the first four lines of stanza 2, where the "I" uses other tactics to praise the glass. At first, he speaks of its dual nature and attempts to solidify his manic vision by making the glass a container big enough for both of them:

> 'Tis much that Glasse should bee
> As all confessing, and through-shine as I,
> 'Tis more, that it shewes thee to thee
> And cleare reflects thee to thine eye. (p. 64)

In these four lines, the glass contains both his all-confessing self and her all-reflective self. He is associated with the glass as window, she with the glass as mirror. He is transparent, she, luminescent. According to those "rules," each retains his/her identifying properties—he, his constant openness; she, her constant light. Transparent in its openness and dazzling in its brightness ("Tis much / tis more"), the double function is fixed by what he demands: her constancy. Standing in front of the mirror, she sees the idealized woman the lover extols. Reading his name etched in the glass, she has it framed within the parameters of her bosom. Imprisoned by her double role, she must remain fixed in place at the window even if he travels all around the world. By referring to doubleness, the second stanza's first four lines seem to deny the unity of the opening stanza. The glass compounds two separate intensive selves. But when, in the last two lines, the "I" expands love's magic, he undoes the doubleness. He breaks the "rules" and imposes a singleness whereby he can ensure her commit- ment: "But all such rules, love's magique can undoe, / Here you see mee, and I am you." Thus if he *is* she, then he *was* she when the initial extension occurred. Read retroactively, these lines render his initial firm- ness the source of the extension in the first stanza.

He is at the center and frame, since he is—and always was—she. Like Petrarch's dismantling of Laura-Mercury at the end of *Rime sparse* 23, that undoing has as its origin a refusal fully to recognize the otherness the "I" ostensibly celebrates. It is his vision that reigns. His firmness replaces her hardness and so obviates any doubts. He breaks the rules of "doubleness" by seeking to impose a singleness whereby he can command her fidelity. By the end of the second stanza, the "I" has placed himself in the originating position. If he is her *now*, then he was her *then* when the process of engravement began. The picture was always his.[10] His rhetoric revises the past, rendering his intensity the origin of her placement, even as it com- mands the present, rendering her stability a function of his control. He is therefore eternally the writer, she eternally the reader, of his text. Her bosom frames his name. But she reads what he has written on her. That relationship casts her as secondary to his production even as it denies her both the biological origination he ostensibly celebrates in the "I am you" and the phallic insemination he presumably worships in the stylus of her starry eye-beams. What starts out as an anamorphic vision—with two alternative readings—emerges a single obsession—with the poet's writing at the center.

When, in the third stanza, the "I" gives the woman a proposed task, he encapsulates the process of the poem, referring both to the "rules" of doubleness and the "magic" of extension: "You this intirenesse better may fulfill, / Who have the patterne with you still." In the "intirenesse," she represents the extensive process of the first stanza; in the pattern, she possesses the rules of stanza 2, lines 1–4. The "you" who contains him ("I am you") simply retains the better vision by remaining *the same*, keeping the intensifying selves of stanza 2, lines 1–4 and the extended selves of stanza 1 and stanza 2, lines 5–6. She is both the mold as originator and prototype as copy. The physical immobility of her stillness governs the eternalizing conceit of his rhetoric, as the psychological constancy of her fidelity dictates the imitative pattern of his lines. Immobilized statue, she is the idealized image he projects. Faithful guardian, she is the role model he emulates. Locked in those stillnesses, she is glued to the window. Though her steady gaze keeps him within her scope, his steady rhetoric keeps her "still" in that place. Though her vision allegedly directs his sight, her position—in front of the window—is determined by his despera-tion. Her looking at his represented agency in the window eclipses her look as agent of that representation. Her reading is secondary to his writing.

If the "I" revises the future with the stillness he projects in the third stanza, he also attempts to revise the past by referring to an idealized and paradisiacal beginning. In the fifth stanza, the "intirenesse" widens and she absorbs "all [his] souls" in terms of a remembered loyalty:

> Then, as all my soules bee,
> Emparadis'd in you, (in whom alone
> I understand, and grow and see,)
> The rafters of my body, bone
> Being still with you, the Muscle, Sinew,' and Veine,
> Which tile this house, will come againe. (p. 65)

As mother and lover in stanza 5 she controls his emotional growth ("un-derstanding . . . seeing") and physical anxiety. He acquires a "stillness" with her that pacifies (muscles, sinews, and veins) even as it fortifies. As mother, she provides the initial rafters. As lover, she roofs the house of the self, presiding over his reassimilation. Awaiting his return, she will restore him to what he was. That restoration recalls the initiating firmness of his love and honors his original being in her. Stanza 5 presents a totally revi-sionist history as the "I" proves not only how he is her but how he *was* her from childhood on. She is, and always was, the house of his self. With stanza 5, the "I" returns to the extensive self. If stanza 3 guarantees the speaker's future in the "entireness" of her commitment, 5 guarantees the lovers' past in the "paradise" of her containment. Once more, the woman emerges a projection of the man, her idealization the result of his construction.

As if the "I" hadn't imposed his singleness enough until now, he makes one more attempt in stanzas 6 and 7, where the stars and tears create a natural configuration to match the artistic one he has imposed so far. Having exhausted the glasses of art, the poet reverts to the glasses of nature—shining stars and mirroring tears—to reinforce his vision:

> As all the virtuous powers which are
> Fix'd in the starres, are said to flow
> Into such characters, as graved bee
> When these stars have supremacie,
>
> VII
>
> So since this name was cut
> When love and griefe their exaltation had,
> No door 'gainst this names influence shut;
> As much more loving, as more sad,
> 'Twill make thee: and thou shouldst, till I returne,
> Since I die daily, daily mourne. (p. 65)

As the perceived hardness of stanza 1 traveled from woman to lover through the glass, so the "virtuous powers," fixed in the stars, flow from the heavens in yet another revised past and lead directly to yet another imagined future in the tears of the lady's projected daily mourning at the end of stanza 7. That flow is the "I's" last attempt to legitimize the extensive self. Ignoring the multiple nature of the glass, the "I" seeks to make the world a mirror of his singularly composed self. In the configuration he dictates, the constant pattern of her mourning would mirror the daily death he dies from her denial. At the center and frame is the "I," who, becoming the woman of the past, usurps her originating power and, controlling the woman of the future, deprives her of any activity but his. The glass becomes an abyss. Instead of building on the accumulated history and anticipated destiny of separate and individualized selves, the "I" attempts to expand the hollow reflection of his expansive self. That last and cosmic idolatry leads immediately to the downward vision of the eighth stanza, where the "I" graphically describes (in the alien lover, corrupt maid, and purloined letter) the betrayal he initially feared. The construct of his effort to combine art and emotion and to impose (with the preserving entirety, initiating paradise, and encircling stars) his chronology on the world is shattered by the imagined lady's insistence on opening the window and thereby inviting in the world. While the "I" seeks the means to make the glass into a mirror of self-perpetuating love, the "she" of his desperate imagination opens the frame (and by implication spreads her legs) to a sequence of new lovers. The betrayal scenario is a déjà-vu, since it is based on an initial fear masked in the desperate enterprise of stanza 2.

When he describes his future as her, it is his fear that dictates the vision. The departing lover attempts to exact a hold on his love which cannot work. In the center of the through-shine glass sits the transparent poet, who, purposefully making his inside the outside, confesses his fear that the initiating source of his poem is not his firmness but her hardness. It is the resistance of the conventionally Petrarchan woman that leads to the scene of the conventionally libertine betrayal he imagines. To imagine a separate other is to predict the benighted self. At the outside of the shine-out glass is the woman who, through the magical charm of poetic art, sees not herself but him, since in his obsession he is she. Her outside, he insists, is his inside. Since he is calcified in his obsession with her, she must be similarly stilled by his fixation. The reflections of the mirror, stars, tears, and poem have at their center the "I" who wills the ensuing vision into being. In the multiplying stanzas are multiple versions of himself, not the he/she of a couple united despite their polarity but the he/he of an insistent vision which attempts to stamp itself and impose itself everywhere. When he imagines himself in the role of the next lover and in the head of his beloved, he only affirms his failure. Despite the sustained reference to the dual nature of the glass as vehicle for joined individual selves, the "I" reverts to extension as he remakes the woman into a reflection of his vision. Because the "I" obviates the intensive other, the firm love of the opening becomes the insubstantial image of a self unable to form another. In the end, he has only his private vision.

That the poet understands the failure is clear at the end when he refers to the whole poem as "dying talk," the ramblings of a self who seeks, by talking, to avoid and deny the reality of the other his imposition contains. Claiming that "all times finde mee the same," the "I" attempts to keep the woman in place despite his departure. Moreover, the burden of that departure falls on her. She must retain the status quo ante since she has the presumably original "patterne . . . still." The accommodation is hers by an act of rhetorical fiat. When the speaker says "I am you," and when he proceeds to elaborate that becoming through a framework that makes her "you" into the "I," he attempts to forestall a vacuousness caused both by the present physical separation of the lovers and by what may have been their past psychological separation. That manic enterprise fictionalizes not only the future so he can control it but the past so he can believe in it. The "I" of "Window" is so intent on rearrangement that he ignores the possibility of a restless or evasive "other" who may not fit into his scheme. It is his picture that dominates the poem just as his vision initiated it. Seeking eternity through an immobile art, the "I's" crystallization at-tempts to lock the woman on to him. When that fails in the end, he has only a memento mori, a hollow image of his "dying talk."

Claiming to move into the medium of another art, as he moved into the body of another self, the "I" of "Window" devises two counterproductive strategies. First he attempts to write out Petrarchan insecurity by replac-ing its divisions with a unified self. Then he attempts to retain Petrarchan inspiration by legitimizing the woman's divisive power. He ends up cre-atively locked in his own devices and sexually replaced in his own sce-nario. The "engraving" of "Window" emerges an engravement, a burial of the lover caught in his single self.[11] Contrastingly, in "Change," the lover is freed from the confines of his own vision as he slips into the lady's expansiveness and recognizes the connection between a fluid self and the larger movements and music of the world. "Window" indicts Petrarchan appropriation, as the narrator—attempting to impose his vision on the woman's gaze—finally sees the reductiveness of his mania.

Taking Leave, Leaving Taking

The remarkable change of "Change" is that the distrustful "I" at the opening speaks the exuberant lines of the conclusion. The narrow-minded hater of art emerges the open-minded lover of music. The misogynist becomes the woman he initially challenged and, like Yeats's "passion-driven exultant man, sings out / Sentences he has never thought."[12] Fi-nally, the "I" ends up arguing with a motherly certainty that "Change' is the nursery / Of musicke, joy, life, and eternity" (p. 20). The "change" he originally doubted becomes the seedbed (as womb) of perpetual exten-sion. The music and joy he speaks of here reverse, in the echoing craft he praises, his initial condemnation of the arts. And the easy flow from life to eternity contrasts to the "hard seal" demanded by his opening fear. The poem has three stages: part 1 (lines 1–14), where the "I" voices his doubts about the "you" and then launches into a disquisition about the connection between women and the arts; part 2 (lines 15–24), where the "I" reverses himself and describes man's inevitable link to women and their natural largesse. That section ends with the woman as river-mother and the poet (as jealous child) begging for her attention. Finally, in part 3 (lines 25–36), the poet no longer addresses the woman. He neither challenges her faith nor begs for her faithfulness. He simply crosses over into her, speaking as she would.

In the poet's initial diatribe, the arts are flimsy, ephemeral, and feathery—as fluffy as the women they represent. But in the ecstatic vision at the end, the arts emerge what the poet wanted at the opening—a link to eternity and a connection that lasts. "Change" begins as a challenge to libertinism and ends as an invocation to liberalness. The exuberance of the last lines suggests something more than what Helen Gardner calls Donne's "sophistry."[13] The speaker does not merely echo the lady's view out of revenge. Rather the change is Ovidian as the speaker moves from a rigid, judgmental self into the restless and flowing other. The concluding epigram represents the poet's acceptance of the woman's restlessness even as it includes his early fear that the willingness by which the lady became his lover merely supports her openness to the next lover. The self-doubt that inscribes the manic enterprise of "Window" surfaces in the accusatory tone of the opening.

Initially, part 1 revolves around two premises: (1) the speaker is all powerful and (2) woman's relationship to man is dependent (as in Genesis 2). In rapid sequence those premises are overturned. The woman emerges dominant and independent in herself (as in Genesis 1) and the speaker is reduced to an observer and cataloger of her power. The reversal occurs early in the poem with the comparison "women are like the arts." An echo of Donne's cynic in the *Paradoxes*, the speaker transforms his fear of the lady's faithlessness into a fact he condemns:

> Women are like the Arts, forc'd unto none,
> Open to'all searchers, unpriz'd, if unknowne.
> If I have caught a bird, and let him flie,
> Another fouler using these meanes, as I,
> May catch the same bird; and, as these things bee,
> Women are made for men, not him, nor mee. (ll. 5–10)

In this section, the "I" moves from arts to birds, inverting the direction of his paradox "Why doe Woemen delight so much in Feathers," where Donne claims both that women admire feathers and that they resemble them. In the first case, they like feathers because "they thinke that feathers imitate wings and so shewe theyr restlesnes and Instability."[14] Their love of feathers confirms their love of change. But that love of change is connected so closely to *plumarios* (artists) that instability emerges as the source of art. In the essay, Donne sees the arts as contingent on a superficiality which he links to a womanly source. Not only does the essayist remove himself from women, he also divorces himself from those men who depend on women: "It must bee confest that some men also love feathers, but they are courtiers or souldiers, men (though perfectly contrary in theyr courses, yet) concurring in a desire of pursuing woemen, and assimilating themselves unto them."[15] Conflating the pursuit of women with an "assimilation" of them, Donne argues that an admirer of women becomes like what he admires. Since the cynic denigrates women because of their artifice, he also disdains artists who love women. All share a flighty featheriness. The equation establishes women and art as independent entities since both have as their uniting force a sense of freedom from ties. Like the feather plucked from the bird who is himself a creature (a fowl of the air) free from bounds, the woman and the arts have a life of their own. In the essay, Donne maintains: feathers = women = art. All three have in common the inconstancy that seems to separate them from their origin, a point which Donne enforces, by contrast, when, distinguishing men from women, he refers to a Latinized Plato: "*Animal bipes implume* (man is a two-footed animal without feathers)."[16]

The male is disassociated from the arts and women by his feet—planted firmly in the earth and his featherlessness—permanently grounding him. Since feathers are for birds of the air, to be featherless is to be earthbound. The presumed heaviness of men contrasts to the asserted lightness of women, a flightiness (resembling Cixous's *voler*)[17] that negates all attaching impulses. Like the two-footed animal, men are tied to their earthly origin. Like the feathered bird, women are frivolous creatures—unconnected to anyone and, by implication, open to all. In the comparison of the arts, Donne, the essayist, emphasizes that what is conventionally thought of as the *dependence* of women on men is less important than the *differences* between women and men. Contemporary women, like the arts and like the woman in Genesis 1, seem to have emerged full blown. Similarly, the initial speaker in "Change," so hoping to establish the dependency of women on men that he sets himself up as a god at the opening, concludes, in the simile of line 4, that women are "forced unto none." That lack of obligation eventuates into the lady's reduction from prized bird to consort for foxes and goats. The speaker in the first part of the poem establishes the woman as object to be discovered, her visibility overhead rendering her fair topic for the fowler who identifies (and befouls) her as his target.

Like the god in the opening section, the searcher and fowler cling to Genesis 2 when they demand a seal—something that confirms a relationship. Both the searcher and the fowler (the other men who covet what the speaker has) attempt to capture, define, and confine what—in its feathery flightiness—is free. Both identify what should be in the public domain as theirs. Thus the conventional idea that women are made *from* men becomes another conventional idea: women are made *for* men. They are made for men to discover, search, make known, and appropriate. Searching and fowling here emerge what hunting and helasing were for Wyatt: male inscribing pursuits. Like Actaeons, Donne's hunters become violators. Their acts of discovery materialize as acts of publicity through which the women become prized by other men. Once freed from the anterior dependence of contingency, the woman is open to a subsequent perusal of curiosity which unleashes the cycle leading to fear. In the opening lines the "I," who begins as empowerer, ends by recognizing that he is only an admirer of what already exists. *The lady* is the deity, the independent creature, that he initially fears. That independence becomes, in the final image of section 1, a primitive savagery: "all beasts." Idealization and vulgarization emerge functions of male name-calling. In both instances, the woman remains the object men define. When the "I" discovers his logical diminution, he defines the terms of her reduction as a fact of reality: "as these things be." Art and nature resolve themselves in an annihilating bestiality. The "I," who began by asserting his authority, ends this section by acknowledging anarchy.

In the opening section, the woman is defined by the man. In the middle section, the "I" seeks the reverse—to define himself through her. She becomes the container, he the thing contained; she, the mother, he, the child. Instead of viewing the female as "a mode of desire which challenges masculinist epistemology,"[18] he sees it as a vehicle that might now include him. But the inclusiveness is complicated in a way opposite to Shakespeare's "Th' expense of spirit in a waste of shame / Is lust in action." Whereas Shakespeare makes the woman into a wasteland, the "I" here makes her into a fecund-land, ever open (because of her freedom) and ever fertile (because of her liberality):

> They'are our clogges, and their owne; if a man bee
> Chain'd to a galley, yet the galley'is free;
> Who hath a plow-land, casts all his seed corne there,
> And yet allowes his ground more corne should beare;
> Though Danuby into the sea must flow,
> The sea receives the Rhene, Volga, and Po.
> By nature, which gave it, this liberty
> Thou lov'st, but Oh! canst thou love it and mee?
> Likenesse glues love: Then if soe thou doe,
> To make us like and love, must I change too? (ll. 15–24)

In part 1, the woman is art; in part 2, she reverts to nature. And if, as art, the woman denies all origins, as nature (land and sea), she is the destiny to which he (as seed and river) tends.

Swelling (as corn and sea) into a Demeter and Poseidon, she thrives as he shrinks into the seed and river that feed her. Moreover, the "I" who started out as god ends as child to her whims, as jealous child who sees liberty as a rival for her affections: "this liberty / Thou lov'st, but Oh! canst thou love it and mee?" The only way out of the dependent situation the "I" is in here is to begin a new tactic. That new tactic makes him, however, totally dependent on her re-creation. Childishly he proposes a formula for fidelity: "Likeness glues love." Playing on likeness as similarity and likeness as affection, he attempts to apply to her the lesson which applies to him. If they are cemented to each other—according to his ploy—then she won't leave. But that ploy fails as he—in likeness (both because of his affection and imitation)—emerges the "you" who overpowers him. The transformation of him to her in line 28 results from his statement in line 25 that the only way to render love permanent is to become the other. His hope is that she will become him. His reality is that he must become her. The "I" who begs here as child and who asks "must I change too?" emerges in the end the "you" who originally prodded him. His metamorphosis into her occurs as he diminishes and is so swamped by her that no self—no resistant memorializer—is left.

The change at the end results from that loss of memory. At the opening of "Change" the "I's" fear is based on what he imagines the lady's past to have been, but at the conclusion he ceases to worry about history. He is reborn. When, at the opening, the "I" said women and the arts were "enforced unto none," he referred to a detachment that rendered them irrelevant and flighty, superficial and flimsy. But that judgment is nullified at the end when the "I" reverses direction to arrive at the same word "force," used now as an initiating source. The change at the end eliminates both the retrospect of Petrarchan obsession and the prospect of Petrarchan obligation. Since there is no need to possess, there is no presumption of return. The elimination is twofold—first the false relationships are denied; then the real ones are affirmed. The "I" redefines force:

> And soe not teach but force my'opinion
> To love not any one, nor every one.
> To live in one land, is captivitie,
> To run all countries, a wild roguery;
> Waters stincke soone, if in one place they bide,
> And in the vast sea are worse putrifi'd:
> But when they kisse one banke, and leaving this
> Never looke backe, but the next banke do kisse,
> Then are they purest. (ll. 27–35)

When the early "I" speaks of the arts being "enforced unto none," he clings to the standard of male memory. When he now speaks of "forc[ing his] opinion," he means a future, female initiative. The word "opinion" retains its currently obsolete meaning of expectation. Speaking of himself as the instigating womanly force, the "I" moves only forward. He will now "expect" to act as she does. There is still another alternative to remaining and spreading thin: leaving without looking back.

When he redefines change, the "I" calls it a sequence rather than a conversion. The woman, who in the opening sections was the single sea, here is numerous waters, and he, one of many banks. Earlier, the god fixation insisted on oneness; here the human opportunity is manifold: many waters; many banks; and, finally, many kisses. At first, there was a clear barrier between land and sea. Here the borderline between sea and land is uncertain. All the old distinctions are broken, including the critical one of the poem: that between man and woman. When he turns forward, the "I" dispels his initial fear, based as it was on his assumptions about her past. He argues as she would. Loving one is to remain forever captive in space; loving all is to remain forever diminished by disease. The quality the "I" originally demanded (faithfulness) and the quality he subsequently sought (saintliness as opposed to animality) end in a similar annihilation, the former because it demands a permanence of place (an unchanging one), the latter because it demands an allegiance of self (to a predetermined standard). Neither of these possibilities produces life. The first ends in a stinking solid, the second in a dissolving ideal.

Speaking as the woman, the "I" connects the spirit of Genesis 1 to the spirit of Revelations 4. He undoes the "ragges of time" Donne deprecates in the Christmas Day sermon. To be in the spirit as omega, it is possible to be in the spirit as alpha. Life and eternity stem from the point of least contact: "And the spirit of god moved on the face of the waters" (Genesis 1.2). When the spirit moved upon the face of the waters in Genesis, God said "let there be light." The brush stroke is implicated in the sun. The emphasis here is on the lightness, or the blush of light, and the featheriness, or brush of gossamer, in the stroke. The spirit initiates creativity by touching the surface ("on the face of the waters") and releasing the substance (moving *on*). In fact, the touching ("moving on" the surface) signals a departure ("moving on" to the next). The alternative comes finally in the last lines:

> But when they kisse one banke, and leaving this
> Never look back, but the next banke do kisse,
> Then are they purest; Change'is the nursery
> Of musicke, joy, life, and eternity. (ll. 33–36)

Speaking as the woman, the "I" converts the vertical contact of Genesis 1 into a horizontal crossing. The man and woman intersperse not by containing each other, as land receives seed or ocean absorbs rivers, but by a process that anticipates retreat. Life (Genesis 1) and eternity (Revelations 4) are connected through an understanding of movement. The spirit is what moves the waters in Genesis; in "Change" that spirit becomes desire. As the movement in Genesis precedes the light which is the source of life so the movement here—a departure—is a beginning. As the "I" of the poem becomes the woman and the waters overswell the shore, so the kiss signifies an entrance which is also an exit, what Groucho Marx might call a "hello, I must be going." When Donne speaks of assimilation in the essay on feathers, he means a total absorption that is end-stopped. When the "I" speaks of "purity" in part 3, he means remaining untouched, a kind of emotional innocence which results from "never looking back." That passage ends in freedom.

Life, as defined in Genesis 1, and eternity, as defined in Revelations 4, have to do with a being in the spirit, an entrance into the other, which presupposes an exit from the other—like a kiss. To connect life and eternity, the alpha and omega, is to see every moment as the point of initiation signaled by the kiss, a moving on the waters which, like music and joy, is a moving *to* the next water. There are no backward turnings, only looks ahead. The "I" of the opening of "Change" insists on recalling the past even as he fears the future and other fowlers who might, at some subsequent time, catch the same bird. The "I" at the end of "Change" has no need to recall the past since he espouses a poetic which blurs the rigidly established borders of the opening. As the waters kiss the bank, and life evolves into eternity, so the "I" emerges the "other," which was initially so repellent to him. He simply mouthes her words. It is a womanly spirit in him that speaks the joyous lines at the end. "Change" is not an attempt to justify male promiscuity by calling the woman restless. It emerges an exploration of a poetics that results from a desire to emulate—rather than append or write out—the woman. For the persona, the "nursery" progresses beyond sexual completion into maternal anticipation. The "after" of sexuality is turned around to the "before" of reproductivity. That fluidity mitigates between the flightiness of feathers and the immobility of idolatry, to make way for music and joy. The spontaneity of those last lines—the way they open the self into the other and both into the motion of the world—attests to how the "I" of "Change" has become the inspiring "you."[19] Citing differently, the "I" returns to the nursery and gives birth to a new language even as he is reborn as the woman who speaks it.

In "Window," an "I," claiming similarly that he is the woman, ends by remaining fixed in himself. Despite his pretensions, he is reduced to a lethargic, a dying, a single self. In "Change," the single "I" is strengthened by a "you" who celebrates the departure feared in "Window." The easy kissing and leaving of "Change" point not (as in "Window") to the graveyard of memory but to the nursery of anticipation. Like the "seminarie" of Spenser's Garden of Adonis (*TFQ* 3.6.30), that nursery is "by succession made perpetual" (*TFQ* 3.6.47). But the succession is ultimately different from Spenser's Petrarchan returns. The Adonis in Spenser's garden is *replaced* (as are leaves on trees) by newer versions of the same original. The sequence solidifies the original tie. In "Change," replacement is subsumed by something genuinely new—a feeling (joy) and a state (eternity) that result from letting go. In the Petrarchan ethos, an initial break causes a loss which the poet seeks, in poem after poem, to repair. At best, his joy is approximated by, his eternity sublimated in, the laurel.

In "Change," such feelings and states *evolve* so that eternity is a result, not a reaction, and joy is a product, not a contrivance. Similarly, the lovers in Donne's "Change" succeed each other and move (as part of nature's continuing cycle) into the arena of an eternity whose fluidity is already enacted on earth. The "I" of "Window" seeks eternity through an immobile art. His crystallization attempts to lock the woman unto him. But in "Change," the "I" has been so swamped by the "you" that a return to an originating selfhood—separated or extended (as in "Window")—cannot occur. Once kissed, the "I" is so "you'd" that he can shore up neither the props of remembered dominance nor the stays of future continuance. In both poems, Donne spawns and exposes selves who are struggling to be born from or absorbed by an "other" imagined for the struggle. In both poems, the arts are central. In "Window," the triple function of the glass—as window, mirror, and engraving—produces a narrowing frame that reveals the poet at the center, imposing and recomposing an increasingly manic self. In the exuberant conclusion of "Change," the "I," who opened by doubting the stability of all relationships, affirms a fluidity that closes up the gaps in the universe. He connects waters to firmament, the self to other, and life to eternity. The links facilitate an expansiveness found only in the exhilaration of letting go. For the eternalizing conceit of the Petrarchan image, the "I" of "Change" proposes eternity itself, undefined because not yet experienced, still connected because not yet born. The nursery is the seedbed where everything exists in potential and everything is connected because undifferentiated.

In "Change," Donne contrasts the annihilative Petrarchan pursuit (Apollo chasing a woman who only runs away) into a sequence that collapses the quest (Apollo becoming a woman who seems to have an agenda of her own). In acknowledging the existence of the woman's vision, Donne revitalizes the chase. The inamorata no longer flees from the poet; instead, she runs *to* something she desires. That shift, in turn, frees the poet to move from the cognitive, through the intuitive, to the abstract. The woman's desire leads the man to discover something she sees which he has never thought. In the transformations of "The Dreame," the woman embodies the man's thought. The poem reflects that desire and presents a mirror of returns which is at once gratifying and stimulating. As reader, the woman experiences the joy of the ultimate compliment. She is deified. As inspirer, the woman prompts the man to sustain a realization she enjoys. He is ratified, returning to her what she wants him to want. In that mutual fulfillment, the lovers create the poem that describes them. But in "Change," Donne transforms the woman's role so that she is no longer the reader who views the poem as a product of the speaker's rhetoric (the argument of "The Extasie," which insists on a dialogue of one, *overheard* in the "marking") or as a product of her direction (the argument of "The Dreame," which imposes a unity of desire overviewed in the *showing*).

Even in Donne's happy poems, the mirror is set up (the violet reflecting the heavens in "The Extasie," the beloved imitating the lover in "The Dreame") so that the woman doubles the man. The woman responds to the initiative of his wit and ultimately returns him to himself. In *Rime sparse* 23, Laura reads Petrarch's reading of her and voices the devastating critique; in "The Extasie" and "The Dreame," the woman reads the speaker's revisions of her and voices her assenting "yes." "The Extasie" renders her an Echo who repeats the overheard word. "The Dreame" renders her a Narcissus who revives the image seen. Both poems flesh out the hollowness of Petrarchan desire, filling in the empty self with a respectively choral and mirroring other. In both poems, the woman observes the man, in "The Extasie" by hearing, in "The Dreame" by seeing. She responds to the clues in his text as the ideal *man* might: she perceives what needs to be done and does it. The vision of "Change" bypasses such returns. Rather, it never looks back. Its nurseries yield first to life and then to what lies beyond it.

When he follows the womanly lead, the "I" is not smothered as he is in the maternal embrace of such poems as "A Valediction: Of Weeping." He is othered, swept along by the excitement of expectancy, as music flows into joy and life evolves into eternity. In "Change," the "I" initially fears the "you's" volatility, attempting at the opening to fix her as the subject of all men's gaze, as the "I" of "Window" frames the "you" in the projection of his fixation for all the world to see. "Window" remains locked in the dead end of thought, the "I" unhinged by the lady's simple act of defiance, the small opening of the window that shatters everything. But in "Change," the "you" breaks the frame altogether and the "I," already contracted (as seed to her Demeter), passes through her passage into a territory the woman stakes out.

That transformation involves a substitution of the hazy sight and subtle soundings of the wave against the vague shore for the fixed demarcations and rigid vitrifications of mirroring windows. Unsealing the boundaries between sea and shore means unfixing the distance between "he" and "she." Such an unraveling regenders the poem. As the hillside expansiveness of "The Extasie's" pregnant "bank" prefigures the journey from earth to heaven that encompasses the poem's argument, so the watery limnology of sequential "banks" in "Change" represents the imprecise borders that lead to its openings. The purity the speaker of "Change" exalts is not the virginity of Petrarchan denial where "no" cuts off contact, but the expansive labial of womanly assent, where the two lips that embrace in identity with each other include, in the next bank they touch, the new life they formulate.

In using the minimal embrace as the point of contact—the light touch of the kiss equated with the gentle brush of the waves against the shore—Donne attaches the open anatomy of the female body to the pluralizing form of the poem's body. Petrarchism reiterates an already realized form. The image represents a previous thought. "Change" moves into a nonexistent form. The movement yields to expectancy. The lips are their own double, the act of kissing an imprimatur that passes on the double. Voicing the kiss, the poet's outside reflects the woman's inside. If the change of "Change" represents a sequence emblematized by the flowing river, it also suggests a transposition, a topsy-turvy shifting between the two principal loci of the female anatomy. The self-duplicating lips of the mouth opened in the kiss begin to animate the fund of language they contain just as the embracing lips in the nursery of the vulva, as Luce Irigaray maintains,[20] already intimate the stores of lives they enclose. The woman's procreative parts reflect her creative (linguistic) energy. Her upside-down self is her down-side-up other. When he calls "Change" a nursery, the "I" makes it a breeding ground and turns static place into mobile habitat, an enclosure meant to discharge its content.

Calling "Change" a place localizes it in about the same way as the "I" localizes the kiss: by describing it as the movement of waters on the shore. It is a loose localization, the shore eroded by what touches it, as the nursery walls are imploded by their content. Somewhere in the imprecise excess of this unlocalized locale is the energy that collapses form by breaking through what contained it. That energy is the paradox of the kiss, a departure that signals an entrance, a greeting that suggests detachment. In its dual role the kiss returns form to energy: the breath of life that animates the poem. Usually, in the lyric, form is the dead end of energy. Laura's static body represents Petrarch's unrealized and unquenchable desire, as, in "Window," the woman's still-life in front of the glass is framed by the poet's desire to render her life his. An act which undoes form by obscuring boundaries returns energy to its source in movement. Unspecified music and unconditional joy break down the walls of the nursery. But it is possible to feel joy or to hear music by yielding to movement or by accepting its pressure, an acceptance Donne concedes in the kiss. In the surplus sounds of music and beyond the confining structure of metaphor, the speaker is Laura-Mercury in joy. When he loosens the boundaries that determine form, he is Laura-Mercury in abstraction. Finally, when he collapses borders in the flow from life to eternity, he erases the frames that distinguish the "what" of lyric idealization from the confines of the idealizing swain. In the nursery of expectation, there is no denial. In the eternity of realization, there is no sublimation. Music absorbs musician and muse. To speak the woman's vision in the poem is to accept her as the destabilizing force whose agency presupposes the "groundlessness of the ground" upon which Petrarchism builds. In "Change," the ground is watered down. The upper reaches are stretched thin. There are no borders and so there are no limits. Petrarch's restrictive binarisms are exceeded even as his codified forms are abstracted.

Donne's watery vision in this poem seems almost to anticipate what Luce Irigaray says of the "woman's voice":

> It speaks "fluid" . . . is continuous, compressible, dilatable, viscous, conductible, diffusable . . . it allows itself to be easily traversed by flow, by virtue of its conductivity to currents coming from other fluids or exerting pressure through the walls of a solid . . . it mixes with bodies of a like state, sometimes dilutes itself in them in an almost homogeneous manner which makes the distinction between the one and the other problematical . . . it is already diffuse "in itself," which disconcerts any attempt at static identification.[21]

Quoting this passage, Ruth Salvaggio maintains that women "dive into the waters and find that there are no words or maps, no comfortably demarcated spatial boundaries."[22] Speaking as a woman, the Donne of "Change" anticipates a theory of fluidity, his exuberance bypassing the imprisoning form that defines him as male poet. That Donne can speak as a woman in this poem, that he can break through the boundaries of music and life to utter yet another dimension, suggests the exhilaration of his transformation. In "wanting to be the woman," the "I" of "Change" wants to have what she wants. And what she wants is to "leave," to move away from the present arena and into the next one. Her movement suggests an opening to what has not yet been thought or said, an opening which will demand new idioms. "Never to look back" is to move beyond nostalgia for Petrarchan form toward a revelation still to come, an eternity the uncovering Laura, and now the uncovered poet, anticipate in unimpeded "joy."

Marvell

The painter's vision is not a lens,
it trembles to caress the light.

Pray for the grace of accuracy
Vermeer gave to the sun's illumination
stealing like the tide across a map
to his girl solid with yearning.

ROBERT LOWELL,
"Epilogue," Day by Day

"BUSIE COMPANIES OF MEN"

Appropriations of Female Power in "Damon the
Mower" and "The Gallery"

While the Donne chapters focus on personae who bend Petrarchism to suit their amorous designs, the Marvell chapters uncover personae who "muddy" the conventions by finding new ways to love or by avoiding desire altogether. "Marvell's Nymph and the Revenge of Silence" describes the female poet of "Nymph complaining" as she regenders Petrarch and the following chapter records the adventures of the "Appleton House" poet who seeks his selfhood in the space between temporalities and designations[1] even as he severs all cultural ties. Chronicling histories that seem more overtly Petrarchan, the present chapter centers on "Damon the Mower" and "The Gallery," where Marvell distances himself from the ambitions his narrators pursue, as they distort the original and become the women who torment or inspire them. The mimetic mower acquires Juliana-Laura's deadliness; the imitative "Gallery" collector imbibes his Clora-Laura's fertility. In the death-dealing Damon, Marvell twice removes himself from the story, framing Damon with a Petrarchanly conditioned narrator-reader who, hearing the song, comments on it. Similarly, in "The Gallery," he creates a Petrarchanly oriented viewer who, collecting paintings by an unknown artist with himself as subject, renders his gallery a hall of mirrors to a previously fixed contrivance. As center of the man's centrality in both poems, the woman is allegedly the source of vision, Juliana the Petrarchan ice goddess of Damon's idolatry, Clora the Petrarchan earth mother of the collector's artistry. But the self-enclosed system of both poems demands that the woman be what her idolator wants. In "Damon," what the man wants is what the woman gives: death. Marvell's narrator in "The Gallery" wants what she takes: life.

In "Damon," Marvell stages two Petrarchan narrators, the limited reader-observer who establishes the conventional scene in the first three stanzas and stanza 10 and the expansive Damon who grows in the course of the poem both to acquire Juliana's destructiveness and to set himself up as mythological model. In "The Gallery," the narrator is the collector and subject of the paintings. His control of Clora issues from the seeming stages of her control. In "Damon," Marvell comments on Petrarchan fatality by moving into its conversional premises. In "The Gallery" Marvell comments on Petrarchism's hubris by moving away—with another art to which the poem alludes—from its possessiveness altogether. But in both poems Marvell himself has the last word. In "Damon," he suggests that the demonic power the mower acquires from the woman is the dizzying prospect of multifoliate, actually defoliative, ruin. In "The Gallery," he argues that the self-aggrandizing art the woman mimics is the claustrophobic passion of the speaker's single-chambered, actually single-minded, obsession. In both poems, speakers who take on women's power find themselves contracted to their transformations. As Marvell—framing lens in hand—moves away from the enclosures of Damon's deadly scythe and the gallery's narrowing closet, his personae move inside their creations. Damon is encircled by the sharp-edged scythe that cuts him out. The "Gallery" narrator is constricted by the heavily laden walls that shut him in.

Both "Damon" and the "Gallery" narrator follow the habit of self-doubling established in Renaissance mythographies that render to male animals the priorities of female earth-motherhood and to female Time the properties of male Eternity. These fusions cross genders and confuse function in the same way that Damon acquires Juliana's deadliness and the "Gallery" narrator appends Clora's fertility. When it describes the life-giving woman, Richard Linche's late-sixteenth-century translation of Cartari resorts to an atmospheric ambivalence that denies gender differences. The conversion of kinds in the metamorphoses Linche enumerates simply prepares for the appropriation of female functions by the men Linche empowers. First he disputes chronology; then he dismisses clearly defined roles. Linche quotes Diodorus's speculations about the animals that surround Mother Earth in the ancient statues dedicated to her:

> *Diodorus* and many others are of opinion that the Lyons so dedicated unto [Mother Earth] signified that she was once fed and nourished by them on that Mountaine Sipilus, as it is read also of many others that have beene kept alive and preserved by wolves, warts, Beares and serpents. The Naturalists, and such as have laboured for the vertue and nature of things produced, say that the elements admit in themselves such a coherence, communencie and coniunction, that one is easily changed into the nature of another, according as the air becometh insensate and grosse or pure and rarified. And in that regard there ought

to follow lesse admiration among us of such intricate names, effects and properties of the gods of the auncients, as the one sometimes understood for one thing, and sometimes for another.[2]

The lion suckles the earth and so seems to have been created first. In the myth of Romulus and Remus, the female animal nourishes and protects its royal foundlings. She thereby proves more gentle than the human parents who abandoned them. But in Linche's approximation of this myth, the male lion mothers Mother Earth and thereby claims the nutritive powers that give him both ascendancy and primacy. That is, since nurturers are always older than the creatures they suckle, the male lion or boar fathers must have preceded the earth mother they project: "she was once fed and nourished by them." Such transformations—verified by the Naturalists— dissociate nurturing from gender.

Linche's answer to the riddle he himself invents speaks to a transformational ethos that presupposes the fluidity necessary for the leaps he takes: "One is easily changed into the nature of the other." In *A Midsummer Night's Dream*, Demetrius dismisses his past exploitation of Helena when he pleads that "these things seem small and indistinguishable / Like far-off mountains turned into clouds" (4.1.185–86). Here Linche similarly fuses boundaries to justify male proprietary rights. As interchangeable parts, the properties of the ancient gods become the changing instruments of a male-dominated hegemony. The king of beasts comes first. He attributes to himself the nutritive function of the female and then redistributes that function to his fellow wolves, warts, bears, and serpents. If, as rock in *Rime sparse* 129, Petrarch "thinks" and thereby fathers the world, in this passage, as nurturer, the male wolf precedes and subsequently masculinizes Mother Earth. A loss of "coherence, communencie and coniunction" is caused when one thing implodes into the other. In the first case, definitions don't matter. In the second, opposites converge. The first conversion clouds over differences. The second mirrors likenesses so there can be no differences.

As an example of the mimesis whereby men claim for themselves a power traditionally assigned to women, Linche describes how female Time imitates its seeming opposite—eternity:

And therefore Trismegistus, Plato and the Pythagorickes, called Time the Image of Eternitie: in that it is revolved in itself, and admits no date. Whereupon for the more ample and copious manifestation thereof, we will heare the opinion of Claudius in his Stiliconyan commands who there makes a description by a Serpent that compasseth round with her bodie the denne or cave wherein she lyeth, in such sort, that making as it were a circle, she holdeth in her mouth the end of her taile: by which is signied the effect of time, which in itself alwaies goeth round: which description is taken from the Egyptians, who before that the use of letters and of writing was invented signied the circumference of a yeare by a serpent with her taile between her teeth.[3]

If time is the image rather than the opposite of eternity, if woman is the image rather than the opposite of man, then the objects of the world are always self-referential. To be "revolved in the self" is to have had no chronological beginning, to have always been in existence—like eternity. As female serpent, Time seems to have sprung, full blown, from the eternity she mirrors. She realizes in her physical body the ordinarily unseen visionary state. After feeding by male lions, female earth motherhood becomes possible; similarly, *after* imitating male eternity, Time initiates the sequence of division for which she is destined. In both cases, male models determine the respectively life-giving and life-denying female roles. Depicted as the female source of endings, Time mirrors Eternity—here characterized as the male stay against endings. Female time is a weak, and hence unstable, version of male immortality.

In "Damon the Mower" and "The Gallery," a male "I" who has been victimized by a woman similarly finds the means to mirror the female power he fears. Thus each becomes the avenger Julian Pefanis describes in "the revenge of the mirror people."[4] In both poems, the "I" masters the woman who initially mastered him. Through a process of appropriation and mimesis, each speaker names himself the sole arbiter of his universe. In "Damon the Mower," Damon emerges the female siren. In "The Gallery," the narrator retrieves beginnings, turns life into art, and mirrors the female earth mother he names. Standing apart from the men who would be women in "Damon the Mower" and "The Gallery," Marvell demonstrates how their egocentricity distorts the world they seek to control. Both poems present narrators who are dramatic representations of opposite sides of the Petrarchan spectrum: Damon sides with the death-dealing woman; the "Gallery" narrator appends the life-giving woman. Both narrators end up triumphantly energetic despite the unmanning experiences recorded in their poems. The "Gallery" speaker occupies a visual space that centralizes his control. "Damon" moves into the Petrarchan linguistic space as the narrator and Damon set up competing stories. The narrator issues the conventional plot of the lover's victimization. But Damon offers a counterplot. First he frames Juliana in the scythe-phallus of his conversionary art. Then he comes in for the kill with the scythe-penis of his penetrative power. But what he kills is the poem. Castrating himself, he stops the cycle of desire at its physical and imaginative source.

By His Own Scythe: Damon as Demon

Paul Alpers maintains that Damon grows in the course of the poem so that he seems more compatible to the sophisticated narrator who initially tells his story.[5] But it might be argued that Damon moves beyond the narrator's Petrarchan conventionality into the arena of Petrarchan self-creation. In Virgil and Theocritus, as Alpers shows, the shepherds comfort themselves in the life-possibilities of other loves; in Marvell's poem, Damon finds solace by absorbing Juliana's deadliness. He progresses through three stages to acquire from Juliana the demonic energy which she seems at the opening to be hoarding for herself. The initial view of Damon comes from the narrator who establishes the typically Petrarchan situation of the poem. The next Damon to emerge is the one attached to an un-Juliana-ed past. In this revisionist chronicle, Damon is both the beloved child of the world and its originating center. Finally, appropriating Juliana's power through the transposed chronology the mythographers derived from Mother Earth and approximating the power of Time from the mimetic capacity the mythographers attribute to it, Damon emerges the destroyer Juliana originally was. He replaces the history Juliana gave him—a past in which he is totally devalued—with an earlier time he creates—a past which is based on his potency. Both histories seem to be vying for space in the present of Damon's psyche. How can he reconcile the time when he was "the mower Damon known" to the time of his insignificance, a time determined by Juliana's indifference to his being?

The answer to the conflict comes in stanzas 8 and 9. First, in 8, Damon demonstrates how he absorbs the capacities of Mother Earth to become the formulative center of his world. Then, in stanza 9, he adopts the destructively female trait and, like Linche's Time, emerges capable of requiting Juliana in kind. When he renders to himself a power beyond the limitations of the biological and psychological constraints of his actual situation, Damon first absorbs what the mythographers call female earth-motherhood and then what, in the opposite mood, they label as the femme fatale. In both cases, he is seductive. He sets himself up as the center of attraction and thereby reverses the narrator's Petrarchan impasse. Fashioning Death after himself, Damon establishes his cutting edge. He is first in line. In the self-enclosure of her encirclement, Linche's Time consolidates her identity. Similarly, Damon establishes his profession as the original that Death emulates. Death is a mower *too*, the feared divider modeled after, and therefore secondary to, Damon's divisiveness. As prototype, Damon establishes boundaries, the Petrarchan formulations of maleness dependent on his consolidation of self. But that oneness is almost immediately complicated as Damon merges with Juliana. When he mows himself, Damon literally effects the castration Juliana symbolically enacts. When he cancels desire, that castration ends both his Petrarchan bondage and tribute: the Petrarchan sigh scythed. At the height of his originating power, Damon stops the poem. The scythe short-circuits the idolatry of Damon's infatuation.

Contrastingly, the narrator is mired in a Petrarchism he can't escape: his view of nature is a sympathetic reading of Damon's plight; his view of Juliana, an automatic indictment of her cruelty. Conditioned by his expectations, the narrator reads the world to isolate and condemn Juliana. He fixes her as the Laura-Daphne of Damon's trap. What the narrator-reader is unprepared for, finally, is Damon's transformation of himself from first-person recorder of his own plight in 4 and 5, through first-person historian of his own evolution in 6 through 9, to first-person director of his own metamorphosis in 11. Once he appropriates Juliana's deadliness, Damon makes her over into *his* image. In the opening sections, Damon has two detractors: the first, the Petrarchan narrator who fits him into a conventional plot where Damon is the frustrated singer of, and Juliana the frustrating source of, romantic failure; the second, Juliana, who refusing both his tributes and his sex, denies him any primacy at all. To defeat the narrator, Damon slides into Juliana and amplifies her denial of his love into a denial of all life. To defeat Juliana, Damon turns her into himself. He preempts her impulse to deny and thereby emerges the ultimate "naysayer," Death. At the opening, Damon is the fool in love, totally victimized by Juliana. At the end, he is Juliana, the poem totally decimated by his emergence. In aligning himself with Death, Damon fits into the image of Laura-Mercury who cuts out the heart of Petrarchan narrative.

Incorporating Juliana-Laura, he eliminates her. Subsuming Petrarch, he cancels the narrator. Damon, not the narrator, speaks the last lines of the poem. In Wyatt's "Process of time" and "Go, burning sighs" or Donne's

"The Broken Heart" and "The Funerall," the Petrarchan speaker makes a compact with the audience against the lady he refuses to laurelize and holds up the prospect of future poems with a better lady. Here there is no future. There is only death in the figure of Damon, whose scythe-pen-phallus replicates—by annexing Juliana—images of its own self-cancellation. With an appended Juliana, Damon writes out the narrator. He tells his own tale only to define himself in alienation. Doing to himself what Juliana did to him in the Petrarchan narrator's story, Damon cuts out the Petrarch essential to the dyad.

"Damon" imbricates several stories. In the first five stanzas, he is the victim of love. In the last six, he is the victimizer, mirroring the woman who hurt him. Stanzas 1 through 3 reflect the narrator's conventional Petrarchism. In stanzas 4 and 5 Damon himself follows the narrator's role, depicting himself as tormented oxymoronically by the fires of Juliana's heat and the cold of her icy breast. But in stanza 6 a new portrait is uncovered as Damon revises his genealogy and recalls another past, the one behind the before of his life with Juliana. As he takes himself out of the narrator's Petrarchan story, he removes himself from Juliana. He defeats both enemies by defining different friends. In 6, he revives the pastoral enclave where he felt protected. The pre-Juliana world is safely encompassed by the circumference he designs through his work. He is the royal scion in the safe garden:

> VI
>
> I am the Mower *Damon*, known
> Through all the Meadows I have mown.
> On me the Morn her dew distills
> Before her darling Daffadils.
> And, if at Noon my toil me heat,
> The Sun himself licks off my Sweat.
> While, going home, the Ev'ning sweet
> In cowslip-water bathes my feet. (p. 46)

Coming "before" the "darling Daffadils," Damon is the favorite child of the world. Aurora is his generous mother, Apollo his protective father. His pre-Juliana infancy usurps Juliana's Petrarchan power; the gods are his progenitors. He is clearly the child of the world, Apollonian energy a birthright he inherits rather than (as Juliana's was in stanza 3) a Laurarite of the Petrarchan construct. As child of a protective Apollo, Damon reconstructs his origin.

In stanza 8, he uses the formulative powers his mythical parents initially bequeathed him:

VIII

Nor am I so deform'd to sight,
If in my Sithe I looked right;
In which I see my Picture done,
As in a crescent Moon the Sun.
The deathless Fairyes take me oft
To lead them in their Danses soft;
And, when I tune my self to sing,
About me they contract their Ring. (p. 46)

Speaking now of the time *after* his separation from the world of his parents (but of the time before his connection to Juliana), Damon defends his being by replicating it. In the "deformation" of that reformation, the scythe at once mirrors and extends his power. His sexuality (what Juliana rejects) is his source (what the sun projects). In creating another "picture," Damon renders his portrait anamorphic. Reframing the image drawn by the narrator, he undoes conventional Petrarchism. Whereas in 1–5 the narrator fleshes out a besieged lover, in 8 Damon establishes a new frame, with the deforming scythe becoming the locus of his reformed image. In the second projection of himself, Damon steps out of, and so leaves behind, the child who depends on Juliana's sustenance and the man who feeds on her denials. The commanding Damon of this vision is totally different from the unnoticed Damon of Juliana's world. Though he speaks in the present tense, Damon's image is untarnished by Juliana's influence. The professional Damon wields the very manly power Juliana denies.

When he looks "right" into the scythe, he sees the now fully grown self who has inherited the creative powers of the sun around which the imitative substance of the moon gathers. "Ey[ing] awry" produces that right image. Shaping himself to conform to his projection, Damon consolidates his role as shape-changer. Framing himself in the scythe, Damon wears its deadly divisiveness. Everything conforms to his edge. Like the restored Charles in the cylindrical mirror, the Damon of the scythe image returns to his earlier held and inherited prowess. No revolutions unseat his dominion. No woman challenges his supremacy. In the anamnesis of his forgotten past, Damon determines the fullness of the moon and the expectancy of the fairies. In the same way, Damon is both the leader of the fairies' dance and the musical source seducing them. The nymphs he inspires imitate the pattern he sets. As solar energy, he instigates their life even as he shrinks them to his form. His sighs/scythes are eternally calmed by the song which they repeat in the ring of their unanimous approval. The stanza that begins in sight ends in sound. Mirror dissolves into Echo as Narcissus gives to his admirer the phallic being she seeks. Adored, Damon offers himself as man to the female fairies who follow him, taking from the myth any trace of its sad end. "Looking right," Damon rewrites his life in his own image, the scythe the vehicle of his reorganized self.

By pulling back the myth of Echo and Narcissus to its early stages, where the nymph follows the arrogant swain, Damon retracts its tragic conclusions. Preempting endings by absorbing beginnings, crawling back into his solar father and becoming him, Damon rewrites the myths so that they are always at the point of innocent initiation. He is a Narcissus perpetually attractive to the nymphs and continuously reflecting on himself. In the fairies' ring, his song is always echoed; in the moonlight, his image is perennially projected. As he tunes himself to sing, the fairies are attuned to the music of his sphere. In the circle of their desire, they follow the aroused being he has become. As child in stanza 6, he corroborated his aristocracy in the progress of the day from morning to evening; as man in stanza 8, he determines that progress from his own daily awakening in the sun to his extended nightly emergence in the moon. He has usurped Juliana's illuminating capacity by holding the moon in his hand and absorbed her originative powers by flaunting his energetic manhood. As phallic moon, his "tool" reflects his sun—the masculine head. As inscribing instrument, his "tool" controls the moon's emergence, just as his inspiring maleness shapes the fairies' song. In fact, he reinscribes the world. Like the wolves to Mother Earth, his invention fathers the female worshippers of his organ. In this new text, Damon multiplies his female readership. He substitutes the sympathetic fairies for the sympathetic fellow poets Petrarch sought in *Rime sparse* 1.

In stanza 8, he makes all Lauras into admiring echoes of his Petrarchan initiative. Later, in 11, he will make all Petrarchs—all mowers—into worshippers of his destructiveness. The scythe-mirror reflects him in the first half of the stanza. The scythe-horn heralds him in the second half of the stanza. Tuning himself in the first half by looking right, he controls and inhabits the moon. He frames the world as he completes his circle. Tuning himself in the second half of the stanza by sounding right, he is surrounded by the fairies who *contract*. They shrink themselves to his dominating form and subject themselves to his controlling power. Defining themselves around his shape, they enclose him. His enlarged pipe determines their reductive following. The ring of their music echoes his voice. The ring of their dancing takes on his shape. As circles completed by him in the opening, as circles dominated by him at the end, the moony females find their voices and bodies in his origination. As mirror, the scythe reflects and completes his mind. As horn, the scythe heralds and enlists his audience. Finally, as song of himself, his music celebrates auto-inspiration. He is the center of the world he invents. He is the source of the women who enclose him, his phallic original, their controlling model. "Ey'd awry" in stanza 8, he recovers an originary self.

When the narrator spoke at the opening, Damon emerged hapless child and hopeless lover. When Damon speaks, he reverses that past to create a history that conflicts with the narrator's Petrarchan assumptions. He pits the competent "I" before Love's "Thistle sowing" against the complaining "I" after. His sighing increases his scything. The phallus grows as his grief remains static. The day of Damon's empowered self waxes and wanes at his will, rises and sets to his decrees. The "day" of Damon's Juliana-ed self is endlessly aggravated by her. In the world of Damon's childhood self, wounds can be healed: the julienned Damon can be put back together; the Juliana-ed one remains forever torn. Once he recalls his history before Juliana, Damon needs to reconcile that past with Juliana's presence. It is the narrator, viewing the scene in stanza 10, who falsely concludes that Damon's end comes from failed love, that his preoccupation with Juliana causes him to slip in his occupation. In the narrator's view, Damon's obsession renders him fragile as grass, subject to his own subjugation.

But though the eleventh stanza is told in the third person, Damon there resumes the role of narrator. His transmogrification from first-person mower to third-person subject of his own narration is part of his final assimilation of Juliana. When he appropriates her deadliness, he outdoes Petrarch. In the manic person of the Ur-Mower, he enacts the separatist impulses of Petrarchan formalization. By identifying the beloved, Petrarch carves out his love in her shape—severing it from himself. By moving into the severed beloved and voicing Juliana's deadliness as his own, Damon cancels his loving self. What takes several steps in the *Rime sparse* is immediate here. Petrarch transfers his amorphous desire into the solidified Laura. Her consolidated presence contains his prolonged love. Her continued denials in turn effect his longing for death. When he reverts to the death-wish directly by assimilating Juliana's denials, Damon waxes into a menacing figure. His scythe cuts down the idealized woman Petrarch sublimates even as it cuts out—and so defines—the desiring self. Petrarch is ancillary. Laura is unnecessary.

It is Damon, not the narrator, who speaks the last four lines. Writing out the wounded lover, he writes in his own apotheosis:

> XI
>
> Alas! said He, these hurts are slight
> To those that dye by Loves despight.
> With Shepherds-purse, and Clowns-all-heal,
> The Blood I stanch, and Wound I seal.
> Only for him no Cure is found,
> Whom *Julianas* Eyes do wound.
> 'Tis death alone that this must do:
> For Death thou art a Mower too. (p. 47)

In the scythe image of stanza 8 Damon placed himself at the center of a circle where "life kept its court"; here, Damon sits in a crown where "Death keeps his court" (*Richard II*, 3.2.162). Damon reduces Death—the great abstract other—to his powerful, now concrete self. With death reduced to the sphere of his jurisdiction, he emerges what Juliana was at the opening: cold to desire. He can cure his physical self by stanching and sealing; he can cure his psychological self by ending his paean. If death is a mower *too*, then Damon came first. He determines the pattern imitated by the formerly divine power. At one with Death, he can end all his ties with Juliana, the source of his wound. He has found a better origin and a surer destiny. Mirroring Juliana in his anamorphic portrait, Damon absorbs her beams, their illuminating brightness now his originating light, their phallic lengths now his destructive instrument. Allied to the great ender, as his being in 8 patterned itself on the great beginner, Damon brings the feared other into the circle of his own power.

Thinking of his love sighs as the source of his deadly Petrarchan wound, the narrator in stanza 10 fails to notice Damon's triumphant fall: "By his own Sythe, the Mower mown." But the connection between sighing and scythe that Damon builds upon in stanza 9 to signify (in the whetting) his increased appetite actually heralds the end of his longing. Once he castrates his Petrarchan self, the mower reverts from love-sigh to death moan. He shrinks as lover and grows as demon. In addition to the pun on sighs/scythe, there is one on mown/moan.[6] The way to escape desire is through death. In his self-portrait, Damon replaces the instruments of longing—

the phallic scythe and the Petrarchan sigh—with the insignia of shortening—the retracted scythe and the last moan. Propped up by his love, he sighs; self-mown, he reverts to "moaning." The dying sound reflects his deadening stroke. "Wetting" his sighs, and thereby dampening his enthusiasm, Damon quenches his fire, having found a way to put it out. Making Death interchangeable with him, he presides over his own replication. If Death can take his place, then he can stanch the pain of love and remove himself from the scene. When he slips out of his intensity, Damon assumes the necessary coolness. He finds comfort in his profession (the arena where he established his confidence in the behind/before Juliana). As *a* mower rather than *the* mower, he hides behind the facade of his destructive occupation and engineers his withdrawal into a sociological guise. Linked to Juliana, Damon takes on her deadliness. In replicating his cutting self, Damon incorporates Juliana and alienates the reader. As Juliana pushes Damon away by denying his tribute, so Damon pushes the reader away by ending the tribute. In a world of endings, there is no need for connection, the self sufficient unto itself as originator. If Petrarchism is contingent on a dynamic of desire extended to the body of the denying Laura, Marvell's Damon becomes what he desires. His formulations mirror his own deforming vision.

Setting himself up as the original, he moves from the mirrored image of stanza 8 to the original model of stanza 11. He now tells his own story. Having incorporated Juliana, he eliminates the original narrator and speaks of himself in the third person:

> Only for him no Cure is found
> Whom *Julianas* Eyes do wound.
> 'Tis death alone that this must do:
> For Death thou art a Mower too. (p. 47)

The rhyme of found and wound emphasizes the connection between the beams of Juliana's eyes in stanza 3 and Damon's scythe here: "Not July causes these extremes / But Juliana's scorching Beames." In the winding reformulation of his instrument, Damon outlines a vision of shadowy Death who, as Mower, frees him from the Petrarchan dependency of female origination. It is Damon's vision that masters. The shining mirror of his scythe short-circuits the controlling gaze of Juliana's wounding eyes. If the lively, connecting scythe of stanza 8 assured Damon's place as originator of woman, the deadly, divisive scythe of stanza 11 heralds his independent state. As wounded lover, Damon is victimized by Juliana's

238

extremes. As re-winding Death, Damon ends his relation to her. He is now the formulating model. In his self-perpetuating likenesses, he fragments Petrarchan attachment as, in his third-person summary, he assumes the detached voice of his own suicidal impulses.

In the alienated Damon, Marvell sidesteps both the sympathetic reader-narrator conditioned by three centuries of Petrarchan rhetoric to sirenize the lady and the sympathy-seeking Petrarch who looks to that reader for the validation Laura refuses to give. If poetic laurels are to rescue Petrarch from the denying Laura, the reader must be brought into the conspiracy against her. Becoming Juliana by extending her beams and using them to create a self-replicating form, Damon appends to the man the deforming impulse Petrarchism attributes to Laura. He no longer needs a reader. Scythe in hand, Damon is an inverse mirror of Laura-Mercury, knife in hand, in *Rime sparse* 23. But the cycle begun there stops here, as the mower emerges the inventor of his own progressively diminished image. Laura's denial shrinks Petrarch. Sufficient unto himself, Damon cuts out replicas of his own deforming impulses. His mirror is an abyss with Death at the center.[7] In stopping the future by severing the flow of his desire, Damon stops the poem by stepping into the demonic center of the Petrarchan formula. As his own Laura-Mercury, he engineers the end of the Petrarchan construct and aligns himself with the woman whose destructiveness he defines. When he joins Damon to the demonic woman, Marvell dramatizes the ambivalence—the desire not to be, the impulse not to write—which Petrarch situated in the life-blighting and poem-canceling Laura-Mercury.

By appending the woman's destructiveness to the man and by rendering Damon the angel of death to his own voice, Marvell fuses the sexually castrated man unto the verbally disempowering woman. If the Petrarchan *sigh* signals the poet's desire for a body he can't have, the Marvellian *moan* signals the lover's dismissal of the forms the poet *can* have. If Petrarch used Laura-Mercury to speak his ambivalence about representation, Marvell directly assails the image-making complex. When he replicates his own form in the mirroring scythe, Damon calls the death wish his own. "The Gallery" narrator does the reverse. He renders the woman the model for the man's discursiveness even as he paints her in *his* image. Damon's silence cancels the woman. "The Gallery" narrator's voice annexes her.

Damon's poem presents an anamorphic portrait of the artist revealed by cutting out, or scratching away, the Petrarchan surface of the narrator's story. Then it presents Damon's story, one designed to end all tellings. "The

Gallery" alternates between stories only to reveal, by innuendo, a totally different portrait. Thus "The Gallery" is anamorphic from the start, hovering between women who alternatingly victimize and nurture the narrator; at the end, it is revealed that those women imitate the narrator, the mirror mirrored. Finally, "The Gallery" imbricates a third image in Marvell's own projection: a portrait which cancels the two earlier ones by rejecting their contrivances. If, as Lyotard argues, the force of desire "compresses the primary text, crumpling it up, folding it, scrambling the signs it bears on the surface" ("The Dream-Work," p. 24), in "The Gallery's" two polyptychs Marvell doubles the fold and presents a commentary that "scrambles" up the safely humanistic complacency of the narrator's self-aggrandizing control.

By His Own Art: The Collector as Originator

Damon seems to strike preemptively. He finds a way to forestall Juliana's rejection by catapulting himself into the prominence of a larger denier—Death. Like the speaker in Donne's "The Broken Heart," he reduces his passion by increasing the number of selves who feel and then behave as he does. Death is simply one of many mowers. The speaker in "The Gallery" admits to still more options. He matches not only the denying but the nurturing other. Where Damon multiplies selves, "The Gallery" narrator subtracts them. Damon retreats to his beginnings before love, "The Gallery" speaker to his beginnings in love. He moves backward at the end to a re-created "entrance." Damon remembers another world whose nurturing arms him against Juliana. Shepherd to Clora's shepherdess in an idyll he invents, the "I" of "The Gallery" can remain unarmed. He perpetuates love stories that match his contrivances:

> I
>
> *Clora* come view my soul, and tell
> Whether I have contriv'd it well.
> Now all its several lodgings lye
> Compos'd into one Gallery;
> And the great *Arras*-hangings, made
> Of various Faces, by are laid.
> That, for all furniture you'l find
> Only your Picture in my Mind. (p. 31)

The second sight—the view from the gallery—and the first sighting—the look of the painting—invite further musings, as the narrator uses the past to affirm his origination. The history of the world is reduced to the pictures "in [his] mind." Clora is sent on a quest, the outcome of which is determined by the speaker's single vision. Though he is obsessed by her, she is possessed by him.

Once having agreed to play the roles of reader and spectator, she will emerge, as his confident "you'll find" indicates, heroine and spectacle of the pictures she sees.[8] The recognition in her anterior reading seems to corroborate her interior and prior being as source of the narrator's obsession. But her discovery of him cements his recovery of her. As spectator, she objectifies him. Her gaze controls his soul. But, if what she sees there is herself, then her objectivity is his subjectivity. With the woman as the viewer of his soul, the narrator renders himself as the specular object. But if she is his soul, then he simply turns the lens into a mirror. As subject of the paintings, "she" is "he." Her inside, as Butler might put it, is his outside. As object of his vision, "he" is "she." His inside is her outside. Her gaze controls him in the painting, even as his gaze controls her in the gallery. The images are his. His "confession" exposes her. While Damon ends with many selves, the "I" of "The Gallery" ends with *one* self, fully in control of his mind and *one* Clora, its "only" picture. As its sole occupant, she duplicates his mind, her being determined by his thought. Though he allows other views, and though they are painted with hyperbolic vivacity, he has a single purpose. Saving the center for last, he gives the illusion of progress. But he ends where he wants to begin, with a Clora whose maternal bosom is the "ground" of a landscape he contrives and a Clora whose fertility is the source of his invention.

If "Damon" presents the linguistic space of two poetic histories that merge to voice a critique of Petrarchan destructiveness, "The Gallery" presents the visual space of two pictorial histories, figured, first, by the guided tour of the Italianate studio the narrator traverses;[9] and, then, by the gradual allusions to the religious polyptych (possibly the Van Eyck Ghent altarpiece) Marvell himself presents. In "Damon," there are two Petrarchan narrators, the ostensible Petrarch replaced by the deadly mower. In "The Gallery," there is only one narrator. But behind him, the poet stands with an alternative serial picture. Both pictures uncover an artistic acquisitiveness that uses the woman to enact the man's ambition. The imbricated religious polyptych Marvell may have had in mind ends in the "blame" after the fall, the studiolo in its prelapsarian guilt. While the

narrator presents one scene of alternating portraits, figured by the walls of
the studiolo, Marvell implies yet another serial painting framed by the
walls of a church. The studio is the presumed scene of the poem. The
religious polyptych is its absent space. In the studiolo history, the narrator indicts himself. In the polyptych allusion suggested by the enfolding
scenes, Marvell indicts the narrator. In the narrator's portrait, Clora may
be the spectator but the narrator tells her what to "find." She may be the
spectacle but the narrator determines how she acts. As model, she obeys
Hélène Cixous's dictum that art is male-centered: "Hold still, we're going
to do your portrait so that you can begin to look *like* it right away."[10] As
viewer, she obeys the narrator's dictum that criticism is male-dominated:
"Hold still, we're going to frame your portrait so that you can begin to look
at it right away." Her look in the paintings and her looking at the paintings
are responses to his direction. As subject and reader, she is controlled by
what he "likes." As portrait subject, Clora is the narrator's image. Her
seductiveness in the paintings is governed by the reductiveness of his
thought. As portrait spectator, she is the narrator's lens. Her reaction to
the portrait is dictated by the seduction of his narrative.

Pulled into the pictures, she is sucked into his fiction. Her image and
her "reading" are his projections. But beneath this spectacle of spectators
is the one Marvell asks his readers to see. He poses both narrator and Clora
on the backdrop of yet another picture. By contrasting the narrator's
second nature in the secular polyptych to the religious polyptych's second
coming, Marvell exposes the narrator's centrism, his conception of a Clora
whose budding maternity mirrors his incipient thoughts. The gallery is a
hall of paintings whose center and frame the narrator commissions; the religious polyptych is a center whose frame—the church—broadens the
context. The gallery narrows to the speaker as it moves toward the center.
The polyptych advances to the heavens, as its center (Christ's ascension)
opens up a different prospect. In the studiolo, the earthly "other"—the
woman—becomes the earthly self; the religious polyptych poses an alternative—the heavenly other—whose being cannot be reduced or transposed.

Using a form of religious painting as a counterpart to his narrator's
story, Marvell comments ironically on the artist as overreacher. He distances himself from the Italianate ornamentation of the gallery and suggests a northern construct. The tension between the puritan Marvell and
his sophisticated narrator may lie in the disparity between the art forms
the narrator chooses and the artistic vehicle to which Marvell himself

inclines. In the hall of mirrors represented by the gallery, both artist and subject, narrator and Clora, emerge as power seekers. Turning love into art, the "I" re-creates the history of its progress. He seizes the green hill of nature as the fecund scene for his designs. While the narrator invites Clora to walk with him around the enclosure of his mind, Marvell himself presents, in the allusion to the Ghent polyptych, an overview of a scenario that falsely enthrones man and treacherously idealizes love. While Clora and the speaker physically travel the psychological time of their lives, encircling the same room and returning to a chamber (like that of "They flee from me") where they mutualize their identity, Marvell, the poet, allows the reader to see, all at once, how this process is idolatrous. With the folding parts of the Ghent polyptych, he accounts for the passage of time; with the central picture, he demonstrates how what looks illustrative is really constitutive of a woman-denying rhetoric. The narrator's studiolo is contemporaneously fashionable. Marvell's polyptych speaks of a perennial truth that undermines the collector's self-determined confession. The poet's allusion to an older art form subverts the narrator's acquisitiveness by pulling the seemingly multiple paintings into one apparent picture. While the narrator ends in Genesis 2 and the Petrarchan Ur-myth, Marvell's allusion to the polyptych reverts to Genesis 3 and the world after the garden.

During the tour, the "I" changes his perspective. In the opening stanza, he is both artist and creator, while Clora is subject and audience. She fills his mind and becomes what he designs. In stanza 6 he reverses roles, she emerging artist and collector, he, subject and audience. As the opposite sides of the gallery unfold, so do the viewing possibilities until, finally in the last stanza, with yet another reversal, the "I" revives his controlling position. As there are two sets of opposing pictures, showing the pleasing and teasing Clora, so there are two sets (in stanza 1 and stanza 6) of opposite viewings. The artist-narrator takes Clora on a guided tour of the gallery—itself anamorphic—as he presents alternative readings of the love relationships, alternatives that, in stanza 7, reveal a mutual center:

Stanza 1

narrator-artist-collector   ∽   Clora-model-observer

Stanza 6

Clora-artist-collector   ∽   narrator-model-observer

In the first stanza, the "I" is in control; in the sixth, Clora takes the reins, as the "I" becomes what she was. Stanza 6 reverses stanza 1 as the panels merge with—and so converge on—each other. Four pictures frame the center and two narratives mutualize the roles of artist and audience. But the conversions merely shift the players. They do nothing to transform the game. The subject of the pictures (the relationship of lover and beloved) and the subject of the commentaries (the relationship of spectator and spectacle) are reflective. If Clora can do what the narrator does, he can become to her what she appears in the paintings to be: the mastering/mistress of his passion. Controlling the central image in the last stanza, the narrator also turns life into art. He thereby reduces passion into something he can invent and renders Clora's devices his. If Clora can see what the narrator sees, then she can become what he pictures: the fathering/mother of his art. While Damon escapes Love by imitating the siren Juliana, the "I" of "The Gallery" passes through the siren stage—with the pastoralized scene at the end—and turns even the tender Clora into an imitation of his artistic "contriving" self.

In the sequence of the sequence, the "I" speaks of his sirenized self, victimized even beyond the borders of death:

IV

Like an Enchantress here thou show'st
Vexing thy restless Lover's Ghost;
And, by a Light obscure, dost rave
Over his Entrails, in the Cave;
Divining thence with horrid Care,
How long thou shalt continue fair;
And (when inform'd) them throw'st away,
To be the greedy Vultur's prey. (p. 32)

Not only does Clora play with the mangled corpse of the lover, she decides, like a judge, when it shall disappear completely and become prey to the vulture. While Damon thinks he can ease his pain in death, the "I" of "The Gallery" finds no such escape. The woman of this panel answers the "how long" of her lover's lament by determining "how long" the speaker has left to remain anything at all. She devises his end and casts his innards out even as she pulls him inward to her cave. The male fear of disappearing inside the woman, of being sucked back into the womb, is here heightened as Clora dismembers and teases the narrator. She presides over his gradual incorporeity. Exposed, he is nothing. Transposed, she is everything. In the oxymoron "light obscure" she plays with his ghastly remains as he becomes all ghost. The split between body and mind gradually erodes. The split between light and darkness gradually disappears. When the vultures finish him, the still conscious "I" witnesses his own disappearance into the fading light. The "I" presides over his mutilation as the woman presides over the absorption into nothingness. She plays with space in the "obscure light" of her cave and distorts time (in the *how long*) of her game. She taunts until the end, allowing the "I" to imagine, like Actaeon in his skittish panic, his disappearance. She divines; he decomposes, waiting for her to determine his final dissolution. At the door of death, she is the opposite of the milky aurora who slumbers in the maternal plenty and the falling manna of stanza 3. She is a Diana who controls the sight-lines. She taunts the speaker with images of his dissolving form even as she teases him with visions of vanquished Time. Her cave is the devouring hollow of the female monster. Like Juliana, whose beams are maternal origin and divining attraction, the Clora of stanza 6 reflects male fear and turns her cavy womb into a death trap.

As he alternates from murdered victim, to fed baby, to dismembered ghost, to revived body in stanza 5 so in stanza 6 she surfaces as the "inventor" of those scenes in which he, as object, is pleased or tormented. Watching the unfolding scene, he revives not just the physical self epitomized by the sensualist of 5 but the artistic self represented by the collector of 6. The reversion of power—he controlling Clora's sight lines in the gallery, she determining their relationship in the paintings hung there— moves chronologically backward as the "I," who begins in male retrospect, ends in a female prospect, controlled by the competitive woman who collects men. As collector of men, she mirrors his harnessing power. As subject of the paintings, she reflects his centralizing impulses.

The last stanza is unbalanced—as is the central picture—and it is there that the "I" wrests back control to gain both inventive capacity and originative place. He emerges Adam to Clora's Eve:

> VII
>
> But, of these Pictures and the rest,
> That at the Entrance likes me best:
> Where the same Posture and the Look
> Remains, with which I first was took.
> A tender Shepherdess, whose Hair
> Hangs loosely playing in the Air,

> Transplanting Flow'rs from the green Hill,
> To crown her head, and Bosome fill. (p. 32)

As "tender shepherdess" and participant in his tour, she returns to what she was, the subject of his painting and the audience of his art. Yet he, too, is pleased (he *likes* the last picture) even as he is duplicated (the picture is a *likeness* of him). Using the verb reflexively, the "I" continues to play on "reflection." Was it, as Phoebe Spinrad suggests,[11] Clora's eyes that "took" him with their "look," or was it he who, in admiration, discovered her? Does she actively seduce him, or is it his pleasure in what he invented that predisposed him to "like" her? "Posture" and "look" suggest created, painterly poses, as if even the tender Clora were already practicing for her appearance as his model. The narrator plays with the possibilities for control here, conflating the hook of female attractiveness with the eye of male imagination.

Though he can't say for certain how it started, he can, through the power of his art, revive the feeling of excitement with which he was initially "taken," a power which gives man the shifting postures the mythographers appropriated from the gods. Since "took" means both captured and excited, since it suggests both a passive surrender and an active choosing, the "I" places himself at the entrance to the relationship. In the last lines he converts Clora, the tender shepherdess, into the conscious model for the role she will play. Her attractiveness extends her acquisitiveness. As she transplants the flowers, she transforms herself into Mother Earth and prepares the posture she will assume in the painting. In crowning herself, she becomes both queen of the May and Flora. In arranging herself, she takes from the "green hill" its fecund and nurturing resources. Eternal spring in the painting, she acquires its greenness and "plays" at life by centralizing herself. When she fills her bosom in anticipation of the "I's" "look" as spectator to the spectacle of sexual arousal she devises, she prepares to "please," and later to "torment," him. Her posture energizes her as erotic object and crowns her as powerful subject. When she flaunts her femininity to attract the "I's" masculine scrutiny, she also uses it to present herself in a way that seeks, and hence provokes, his approval. But he manipulates her seductiveness and incorporates her into the frame of his mind just as she grafts the earth onto her body. The mirrors of their mutual plunder make her appealing to him in her sexuality and revealing of him in his power. Both are artificers, appending to themselves, as the wolves and warts in Linche's mythology did Mother Earth, nature's creative capacity.

Like the narrator in Marvell's "Garden," they turn the "green shade" of the hill into a "green thought." She uses her bosom as fertile ground for the flowers. He views her bosom as erotic source for his imagination. As surrogate mother to the flowers, Clora cuts off their growth. In the same way, her artistically preserved erotic beginnings block the uniting closure of desire. The deadly womb of her cave in the fourth stanza completes the deadening impact of her artifice here. The poet's image of her biological body is shaped by his image of her artistic body. Pygmalion to her own Galatea, she renders herself his rendering. Clora and the narrator crown themselves in artifice and divert the origins of power to themselves. That appropriation places man—seen as the force behind the tender maiden— at the center of his created universe. As specular object, Clora invites the narrator's gaze and calls him into the picture he arranged. But as pictorial subject, Clora mirrors the narrator's appropriating. She takes from the green hill of nature the reproductive potential he arrests by capturing her controlling power in his dominating image. As she tops her originative head in a self-idealizing image, she fills her maternal bosom in a self-replicating tribute. Crowning herself, she confirms her originality, an originality which, however, mirrors his. It is his mind that is on display, that laurelizes itself in her crowning. As idealized object, her dominion over air and hill turns her into Botticelli's centralized Venus whose presence in the painting concretizes her Cronos-collector-father's phallic emergence. Defoliating the green hill, Clora mirrors the narrator's ambition. She sucks him in by suckling his desire to assimilate the landscape.

Another Unfolding

The series of unfolding portraits transfers to a mythological form the creative energy that religious polyptychs place in a spiritual context. The narrator's allusion, in the sequence of paintings, to his own originality ironizes his Italianate usurpation of the Northern construct. The dominion of his visual dictatorship corroborates the idolatry of his formulative mastery. In the second serial painting, the religious polyptych to which Marvell secretly alludes, God himself is the central subject. In the narrator's story, the "I," like the Renaissance mythographers, humanizes the gods and crowns himself as one. That coronation gives the narrator power over life and control over the woman. Damon finds a way to deal with his hurt by turning the great abstract other—Death—into the ordinary working man—the mower. Enfolding himself into the circle of endings, as his sun went round on the orbit of its own beginnings, he slips into the self-protective guise of indifference. The replication creates a siren-self to match the elusive Juliana-other. In "The Gallery" the narrator converts the beloved into himself more directly. He poses her in the posture of imposture, the eternal artifice of art. The rhetorical thrust of that conversion is to flatter her with the eternalizing conceit of the Petrarchan laurel in order to grant himself the eternal opportunity of her youthful pursuer. In the Shakespearean sonnet, the beloved's summer will never fade—though death's shade prevails over his actual person; in Marvell's "Gallery," Clora survives her own monstrosity to return to the entrance and view her lover's still active mind as it reflects what the narrator suggests is her eternally creative self. Damon is demonized by the toughness he realizes when he effects his own death. The speaker in "The Gallery" absorbs the sources of renewal and gives birth—by duplicating Clora—to the youth and femininity of his own "tenderness."

Alternating the perspective of "The Gallery" within a constant format, Marvell links the painted scene to the real frame wherein it is placed so that the "lodgings" are part of the paintings, the way the great polyptychs were part of the churches for which they were designed. That fusion allows Marvell to comment on his narrator's controlling rhetoric. The individual events of the narrator's life are connected to each other by their presence in his mind, just as the paintings in the Gothic cathedral are enclosed by the upward spirals of the church itself. While the narrator evolves his life in art, Marvell's imbricated polyptych alludes to another picture—one where art yields to life and life is crowned by eternity. With the dual references, Marvell creates individual scenes and places those scenes within a critical context. About the differences between Northern and Italian Renaissance art, Lotte Brand Philips comments, "In Italy, the painted or sculptured work powerfully maintained its own sphere of existence, asserting itself against the sacred architecture surrounding it. In the North, however, this sacred structure, the Gothic cathedral, had long since completely absorbed the painted and sculptural art, which had lost their own realm of existence and had become entities directly connected with the architecture and with the space of actual reality."[12] Placing his narrator in the context of a still larger structure, Marvell exposes him.

As the narrator contrives, in the last stanza, to render his acquisitiveness innocent, so the second story Marvell tells (with the imbricated allusion) describes an innocence that is uncontrived, an innocence based on loss. In many ways the serial painting is a forerunner of the hypertext; the painter gives a "range of choices" and the viewer chooses where to cast his eye. But the anamorphic image of Marvell's alternative polyptych obviates the choices. In the shadow of the Ghent vision, the gallery unravels. Its insistence on human centrality is overcome by another narrative series which renders the human gallery trivial. Thus the anamorphism of the implied polyptych erases the "good form" of the narrator's gallery by proposing Christ's ultimate formlessness as a substitute for the self-promoting human artist.

In the Van Eyck polyptych which Marvell may have seen at Ghent (see figure 2), the sacrificial lamb is at the horizontal center of the work and the risen Christ at the vertical crux.[13] Sacrifice and life in the New Jerusalem are the ends which parallel and therefore contrast to the narrator's "Entrance." The Adam and Eve of Genesis 3 frame the Ghent polyptych (figure 3). Eve stands underneath the carved images of Cain and Abel. Adam is crowned by the image of Abraham and Isaac. Equally covered, each looks downward, toward the viewer. Each wears the fig leaves that mark the fall. Eve still holds the bitten apple; Adam stands with his arm folded across his chest, as if to say "don't come near me," in order to heal his aching rib, to protect himself from what has already happened, or to ward off the slaughter—Cain/Abel; Abraham/Isaac—still to come. Engaging the viewers, Van Eyck's Adam and Eve seem to acknowledge that they replicate what the biblical couple repudiates. Since Adam and Eve are at the edge of the scene, and since the viewers are already apart from it, all are excluded from the garden of enfolding paradise. With his hand on the rib from which she sprang, Adam seems also to misprize the Eve he disengages. Does he wish she had never been formed or does he wish—with the off-putting gesture—that she never would come back? Is Adam repulsing Eve—denying the other—or is he repressing sexuality—denying the self? Is he pushing her—or his progeny-audience in the chapel—out of the picture? In the shadows, Adam and Eve counter the perspective of the central panel, which leads from lamb to dove to the risen and light-yielding Christ. Leaden-eyed and heavy-limbed, they seem to prophesy nothing but death. Brandishing his scythe, Cain is a "mower." Sacrificing his son for his faith, Abraham is a "collector." Adam and Eve precede generations of sacrifice—Cain and Abel, Abraham and Isaac—that eventually yield to the hallowed/haloed lamb and the crowning, rising, sun/son. But the narrator of "The Gallery" thinks only of his own rising sun and consequential Apollonian dominance. He controls vision and language, as he pulls the woman and audience into the frame of his discourse. His pictures are united by the revised innocence of the centralizing Clora

Figure 2. The Van Eyck Altar-Piece, photograph by permission of Fotografie Paul M. R. Maeyaert.

Figure 3. Detail of Adam and Eve: The Van Eyck Altar-Piece,
photograph by permission of Fotografie Paul M. R. Maeyaert.

who mirrors his self-aggrandizing ambition. The Ghent polyptych asserts man's separation from God. Outside the frame, Adam and Eve corroborate by their gaze a cycle that excludes man from the divinity. In such a view, Adam and Eve and Abraham and Isaac do not automatically become the second Adam or the hallowed sheep, symbols of the rising Christ. Something miraculous has to intervene.

In the self-enclosed rhetoric of "The Gallery," Marvell's shepherdess looks to the shepherd, calling him forward into the picture and backward into his past. The many stages of the Ghent polyptych advance to resurrection through sacrifice; the many stages of the narrator's "Gallery" revert to an Eve who, out of the shadows, assumes the fiction of her central place. That centrality occurs through the artist's contrivance so that her "look" becomes his insight. In the religious polyptych, such appropriations are impossible. A fallen Adam and Eve stand fixed at the outer frame as a transfixed Christ rises to a central place. For the Marvell who comments on the narrator, memory gives way to vision. Marvell's juxtaposition of the religious form with his narrator's pagan content contrasts divine inspiration to human creativity. For the narrator who comments on himself, vision gives way to power.

Through his ironic allusion to the polyptych, Marvell himself offers a critique of the Petrarchan narrator whose deliberately classical persuasion, like that of the Medicis and Gonzagas he rivals, is itself a form of self-referential self-aggrandizement. Resembling the circles of Linche's serpent, the cabinet revolves in its repetitive orbit. At the center Clora emerges with her hair "loosely playing in the air." The Chloris-shepherdess of the Botticelli painting is now enshrined as the Clora-Venus of the narrator's experience. That coronation enfranchises the captivated artist, who captures her "look" and assumes her "greening" maternity just as Damon's blackening deadliness allows him to surface as the siren who, at the opening of the poem, reduced him. As appropriators of female power, Damon and the "Gallery's" narrator testify to their ongoing desire not to meet the woman as an independent other but to use her in the arsenal of self-realization. When they mirror her destructive and creative capacities, they incorporate the "look" that initially "took" them and turn the woman's dazzling gaze into their own—doubling and redoubtable—perspective.

Marvell's double layer of painterly allusions, like the double distance of his narrational devices, allows him to unveil the appropriation of female power in the poem and to deny its appropriateness. That denial is not a restoration. Marvell does nothing to return to women the maternally creative powers usurped by his acquisitive narrators and characters. Instead, he renders men and women equally exploitative. Locked in self-reference, Clora (with her transplanting narrator) and Damon (with his demonic Juliana) endlessly mirror their dismembering and remembering of a nature circumscribed by the confining gallery and serpentine scythe. Clora cuts flowers to insert them into the bosom of her maternal expansiveness. Damon cuts grass and extracts himself from the reproduction of art. To read Marvell as separate from his characters is to see how he reads their distortions of gendered experience. As they elevate their women into goddesses (Juliana the demonic siren, Clora the fecund earth mother), his narrators turn themselves into women. They acquire *from* them powers they originally ascribed *to* them. Separated from his narrators, Marvell speaks to the layers of experience; pitted against the narrators' classical shepherds and shepherdesses and exposed in the pentimento of the poet's art, Adam and Eve are distanced from the self-idolatrous artists, as they are from each other, in the gendered generations of their human limitations.

The Marvell of "Damon the Mower" and "The Gallery" rejects the reflection Donne glamorizes in "The Dreame" to identify (in the mimetic emergences of Damon) the destructive nexus of Petrarchan deformation and (in the contrived postures of Clora) the aggrandizing impulse of Petrarchan appropriation. Bringing in Genesis 3 via the reversion to death in "Damon" and the painterly allusions to the world beyond Eden in "The Gallery," Marvell links the denying other to the conversionary lover. In the mirroring scythe and claustrophobic gallery, he represents the imagined as imaginer. That spiral suggests the limits of representation, as Petrarchan enclosures lock poet and woman in mutually confining likenesses. In the death-dealing Damon, Marvell extends the Petrarchan desire not to be into a desire to unmake the world. The scything Damon is a model for death. His castration transforms sexual disinterest into poetic and reproductive sterility: Damon as de-populator. In the life-loving narrator of "The Gallery," Marvell extends the Petrarchan desire to turn the other into the self into a desire to turn the self into god: the narrator as re-populator. The visual portrait behind the portrait imbricated in "The Gallery" mocks that desire and inexorably separates Christ's ascending vision from Adam's deformative gaze. By superimposing one text and its concomitant value systems on another, Marvell initiates a set of appropriations and criticisms that call into question the fundamental premises of

both. The anamnesis of the forgotten Ghent polyptych projects an anagogic vision the Petrarchan narrator could not imagine. At the same time,
the narrator's worldly openings suggest possibilities for gender reformulations unfathomable in the hierarchical structures of the Ghent polyptych.

And, while "Damon" and "The Gallery" narrator retain the male hege-
monies of Petrarchan discourse even as they double their respective destructiveness and creativity, the female poet of "The Nymph complaining
for the death of her Faun" invents a hierarchy that bypasses both the
death-wish and art-desire that seem so final in these poems. Re-creating
her life, the nymph achieves the fleshly union Petrarchan laurels sublimate. Commissioning a self-destructive art, she dismisses earthly laurels
altogether.

"PREPARING FOR LONGER FLIGHT"

Marvell's Nymph and the Revenge of Silence

The time is out of joint. O cursed spite,
That ever I was born to set it right.

Hamlet 1.5.187–89

Go, intercept some Fountain in the Vein,
Whose Virgin-Source yet never steept the Plain.
Hastings is dead, and we must find a Store
Of Tears untoucht, and never wept before,
Go, stand betwixt the *Morning* and the *Flowers*;
And, ere they fall arrest the early *Showers*.
Hastings is dead; and we, disconsolate,
With early *Tears* must mourn his early *Fate*.

Andrew Marvell, "Upon the Death of
Lord Hastings"

When he separates himself from the personae of "Damon" and "The Gallery" narrator, Marvell critiques the Petrarchism they embrace. Through Damon, he comments on the implicit deadliness of the construct; through "The Gallery" narrator, on its deferred acquisitiveness. But in "The Nymph complaining for the death of her Faun" Marvell begins with a woman poet and so recasts the nature and the form of Petrarchan desire. With that becoming, he goes one step beyond the woman-sympathizer in Wyatt's "Whoso list to hunt" and the woman-ventriloquizer of Donne's "Change." Trapped like the woman he imagines, the exhausted Wyatt of "Whoso list to hunt" comes to understand her desire for flight. Absorbed into her anomie, he loses interest in the chase. In "Change," Donne follows the woman into an art whose form is so open-ended that it enlarges with, rather than shrinks from, the impulses engendering it. The woman's feeling of freedom inspires the man's freeing poetic. Wyatt stops beginnings; the Donne of "Change" denies endings. For both poets, the woman's resistance to her representation in the dyad is the first step in the poet's dismissal of the whole poetic. When he sides with the woman, Wyatt retracts the male hunter of words. When he slides into the woman, Donne acknowledges the female nursery of language whose origin depends on a primary, not an imagined, replacement. In Petrarch, there is a secondary consolation. The poem remains as next best thing. Its permanence often emerges as the very best thing. Since sublimation is insubstantial, nothing real is risked; reality remains unchanged. Contrastingly, the initial literal transfer of bodies in "Change" prepares for the subsequent bodilessness of the exultant conclusion. Letting go of what matters facilitates matterlessness. If Petrarchan poetics is fixed on one, the poetic of "Change" engenders many. But the opening is into "eternity." The pluralizing prospect of vastness is attained as the poet forfeits the consoling security of sublimation.

Stretching the form still further, Marvell's female narrator in "Nymph complaining" takes on all the risks of "Change." But her abstracting impulses come only after she achieves the material love that transforms everything. In her triumph, the nymph creates a passage that at once galvanizes the flowing movement of "Change" and realizes the unifying communion Petrarchism only proposes. Like "Whoso list to hunt," "Nymph complaining" alludes to the Actaeon myth and turns Petrarch around. A hunter who feels the woman's situation as his own, Wyatt gives up the brutalizing maleness of pursuit. He apologizes to his fellows as, in pointing them toward a real find of a hind, he allows them to take his place. "Nymph complaining" has its savage hunters in the wanton troopers. But as woman, the nymph separates herself from them, cements her ties to the Petrarch that Wyatt abandons, and takes her deer out of the range of all hunters. She desolates the legions and generations of male viewers Wyatt addresses in "Whoso list to hunt." In so doing, Marvell's imagined nymph parallels such Renaissance women writers as Louise Labé and Veronica Franco, who, as Ann Rosalind Jones maintains, "take possession of masculine discourses even as they desublimate amorous conventions."[1] Marvell's nymph achieves the desired sympathy and cancels the sublimating memory of the Petrarchan poetic. She enacts a peculiarly female revenge, one which deals both with the arbitrary necessity of chance and the deliberate cruelty of men. When she inverts the Diana-Actaeon myth of *Rime sparse* 23, Marvell's nymph transcends the limitations of Petrarchan form and realizes the expectations of Petrarchan desire.

In their denial of the future, the two most famous Diana stories identify the locus of female revenge: hostaging Iphigenia and taking the child away, the Diana-Agamemnon story threatens *nature* and the Greek procreative dynasty; arresting language and taking the word away, the Diana-Actaeon story subverts *art* and the narrative, creative future. The nymph embodies both versions as she bespeaks her revenge and magnifies her little story into global proportions. The peculiar silence of her retaliation separates it from the traditional revenge plot and aligns it with another revenge to which Marvell alludes in some of his most famous poems. The nymph's revenge is different, too, from the vindictive Petrarchan withdrawals of Wyatt's "My lute awake" or Donne's "The Funerall." Aligning themselves with their male readers and pitting themselves against the female audience they ostensibly address, the anti-Petrarchan Wyatt and Donne suspend laurelization but entertain its possibilities in poems they might someday write. Their "telling silences" retaliate against the woman but negotiate a promise to the reader: "I will deliver a proper tribute, when I find the right Laura"; the ideal is retained, the failure to laurelize on some occasions, a rhetorical device promising future occasions. Even as he withdraws his tribute, each poet holds on to Petrarch's vision of perfection.

In "Nymph complaining" the sexual identity of writer and reader in the Petrarchan dyad is reversed. When the writer is a woman who realizes the ideal communion Petrarch sought, then the parallel party in the dyad—the male audience—loses out. Creating in the fawn the Laura she needs, and succeeding by rendering him the only reader and only beloved, the nymph does not need the outside sympathy Petrarch sought in *Rime sparse* 1 when he identified his audience as those "who understand love through experience." Blessed in the deer with the one "you" who responds, the nymph can do without the many others who sympathize. The wanton troopers resemble Shakespeare's swains from *Two Gentlemen*. In the hunt, the troopers treat all nature as inherently theirs. In the play, the "swains" identify themselves as owners of the ideal woman they invent. The nymph's revenge suggests not so much a poem she won't say but a vision she won't yield to such men. She is wronged not only by the indifference of a lover but also by a craven world. In turn, she punishes readers who don't care. Robbed of her fawn, she deprives troopers, swains, everyone, of the automatic entitlement their appropriations reflect. Hunters and soldiers emerge similarly exiled purveyors of dead masculinity. Naming them as wanton, the nymph at once infantalizes and feminizes her enemies. They are objectified both as Lear's fly-killing boys and the misogynist's unchaste whores.

When he is absorbed by the female feeling in "Whoso list to hunt," Wyatt fails to become the Petrarchan hunter/poet he elsewhere so eagerly embraces. Contrastingly, the nymph achieves a communion Petrarch never realized, even as she destroys the laurel, the eternalizing form, that constitutes Petrarchan sublimation. In "Whoso list to hunt" and "Change," the narrators acquire the woman's vision but speak in their own voices. The resulting split produces an overwhelming impotence in Wyatt and an overflowing exuberance in Donne. Each speaker gives in, Wyatt reluctantly, Donne enthusiastically, to the other. With a female Petrarch, Marvell recharges the system of Petrarchan formalization and the dynamic of Petrarchan revenge. If Petrarch makes up for his romantic failure by succeeding poetically, the nymph experiences both romantic and poetic success. If Petrarch enlists sympathetic males to corroborate his fame, the nymph excludes men who marginalize women from her vision. Her Petrarchism reinvents revenge and changes the dynamic of her poem from passive complaint to active retaliation.

At one extreme of the conventional retaliatory dynamic is Hamlet, whose imposition of revenge weeds the garden of Denmark to make it grow again. At the other extreme are the male narrators of Marvell's lyrics, who, seeking to right wrongs done to them, struggle to make a wronging world wronger. Like Atlas shouldering his burden, Hamlet responds to his father's murder sociologically and registers a filial obligation to return the world to its correct and previously held position. Of the vision at the end of revenge tragedies, Wendy Griswold writes: "A ritual feast is often undone in blood. In its place what is celebrated is the return of order following the period of disorder represented by all those dead bodies lying about."[2] The purging restores the world to health. But in an early poem, "On the Death of Lord Hastings," Marvell illustrates yet another motive for revenge: that of depriving, not reviving, the world. The "deflowering" the speaker envisions responds in kind to what the gods did to Hastings. In his vengeance, the speaker attempts rape by defoliation. Seeking to reverse the flow of nature while appropriating the best of nature to provide the substance of his mourning, the disconsolate narrator enjoins his fellow mourners to intercept the early showers and so prevent a normal spring. Similarly, in "To His Coy Mistress," the lovers "break through . . . life." As their fantasy disrupts the orderly process of the heavens, they smash restraints. The revengers of both poems project cosmic changes. Hastings enlists already sympathetic others to effect the blockage he envisions. The "Coy Mistress" narrator persuades the woman to join him as, together, they outwit time. Destructive impulses spur many of Marvell's narrators on to visionary heights from which they later voluntarily descend. The social disengagement of "The Garden" is canceled by the orderly acceptance of time in the last stanza, that of "Appleton House" by the complacent return of the concluding "let's in." In "Hastings" and "Coy Mistress," the cosmic subversion results in a similar social impasse, acknowledged as the impotence of poetic vision ("Art . . . is Long but Life is Short," 60) in the early poem and the oblivion of sexual rapture (act *now* and forget time) in the later one.

In "Nymph complaining," Marvell invents a narrator who remains steadfast where the others fail to follow through. When she refuses to come back to an orderly fold, the nymph retreats entirely and single-handedly enacts the deprivational revenge the bereaved speaker of "Hastings" and the argumentative lover of "Coy Mistress" only propose. She *does* deny her enemies a richness defined in the course of her poem. The most interesting fact about her success is that Marvell chooses a female speaker to achieve it. In her denial, she answers those who wronged her. She takes on the unfaithful Sylvio and then the murderous soldiers. Her answer to Sylvio opens up a mythical world based on the fact of her loss. Her rebuttal to the soldiers, corroborated by her silence, consists of a refusal to share the world she initially created. Hamlet may "unweed . . . [an old] garden" (1.2.134), but the nymph invents a new one. The play ends with a reaffirmation of the social order. The world rests on Fortinbras, whose ("strong-armed") name itself carries the burden of Hamlet's initial shouldering. Wholly otherworldly, rushing to the eternity the speaker of "Change" identifies but never literalizes, the nymph is utterly indifferent to setting anything in the earthly realm right.

While taking into account the nymph's retaliations, recent critics have failed to emphasize the relationship of gender to the revenge genre. In so doing, they make less of the initial libertine violation in Sylvio's abandonment and elide it too easily with the soldier's callous indifference. Such readings imply one revenge, whereas the poem actually details two: the story of the nymph's triumph over Sylvio's dismissal (her re-creation of his gift) and the story of the nymph's triumph over the soldiers (her decreation of the world she made to rebut Sylvio). The first story describes her artistic success in the form that celebrates male sexual failure. Her second story reveals her dismissal of the form that consoles men who fail. In the first story, the nymph inverts the conventions of the Petrarchan situation. She expands the *Rime sparse* conversions and renders herself a Petrarch who succeeds and the deer a Laura who listens and responds. In the second story, the nymph turns from tale to tableau. She refers to a statue in Diana's existent shrine and commissions one in the memorial she envisions. Her first revenge lies in her success; her second, in a deliberate failure. Jonathan Goldberg alludes to the retaliative impulse in his seminal essay on "Nymph," when he calls it "a poem whose plot entirely comprises the moment of creative annihilation," and when he refers to the nymph's statue at the end as "created in dissolution, made by erosion . . . a self-consuming artifact."[3]

But Goldberg's claim that the poem offers "Marvell's most elaborated version of the meaning of the [annihilating] moment for his poetry and for himself as poet" (p. 14) does not go far enough in categorizing the poem as a peculiarly female vision. Goldberg accepts Geoffrey Hartman's conclusion that "we must assume a . . . unity between the poet and his persona. Once we do this, the Nymph begins to appear as a Muse in little, a figure created by the poet to mourn his own loss of power or perhaps that of poetry."[4] In "Nymph complaining" Marvell fabricates another poet, one who goes beyond lamentation. The counter-self Marvell invents for "Nymph complaining" is a counter-gender and that contrariety is itself significant. The woman's voice renders Marvell's Petrarchan inversions qualitatively different from the impotence of "Whoso list to hunt" and the magnificence of "Change." Through it, Marvell formulates a separate category of revenge which places "Nymph complaining" in a genre which relates to (but is ultimately at variance with) *The Duchess of Malfi* and *The Winter's Tale*, works in which women answer the men who deny them by creating enclaves of self-enabling silence.

Marvell's empowerment of the nymph neither annexes nor avoids the female vision. Instead, it turns the interior life, essential to the dynamics of Petrarchan poetics, into a communicated experience, even as, in the end, it fails to expand the circle of communication to include the reader it tantalizes. The nymph's initial poetic triumph and her final artistic destruction redefine the poetics of failure. "Nymph complaining" does not mourn losses; it creates loss. Its revenge is double: first, as Goldberg and Hartman imply, it portrays an artist who invents a new form of expression by finding a figure for her expressiveness and a receptacle for her inventiveness. In the garden, the nymph creates artist, art, and audience, a representation in miniature of the poetic process. She has *one* lover and one reader. The deer's understanding of her message eliminates any need to record it. When he eats the roses of her words, the fawn absorbs the text that names love; the second revenge is enacted when the nymph commissions a statue that will eventually corrode. She thereby destroys the text that commemorates love. Harry Berger, Jr., calls the nymph a "refin[er] of the escape artistry of the ovidian sculptor, Pygmalion as well as her statue."[5] But he refers to the nymph at the end and therefore doesn't recognize (as Goldberg does) that her art there is intended to be annihilating. The revenge within the garden is an artistic retaliation; new life substitutes for loss. The second revenge, after the garden, represents the destruction of that art.

"Nymph complaining" clearly imbricates two stories. Each of the nymph's dilations (in what will be called, respectively, the inside story of lines 25–92 and the framing story of lines 1–24 and 95–122) enacts a different aspect of the Petrarchan process. In the inside story, the nymph's strategy reverses Petrarch's. Where he seeks to displace the always psychologically and sometimes physically absent Laura with the presence of his poetic laurel, the nymph achieves the Petrarchan desire for sympathetic "pity" (*Rime sparse* 1) and generates the understanding presence Petrarch never realized.

With the nymph, Marvell invents a poetics in which immediate gratification obviates the need for sublimation. That is, for a Laura who refuses to listen and therefore who refuses to react, the nymph engenders a lover who acts out her fantasy. She rears the deer to be the sympathetic reader she wants. In the fawn, she retains all the qualities of the idealized Laura—the purity, the pastoralized loveliness—and dismisses all the traits—the denial, the hardness—of the vindictive Laura. The nymph is not just a woman who realizes and then loses her mixture of amorous and maternal desire. She fabricates the situation in which her desires can be understood and thereby finds a vehicle of expression that transmits the feelings Sylvio abused. The nymph's motherly fostering of the fawn earns her the responsive lover she wants. Restoring to a woman the creative wellspring of language Petrarch appropriated from Laura, Marvell regenders identification. The nymph first nurses the fawn as child-object and then names him as love-object. Her sublimation (the deer for Sylvio) turns Petrarchism around. Where Petrarch accepted the laurel of poetic fame as a substitute for Laura, the nymph uses poetic transference as a means of realizing her desires. Her exploitation of the Petrarchan model reifies its transactions. The fleshly deer responds to her expressiveness in the inside story. But her Petrarchan variations extend one step further, as (in the framing story of lines 1–24 and 93–122) she converts the public homage of Petrarchan fame into the private victory of original vision. When she withdraws at the end, she takes her laurel with her and leaves only a fading sign of what she realized in the garden. Since she finds the solace of Petrarchan sympathy in the inside story, the nymph has no need for the comfort of Petrarchan fame in the framing story. Petrarch wooed his readers and accepted their laurels instead of Laura. Having persuaded her Laura inside the garden, the nymph has no interest in the future laurels that lie beyond.

Marvell's female voice of revenge is the absence of voice—and it is that absence that enables Marvell to create a heroine who withstands the usual accusations against women's anger. Carolyn Heilbrun summarizes the history of literary misogyny by quoting Mary Ellmann, who argues " 'the most consistent critical standard applied to women is *shrillness:* blame something written by a woman as shrill, praise something as not shrill.' " Then Heilbrun adds, "The other favorite term, of course is *strident*."⁶ Shrillness and stridency are tones that wanton soldiers and diffident lovers—who expect women to react hysterically or violently to their betrayals—might anticipate. The nymph's silence is strident in a way that neither Sylvio nor the soldiers imagine. As the Duchess of Malfi creates a life for herself by not answering her brothers, as Hermione, in *The Winter's Tale*, creates a death for herself by withdrawing from Leontes, the nymph shapes both her life and death. First, she avenges Sylvio, then the soldiers. The Duchess of Malfi and Hermione react by not reacting directly. Refusing to allow their victimizers the pleasure of dismissing them from the living world, they strike preemptively. In their retreats, these women dismiss the world. The nymph's strategy is different. While the Duchess and Hermione bury their resourcefulness only to disclose it later, the nymph initially confides in her readers, persuades them of her accomplishment, and then stops telling. Her silence is unexpected. Beginning by opening up, before the poem to Sylvio, in the poem to the reader, she concludes by retreating. Her closure cuts off disclosure and so disrupts the continuing story that creates the Petrarchan legacy.

Unlike the conventionally Petrarchan heroines of so many other Marvell poems, from the coy mistress to Damon's Juliana, who refuse to say "yes" to their beseeching lovers, the nymph has acquiesced before her poem even begins. When she says "no"-thing at the end, that refusal punishes not just the lover but the world. Her silence, too, is qualitatively different from the vengeance at the end of Donne's "The Funerall" or "The Dreame," where the male speaker threatens to stop praising the woman he had previously deified. Donne's promised silence takes away nothing but his earlier—conventional—compliments. The nymph withdraws the substance of a realized—and original—vision. Having penetrated the "mystery of things," Marvell's nymph becomes mysterious herself. In *The Duchess of Malfi*, Ferdinand and Bosola are punished by the demons they unleash. In *The Winter's Tale*, Apollo helps Hermione work her retribution. But Marvell's nymph designs and executes her punishment on her own.

The double invention enables her to wreak a revenge that lasts. The nymph remains firm in her withdrawal and achieves in fact what the Hastings narrator only wished to do. However, that double power distinguishes her from those Renaissance dramatic women with whom she is most closely aligned. Their classical model is Demeter, the goddess who withdraws and then forgives by taking the future into account. Similarly abused by men, the Duchess of Malfi, for example, still plans for the normal lives of her children: "I pray thee, look thou giv'st my little boy / Some syrup for his cold, and let the girl / Say her prayers ere she sleep."[7] In *The Winter's Tale*, Hermione—who retreated into silence for sixteen years—nevertheless comes back to see the daughter she lost. Hermione and the Duchess share a tender concern for what comes after. Initially hardened, they soften in the end. Marvell's seemingly tender nymph calcifies and damns the future in her silence. She suffers on a smaller scale than the Duchess or Hermione. In fact, the crisis in "Nymph complaining" borders on the absurd.[8] Modern instances of the revenge plot as Marvell uses it are indeed parodic: Poe's raven; or Irving's Ellen Jamesians; or Beckett's endlessly spinning silence at the end of *Krapp's Last Tape*. What saves Marvell's nymph from the ludicrous is the psychic and spiritual breadth of her vision. She dares to go beyond the limitations thrust on her because she moves into a self-created mythical sphere. In the process, she challenges men who marginalize women and escapes their confines altogether.[9] She moves out of bounds.

In "Nymph complaining" Marvell's classical model is neither the passive Philomela, whose nightingale beautifies the bloody landscape that shaped her, nor the forgiving Demeter, who restores the landscape she temporarily withdrew. As the Actaeon-Diana, the nymph takes hold of vision. Initiating a tableau, she turns the bower nature made in Ovid into "a garden of [her] own." As the Agamemnon-Diana,[10] she seems to commit herself to the future in the memorial. But, in allowing it to corrode, she turns Petrarchan expectation into disappointment. The nymph connects the two myths. The privatization in the Actaeon story inside seeps out onto the public domain of the Agamemnon myth. Conversely, the dismembered statue in the outside Agamemnon story mirrors Actaeon's lacerations. The inside story of the Diana-Actaeon revenge renders the text unnecessary; the outside story takes it away and deprives the world of the usual poetic consolation for loss.

The nymph's statue at the end solidifies her as Agamemnon's Diana, wreaking her displeasure by depriving the world. Hamlet tries to cure the world; the nymph takes her cure with her into the death she carefully stages. Turning herself into a statue, she creates a mirror with nothing to reflect. Her displeasure is measured by the Petrarchan inversion she sustains with her hart. Where the original Petrarch's hope is based on marble melting, this Petrarch incorporates the hope to illustrate its vanity; having realized in the beginning the union Petrarch sought in the end, she wipes out the memory of Petrarchan consolation. In *Rime sparse 265* Petrarch "lives on hope," remembering that [he] has seen "a little water, by always trying, finally wear away marble and solid rock." Petrarch turns that hope for a melting Laura into a justification for his sustained poetic complaint. He aligns himself with the readers who, as they applaud his persistence, will see it corroborated in the stone of his metaphor. The nymph literalizes the metaphor. She plays both parts, persevering water and corroding statue. Her vision disappears, its form eaten away by its content. When she interiorizes the metaphor, she wipes out the male art her enemies expect. By rendering herself the melter (in the weeping) and the melted (in the statue), the nymph turns Petrarchan illustration into self-consuming art.

As both Dianas, the nymph projects a twofold revenge. In the interior story, she creates a revenge of mirrors. Living well by living doubly, she inverts the Diana/Actaeon myth and avenges Sylvio. She wreaks her second—and silent—revenge in the framing story where she evokes the Diana/Agamemnon myth. She responds to the murder by taking the deer out of the human realm as Diana took Iphigenia and made her a priest in Taurus. With the second revenge, she dies well, privileging what she earlier shared. In *Romeo and Juliet*, Shakespeare undoes the damage of Petrarchan self-cancellation. Romeo is cured of his earlier sickness from the moment Juliet participates in the sonnet of 1.2.92–105. Juliet "speaks" as a second Petrarch, sharing the very form whose content signaled Romeo's damaged psyche in the opening scenes. Here Marvell goes beyond Shakespeare in granting a woman artistic power. The nymph succeeds at Petrarch's quest. She finds a way to convey her inner life by transmitting it *safely* to an audience she creates. When the sympathetic other is taken away, she annihilates all others. If, as Patricia Fumerton argues, the limning of miniatures details a private, secret art,[11] here the nymph turns the large scale of ostensibly public art into a private memory. In the corroding statue, the nymph leaves nothing behind. She teases with possibility but retracts all concrete evidence. The golden statues in *Romeo and Juliet* preserve a love outdone by life. Obliterating the vision it seems to be commemorating, the marble statue is a monument whose ruin is part of its original design.

Roses Within

When she alludes to Diana/Actaeon, the nymph suggests how the idealized communication in the garden (the nymph using her body as her text, the deer receiving her text as child and responding to it as lover) is a function of the transferences the myth presupposes. She turns Actaeon's awful discoveries into elements of shared sympathy. The deer may be the inspiration of the nymph's creativity but he is also its audience, an audience the nymph molds by sensitizing him to her. In the complex mirrorings of the Diana/Actaeon myth, the nymph weaves a foundling plot, complete with abandoned child and pastoral retreat. That life answers Sylvio's trivialization of her love and inverts the myth. In Ovid, a man becomes a deer; in the nymph's versions, the deer becomes a man. In Ovid, the "bare" Diana withholds her secrets. She underscores Actaeon's impotence to tell by urging him to "tell if he can." In this version, the nymph encourages the fawn. She allows him to absorb her and, finally, to print that knowledge in the kisses he returns to her. He knows and tells. As Petrarch drifts into Laura in the *Rime sparse*, calling himself the laurel tree that her name initially signifies or converting Laura into the deer he becomes in his numerous allusions to Actaeon, so the nymph mirrors, and plays with, the mythic possibilities of transformation. She uses the Petrarchan poetic situation to demonstrate the shifting possibilities for success. She triumphs by fashioning the sympathetic "other" that Petrarch lacked and by controlling his otherness. Her dismissal in one story (Sylvio's suggestion with the gift that she busy herself with the fawn so he can be free to busy himself with others) prompts her invention of a new one where the fawn becomes literally what Sylvio casually suggested: his replacement.

The substitution initiates a reversal of narrative sequence which allows the traditional ending of the family plot (culminating in the birth of a child) to serve as the opening event in the courtship narrative (usually initiated by the discovery of a desirable other). As she condenses the fawn's life, the nymph becomes first the mother in the family plot and then the lover in the courtship plot. In that process, the fawn waxes from infant to man. When she pairs a familiar plot line with a familiar myth, the nymph makes herself the fawn's savior. Her version of the family plot is further complicated by its conversion into a foundling story. For the literal birth, the nymph stages an adoption. Her foundling story traverses social, generic, and gender barriers. In most foundling plots, a royal scion is adopted and raised by peasants in pastoral surroundings. The royal acquires for a time at least a hardiness and innocence he could not have had at court. In the nymph's telling, the adoption works two ways—lending her an animal resilience and allowing the deer a human understanding. Her pastoral retreat gives him a privileged status; his acquired sensitivity galvanizes her inventive powers.

If the nymph imbricates one genre—first the Petrarchan poem, then the family plot—behind another, she also imbricates species, moving from human to deer and back again. Deprived of human contact, the nymph becomes one of a kind with the beast. The movement downward through solitude, which is a movement inward toward her animal nature, reduces her to the fawn's level and raises him above the humans he replaces:

> But I am sure, for ought that I
> Could in so short a time espie,
> Thy love was far more better then
> The love of false and cruel men. (ll. 51–55)

The fawn is doubly better than "false and cruel men." As prelapsarian animal, it is superior in *genus* to mankind; as spawn of woman, it is superior (in loving) to the *gender* of men. His adoption by a woman renders him closer to a woman; her adoption of an animal arouses her promiscuity. He imbibes her femininity as she acquires his robustness. The conversion of kinds occurs by a progression of similarities. The nymph merges the separated parts of her body and world as the first stage in crossing over into the fawn's being. Her extension turns her into the fawn's wet-nurse and facilitates the adoption of the foundling plot:

> With sweetest milk, and sugar, first
> I it at mine own fingers nurst.
> And as it grew, so every day
> It wax'd more white and sweet than they.
> It had so sweet a Breath! And oft
> I blusht to see its foot more soft,
> And white, (shall I say than my hand?)
> NAY any Ladies of the Land. (ll. 55–62)

The process of extension begins as the nymph replaces breasts with fingers and stretches "sweetest milk" into sugar. The redundancy—the overflowing sweetness (like the excess "world enough *and* time")—is almost immediately received and given back as the nymph realizes the first return ("it had so sweet a breath"). With the second elongation from her hand to his foot, the nymph transfers the purified whiteness of the milk and sugar to the fawn's body. Nursing replaces *in utero* feeding. Fingers substitute for breasts; feet link up to hands. In Golding's Ovid, Actaeon's *endeerment* similarly begins with an elongation: "She sharpes his eares, she makes his necke both slender, long and lanke. / She turnes his fingers into feete, his armes to spindle shanke. / She wrappes him in a hairie hyde beset with speckled spottes, / And planteth in him fearefulness."[12] The deer's softening and whitening in the nymph's story is a reverse mirror of Ovid's descriptive roughening and darkening, the fawn's feet whiter than any lady's hand. The whiteness excels in refinement and the foot exceeds in dexterity the ordinary human dimension: "NAY any Ladies of the Land." Establishing "kinship through the interpellation of gender that . . . contests a naturalized effect" (*Bodies That Matter*, pp. 7–8), the nymph takes the fawn into her imagination and then re-creates him as her child in this new "domain of language" (*Bodies That Matter*, p. 7).

The extension of mother into child subsequently fosters another attachment as the deer returns the maternal love the nymph gave with the sexual love she wants. In Ovid, fingers turn to feet. In the nymph's story, feet are "softer" than "hand[s]." Yet their softness makes the nymph blush, presumably because they suggest other organs she manipulates. The phallic extension of her hand in the script she writes is matched by the physical enlargement in the body she covets. Hand descends maternally into breast. Foot rises sexually to penis. Softness waxes into form as the nymph shapes the

fawn's desire. The fawn emerges from her—a double she creates, and returns to her—the lover she needs. As child, the fawn reflects her; as man,
he corroborates their similarities by recompensing her support with his
understanding. The sexual-procreative process resolves itself into a vegetative organic cycle. The feeding and bleeding (lines 82–83) issue from the
nymph's breeding. With the story her writing hand records and with the
child her breast hand nurtures, the nymph brings female reproductivity
(and the family instinct) into the Petrarchan plot. Her sexual re-member-
ing of the deer inverts Actaeon's specular dis-memberment.

When she refers to the garden where he becomes most like her, she
switches stories. Now adopted by her, the deer-child emerges a deer-man.
And the emergence is complicated because the mirrorings are doubled.
Earlier, as child of woman, the fawn is softened and feminized; later, as
man and lover, the fawn is sensitized and responsive. Similarly, the femi-
nizing nymph is masculinized by the fawn, gaining from him a confidence
in herself. But as a woman, she awaits the response she taught him to give.
The earthly bower signals the nymph's entrance into the mythical realm
where sexual thoughts sexualize the landscape. The conversion from boy
to man through the perception of the woman is very much like the transformations in "The First Kiss," part of a series of Ovidian imitations by the
Dutch Neo-Latin poet, Joannes Secundus (1511–36):

> When Venus carried the sleeping Ascanius off
> to her mountain of love, she laid him on soft violets
> in a white thunder of roses she drenched him, and left
> Her liquid fragrance everywhere like dew.
> And then she remembered Adonis; and the old
> insinuating fire burned
> in her marrow bones.
> How often she longed to embrace him, flesh of her own
> flesh, exclaiming, "Adonis has risen again!"
> but afraid to arouse the boy in his innocent dreams
> she kissed a thousand nearby roses instead—
> and suddenly they flush crimson, a low
> passionate moan parts her astonished lips:
> on every rose she touches a fresh kiss blooms,
> and in the goddess herself shivers of multiple joy.[13]

The nymph's Diana parallels Secundus's Venus. Like the nymph, Venus has
a garden. As the nymph adopts the fawn and makes him her lover, so Venus

kidnaps her grandson and turns him into Adonis. Both Venus and the nymph raise their boy-children into men-lovers: "Adonis has risen again." And, as the nymph moves from child to man, so the thought of Ascanius revives in Venus a longing for her earlier love. That longing is transferred to the reddened blooms which record her self-induced orgasmic pleasure.

If the nymph blushes, admitting her physical excitement, Venus flushes the world, expressing her sexual release in a roseate shiver. The protective Venus emerges as the emblazoned lover. She extends her body into the landscape. The red roses signify her union with the gored Adonis. Her love is linked to death. Where Venus reddens the landscape, transferring her unrealized feelings to it, the nymph whitens it. As her sexuality is experienced, the red roses are ingested. As her purity is sanctified, the lilies are thickened. The nymph's landscape is milky. Her nutriment spreads to fuse maternal instinct with sexual desire. The nymph's landscape is also rosy. Child and mother are eroticized as each feeds on returned love: lilies without, roses within. Their insides absorb the outside as they exchange identities. Both the nymph and Venus create the enclaves where their fantasies are fleshed out but, while Venus's pleasure is self-contained, the nymph rears a child who is awake to, and aware of, her needs. Extending her being into the fawn, she initiates the sexual cycle predicated by his responsiveness. The circle of love the nymph describes is incestuous. She mothers the fawn's love as he arouses her sexuality; she fosters the fawn's manliness as he corroborates her womanliness.

Unlike Ascanius, who cannot know his relationship to Venus and cannot resolve his destiny through her, the nurtured fawn recognizes his maternal origin in the nymph and publishes his erotic future with the kiss. Ascanius sleeps through Venus's transformation. The fawn awakens to the nymph's desire. His is a knowledge that registers in acknowledgment. Hers is a desire that can be realized. Within the circle of the garden, the deer is a Laura who says "yes," the nymph a Petrarch who shapes her audience. His rosy kiss not only corresponds in kind to the nymph's rosy blush on discovering his white foot; it satisfies her being and appeases, in kindness, a longing that led to the initial prolongation. With the returned kiss, the nymph explores one more version of the Diana/Actaeon myth, turning what Actaeon lost into what the deer discovered: the woman's desire. The deer does know the nymph and he responds to that knowledge the way Petrarch wishes Laura had: with a kiss. As the deer whitens, his outside reflects the nymph's inside, even as his rosy innards reflect her former blushes. Each becomes the other in drag, as if Diana were a deer, Actaeon, a woman. With the Diana of the inside story, Marvell identifies a form of communication that builds on the cycles of the love poetry convention. It begins with the nymph's "blush" and its initial corroboration of longing and progresses through the transference of desire into an object of desire (the fawn-child). In Wyatt's "long love," a blush starts a cycle of noncommunication that ends in impasse. Here, the "blush" is returned. The sign of initiation results in an active response. The "heart's forest" of "Long love" exposes man to his own bestiality. The garden of "Nymph" exposes the beast to femininity.

The multiple transformations of the garden—the deer's conversion from animal to child, child to man, offspring to lover; the nymph's reversion from victim to creator to recipient—suggest a circle of connection (mirrored in the multifoliate rose, the understanding reader, the embracing lover) that at once underlines the object of poetry and eliminates the need for it. Petrarchan poetics are based on absence. As Kenneth Cool observes: "Every object in the landscape has the metonymic power to evoke the beloved's total presence. And to this end, the entire natural scene becomes a vast sign system jogging the lover's memory of its absent referent."[14] The nymph's garden contains all the conventionalized flora and fauna of the Petrarchan landscape, but the objects fade into abstraction (the roses are eaten, the deer hides) as the thoughts are materialized in the realized kiss. The text is immediately read and the response is an instant return. As she condenses the fawn's life, raising him from child to lover, so she lives the Petrarchan process, turning its desired end for a sympathetic other into her conversional premise. If, as Gordon Braden suggests, Petrarchan poetics are based on the equation between failed love and poetic triumph,[15] the nymph changes the dynamics of the equation. The Laura-fawn satisfies her. He reads her desire and fulfills it. The nymph subtracts the usual Petrarchan repertoire of loss. Once she gets what she wants, she no longer needs to sublimate her desire in its replacement, the poem, or to sublimate her presence in its denial, the self-canceling metaphor.

As a woman who realizes her femaleness through an art usually privileged to males and as a writer who enacts the reproductivity Petrarchism avoids, the nymph eliminates the end product: the text. She replaces its phallic inventions with her physical realizations. The nymph's feminization of the deer in terms of sensitivity and his empowerment of her in terms of initiative suggest how the poetics of failure can be reversed. At the same time, the nymph and fawn reverse the reversals. He is both male lover responding (with the roseate kiss) to her female desire and a female reader who understands—and hence obviates the need for—the poem. The deprived Petrarch of the *Rime sparse* is immortalized in the laurel of his poetic remains. A satisfied nymph can dispense with the remains. Inventing a woman who creates a vanishing text even as she points to a triumphant love, Marvell reverses the laurels of Petrarchism. Instead of an immobilized tree, the nymph envisages a mobile paradise—the divine landscape imbricated beyond the garden. Her Elizium is a projected painting, one which the reader, remanded to the steadily deteriorating statue, will never get to see. Here, the web-work of the hypertext is tantalizingly dangled before the audience even as its purified whiteness renders its links both invisible to earthly eyes and beyond the reach of mortal hands.

Nothing Without

Outside the garden, the text seems much more important, its context visualized, statue rather than poem. Inside the garden, the nymph suggests ideas which are then enacted. Outside, the nymph "bespeaks" images which she then withdraws. There's the rub. The statues are necessary reminders which the nymph dangles and then, retaliatively, renders fragile. The statues become "the absent referent" of the naturalized landscape, recalling both garden and beloved. But, whereas Petrarchan poetry replaces the missing beloved with a verbal image that lasts, the nymph's retaliation elaborates a concrete image which will eventually dissolve. In the bower, the fawn is an Actaeon invited to join and read Diana. Outside the garden, the Diana of the Iphigenia myth takes over and subtracts what was engendered, pulling fawn, child, and lover into a privileged country. In the framing story, the nymph withdraws the idealized text she created in the bower. After the heavenly landscape to which she runs, and the love landscape from which she withdraws, the nymph imbricates two more tableaux, one which hardens gradually as she speaks, the other which softens gradually as she invents. In the first, she reflects her situation, the nymph and fawn in a last moment of impassioned communication; in the second, she deflects her vision, ostensibly preserving the marble tableau but actually effacing its eternalizing possibility.

The first image turns backward toward the lost garden:

> The Tears do come
> Sad, slowing dropping like a Gumme.

> So weeps the wounded Balsome: so
> The holy Frankincense doth flow.
> The brotherless *Heliades*
> Melt in such Amber Tears as these. (ll. 95–100)

The scene (he weeping her tears / she weeping his) is first crystallized in amber to emerge eternally self-referential and then (the shining crystal, the sparkling gold) eternally blocked by Diana's shrine:

> I in a golden Vial will
> Keep these two crystal Tears; and fill
> It till it do o'reflow with mine;
> Then place it in *Diana's* shrine. (ll. 101–104)

Sequestering the vial from the marble statue she commands, the nymph closes off from posterity the "whiteness" she experienced with the fawn and the Elizium she projects for him. When the nymph places the "crystal" tears with her overflowing ones inside the golden vial, she hides (in the darkness) what she now sees. Depriving the world of the sight of saint and hagiographer, her "keeping" becomes a guarding of the secret, the golden vial, a grail reserved only for the initiate. The nymph preserves the first tableau but privileges it only to Diana.

In sonnet 65, Shakespeare similarly plays with hidden and exposed jewels. Seeking immortality, the speaker states the problem and finds a solution:

> where, alack,
> Shall Time's best jewel from Time's chest lie hid?
> Or what strong hand can hold his swift foot back,
> Or who his spoil of beauty can forbid?
> O none, unless this miracle have might,
> That in black ink my love may still shine bright.[16]

The nymph hides and so keeps the crystal jewel of the fawn in the golden "chest" of Diana's shrine; Shakespeare transcribes his love in "black ink," imprisoning him in his arsenal against time, even as he exposes him to future observers. While the nymph retains two distinct selves, Shakespeare contracts lover and beloved to the bright shining of "my love." In "penning" immortality, Shakespeare enlists his lover in the conspiracy he leads and thereby celebrates his own origination. An outward expression of his private vision, the "miracle" signals his own reincarnation as desirer. His "love" ignites the shining torch that turns the spotlight on the poet. The nymph's expanding feeling crystallizes two earthly selves—she hiding their remnants by burying him with her—and anticipates two heavenly selves—the deer effecting her transformation by leading her to it. When he promises exposure, Shakespeare confines the lover to the blackness of his objectification. His immortality *later* confines the beloved *now*. When she promises secrecy, the nymph transcends time and frees her lover in milky whiteness. Her shining shrine blackens the memory of the fawn simultaneously as it releases him to romp in Elizium now. Her future obscurity facilitates his momentary release. Shakespeare's confining words promise an earthly eternity. The nymph's hidden treasure subverts the earthly and frees her to follow the fawn into the Elizium that excludes posterity. For Shakespeare, memory is art. For the nymph, art dissolves along with memory. Shakespeare's immortality is textual; the whole world has access to his innerness. The nymph's is material but it is a materiality whose confines emerge untouchable, always out of reach of the uninitiated. If, as Butler argues, there is a relationship between citation and materiality, then the nymph's refusal to cite or to tell means that her Elizium is not to be shared. Her materialization there presupposes a radically anagogic formulation.

The nymph preserves her reflective image in the golden shrine of Diana's statue, but her second image (the ostensibly public tableau of the marble statue) self-destructs. First the nymph freezes her tears in the amber she hides. Then the nymph melts her tears in the marble statue she erects. The sequestered amber immediately denies the world of the brightness she projects. The public tribute erodes gradually. Its whiteness fades as the nymph seems to give what she withholds for a second time. In the carefully designed double tableau, she seems doubly victimized as woman. But does the tear fetish render her what the audience "think[s she is]": the weeping victim of the world's brutality? Or does she turn what seems to be the source of her misery (the amber tears reflecting what is lost) into the arsenal of her defense (the fountain tears obliterating the little that is left)? The statue brings up the question of posterity and underlines the audience's exclusion from the vision. Like the decimated Actaeon, the statue falls apart. Like those of the threatened Agamemnon, dynasties are endangered. When she runs away, the nymph suggests a finality that Petrarchan remembrance overcomes. Her monument corrodes the form that consoles Petrarch. If Petrarchan remembering reconstitutes the male inscriptions lost in the Actaeon disintegration, the nymph's incipherability emasculates and erases. By the time she gets round to the second tableau, the nymph has aligned herself with a separatist vision. She is unknowable. Petrarch's Diana withdraws from the deer and dismembers the man: "I felt myself drawn from my own image" (*Rime sparse* 23). Unrecognized, he emerges, like Ovid's Actaeon, only a hunted object. Like Actaeon's dogs, the wanton soldiers see only the deer-as-hunted-object. Because they cannot possibly understand it, the nymph pulls the text out of sight (inside the inside, tears enclosed in vial, vial hidden in shrine) and so guards its secrets. To the many Sylvios, she leaves a fractured world, her statue one of many adornments Marvell's mower cited "against gardens." She bequeaths only a decaying reminder, taking with her into Elizium the reflective crystal of her exclusive vision.

For a brief time simultaneous to the interior story, the reader saw what the fawn read. Now the reader stands outside the discourse. Without the deer as first reader, the nymph loses her desire to play with the inversions of love poetry. Marvell's nymph plans her silence. She substitutes deprivation for violation and renders herself fundamentally inviolable. The revenge of silence makes the world seem "wronger" than it ever was initially. Though Hamlet rambles and Lear rages, their worlds are purged by their violence. The quiet withdrawal in this poem deprives the world of a richness the nymph takes with her into Elizium. As she follows the fawn into the heaven she projects for him, so she tempts her audience, through the story she tells and the statue she designs, to follow her sightings. But when she arrives at Elizium, her story will end; when future generations arrive at the statue, it will be gone. She enlists no Horatios to tell and retell. The transforming power of her imagination—the elisions of gender and genus she made possible—constitutes the private genius she withdraws.

Unlike Petrarch, who reverts to the eternalizing conceit and finds solace in the poetic rather than fleshly laurel, the nymph leaves no artistic comfort. Petrarch violates Diana/Laura's command. He makes "word" (p. 62), recording what she forbad him in *Rime sparse* 23, of his heart/ change and ends hart/changed. In the inside story, the nymph begins with the hart/change and ends with an exchanged heart. She extends her vision and fosters in the deer a sympathetic other. But in the revenge of silence, she privileges that mutuality, taking the deer out of range. There can be no earthly reprintings of the responsiveness (the blush of desire / the rush to requital) imprinted by the kiss. The kiss is an immediately sympathetic reading of the love-text she creates. When she effaces the vision, the nymph severs all ties with her listeners. Geoffrey Hartman is right when he says that the subject of "Nymph complaining" may be "musings generally,"[17] both as poetic kindling and reflective afterthought. Inspired by the deer, the nymph reared him to be the ideal reader. Each sustained the circle of mutual support essential to the creative act. Deprived of that responsiveness, the nymph by her silence deprives the world. She keeps from it what she gave.

While Hartman, Berger, and Goldberg see the nymph as a figure for Marvell, their elisions fail to take the nymph's success fully into account. With the nymph's realized love, Marvell questions the Petrarchan poetic of loss even as he uses its dynamic of desire to flesh out female invention and voice. The nymph's procreative powers (her motherly instincts toward the fawn) energize her creative powers (her poetic wooing of the fawn). The fostering of the deer guarantees her what Petrarch lacked: the sympathetic other. Her Petrarchan "complaint" celebrates her love by inflicting Diana-Actaeon's revenge; the "death of her fawn" silences future complaints by inflicting Diana-Agamemnon's punishment. As her child, the fawn imitates the nymph even as he instills in her the need to draw him back, to get him to respond at the end with the reddened kiss that matches the initial reddening blush of her desire. That he does respond is a tribute to the nymph's power to direct his response. As her reflection, he is a Narcissus whose object of desire is still an other, she an Echo whose voice is her own. In the garden, the nymph and fawn form an enclosed pair, organically self-referential.

The nymph avenges Sylvio (the lover who, like the lady in Donne's "Jeat Ring Sent," gives a gift as a way of writing the beloved off) by creating a lover who writes her in. The deer responds fully to what she feels. His instinctual sympathy immediately absorbs—and so eliminates the need for—a text. She avenges the soldiers by creating an art that fades. Her garden pales as her red roses are ingested. In the second story—where the tableau becomes the presence that evokes the absent referent—she mocks the eternalizing conceit in the Petrarchan convention by annihilating its sign. With a female Petrarch, Marvell reempowers the source and returns poetic privilege to its original wellspring. Petrarch wrote for two audiences—the unyielding Laura who rejected him and the pliant readers who would give him, beyond his life and hers, the sympathy he couldn't immediately win. The nymph writes for one audience who returns, with the response she shapes, the spirit of her letter. When she takes the spirit with her, she renounces the form and eternalizing baggage of sublimation.

Her secrecy constitutes a critique of the Petrarchism that initially energized her. In letting go of sublimation, the nymph dissolves Petrarch's
sympathetic others. The little story of the nymph's triumph has a larger
critical context when seen in the light of what the nymph takes away.
This wallflower's revenge constructs a wall between her private visions
and the world's image of her. Her form prefigures formlessness, her formulations privileged only—as with Iphigenia at Taurus—to the initiates now
sequestered in Diana's shrine, now hurrying to Elizium.[18] Like the dissolving manna in "On a Drop of Dew" and the sun in "Coy Mistress," the
nymph and fawn *run*. They find a resolution in dissolution.

In "Whoso list to hunt," the deforming and transforming wind describes the woman's restlessness and her impulse to resist poetic materialization. Implicated in her elusiveness, Wyatt feels incapable both of
holding the shape eluding him and arresting the thoughts pursuing him.
But with the nymph's evaporation—her dying into an Elizium she envisions and her escape from the engravement she commissions—Marvell
gives formlessness wings of thought. The whitened fawn follows the pure
"swans and turtles," the redness of the digested roses now totally within,
the unrealized passion they symbolize already experienced. Diffusing her
redness with his whiteness, the deer passes it back to her. She absorbs
inwardly with the kiss what, in her blush, she showed outwardly. As it
courses through her veins, the nymph's passion is realized rather than
symbolized. Understood by the fawn and returned, her feelings become
acts rather than thoughts, expressed energy rather than repressed libido.
Inside the garden, the deer reads her heart and returns with artlessness the
rose of her blush. When the roses are ingested, the bower itself is whitened,
its purity the earthly *footing* for what will become the heavenly wings.
The rose of idealized love is replaced by the lily of transposed divinity. The
nymph's garden is a rehearsal stage for the grand theater in Elizium; its
processes, the whitened statues worn down, the running deer headed up,
are preparations for the longer flight, anticipations that, like the dew's
self-enclosing roundness, already enact their expectations.

If statues are visual representations of the sublimations engendered
by Petrarchan fame—words solidified as things—the nymph's corroding
monument demonstrates how little she relies on substitution. Her things
fade into words. Her words fade into silence. Petrarch marbleized Laura,
calcified her hardness, and eternalized his tears in distilling and stilling
words. In *Rime sparse 265*, he imagines a time when the marble will melt,
a millennium Wyatt undoes in "Process of time" when he puts the lady out

of frame. The nymph doubles Petrarch's wished-for eventuality. First, she turns it into a psychological fact as she softens the fawn's mind in her garden realization. Then she renders it a physical certainty as she escapes with the fawn into the paradise of Elizium. Her private triumph outfaces the consolations of public fame. Mystifying herself and escaping with the fawn to an Elizium men cannot fathom, the nymph dissolves her Petrarch into a Laura-Mercury who, having proven her shaping powers in the dilation of the inside story, follows her evasive impulses by deconstructing the frames of discourse.

In the nymph's revenge, Petrarchism is regendered. Its achieved love renders the other whom Petrarch couldn't convince totally sympathetic. Its projected transcendence renders all the others Petrarch recruited wholly unnecessary. If "Change" breaks down boundaries to liquify forms, "Nymph" dissolves boundaries to abstract them, unshaping solids to evolve a female vision of space *beyond* signs, a female version of language that moves—through earthly silence and heavenly play—elsewhere. That revenge imbricates—and then destroys—two stories: the first that of the nymph's fleshly triumph; the second that of her artistic destructiveness. In the flesh, the nymph reaches heaven and so eliminates the earthly picture. In the art, she destroys the statue and so flattens its material reality. Thus there are no layers left, no sign of the complications she evolved, no remnant of the love she preserved. In "Nymph" Marvell speaks a female revenge. In "Upon Appleton House," he goes one step further in flexing gender, moving into the space *between* signs that eliminates the opposition between self and other. He thereby annuls the need for revenge. The nymph moves on to an Elizium that occurs after forms have evaporated. The "Appleton House" poet returns to a time when forms have not yet materialized.

A-MAZING AND A-MUSING

After the Garden in "Appleton House"

In "The Nymph complaining for the death of her Faun," the female narrator flattens out the anamorphic portrait that Petrarchism generally produces to tell a single-dimensional story she gradually erases. In "Upon Appleton House, to my Lord Fairfax," imbrication once again reveals a narrative doubleness and so uncovers two selves—first the historian, an "I" who, chronicling patriarchal marriage, sees women as ornaments to be appended; then the poet who, idealizing freedom, follows the Petrarchan woman's desire for detachment by unhinging himself. In "Change," Donne speaks the force of the woman folded over into himself. He is Van Gogh's sun to her brush stroke. In "Appleton House," the self unfolds, totally relinquishing force. The sun reflected in the encircling river of the crucial stanza 80 is diluted in its own watery image. If Wyatt and Donne connect Petrarchism, with its desirable *one*, to libertinism, with its desiring *many*, the "Appleton House" Marvell ties marriage to Petrarchism. The mania of idealization fuses with the manacles of family. In his subversion of the Fairfaxes, whose history "Appleton House" ostensibly records, Marvell pulls away from the heritage of Petrarchan success to find in private poetic mindlessness the release necessary for his new vision.

The movement beyond the form of poetic and social convention in the "abandonne" of stanza 81 links Marvell's poet to Laura-Mercury's deforming impulses. When he demystifies the poet, the Marvell of "Appleton House" "eases" into sexual neutrality. The idyllic languor—the relaxation from the pressure to formulate the self or to be a formulating self—extends (into the late seventeenth century and beyond) the womanly vision Wyatt and Donne acknowledge more violently as they pull away from Petrarch. If the Wyatt of "Whoso list to hunt" stops the poem by assimilating the woman, the "I" of "Appleton House" experiments with formlessness by similarly bending gender rules. In the watery kisses of "Change," the man espouses a poetic too large for concrete comparisons. The eternity he envisions as the woman is an expression of her excited feeling about a future openness. In the watery immersions of "Appleton House," the poet doesn't get much beyond an earthly desire to bypass conventional forms. But his rebellion involves a similar break with the restrictions of lyric exactitude. When he explores the aftermath of Petrarchan appropriation and familial enclosure, the Marvell of "Appleton House" achieves poetic license and subverts the courtship and marriage negotiations that structure narrative. The nymph forges her imagined Petrarch and her family too. In "Appleton House," Marvell rejects both. Having exhausted Petrarchism, in the vanishing text of "Nymph," Marvell observes marriage in the chambers of the Fairfaxes and invents a persona who prefers to remain outdoors. Freeing himself from all confines, the poet speaks for "marginal space and . . . liquid space."[1] Like Laura-Mercury in joy, he moves into the unlocatable. Unrecoverable, he has "gone fishing."

"The Garden" begins with a similar desire to escape the traditional poetic muse but its critique reverses hierarchies without eliminating them. It strengthens—rather than questions—the appropriative male. Where the Petrarchan woman runs away from man, the flirtatious nature of "The Garden" runs into him:

V

What wond'rous Life in this I lead!
Ripe Apples drop about my head;
The Luscious Clusters of the Vine
Upon my Mouth do crush their Wine;
The Nectaren, and curious Peach,
Into my hands themselves do reach;
Stumbling on Melons, as I pass,
Insnar'd with Flow'rs, I fall on Grass.

VI

Mean while the Mind, from pleasure less,
Withdraws into its happiness:
The Mind, that Ocean where each kind
Does streight its own resemblance find;
Yet it creates, transcending these,
Far other Worlds, and other Seas;
Annihilating all that's made
To a green Thought in a green Shade. (p. 52)

The fruits of stanza 5 may be feminine but, in their extensions, they inseminate the "I" who gives birth to landscapes that project male vision. As the ocean in stanza 6, the mind becomes the nurturing womb of resemblances, where metaphor emerges in "streightness" what William Kerrigan calls "the clearest thing around."[2] That clarity is phallic. Whatever Venuses rise from the mind's ocean in stanza 6, they stem from the extensions of stanza 5. "The Garden" does without the woman of Petrarchism in the same way as "The Gallery" narrator resolves his misogyny: by turning the woman into a man. As Cronos to the emergences, the "I" cuts his metaphors out of a re-membered patrimony. Each kind "finds" the resemblance it "creates." Invention is a recovery of self. When he identifies the male Apollonian imagination as the origin of other worlds and other seas, the "Garden" poet obviates women by writing out Daphne. First he establishes in the resources of his own mind the pool of Petrarchan metaphor; then he achieves, in transcendent "other worlds," the eternity of Petrarchan sublimation. Idealizing sexual loss without risking sexual encounter, the "I" of "The Garden" engineers the poetic success that maintains the Petrarchan balance. Despite its rejection of love and war, "The Garden" is Petrarchan in its methodology, heroic in its idleness. Its mind produces clear images of its desire for itself.

In "Appleton House," Marvell finds in looseness what "The Garden" forges in "streightness." His poet imitates, rather than appropriates, the woman. That imitation involves a pleasure in less. Formless, boundless, selfless, the poetic "I" of "Appleton House" ceases to impose. Though "The Garden" vision begins in "streight" resemblance which it then transcends, it still remains within the vocabulary of male origination. Its other worlds require no other words. In "The Garden," ripeness is everything. In "Appleton House," readiness (for what might still be expressed) is all. The bird-soul of "The Garden" knows where it is going. With its appetite stimulated by recollection, its wings wave upward and carry the image-making complex of the oceanic mind into a light its maker already knows. Suspending his foot, the "I" of "Appleton House" slides downward and into the osier, sidestepping the familiar. It *hangs on* and *leans over* the unknown elements it bridges:

> Abandoning my lazy Side,
> Stretcht as a Bank unto the Tide;
> Or to suspend my sliding Foot
> on the Osiers undermined Root. (ll. 643–46)

When he attaches himself to the osier, the "I" acquires the haziness of its bent, the opposite of the straightness of "The Garden." If the tree of "The Garden" is a laurel, the trees of "Appleton House" are, first, the pine of stanza 80 and, then, the willow of stanza 81. In the pine, Apollo mourns female loss. In the willow, the poet follows female openness. The "Garden" tree is fixed firmly in the masculine self. Its laurel is phallically upright. The osier's undermined roots straddle the elements and therefore are obligated to neither. Folded over, the "I" of "Appleton House" similarly dangles his line and remains part of both worlds. Whereas the "I" of "The Garden" "amazes" himself with images that replicate his own imagination, the "I" of "Appleton House" amuses himself with images that have not yet happened. Whereas Petrarchism establishes itself heroically against the woman's resistance, the poetic "I" of "Appleton House" forgoes heroics. His unruliness eliminates the clear thought and masculine assertion that characterize "The Garden." He gives up and abandons himself *to* his female proclivities even as he gives *in* and acknowledges the female always already there, at his side, as Eve.

Monique Wittig argues that, in order to reflect on women's situation in history, it is necessary to interrogate the dialectics that were used to determine it. That means going back to Plato and Aristotle "to comprehend how the categories of opposition that shaped us were born."[3] Wittig then shows how Aristotle's sexual divisions were at first merely descriptive variations of "a kind of carpenter's square" which only belatedly became "a means of creating metaphysical and moral differentiations in Being."[4] What Wittig wants is to dialecticize the dialectics or to question what will really happen to "humanness" once "all categories will be transferred onto the side of One, of Being, of the subject."[5] Such a fusion, she argues, can "only be helped by the process of abstraction, where the Other, whatever its kind, is included."[6] It is at the level of inclusive otherness that Marvell's "I" floats between signifiers, as the poet "suspends" his sliding foot to indulge in a poetics of "in-between." Letting go, he loosens his hold on the old polarities and, becoming the other, widens the self.

In stanzas 71 through 81, the "Appleton House" poet finds himself in that stretching, his "fishing" an activity that feminizes him by being what Aristotle defines as unresolved, ambiguous—bent. In losing himself, he exposes himself as already female:

Male	Female
limited	unlimited
one	plurality
at rest	moving
straight	curved[7]

This plurality of possibility replaces the male limits that Petrarchism invests in the "one" with a female appreciation of openness. The revelation of doubt and the impulse to keep moving stops the "Appleton House" "I" from simply projecting the "other" through which Petrarchism identifies the self. If we begin an analysis of the self producing the poem by examining what Judith Butler calls the string of performances in the poem, what we uncover is an "I" whose being is curved and whose self-portrait bends to include the other. "Transferring the categories," Marvell reveals his female inside, rendering Aristotle's polarities what Wittig would have them be: descriptive, not prescriptive. Mimicking the osier's curve, he abandons himself to the "laziness" of the unformed Eve. What he wants is what he already has: the potential for a loosening of self. He enacts that potential as he moves away from the limitations of male form and into the excess of the in-between. While the Wyatt of "Whoso list to hunt" remains unhappy in impasse, the "I" of "Appleton House" enjoys going nowhere. Undoing the physical locus by obscuring the visual focus, Marvell glides into an anagogic territory which eroticizes the inspirational wind even as it feminizes the inspired poet. But it does so by a process of what Wittig calls abstraction, a departure from preconceived notions of gender and genre that simultaneously allows an inclusion of the other in the self.

The historian chronicles the private life of public figures; the poet outlines instead a hitherto unrevealed life figured by his own joyful emergence in stanzas 71–81. By finding a self totally apart from the history it seems to praise—the mosaic of Old Testament violence and New Testament sacrifice—Marvell evolves an "I" for "Appleton House" which frees itself from the pressures of all traditions. Generically a "country house" poem,[8] "Appleton House" bypasses its own conventions and subverts the dynastic impulses it seems to celebrate. If the Donne of "Change" escapes the repressive returns of Petrarchism by espousing a female nursery, the poetic "I" of "Appleton House" does away with nurseries and their rhymes, lovers and their narratives. He eliminates the reproductive baggage of the maternal other by mothering his own deformations, inventing an alternative to Petrarchism *and* marriage.

Marvell's subjectivity in "Appleton House" is solipsistic. The "I" in the forest sequences is happy. The self revealed there undermines the history it chronicles by seeking to go "behind" the "before" and to get back to that place preceding beginnings. In *Rime sparse* 237, Petrarch prays to get through history, hoping for "the last evening / which will separate in me the living earth from the waves." In "Appleton House," Marvell attempts to escape history altogether by regressing to a period before—or at least apart from—chronological time. In that respect, "Appleton House" denies both the sublimations of Petrarchism (the poem as replacement for the desired person) and the consolations of the familial (the person as replacement for idealized desire). Maria's vitrification (as Jim Swan writes)[9] therefore appears Medusalike, the fluidity of deific communion in nature replaced by the calcification of hard shells. Her marriage is a union that stops growth: "the priest shall cut the sacred Bud" (l. 740). Marvell's familial doubts surface only after a reading that undercuts the sequences of seeming praise. To understand the poet's self-story, it is necessary to unravel the historian's "other" stories. Marvell's history works to reveal an uninvolved self—the "I" who makes an appearance only briefly in a sequence totally apart from the chronicled enterprises. Lacking both mother and lover, the poetic "I" has no history and no destiny. In the osier sequence, the "I" experiences what Laura-Mercury wants—freedom from the restrictions "thinking" imposes. To get at this abstract self is to delve beneath the surface, to uncover the self apart from history.

Harry Berger, Jr., argues that "Appleton House" has a single speaker who is "staging himself, trying on (and trying out) certain conventional 'roles'—attitudes, gestures, habits of mind—and delighting in his play both as participant and audience."[10] Writing specifically about persona, Charles Molesworth similarly refers to an umbrella personality, embracing three integrated roles—historian, philosopher, and priest—whose function is to praise a praiseworthy house.[11] More recently, Harold Skulsky calls the narrator a guide who, as performer, plays with "the amphibiousness of discourse"[12] to challenge the place a bit even as he undermines his own semantic tricks. Most readings of "Appleton House" imply one complex (multi-mooded or multi-voiced) personality presiding over the tour. The single-speaker theory strengthens the historical case, situating the "I" as tourist-recorder in the house of Fairfax rather than explorer-poet in the house of the self. But Marvell has two stories to tell, for which he paints two portraits: first the narrative of the family; then its counterstory in the antifamilial plot of the poet.[13] One persona even stages his own disappearance to make way for the other. Both cannot exist simultaneously nor do they build into one larger all-embracing self. As Lyotard writes of the anamorphic portrait, "what is recognizable in one space is not recognizable in the other."[14] The first persona, the historian, follows the experience of the events he records. His function is to try on—by writing about them—the lives he chronicles. He covers the self in multiple guises. The second persona, the self here called the poet, struggles to find something more personal and private. He uncovers the self and finds multiplicity. The two narrators are mutually exclusive. The "historian" is committed to narrative and its imperatives. The poet's commitment is to lack of commitment. The historian gets caught up in sexual politics. The poet's story is gender neutral.

While the historical "I" is quickened by the women of the poem, the poetical "I," seeking a deformation where he can become yet another self, finds his inspiration in something older than Eve. Oblivious to the sexually generative cycle through which the rest of the world evolves, the poetical "I" is formed not by the womanly other Petrarchism appropriates but by the zephyr of poetic license. The central biblical moment for the poet is Genesis 1, particularly its earliest sections. Joined to the wind, the poet moves before even the sibyl to a time predating prognostication. Unraveling himself to a place *behind* the *before*, he is no longer mourning a lost innocence but prophesying one yet to come. In terms of the locus of the poem, he has to be neither "in nor out." He remains totally apart from the world absorbing the historian. Through the poet's persona, Marvell evades the chronological world altogether. He eliminates what happened by consuming it beforehand. The birth of the poet who finds himself is facilitated by the historian who never seems able to be himself as, in a series of historical impersonations, he leads the objects of his admiration to their inevitable demise. While most autobiographies insist on the family story and its formative influence, Marvell invents an "I" (in the poet) who has no history. Without mother and lover, the poet finds his pleasure in relinquishing ties, despite the fact that the historical "I" is fixated, from his nunnery opening to his saintly conclusion, on versions of idealized enclosure. Thus the anamorphic portraits in "Appleton House" resemble, in their techniques, the two focal points of Holbein's *Ambassadors*. But if Holbein's portrait imbricates death, Marvell's imbricates life and so resolves itself in opposing formulations: the first, a series of solid architectural shapes, returning inevitably to the house of the Fairfax demesne; the second, a series of vague spatial abstractions, loosely related back to the wind and water of Genesis 1. Marvell's imbrication of the poet is postmodern. He returns, through anamnesis, anagogy, and anamorphism, to an earlier time, a place before the world began, to recover a self "initially forgotten." But, in that recovery, he also uncovers a dematerializing desire. This movement backward is never over because it establishes the realm of the not-yet-born. But it also is never total because history has the first and last word in this poem. Before the poem gets too comfortably away from boundaries, the patriarchal forces coalesce in Maria, who, dismissing the poet and his "Toyes," draws the historian back "in."

Deconstructing History

The cycle so seductive to the historian at first builds into more and then shrinks into less. It thereby summarizes the family plot from which the poet will withdraw: first, the nuns speak of spiritual growth; second, Fairfax plans a familial dominion; third, Thestylis secures her expansionist empire; in the next two sequences, flora imitate fauna. The meadows double through mirroring, gathering the metaphoric dimensions of the river. Through flooding in the fifth story, the river expands its dominion. Its literal overflow equals the meadow's aggrandizing ambitions. Finally, reorganizing the landscape so that it once again frames its inhabitants, Maria will recapitulate in her future marriage the lives already lived by her family. The overweening impulses in the first five stories lead inevitably to diminished conclusions, which the historian struggles consequently to tell. In the case of Maria, he only implies the decline when he links her future to hopes already dashed.

Pointing to the pointlessness of his situation, the historian presides over his own disappearance. When he subtly admits, in the middle of the forest sequence, how he has been included in the historical indictment he issues, the historian devises an escape that facilitates the poet's emergence. There is only the short sequence in the forest where the poetic "I" flourishes. His domain ends when Maria appears on the scene and her centralizing powers call the historian out of retirement. Yet that brief moment is the climax of the poem. In it, something new is formed that obviates Genesis 2 (and the subsequent fall), by remaining asexual, and antedates humanity's appearance in Genesis 1 (and its consequent "dominions"), by being allied with the earliest movement—that of the wind upon the waters. The interior sequences first reveal the trick whereby the historian allows the poet to emerge in stanza 70; then they revel in the freedom the poetic "I" achieves in 71–84. Both interior sequences are original and remarkable. But they can occur only after the, at first, seemingly remarkable Fairfax history is followed and cast off.

In the historian's sections, the nuns, Isabel, Thestylis, the mowers' partners, and, finally, Maria dramatize the constrictive bonding described at the end of Genesis 2. Circumscribed by "cleaving and leaving," that union is based on loss. Watching the unfolding scene before him, the historical "I" sees it as a refolding of an earlier story, as if all the enclosures of the poem finally nested in one box: the original pairing of Genesis 2. These stories operate on the inspirational premise of seduction into the sexual generational cycle which eventuates into a destructive, warlike sequence just as the story of Adam and Eve leads to Cain and Abel. The historian's section has two main loci: the lives the historical "I" follows: Fairfax, Thestylis, and the birds; and the landscape the historical "I" opens up: the meadow and the river. They unfold through distorted auditory *echoes*, which offer different versions of the same plot, and curved visual *mirrors*, which return negative images of an identical picture. As echo, Thestylis repeats Fairfax's story. As mirror, the meadow reflects the river. Then, in turn, the river closes in on, and doubles, the meadow. All those reverberations suggest a theory of history which is part of the historian's impasse: an abyss with Genesis 3 at the center. To get at the poet, it is necessary to get through the historical stories, to see them as sequences that are merely variations of the same plot. If, in Petrarch, women are idealized versions of what men project, in the historical sections, they are realized versions of what the men *are*. The women equal the men in their need to extend power. In Petrarch, women define, in their otherness, what the self is. In the historian's section, women achieve, in their acquisitiveness, what the men want.

Attempting to append Isabel, the nuns are masculinized in their uses of her, as, having incorporated her, Fairfax is feminized in his appendages. Both begin preaching insemination and end up—in the preparation of nun Appleton House as seedbed—undermining the comfort of gestation. Both turn the protective womb and nutritive impulse of the woman into the military arsenal of a man. The marital Thestylis is the logical culmination of the martial Fairfax. Similarly, the sowing nuns anticipate her reaping. The conversions of the poem render each subsequent event a version of the original. The denial inherent to the unrequited love of the lyric poem and the affirmation derived from the returned love of the family chronicle emerge identical. The "not having" of Petrarchism and the "giving" of marriage provide the same motive for appropriation. Marvell's critique of history—and its chronicle of dominion—ties Petrarchism to militarism in its espousal of conversion. Idealizing the woman and marrying her equals valorizing the man who dominates and appends her. In the historian's sections, "Appleton House" extends the acquisitiveness Marvell noted in the demonic Damon and the manic "Gallery" narrator to the real-life heroes whose lives are chronicled.

Fairfax's story is doubly intertwined with the nuns' beginnings. He reacts to their initiating assault by repeating their acquisitive pattern. They seek to join Isabel's virginity to theirs, as later he will add his sexuality to her and then hook the extended family to his vision:

> 'But much it to our work would add
> 'If here your hand, your Face we had:
> 'By it we would *our Lady* touch;
> 'Yet thus She you resembles much.
> 'Some of your Features, as we sow'd
> 'Through ev'ry *Shrine* should be bestow'd.
> 'And in one Beauty we would take
> 'Enough a thousand *Saints* to make. (ll. 129–36)

Planning Isabel's figurative dismemberment once she is enfolded, the sisters reproduce her. They plant her separated parts—like seeds—everywhere. The nun's flattery operates sequentially: first she compliments Isabel's originating and centralizing similarity to *our Lady*; then she anticipates how that resemblance will produce further converts. Wooing *our Lady* will—in time—produce lots of little Marys whom the nuns can—in turn—plant. The "thousand *Saints*" the nun envisions replicate Isabel's model. The nuns want Isabel "added" to them in order that they might use her seminal force, "take it in" and then spread it out again. The process of dismembering and remembering is achieved in the anticipated promotion of Isabel's image whose power proliferates through every shrine. The nun puns on sow/sew. Even as the sister tears Isabel apart, she stitches her into the solid "shrine" that contains the gathered images. Appending Isabel to them, and nurturing her seedlings, the nuns achieve the phallic extension that will enable them to "touch" heaven. Their appeal is twofold: first they will impress Mary and win themselves divine attention. Their extensions render them the "touching" orphans mother Mary adopts; then they will incorporate followers. Their manic enterprise renders them the formulative models the world emulates. Heavenly children of Mary, they are earthly mothers of the church. For the scattering of the *Rime sparse*, the nun first sows Isabel's image in the minds of the converts and then sews the converts into the body of the church. First she disseminates it; then she stitches them into the embroidered advertisement she will use to pull still other neophytes into the church. As Laura's idealized form wins Petrarch the sympathetic readers who consolidate his fame, so Isabel's enshrined icons will produce loyal converts to promulgate the faith.

While they seek immortality in the thousand saints they will engender in Isabel's likeness, Fairfax defines it in the "offspring fierce" (l. 241) who will perpetuate him with "successive valor" (l. 243), the sequential bravery of future generations. Like the seed stretching into the heavenly kingdom of the nuns, Fairfax's "blest Bed," where all things begin, is linked to his "warlike Studies," where all things end. The heavenly destiny of the nuns emerges the earthly hegemony of the military family:

> From that blest Bed the *Heroe* came,
> Whom *France* and *Poland* yet does fame:
> Who, when retired here to Peace,
> His warlike Studies could not cease. (ll. 281–84)

The bed Fairfax sought as sexual goal becomes the source of his military enterprise. In it, he plants the familial seed and, from it, he plans his "warlike Studies." As conjugal meeting place, the bed is the origin of human succession. As seed base, it forms the bottom of the garden and the poetically connected river. The source of both family and landscape is that "blest Bed" which has absorbed—in its earthly seed—the power the nuns sought in Isabel's heavenly insemination. The male bed becomes the female womb. As the nuns aggressively seek male extensions, Fairfax realizes a female encirclement. His manhood appropriates Isabel's womanhood in order to beget replicas of itself. When he turns the bed into a sexual and spatial origin, the historian anticipates the familial and geographical enclosures of the poem. As the meadows become water at first through analogy in stanza 48 and then literally in stanza 49, so the bed becomes both the grounding of the garden with its overflow in the unfathomable grass and the crib of the banked and then flooded Denton. Similarly, Fairfax, the planter of that bed, sows other beds that lead to the same abyss. His garden mirrors his mind and anticipates its subsequent activation, carried out, in the sequence of the poem, by the army of laborers he commands. He prepares for his familial future in the same way as he designed his military strategy. The contemplative "study" is warlike.

Thestylis's control in the next story is the end result of Fairfaxian design, as she turns the historian's idle spatial ruminations into a story she can pull into her purposeful temporal scheme. She interrupts his digression into the scene with her insistence on a progression into time as she anticipates both the rhythm of the mowers' love dance and the children who will perpetuate it in the yearly ritual of the "hay." *Thestylis's* alimentary aggression in the rail-killing evolves into the marital conquest of the hay-making. The odor of power mingles with the ardor of sex:

> And now the careless Victors play,
> Dancing the Triumphs of the Hay;
> Where every Mowers wholesome Heat
> Smells like an *Alexanders sweat.*
> Their Females fragrant as the Mead
> Which they in *Fairy Circles* tread:
> When at their Dances End they kiss,
> Their new-made Hay not sweeter is. (ll. 425–32)

Serpentine in its undulating sequence, the hay as a dance is equivalent to the just-mown grass in its sweetness. Similarly connected, the mowers are seductive in their power and seduced by what they have made. If man is grass,[15] then his hay is his end, even if it leads to the fairy circle of the dance in which the mowers are led by the sweet females. That circle is bewitching, since fairies entice the mowers into it, and prophetic, since it surrounds the men with encircling women in images that fix their sexual enclosure,[16] an enclosure already nested in Fairfax's bed. The "new-made hay"—a chain beginning with the mowers, followed by the women who then produce the children that replicate the cycle—unfolds from grass, through dance, to the eventually resulting offspring, as all three generations are thus connected by smell to a final fragrance that links the battle to the bed, even as it did Fairfax and Isabel. Alexander's sweat merges with female sweetness to engender the battle of the sexes. As Thestylis energizes the dancers with her inspiring nutriment, so the historian seems absorbed by her vision, himself caught by the odor so closely connected to the initiating plunder. The end of that plunder is the kiss of peace, war reversed. But the kiss, in turn, opens up the sexual cycle as the concentric circles of the fairy dance multiply in the annual ceremony here substantiated—and here "fed"—by an inspiring alimentary sweetness. Eating whets sexual hunger, which in quick succession becomes the aggressive appetite of war.

Thestylis's inspiration spreads, as the historian continues the scene drawn, withdrawing, and finally drawn again in his image of the "Table rase," which is simultaneously the first created world and the arena where the bulls enter to be mangled and—like the mowers who, as soldiers, "feed" into the historical slaughter—ultimately eaten. When he describes the still more leveling cattle, the historical "I" occupies a double place. He both participates in the procession and describes its progress, following the womanly lead already tracked by the mowers in pursuit of the dancers, the cattle in quest of the hay, the meadow in imitation of the river, the nuns persuading Isabel, and Fairfax overcoming them. Like the hungry mowers, the hungry cattle are lured onto the stage by the nutriment that will make them as deadly as the bulls in Madrid. The peaceful circlings of the haying kiss prefigure yet another warry ring. But when he continues to tell Thestylis's story, the historian simultaneously retracts its fierceness and expands its scope:

> They seem within the polisht Grass
> A Landskip drawen in Looking-Glass.
> And shrunk in the huge Pasture show
> As Spots, so shap'd, on Faces do.
> Such Fleas, ere they approach the Eye,
> In Multiplying Glasses lye.
> They feed so wide, so slowly move,
> As *Constellations* do above. (ll. 457–64)

In the alimentary image of the feeding cattle, the earthly landscape is turned around so that it mirrors the heavens. With that inversion, the sequence reiterates the nun's vision of "touching our Lady." The cattle are "drawen" into the looking glass by the seductive food which they, in turn, will "feed upon." They convert their weakness into the energy for multiplication. The hungry child Thestylis nurtures emerges the sexually desirous adult she entices when he seeks to return, by insemination, to his womby origin. As the child "hardens" into the man and Thestylis's vague dew solidifies into edible manna, so the waving grasses emerge the polished glass which seduces the cattle and then reduces them inside the huge pasture. Eager to feed, the cattle are in turn fed upon. The feeders widen to diminish the world. The grass they eat becomes the mirror reflecting them, its size diminished as they are enlarged. But their enlargement is temporary as—approaching the eye—they are in turn reduced, the multiplying glasses alternately telescoped and microscoped. The first glass the poet duplicates is the mirror. It bridges kinds. Grass is glass, reflective and reductive. Its power is relative. Glass is grass, nutritive and reducible. Its function is devoured. The threatening bulls become voracious fleas, feeding on the skin they "spot" even as, approaching the eye that "spots" them, they slowly seem, like the eye-slicing camera in Buñuel's *Andalusian Dog*, to eat it up.

With the Thestylis story, the historian transfers the feeling he had of being dwarfed by the grasshoppers (ll. 370–72) onto the cows who are shrunken by the huge pasture. That diminution of the cattle changes the ominousness of the bull fight into a harmless image, reducing Thestylis's power. Her war story ends as it began, in a benign landscape. When he compares the cows to cow-shaped spots on the face, the historian turns them into grotesque monsters, fleas who, eating the flesh, feed (like Error's children in *The Faerie Queene*) on the face that fed them. Moreover that face becomes (as the fleas grow into stars) the firmament, stretching itself to the heavens. The multiplying glass at once causes an infestation that seems overwhelming and then diminishes (through the feeding) the differences that make shapes discernible. In Fairfax's story, the nuns disappear. Similarly, Thestylis's scene vanishes when the flattened earth is eaten away by the infestation. The sky takes over, reducing the earthly enterprise to a fixed and determined heavenly design. "Approaching the eye," the fleas presage their disappearance as they threaten to absorb the orb that "spots"—and aggrandizes—them in the first place. In its shining, the eye functions as the multiplying looking glass which, when the fleas approach, loses both its power to reflect and its power to observe. If there is no seer, there is nothing to be seen. Everything is devoured, as opposites— earth and sky, fleas and cows, men and women, meadow and river— emerge versions of each other. The conversionary impulses of the nuns and Fairfax are first mirrored in the landscape; then the mirror is again mirrored. The second glass the poet uses is the telescope. It bridges distance. Eye and grass come so close that vista is absorbed by viewer; reflector and lens replicate each other. Grass and glass are as transposable as sky and earth. The glass multiplies like grass. The grass is reflective like glass. Each entertains and absorbs the function of the other. The "revenge of the mirror people" here results in an annihilation of "all that's made."

In the concluding couplet of stanza 59, the historical "I" mirrors once again the imitative and seductive power he has been "drawen" to all along, this time returning to nature itself. Like the nuns, Fairfax, and

Thestylis, the river pulls in the world and then proclaims itself as central: "The River in itself is drown'd / And Isl's th' astonisht cattle round" (ll. 471–72). As the nuns sought to add Isabel to their arsenal, so the river turns the meadow into itself, enclosing the benumbed cattle (who are, by previous analogy and by extension, the dwarfed men in the meadows). First, everything is reduced in size; then it is changed in kind. When it eliminates generic differences, the river inverts the ox and eel, making the water sound (bellows) replace the land sight (cattle). The river opens itself up to take over the world. Principally that takeover consists of a makeover, a transformation which (like the metamorphic pattern already established) begins by an absorption that emerges as a mirroring, what Wittig calls a reversal "where everything everywhere corresponds to the Tweedledum and Tweedledee of Lewis Carroll."[17] When the river "in itself is drown'd," it becomes the ultimate seducer and libertine. It pulls in the water simultaneously as it pours it out. Its power to draw is a self-canceling funnel. Like the disappearing nuns and the castrated bull/fleas, the river vanishes as a contender. In order to be mirrored, the river must forfeit a portion of itself, and that portion becomes the suction cup that absorbs it. The river decomposes itself in the process of recomposing the world in its image. All the historical stories emerge versions of conversions: the desire to draw the world into the self.

When he reverts to the holt-fester, the historian becomes, like everything else, an absorber; only this time he pulls in his own power. The historian includes himself (with the "our flesh" of line 554) in sin and so, like all the other powers in the poem, is sucked up by the narrative flow. Emerging bait to the hewel's young of line 558, he describes his own death. He extends the possible participants in his history (by calling "us" into it) and retreats to its potential center (by including himself with us). For the first time, the historian gets involved and intertwined in the story. He inserts himself in the narration which now seems inescapable. Even the teller gets swallowed up. The history he tells is a sequence beginning with Genesis 3:

> Who could have thought the *tallest Oak*
> Should fall by such a *feeble Strok'!*

LXX

> Nor would it, had the Tree not fed
> A *Traitor-worm,* within it bred.

(As first our Flesh corrupt within
Tempts impotent and bashful *Sin*.)
And yet that *Worm* triumphs not long,
But serves to feed the *Hewels young*.
While the Oake seems to fall content,
Viewing the Treason's Punishment. (ll. 551–60)

The fall of the oak parallels the fall of the world. An auditory equivalent to the dwarfing impact of the meadow's telescoping of space, this reduction condenses time. The historian needs to arrive at the psychological beginning of the nest of stories he has been telling. He has to get to the Fall and that story has to be told in terms of an entrapment, a sucking in like all the others. Universalizing his experience, the historian underlines the ominous possibilities for disappearance. It doesn't just happen to nuns, or fleas, or cows. It happens to us.

In the historian's revisionist interpretation of Genesis, the flesh is the enticer, sin impotent and bashful. The comic role reversal makes the flesh into a mirror of the nuns wooing Isabel. The equation, however, has a retroactive thrust. If sin is Isabel, then she becomes Adam to Eve's temptation; the sexes are transposed as the myth is turned inside out. Finally, there is yet another regression, from Genesis 3 to Genesis 2 as Adam calls Eve back into his own rib. The shift (body tempting sin) reincorporates masculine power, as if the male parent were eating its female offspring. Like the double telescoping of sight and sound, that double exposure repeats the Thestylis episode with the compounding of feeding and breeding. The tree feeds the worm, which in turn is eaten by the hewel's young. And, as the tree disappears with the Fall, so does the traitor worm. It is swallowed up by the voraciously "feeding" young, as the face of the meadowy metaphor was infested by fleas. The punishment allows the tree to fall *content*, satisfied in its demise because what it encloses (the content) has been absorbed in the eating process.

In the hewel fable, the historical "I" eliminates both the temptation and the tempter even as he retreats one step further back toward the early, formless moments of Genesis 1. No longer telling the story of Thestylis or Fairfax by becoming them, the historian personalizes the hewel's story. The flesh of the simile is *our* flesh. The "I" has penetrated the narrative by reining it into his own story. He is the seducer appearing, like Fairfax in the nunnery, compellingly at the center. The history ends with the historian's absorption. The story is no longer "theirs." It becomes, with the "our," all inclusively his. With that admission, history also disappears. If, in the telescoping sections, the visual "I" is eaten, in the hewel section, the vocal "I" is effaced. Without eyes to locate it or tongue to tell it, history is annulled: it never happened. The next step in the deconstruction of time is to eliminate the future: nothing will ever happen. Having been consumed by the history he narrates, the historian is absorbed by what he tells. In the interlude, an "I"—divorced from history—is freed from the destiny of nuns, Fairfax, mowers, cattle, meadow, and river. Dispossessed of his past in stanza 70, he eliminates the future in stanzas 71–81. In the interim, he finds a space where a boundless self, unrestrained by the pressures of gender and genre, thrives. With that elimination, the poet is born. First, the poet dissolves the old forms of expression and unravels the tapestry of Mosaic law; then he eliminates the old need for expressiveness and discredits the philosophy of imposing mind. Unrestricted by the rules whereby one form of oppression simply substitutes for another—as the nuns are superseded by Fairfax, who in turn is replaced by Thestylis—an unruly self comes into being.

Constructing a Poet

As the flesh pulled back anticipated sin, so "Phancy" weaves into the tapestry events that have been prophesied. Like everything else in the poem, the future is devoured, as the most famous sibylline prophecies were burned by the warry fires they predicted. Out of that reassemblage, all history (Rome, Greece, and Palestine) merges into one origin which is at once *consumed* (united in the climactic moment of the tapestry) and annulled (because it has been already lived):

> Out of these scatter'd *Sibyls* Leaves
> Strange *Prophecies* my Phancy weaves:
> And in one History consumes,
> Like *Mexique Paintings*, all the *Plumes*.
> What *Rome, Greece, Palestine*, ere said
> I in this light *Mosaick* read.
> Thrice happy he who not mistook,
> Hath read in *Natures mystick Book*.
>
> LXXIV
>
> And see how Chance's better Wit
> Could with a Mask my studies hit! (ll. 577–86)

As history disappears (having reached, like the self-canceling nun's castle, the absorbing meadow, and the flooding river, its own apogee), so the poet, having emerged the reconstructor of the sibyl's leaves, creates the conditions for his own birth, not only from the love/war cycle but from the Mosaic law of antique, and hence already determined, style. Linked to the seasonal leaf, the "I" detaches himself from history. In a deciduous world, the leaf's arrival is a preparation for departure. Removed from the tree, the scattered leaves of the deciphering sibyl replace the scattered Isabels the nuns consolidate and the scattered rhymes Petrarch reconsolidates. The sibyl's leaves are pages of an unbound book, all causality unhinged.

To be fully released, the poet, now slowly emerging from the historian's dissipation, has to arrive at a mindlessness that allows him to find Chance's wit. The poet's conception eliminates preconception, as his engendering is determined not by a prediscursive sexuality but by the absence of impediments. If Fairfax secures his empire with the deliberateness of his "warlike Studies," the poet makes his "studies" the target of casual chance. He forfeits his power in favor of a better guise, the meanderings of accident. With the elimination of tempting sin, the historical "I" was freed from his sexual need. With the absorption of determining prophecy, the poet comes into a being freed from formulative desires. In fact, the poetic "I" relinquishes his prophetic impulse in the identical way the historian was relieved of his sexuality. He "consumes" it, eats it up. In the self-consuming mosaic of stanza 73, the poetic "I" eradicates the already lived past. With Chance's wit, he awaits the not-yet-lived future, allowing himself to destroy both the artifacts of study and the seduction of prophecy. Whereas in the early part of the poem, the historical "I" sought to become what he admired, here the poetic "I" strives to become a self who is not yet committed. Unlike the stony and leaden tables already lived, this light and feathery mosaic has not yet been thought. In fact, it is thought-free. Released at last from the confines of society and its inherent formulations, the poetic "I" celebrates his birth, entering a realm that undoes gender by masking separations, and then unhinges *genus* by allowing equivocation. The poet appears only after the historian has been defrocked. And he surfaces in two stages, the first straddling gender differences, as the "I" lets go of his formulative mind, the second resisting *genus* dominions, as the "I" evades formal boundaries. The conversions of Petrarchism are abandoned in favor of independent musings.

Sliding from the easy philosopher in stanza 71 to the easy languisher in 76, the poetic "I" is tossed, cooled, and flattered by the sensuality of nature. Removed from his own dominion, he emerges a passive female to the disarming suit of the wind:

> Then, languishing with ease, I toss
> On Pallets swoln of Velvet Moss;
> While the Wind, cooling through the Boughs,
> Flatters with Air my panting Brows.
> Thanks for my Rest ye *Mossy Banks*,
> And unto you *cool Zephyr's* Thanks,
> Who, as my Hair, my Thoughts too shed,
> And winnow from the Chaff my Head. (ll. 593–600)

As rapist, the "flattering" zephyr winnows not the "I's" physical clothes but his mental dressing. That ravishment leaves him metaphysically blank. The wind does not append him as a kind of wraith. It simply gives him a rest by separating him from the sources of his own self-stimulation. The poet has left his mind behind and thereby allowed himself to languish and play. Cooled by the wind and protected by the vines, he is motivated by neither a desire to formulate nor a need to emulate others. Panting in anticipation of Zephyr's winnowing, the "I" allows the inertia necessary to his emergence and permits his outside to reflect his inside. If Wyatt's undoing in "The long love" came when his inner turmoil was reflected in his face, here the "panting brows" mirror a self already female.

But the poet subsequently goes one step further, abandoning both the masculine assertiveness of the historian and the feminine passivity of his initial realization. With the spatial in-between, he establishes a state that encourages exploration. With the temporal in-between, he approaches a borderland, where things are and are not yet. Finally, with the descriptive in-between, he overcomes gender binaries to enter a place where selves are open and not yet committed. His enjoyment derives from "edging," coming close without falling in. In his simile, the "I" himself becomes the river's border; in his alternative ("or to suspend," l. 645), he eases himself unto the water-straddling roots of the leaning osier, itself a suspension between two worlds:

> Oh what a Pleasure 'tis to hedge
> My Temples here with heavy sedge;
> Abandoning my lazy Side,
> Stretcht as a Bank unto the Tide;

> Or to suspend my sliding Foot
> On the Osiers undermined Root,
> And in its Branches tough to hang,
> While at my Lines the Fishes twang! (ll. 641–48)

Banking the river, the "I" obscures the differences between land and water. Hanging his head on the river's edge, his side on the bank, his foot on the root, and his line on the fish, the "I" forfeits his own shape. He holds out by detaching himself. Abandoning [his] lazy [feminine] side, the poet lets go of formulation, his giving into laziness expressed (in abandon) as a giving up of the woman through which Petrarchism materializes. But his giving up (abandonment) is simultaneously a giving in (*abandonne*) to the woman. His equivocation in living at the edge allows him to release, and fall into, the other. To let loose is both to relinquish the recollection of history and to sink into abstraction. If, as Jane Hedley argues, metonymy depends on physical context and metaphor on mental connection,[18] the abstraction here is deliberately unconnected and deliberately mindless. "Groundless," it begins in the undermined root. Boundless, its source is the uninvested self. Abandoning himself to his lazy side, the poet encompasses the Eve not-yet-born. Hanging in suspension, his excess being delights in marginality. He is "both and" and therefore nowhere in terms of gender. He is "both and" and therefore everywhere in terms of genre.

The poet's role is to maintain the *in between* where he can come as close as possible to the other—without becoming or converting it. In fact, he becomes the border as he negotiates between bush and grass, river and land. In an anagrammatic reversal, the "I" plays with the "he" and "she" buried in *he*dge and *se*dge. He is the *edge*. Neither here nor there, he is also therefore totally apart from the struggles of the *he* and *she*, having moved from passive female assaulted by the wind to neutered self indifferent to gender. His "embankment" is an escape from the pressures of history encountered in marital/martial embedding. Breaking loose from the patriarchal nesting impulse and abandoning himself to the "lazy" (female) side of stanza 81, the poetic "I" separates himself from sexual preconceptions and sexuality itself. The play on line and twang, on the poetic measure and musical note, indicates where the source of his inspiration lies. It comes from neither a dominating other nor a formulating self but from a renunciation. Mediating between fish and man, the "twang" is music in its most primitive form, an expression of what Leslie Dunn calls "an excess of meaning"[19] that disrupts the process of materialization by which poetry fixes the other. Unformed, the twang sounds the experimental possibility, the poetic line freed from predetermined shape and premeditated relation. Stretching and suspending, the "I" lets go without being absorbed by anything else. Released, he retracts to a time which antedates form and prefigures substantial being. The pleasure is to hedge, to push away from the temples both the desire to formulate a metaphor and the need to be dominated by a context. Twanging merely pulls the string; it doesn't force the fish out of the water.[20] Being is separated from appetite. It emerges what Lyotard calls "tantamount to Being which is not" (*The Differend*, p. 138).

Enjoying his "not Being," the poetic "I" aligns himself with the interspace, finding himself in loss. To become part of the end of the world—to drift from land to water—is to get close to its beginnings, to arrive on the threshold and to make from the self instruments of departure that emerge instruments of origination, what the "I" in stanza 82 calls "hooks . . . quills . . . and angles." His writing instruments turn the "wavy wing" of the angelic "Garden" bird downward into the water. His quills are "fishing feathers," birds rendered nautical. "Angling" toward vacancy, "hooking" without catching, the poetic "I's" abstracting impulses are represented in the oxymoron "idle utensils." Are they idle because they extend his lazy side? Are they idle because they have nothing to do with fixed knowledge, everything to do with random musing? Or are they the tools of innocence, the way into the idyll, the unstructured realm, of poetic exploration? To have idle utensils is to have everything in potential and nothing yet in actuality.[21] It is both to be before words and to have existed after them. It is to say everything or nothing, to expand into fullness or (as Lyotard says, using a maritime example) "to plunge into emptiness[es]" (*The Differend*, p. 138).

But from Maria's point of view the utensils are childish toys, their *use* arresting development. When Maria comes, the poet casts them aside:

> But now away my Hooks, my Quills,
> And Angles, idle Utensils.
> The *young Maria* walks to night:
> Hide trifling Youth thy Pleasures slight.
> 'Twere shame that such judicious Eyes
> Should with such Toyes a Man surprize;
> *She* that already is the *Law*
> Of all her *Sex*, her *Ages Aw*. (ll. 649–56)

In Wyatt's "Whoso list to hunt," hunting is a shorthand for the scopic vision and verbal revisions of Petrarchism; in "Appleton House" fishing describes the experimental nature of the Marvellian poetic.

Sliding between two elements (not as in "The Garden" between heaven and earth to make birdlike song but between land and sea to make an earthly instrument play), "Appleton House" turns the high seriousness of "Garden" flight into a waggish gesture involving descent. Casting his bread onto the waters, the "I" unhinges the appropriations that feeding usually entails in the poem, his extensions experiments in departure that seek no returns. The "twanging" seems accidental, a simple response to the extension that indicates the responsive possibility. For the poetic "I" there is "no preexisting identity by which an act or attribute might be measured" (Gender Trouble, p. 141). Nothing is preconceived. Everything is possible as the "I" stretches himself to see what might happen. That stretching opens a world beyond both the hierarchical binarisms of Petrarchism and the limitations of the essentialist body. With the pool resembling Diana's bower guarded by trees, Maria appears as a sexually reversed Actaeon, to destroy the communion. The seemingly exalted perspective of her vision reduces the poet's experimental instruments to masturbatory playthings. The critical nature of her "judicious" gaze straightens the unruly impulses—the "angles"—into the hard line of historical imperative. Sexualizing the neutered landscape, Maria heralds the return of the historian whose reversion to Petrarchan idealization anticipates the enclosure of the familial construct.

Going In

In the sections following the windy winnowing, nature imitates the poet's contentment, folding and holding on to its harmless selfhood, as the "I," in languishing, tosses passively. In that passivity, space opens up to obscure the borders between land and water, and the self opens up to merge the boundaries between the "he" and the "she." The poet relaxes; nature unwinds. In the Maria sections, nature finds another model and the "I" tags along. Maria may be the goddess who is honored because she reorganizes the landscape into "worshipful coherence," as Robert Cummings suggests.[22] But her worshipper is not the poet. Maria's ascendancy signifies his demise; the eager-to-praise historian imitates nature's emulative example. As he canonized the personalities and forces in the opening, the newly resurfaced historian praises Maria by describing her organizational and shaping power. Forgoing its looseness, nature puts on its *bonne mine* (l. 660). But when the "I" compares Maria to the halcyon, the imagery becomes, as it so often does in the historian's sequences, deadening. With the extended comparison, the borders (carefully widened before) once more converge. The shade which, in the noontime of the sun's narcissism, remained separated from Apollo, now "creeps" upward. It extends its power until it encircles the river with black shutters and then wraps the water with the remnant of the sky:

> So when the Shadows laid asleep
> From underneath these Banks do creep,
> And on the River as it flows
> With *Eben Shuts* begin to close;
> The modest *Halcyon* comes in sight,
> Flying betwixt the Day and Night;
> And such an horror calm and dumb,
> *Admiring Nature* does benum. (ll. 665–72)

Since the shadows are the remainder of the sun, the ascension emerges a way of shoring up the heavenly power. Apollo comes back into the scene. Similarly, the modest halcyon, the drowned wife of Ceyx, rises from her watery grave to control the processes of day and night. An inverse of the dew's coyness (in "On a Drop"), her modesty pulls the encircling shadows up, as the dew brings the heavenly light down. Nature responds, in admiration, by remaining calm and dumb, stupefied by the sight. What follows is a series of enclosures, as the halcyon becomes a model for containment and nature struggles both to imitate her numbing power and somehow to surround her with itself. So the blackening air denies its blueness by sucking it out. So the gelid stream fixes the bird's shadow, both to become like the air in its rapt following and like the halcyon in its power to draw. Fish, air, meadow, river—all are swept up in the vitrification. The air, for example is sapphire-winged. Its atmosphere, like the bird, has grown wings. Yet it is only "blue winged." Its color fades into the densifying mist. The halcyon is centralizing and overwhelming. It has the power to draw and to turn the world into it. Her power repeats the conversionary impulse exemplified by nuns, Fairfax, Thestylis, river, and meadow. "The dynamic of power" Maria represents is constraining and defining. It controls the direction of bodies and the binaries of difference. Solidifying the world, she brings the exclusionary matrix of gender and genre classification into operation again.

That hardening signifies, as do the creeping shadows, the death that causes the bird's appearance in the first place. The halcyon encloses the world and forces it to come within the spread of her wings; similarly, the world attempts to enclose her; air and stream compact to keep her within bounds and so to separate birds from fish. There are no quills—no fishing feathers—here. The cycle of desire and death ends in the enclosure of marriage and sacrifice of children. There is one centralizing image figured in the swoop of the projecting halcyon, the circle of the stifling air, and the ring of the killing marriage. The enclosures anticipate the patriarchal bind of family. When the historian approves the spatial vitrification that annuls the experimentation in the swamp, he prepares for the temporal solidification of the familial thrust. Mirroring Fairfax and Thwaites, the present Fairfax and Vere will repeat the generational model, sacrificing their "sacred Bud" (l. 742) to prepare for her "blest Bed" (l. 281). All choose the certainty of participation in historical time over the doubt of suspension in loose space. Fatally drawn to Maria's image, the historian ascends in his praise even if that ascent leads him to predict her eventual cutting (like a sprig of mistletoe) into marriage. When he says at the end, "let's in," the historian heads for the house, yet another enclosure which only the poet's twanging in the woods escaped. Inside, the "I" withdraws from the windy winnowing. That protection is a double encirclement, a redundancy, like the nuns' aggrandizement, Fairfax's expansion, Thestylis's acquisitiveness, the meadow's enlargement, and the river's flooding.

The reductive pattern of imitation and seizure is repeated in the last stanza:

> But now the *Salmon-Fishers* moist
> Their *Leathern Boats* begin to hoist;
> And like *Antipodes* in Shoes,
> Have shod their *Heads* in their *Canoos*.
> How *Tortoise like*, but not so slow,
> These rational *Amphibii* go?
> Let's in: for the dark *Hemisphere*
> Does now like one of them appear. (ll. 769–76)

Antipodes are already shod by their mirror images. The phrase "antipodes *in shoes*" merely adds a gratuitous protection, an extra hat for the feet now plodding through the family plot. The leather boats enclose the fishers' heads, moistening the land creature with the sea vehicle. Like tortoises, the amphibia cross over into the other element and push every-thing into one box. In the poet's twanging there were no conversions, merely conjectures about, and explorations of, the other. The instrumental fish stayed in the water. But the house is another version of the enclosing domain, its roof a replica of the sky which mirrors salmon fishers, tortoises, and antipodes. All parade their purposefulness, as they push the earthly element into its heavenly opposite and squash the divine impulse under a confining lid. As the Fairfaxes make their destiny their choice, so the historian, gathering his selves, includes them in the shodding; when he chooses the "housy" covering, he concedes to the hemispheric process. With that concession, he follows the womanly lead already tracked by the mowers in pursuit of the dancers, cattle in quest of hay, meadow in imitation of river, nuns persuading Isabel, and Fairfax overcoming nuns. For the time being, the historian finds closure in the shadowy enclosure and accepts his spatial containment as Fairfax and Vere assume their historical place. Going *in* to the house means going into history. The shodding represses the abstracting impulse.

The only way out of the space/time continuum is to regress to the behind/before that the poet briefly experienced in the interlude of his ascendancy. In those moments, the "I" exists marginally, resisting the enclosures of gender and the formulations of genre. To arrive at the moment behind the before is to write the story of a poet detached from the conventional concerns of historical imperatives. During the forest sequence, the "I" discovers poetic license. He widens the interspace and interim where the self can be un-othered. Detached from the conversionary impulses of Petrarchism, the fishing poet dangles his line somewhere in the region of doubt, committed neither to sea nor shore. Hovering "in-between," the poet experiments with a formlessness that is absolutely pleasurable—both unpressured by the limits of time and unsequestered by the demarcations of "world." That "in-between" is poetically "enough." It beckons Marvell's poetic "I," as it does the Wyatt of "Whoso list to hunt" and the Donne of "Change," into the margins. In the "abandonne" of the osier sequence, Marvell's poet finds himself undefined and unresolved. "Twanging" in-between, he straddles the demarcating elements, experimenting with—but not choosing—gender norms, releasing—but not formulating—sound effects, expressing—but not forcing—possible meaning. Like the subversive Laura-Daphne, he resists the family and turns away from society. Like the unformed Laura-Eve, he abandons the distinctions waking reality demands. Like the detached Laura-Mercury, he eludes the body that thinking determines and evades the form that knowing inscribes. He revels in the groundlessness the woman in him uncovers. Rootless, he is limitless. Twanging, he is wordless.

"Appleton House" does not define a new world. It merely suggests how, in the mire of this one, the self might be released from the pressures that bind him to preconceived norms and the practices that tie him to predetermined forms. Like the womanized "I" of "Change," the poet "liquifies boundaries"[23] to sequester in the osier sequence a self free from the imperializing agency of poetic convention. But he goes one step deeper, to reveal—in his lazy side, as part of his core—the incommensurable Laura. The more he uncovers the woman in the self, the less he seeks the form of control Petrarchism substantiates. If, as Butler theorizes, the self is "always already" the other, the other that Marvell discovers in the self is the self who renounces all cover, the self whose revelations point toward a Lyotardan "Being who is not." Choosing to remain apart from the cannibalizing instincts of family, sexuality, and power (the historian chronicles in the poem), the poet revels in his lazy side even as he postpones the necessity of defining it as woman. In the interim, he discovers the pleasures of the in-between.

MUSING AFTERWARD

Benedick.   I can find out no rhyme to 'lady' but 'baby'. . . . I was not
born under a rhyming planet.

Much Ado about Nothing

He knew the principles of photography but saw also that moving pictures depended on the capacity of humans, animals or objects to forfeit
portions of themselves, residues of shadow and light which they left
behind. He listened with fascination to the Victrola and played the
same record over and over, whatever it happened to be, as if to test the
endurance of a duplicated event.

And then he took to studying himself in the mirror, perhaps expecting
some change to take place before his eyes. In fact, he continued the
practice not from vanity but because he discovered the mirror as a
means of self-duplication. He would gaze at himself until there were
two selves facing one another, neither of which could claim to be the
real one. The sensation was of being disembodied. He was no longer
anything exact as person. He had the dizzying feeling of separating from
himself endlessly. He would entrance himself so deeply in this process
that he would be unable to come out of it even though his mind was
lucid.

E. L. Doctorow, *Ragtime*

Poetry's flirtations with erasure, contingency, even nonsense, are tough
to take.

What may be still tougher to take is that poetry in its figurativeness,
its rhythms, endorses a state of verbal suspension. Poetry is language at
its most beguiling and seductive while it is, at the same time, elusive,
seeming to mock one's desire for reduction, for plain and available order.

It is not just that various meanings are preferable to a single dominant meaning. It may be that something beyond meaning is being communicated, something that originated not with the poet but in the first dim light of language, in some period of beforeness.

Mark Strand, *The New York Times Book Review*, September 15, 1991

Gazing Themselves: Marvell's Release

In the rootlessness of the osier, Marvell frees the "Appleton House" poet from the genders that bind him. In the licking and slicking river of "Appleton House" stanza 80, Marvell liberates Petrarch and Laura from the genres that define them. Because his narcissism is for the woman already in the self, Apollo incorporates Daphne's being without rewriting her body. The revolution—from river to sky and back again—refolds the Petrarchan experience:

> See in what wanton harmless folds
> It ev'ry where the Meadow holds;
> And its yet muddy back doth lick
> Till as a *Chrystal Mirrour* slick;
> Where all things gaze themselves, and doubt
> If they be in it or without.
> And for his shade which therein shines,
> *Narcissus* like, the *Sun* too pines. (ll. 633–40)

Connecting the watery source of life to the biblical agent of death, Marvell robs the serpent of its bite. The reversal effects a retreat from fatality, even as the identification of Apollo with Narcissus redefines the loss necessary for discovery. In the oxymoron "wanton harmless" Marvell writes out the Petrarchan opposition. The wanton troopers of "Nymph" inevitably inflict "harm." Here, wantonness is harmless, its cruelty canceled in benign release, its waywardness helpful. The river "holds" the meadow and thereby becomes supportive rather than limiting, the defining "hold" a function of the temporary fold which "scrambles up meaning" without forcing it. At the same time, the verb "hold" is a foreshortened *behold*; the river gazes at the meadow, the former competitors now mutual regarders of each other. Like Lyotard's folded over dream-work, the regard seems to anticipate—in the doubt it precipitates—a redefinition of self, a "change in nature" ("Dream-Work," p. 24) which includes a revi-

sion of the originary Petrarchan myth. The sting of transgression is removed in the quest for identity.

With the imperative "See," the poetic "I" directs the reader's gaze to a
self-examining construct. His seduction into privacy sounds a bit like
Diana calling Actaeon into the bath. Only here everyone is engaged in the
same masturbatory act, the violation pointless. A world where the self
returns its own gaze is impenetrable. When selves spy on themselves and
the subject is subjectivity, intruders can't matter. A Narcissus who knows
himself has already defused the deadliness in the myth, as the inherently
stingless serpent has lost its poison. The anticipation at the beginning
forestalls the inevitable disappointment, the previously experienced end
eclipsed by the enclosure. Selves that act upon themselves obviate the annexations necessitated by the other that Petrarchism appropriates. Selves
that gaze at themselves turn the looking relations inward as specializa-
tion merges with speculation and thought becomes "doubt." When Apollo
joins in the reflection, he acknowledges the other always already inside
even as he comes to understand, through pining, how much the other
forfeits.

The elusivity of the Petrarchan Daphne is reclaimed by the multiplicity
of the Marvellian selves, calmly contemplating their own status. The
possibility of a self-induced question leads to the alternative of a self-
regenerating answer, the *fictions* of self defined in a narrative experiment,
the line dangled to learn what—unexpectedly—might answer. To see the
world seeing itself is to be called into the harmlessness of self-exposure—a
loss expressed in auto-replication. Earlier eager to encircle the land, the
river now holds the meadow to its bank. Crystallized into a purity that
renders it simultaneously duplicative, the harmless river displaces the
fatal scene of so many Petrarchan episodes, Diana's unsafe pool: "Where
all things gaze themselves, and doubt / If they be in it or without." The
doubting (or doing *out*) of self-contemplation annuls the winning (or
pulling *in*) of Petrarchan laurelization. The pleasure lies in the permutations of doubting, of being neither in nor out, neither before nor after.[1] To
do out is to bring out the other in the self. Apollo pines, experiences loss,
and understands what Daphne feels. When he turns Narcissus into Apollo
and contracts the beginning of the Petrarchan romance to its end, the
poetic "I" accepts its self-imaging as a self-satisfying engenderment. In
stanza 81, suspension describes a self free from the ground that constricts
it. Here, pining describes a self free from the other that laurelization
appends.

The sun pines for its sons, a Marvell pun from "Coy Mistress." The sun also pines for its shadow, a natural pun. Apollo is already the tree, Daphne's end absorbed as his wooden beginning. Pining displaces laurelizing as nature anticipates the losses its deformations necessitate. The self is formulated in the masculinized and paternal pine. The self is complicated in the feminized and pining mother. As combined masculine and feminine feeling, the "pining" of the stiffening phallus in the paternal sun's rays is already a "regretting" for what the maternal center will necessarily yield: the shadow or little sons. Shadows are both lesser lights and ghostly selves, emanations that reflect the heavenly father in the earthly river, reflections that insist on self-loss as part of the transformational process. Unlike Narcissus, whose one self is mirrored in watery death, the sun pursues many selves repeated in watery life. The Petrarchan fixation on memory is annulled by shapes not yet formed. The Petrarchan obsession with the *one* other the poet appends is obviated by the multiple parts Apollo releases: many things vague and still unfocused. The shadows of the river shine in noon-day light, their shapes as irregular as the water. But the two elements—the sense of doubt realized not through a no-saying other but by an indeterminate self, the sense of light wrested not from an inspirational other but from a relaxed self—define in Marvellian terms the deformations Wyatt recognizes in the windy woman of "Whoso list to hunt" and Donne in the river woman of "Change."

When Marvell writes that the sun, *too*, pines, he cancels the difference between the Apollonian original and his earthly sons. When he merges offspring with model, Marvell bypasses priorities, the duplicated self inseparable from the duplicating others. The sun imitates, rather than emanates, its shadows. Like all the earth-bound creatures searching in the river, the sun is engaged in reflection, original and shadow distilled in the mirror. Abandoning all three Lauras, as the historian relinquishes Isabel, Thestylis, and Maria, the poetic "I" of "Appleton House" sees in its extensions visions of its own origination.

If, in the laurelizing of "The Garden," Apollo hunts Daphne for a tree, in the *pining* of "Appleton House" Apollo turns the tree into a process, not an end. Merging Apollo and Narcissus, rendering the snake circular, and giving up parts of the self, the poet begins with losses that have already happened. In the interspace—somewhere between the "in" and "out" of the unspecified region of doubt—is the origin of imagination. The gap reverts to the "first dim light of language" or the "period of beforeness" that Mark Strand describes in the passage prefacing this chapter. Deemphasizing the *one* Genesis 2 made necessary in the other and Genesis 3 made necessary in the family, Marvell returns to the behind/before of Genesis 1, and releases himself from the mediations of Petrarchism and the negotiations of history. Like his "abandonne" in stanza 81, the "wantonness" here reveals how the poetic "I" revels in the not-yet-formed. If "The Garden" names the mind as "that *ocean* where each kind / Does streight its own resemblance find," "Appleton House" represents the fluidity of mindlessness as a more congenial river where each kind seeks (in vacancy) to recover what it has already sacrificed. More becomes less in "Appleton House," as the "I" finds in the harm*less* river essences it could not discern in the larger flood. Laurelizing presupposes increase: the acquisition of a material replacement for loss. Pining gives into loss. Apollo languishes, whittled down to the size of his shadowy sons.

When Marvell's poet evolves another self, his fusion breaks down formal barriers and legitimizes doubt. Like Laura-Mercury, his gazing selves choose inexactitude and, in the discrepancy between origination and image, find a space that unseats thought and reconstructs the thought-out other. The shade is Apollo and something else, his future as son and in death. The spectacle includes the spectator in its shining; the god is subject to his mortality and another life. Auto-replication, as Marvell envisions it, includes Laura-Daphne's rejection of the sexual trap. Auto-reflection, as Marvell relates it, reiterates Laura-Mercury's contempt for linguistic determination. When they connect Laura-Mercury's deconstructions of cultural representation to Laura-Daphne's evasion of the biological family, Renaissance Petrarchists anticipate contemporary poetic and critical theory. They establish a ground where abstraction—in its reconstruction of "form's relationship to the eye"[2]—and feminism—in its reassessment of women's objectification by men—meet. They write the imagining woman back into the poem by recovering the borderland as the space of the woman's imaginings.

Looking Ahead: Renaissance Futurism

The Wyatt of "Whoso list to hunt" complains that he "can by no means [his] mind draw from the deer," and calls his immersion in the womanly element an imprisonment that blocks the poem—the drawing out of male conceit. The Donne of "Change" sees his submersion in the woman as a release. His expressiveness imitates the liberations she initiates: "But when they kisse one bank, and leaving this / Never look back." In these moments, Wyatt and Donne assimilate the female perspective. Wyatt leaves off hunting. Donne voices the woman's evasions. But, in each poem, the woman's *body* becomes the scene of male awakening, as Wyatt merges with the deer and Donne mouths the kiss. Marvell's poetic situates the woman's *spirit* as the source of a vision that further relaxes gender hierarchy. As he abandons his lazy side, Marvell gives into his deformative impulses. His "hanging" on is a letting go of male constructions. But in *abandoning* his lazy side, he moves into Adam's prenatal sleep, forfeits the product of his rib, and yields to Eve's unformed self. That relapse involves a relaxation of control that admits to the mysteries of Adam's dream and therefore to the uncertain origin of the poem. Fusing reciprocation and desire to internalize inspiration, the "abandonne" assumes the woman is always already in the self even though she has not yet materialized.

In relaxing the pursuit, Marvell overcomes history and thereby yields to what came before bodies (the deep sleep of laziness) and before Adam (the light itself). In "Change," Donne also opens an undefined region but he does so by rushing to follow the woman's lead. In "Nymph complaining," the female body and text are similarly resolved in a kiss, the deer's enactment a quick reading, the deer's abstraction, a "race" to heaven. To get to the particular statelessness and matelessness "Appleton House" defines, Marvell's osier poet of stanza 81 moves lethargically, accepts the woman still inside him, and abandons himself, in laziness, to an Eve not yet born. The chapters of his poetic are "slow-chapped." Of course he can languish; his lips have not yet uttered Time; his "lines" have not yet pulled in a body. In the willow, Marvell loosens his hold. In the pine, he accepts loss. In the interspace and interim, he awaits an idiom not yet found. In the freedom of a wantonness rendered harmless, the dream-work becomes dream-play.

With a self already open to plurality and motion, Marvell reshapes Petrarchism, fishing waters still to be sounded and pursuing forms still to be named. It took the modernists to match the nameless curve Marvell follows to a poetic they could call "new," but, even there, they still revert to Petrarchan oxymoron. The experimentation of "free verse" connects to the lines already dangled in the amorphous waters of Marvellian indeterminacy—lines extending from the Petrarchism the poet renounces in "Appleton House." Like the Santayana he admires in "To an Old Philosopher in Rome," Wallace Stevens, for example, is an "inquisitor of [the] structures" he inhabits. As the historian of "Appleton House" inevitably goes "in" to the forms the osier poet abandons, so Stevens inexorably names his last book "The Rock." But the brief experimental moment in Marvell's poem—figured by the "abandonne" of the woman—opens up to visions not yet cast in the imagined stone of the imagining man. The uncontained anomie of the wind in Wyatt's "Whoso list to hunt" and the unraveling departure of the river in Donne's "Change" force the woman's perspective onto the man. In Wyatt, her resistance stops the poem. In Donne, it energizes it with an expectancy for new banks. In Wyatt, the poet looks back to what he can't touch. In Donne, the poet never looks back; instead he flows into what he never imagined. The Marvell of the osier sequence yields willingly to the female vision that causes Wyatt's impasse and promotes Donne's enthusiasm. To argue that a female poetic exists is to take seriously the alternative representation augured by Laura-Mercury's resistance: "I am not perhaps who you think I am." It suggests that the poet imagines a woman as the agent not only of visual but of linguistic pleasure—an agent whose difference demands an alternative to the form that Petrarch elsewhere so insistently imposed on Laura and, therefore, on himself and his followers.

Why is this critical other a woman? That question returns to the Petrarchan paradox and its obviation of the biological reproduction its sexual teasing almost achieves. If Laura-Mercury unhinges the poem by denying language and Laura-Eve undoes it by denying denial, Laura-Daphne threatens *life*. Her initial rejection of sexuality and subsequently static laurelization point to the art of Petrarchan art. When Marvell opens himself up to the feminine, his Petrarchism protects him from the biological and cultural imperatives that exist outside of the poem's fiction. Assimilating the woman's body does not give Apollo the wife and family patriarchy demands. Even when it establishes the woman's experience as the mode of its imitation, the lyric exempts itself from the exactitude of actual biography; its fictive "I" still distances itself from history; its reformations still undermine the reproductivity it seems to advocate. In the comedy of *Two Gentlemen of Verona*, the lyric *what* is subsumed by the dramatic *who*. In the poems of Wyatt, Donne, and Marvell, there is only a *what*—a woman who rebuts sexuality (Laura-Daphne) or invents it (Laura-Eve) but who never will be the cleaved-to wife. Sometimes the poet makes his *what* more of a *who*, as Donne does in "The Dreame," where the woman invents and virtually writes the "swain" of her desire. Sometimes the poet makes his *what* less of a *what*, as Wyatt does in "Whoso list to hunt," where the woman destabilizes the forms that solidify and objectify her. The double pull—the biological reproductiveness of the woman remanded to a realm not yet named and the final detachment in the poem seen in its subversion of the biological—is still part of the death wish in the poem's body. Formalized as an intrinsic element of the lyric, that subversion becomes a rejection of social convention and a negation of the patriarchal imperative to "increase and multiply."

If biography seeks the familial connection, the Petrarchan poetic chops down the family tree, even in those moments when it establishes—in *abandonne*—the woman's vision as the mode of its imitations. It defines the language of the self, rather than the self of father or mother. Like Stevens's "So-and-So Reclining on Her Couch," the poetic "I" is "born at twenty-one" with no biological attachments. The poem is the illegitimate child of invention. The lyric poet is the child who kills off his parents and children. He does that with Laura-Daphne, creating a situation where the family is impossible. Then, as childless orphan, he pleads for the reader's sympathy. He asks for that against Laura-Mercury, pitting his internal softness against the external hardness—the rock—she imposes. Though he imitates female fertility, he reproduces only a fictional self. The lyric "imagination"—even in those moments when it ties itself to the mother— is detached. The lyric's sexuality insists on invention. Its invention insists on abstraction. The Marvellian narcissist's pining and the modernist Stevens's "form gulping after formlessness" are inversions, but still other versions, of Apollonian laurelizing. The lyric's self is language, its being a forgetfulness of things. It's a cold heart that Laura-Mercury steals as she enacts and then speaks her evasions. It's a cold self Petrarch revitalizes as he goes on to materialize the self she invaded. It can function, as it does in the reformulations following *Rime sparse* 23, as if the invasion hadn't occurred.

When he follows the tradition, the English Renaissance poet may—like Doctorow's little boy—be standing in front of a mirror he himself shapes so that he can feel the dizzying excitement of sexuality without risking the confrontational reality of engagement. But even if the poet forms himself out of a dyad that resists what it seems to want, his inclusion of the female imagination complicates the poetic, sometimes even stops it. Mary Jo Salter argues (on behalf of female poets) that "male poets have had a double-barreled power behind them. The female muse inspired them; the male literary tradition, a tradition of accomplishment, gave them fathers to revere and to try to usurp."[3] But Salter isn't taking into account the extent to which, denying its relation to the masculinist image, the female imagination in the dream-work of the male poem undermines the literary father in the life-work. Nor does it factor in the extent to which, denying her relationship to patriarchal life, the female subversive decreates the idea of biological fatherhood altogether. The alternating images of ana-morphism become part of what the poem arrests, not just desire but its per-mutation, not just "me perpetuated in the image I choose," but "why me trapped in the inescapable body I body forth?" Wyatt's anomie, Donne's anticipation, and Marvell's *abandonne* amplify what Petrarch sought to repress: the counter-agent imbricated in the original dyad. Laura-Mercury's challenge to representational legitimacy—of time, place, and substance—takes a woman's form not just because her body seems what Thomas Greene calls "virtually irresistible" as an object to symbolize desire[4] but because her evasions suggest another desire—for formlessness, feeling, and absence—which the poet is reluctant to claim as his own. In those moments, the poet finds himself and approximates what Leslie Dunn defines as "song in its unfixed [and feminine] elements . . . gen-erat[ing] an excess or surplus of meaning and disrupt[ing] the normal process of signification."[5]

When Marvell's poet stretches his lines in the unsponsored fishy "twang," he abandons conventions and identifies a locus of meaning still to be articulated. Yet, when he enters the "surplus" of the osier edge and unseats the etched impressions of gendered identity, he rearticu-lates the dyad and anticipates modernist questions about subject forma-tion. The dyad is complicated by the invented woman whose being is neither primarily sexual nor absolutely fictive even as it is spurred by the invented poet whose being is neither primarily biographical nor defini-tively formed. If the woman's body prompts the poet to imitation (of her doubling in Wyatt's "Will ye see what wonders," initiatives in Donne's "The Dreame," and maternity in Marvell's "Nymph"), then the woman's spirit (in *Rime sparse* 23, "Whoso list to hunt," "Change," and "Appleton House") prompts him to stop what she started: the poem of the body. If the male poet of the Petrarchan dyad builds his poem around the absence of the sexuality he seems to want, the female poet in the Petrarchan dyad begins her dismantling with the absence her biological reproductiveness seems to presuppose. Heard but unseen, the Laura-Mercury of *Rime sparse* 23 articulates the woman's pleasure in also being "disembodied" and in not being anything "exact as a person." But she does something else as well: she evolves a poetics of nonbeing whose tentativeness—"I may not be"—posits a depth that "thinking" cannot fathom and whose evasiveness suggests a spirit that form cannot contain.

Looking Backward: Modernist Pining

In "Desire & the Object," Wallace Stevens rephrases the woman's pleasure in terms of a riddle whose answer the riddler does not define precisely: "It could be that the sun shines / Because I desire it to shine or else / That I desire it to shine because it shines."[6] As critics have argued, Petrarchism is an expression of the self ("the sun shines because I desire it to shine," or "the woman is beautiful because I invent her as sun"). But it is also an imitation of another self ("I desire it to shine because it shines" or "I desire her because she already is") whose existence has a light and a shadow self of its own. Is the shining object the source or the reflector of light? Is the shining object already part of the self? Is wanting to have part of wanting to be? Is the brush stroke of Stevens's desire part of what Lyotard calls Van Gogh's suns? Where precisely does the self end and the other begin? That uncertainty about what constitutes the self—the unwillingness to be "exact as a person"—may mean that the woman who maintains her indefinite status doubly troubles the situation governing the poem. She is, as Jessica Benjamin writes of the woman's position, "both with and distinct from the other."[7] In the poem, she is, as Butler theorizes, "the self's possibility" ("Imitation and Gender Insubordination," p. 27).

Her "trouble" evolves a Laura-Eve whose anterior existence presumes (as in Wyatt's "They flee from me," Donne's "Dreame," or Marvell's "Nymph") the sexual imagination of the woman; her "trouble" corroborates the inventive imagination of the woman whose agency subverts the process of signification by which conventional Petrarchism determines her status. In her *Rime sparse* 23 eclipses, Laura-Mercury expresses Petrarch's ambivalence about the form he invents, an ambivalence which Renaissance writers systematized in certain poems and modern artists call abstraction. The Soviet artist Kazimir Malevich, for example, could be talking of Laura-Mercury's resistance when he argues that Suprematism is "a way of seeing everything in nature not as real forms and objects but as material masses from which forms must be made that have nothing in common with nature."[8] What results is, then, what Lyotard calls "a change in [the understanding of] nature" ("Dream-Work," p. 24). Monique Wittig could similarly be talking of Laura-Mercury's evasions when she speaks of the transformational possibility of abstraction.[9] Laura-Mercury decrees both manifestos as she unhinges the form that confines her. Her lightning shining eclipses her thundering voice but retains the excitement of "storms and the complete stillness afterward."[10]

If metaphor implies connections, then the stormy resistance of Laura-Mercury's "I am not perhaps who you think I am" denies relations and speaks for un-poems. "Clouds do not look like buckets of water," Malevich writes in a reduction to absurdism that connects the Suprematist movement to the unpatriarchal impulses of dadaism.[11] But Malevich might also speak for "mamaism," a creative impulse that similarly defies the matriarchy by producing a nonfigural art in ways that parallel Laura-Mercury's deformations and echo Laura-Daphne's denials. The need to get beyond the forms of nature in abstract art is a variation of Laura-Mercury's insistence on getting beyond the form of the poem and the frame of a woman as she escapes what Malevich calls "the circle of things."[12] Like the reproductive capacity of the woman in the lyric, the fertilizing potential of buckets of water comes close to saying what a cloud is but not close enough. When Laura-Mercury teases Petrarch by hinting at what "she" is *not*, she opens up the dyad into space, and beyond, toward an arena that clouds what a woman is in the way Malevich obscures what a cloud does by saying what *it is not like*. When he links buckets of water to clouds, Malevich nevertheless alludes to their revitalizing and seminal function which, like Chaucer's piercing rain in *The Canterbury Tales*, begins the natural growth process. But in affirming the difference between the man-made object and the natural form, he speaks Laura-Daphne's sexual denials and Laura-Mercury's artistic subversion: "I am not made for the *use* you ascribe to me."

Uncovering Laura's resistance in Petrarch, Wyatt, Donne, and Marvell does not deny that most Petrarchan sequences commodify the female body as "the enabling ground from which transcendent meaning and male figures of the sovereign subject emerge."[13] But it does suggest that (1) the imagined woman provokes new questions about subject formation seemingly denied by the form that contains her; and (2) the imagined woman presupposes a critique of gender that undercuts "the solace of good forms"[14] ostensibly provided by the sublimations she engenders. The imagined woman's presence in the poem defies both the patriarchal and poetic conventions her containment would seem to support. As the sexually unavailable Laura-Daphne, she need not be Benedick's essentialist "lady' who makes babies. As the sexually reflective Laura-Eve, she need not be the repressed other who denies the body. As the verbally "unusable" Laura-Mercury, she need not be the objectified lady who enables the poet to substitute his representation for her body. Laura-Daphne frees men and women from biology. They will never make the babies their bodies seem fated to deliver. Laura-Eve frees men and women to express sexuality. They might actually escape taboos that inhibit physical expression. Laura-Mercury frees the woman from the man's language. He will never find the self he thinks she allows him to become. Turning Petrarch to stone, she makes him her invention and insists that the speaking "I" of the poem is the imagined "swain" in the dyad, a self constructed by the lyric. When the woman in "They flee from me" asks "how like you this," she seriously explores the nature of male sexuality, meeting the man at a point where he might articulate pleasure. When the man of "Change" asks—in a similar vein—about likeness "must I change too," he acknowledges the give and take of a sexuality that seeks to render desire mutual.

Finally, pointing to what Barbara Correll calls "other spaces of signification,"[15] Wyatt's windy woman, Donne's rivery woman, and Marvell's snaky river free the poem from both the cultural expectations it seems to perpetuate and the particular context it seems to illustrate. They free themselves and their poets from the idealized bodies the form demands and suggest that poetic pleasure has a good deal to do with the abstraction inscribed forms preclude. These "excessive," troublesome Lauras offer other ways through the representational maze and other answers to biological imperatives, "discontinuities" (*Gender Trouble*, p. 141) which might be found by asking why the poet invents a woman to reinvent him and to provoke the "gesture that jams sociality."[16] Simultaneously as the gesture "breaks a mold of discourse," it opens poetry up to "the place beyond all places, beyond all boundaries"—the unspecifiable space that remains "unnameable by choice."[17]

In a recent reworking of the Petrarchan poem, Adrienne Rich imagines a contemporary Laura-Mercury who, as the titular "She" evading the "fine nets" of Petrarchan *impossibilia*, speaks her absence triumphantly. Along with the other poets of her generation, linked by David Kalstone in *Five Temperaments*, Rich was taught to read and "sometimes to write" by influential—and exclusively male—literary critics.[18] Coming of age in the fifties or early sixties meant that "for them [unlike for Pound, Eliot, and Stevens] there were, for better or for worse, English Studies."[19] Included in Rich's Radcliffe training were all those poems where she met the "image of Woman in books written by men."[20] "Taught," as Kalstone puts it, to be the "ideal reader of Donne or Marvell," Rich struggles (as she writes in "She") to "balance memory" (of life lived) "and training" (of poems read).[21] As the anamorphic space of the Bordone painting theorizes two stories, so Rich's "She" yields two poems—one where the "she" is the "weir / where disintegration stopped" and the other (the unstable poem at the end) where she is not there. Even in the hands of a twentieth-century female poet, the oppositional pull between self and other, endemic to Petrarchism, reiterates the original dyad. The three Lauras continue to complicate the tapestry of the love lyric. The "trouble" they cause—both by their presence and absence—demonstrates how the multiple layers Petrarch imbricated in the *Rime sparse* remain part of the legacy his followers inherit.

Writing of the writer in the third person and writing of the writer as woman in the poem, Rich acknowledges what Janet Malcolm calls the "unsustainable fiction . . . on which all autobiographical writing is poised, that the person writing and the person being written about are a single seamless entity."[22] Rich emphasizes the gap, and perhaps even the impossibility of the reconstructions that seams presuppose, when she speaks of *elsewhere* as both another text and another life. The anamorphic frame of "She" yields two stories: in the first stanza, expressing the solid rationality of "right gazing," it speaks of the woman's awareness of her role in representation; in the second, delineating the vague abstraction of "eyeing awry," it finds a way to describe—without solidly outlining it—an alternative to the discursive "fix." "Eyed awry," her "I" emerges a third-person presence in the first poem, a third-person absence in the second:

SHE

goes through what must be gone through:
that catalogue she is pitching out
mildew spores   velvet between the tiles
soft hairs, nests, webs
in corners, edges of basins, in the teeth
of her very comb. All that rots or rusts
in a night, a century.
Balances memory, training, sits in her chair
hairbrush in hand, breathing the scent of her own hair
and thinks: *I have been the weir*
where disintegration stopped.
Lifts her brush once like a thrown thing
lays it down at her side like a stockpiled weapon
crushes out the light. Elsewhere
dust chokes the filters, dead leaves rasp in the grate.

> Clogged, the fine nets bulge
> and she is not there.[23]

As woman poet writing about the woman in the poem, Rich faces the same problems Petrarch does in *Rime sparse* 23: what to do with the woman who, as reader and inamorata, is there to implicate the poem and *not there* to be represented by it. "She" is about both the other as "conscious subject" and the poet who recognizes, as do Petrarch, Wyatt, Donne, and Marvell, the imaginative implications of that subjectivity.

Punning in the first poem on "weir" as oppositional union (we're) and as destructive fate (wyrd), Rich's "weir / where disintegration stops" suggests that the "she" of the first poem is fourfold: (1) reproducing woman who, as Laura-Eve, offers her own version of mildewed spores, replenishing the gaps with her generational potential; (2) fated avenger (wyrd), who ends the biological cycle, canceling, with Laura-Daphne's sexual denials, the endlessly repeating vegetative cycle; (3) represented figure who, as the idealized other of the poem, is the male projection against death, filling in (with her fleshed out image) the cycle of nothingness art emblazons itself against; (4) scourge who, as Laura-Mercury to the male enterprise, pitches out the woman-defining "catalogues." In all four roles, she is co-conspirator with the poet, her function as ender of the vegetative cycle linked to the implicit death in Petrarchism's sexual denials. As fated avenger, she cohabits with male destructiveness. As artistic inspiration, she is a poet's projection. And, as reproductive woman, she supplies the needs of patriarchal society. In the anamnesis of the stop-gap weir, Rich speaks of the woman as the source of poetic wholeness. She provides an almost familial comfort to the poet who seeks her solid maternity.

But in the second poem, the titular "She" is anagogic, somewhere undefined and not yet thought. The "initial forgetting" emerges in the last stanza as an abstraction which her absence only begins to convey. The second *where* of the poem is outside the house of poetry and beyond the confines of the frame. Like Laura-Mercury's lightning flash, the second part of "She" calls attention to absence. Even its brevity characterizes the missing person of the woman. Left in the womanless world of the second poem are the remains of the biological and poetic cycle: first, the dead leaves in the grates; then the stuffed doll of the ventriloquistic poet. Without the impulses of the woman's evasiveness, the nets bulge with their own throbbing members. Stuffed, unchallenged, the patriarchy bloats on itself. Trapped in the ballooning nets, as, Merlinlike, Petrarch is trapped in the sterile rock of *Rime sparse* 23, the unwomaned poem goes nowhere.

The world without the critical consciousness of the female imagination is one framed by the prison grate whose clearly defined edges control the dead voices (raspings) of a remaindered culture (leavings). If Rich's "She" is the fourfold weir of the opening, her "she" of the second poem is not there at all: not there as biological Eve to perpetuate the race; not there as elusive Daphne, whose fate is to stop biology; not there as represented figure who might inspire a song instead of a rasp; not there as Laura-Mercury to challenge the netting process.

How do we locate the "she" then, if she is not the co-conspiratorial weir/we're? As Laura-Mercury is not perhaps *who* Petrarch thinks she is, Rich's "she" is not *where* we think she is. Defined only as "not there" in the male image, her "elsewhere" lies beyond the filtering consciousness of entrapping nets. Unformed and unbegun, such a transformative space returns to *Rime sparse* 23. Defiantly abstract, her elsewhere is wholly otherwise, though imbricated in the anamorphic frame. Like Marvell's nymph and "Appleton House" poet, Donne's river woman, and Wyatt's untouchable deer, the "she" who escapes resists all predefined gender and generic categories. What we have left is what we have in Wyatt's "I may no more" and Marvell's "let's in": the confined self of the writer who sees her confinement within what Marvell calls "the iron grates[24] of life." But we also have a notion that *elsewhere* is a viable space although we haven't yet found the idiom to name it. Even when the writer is a biological woman, Laura-Mercury's absence is what empties the poem of the depth—the anamorphic layers—her deconstructions presume. In "She," Rich explicitly writes of the female consciousness which, through the sexual denials of Laura-Daphne, the physical constructions of Laura-Eve, and the metaphysical questions of Laura-Mercury, renders the dyad "dense" ("Dream-Work," p. 24). Even the contemporary lyric still retains the imagining poet who imagines an other—sometimes similar and often larger and more imaginative, more assertive and more daring—than her self. Despite the traditions she breaks, what Rich keeps alive is the uncovering Laura. Rich's "She" is Petrarchan in the plenitude the female presence of the first section represents. And it is Petrarchan in the windy absence the second poem laments. That poem needs the imagined woman, just as Petrarch and his Renaissance followers yielded to their multiple Lauras, to speak the poet's desire *not to be there*.

NOTES

Introduction

1. James O. Ward chronicles the popularity of the Greek romances in early modern Italy. When they were as obviously libidinous as *Daphnis and Chloë*, they were read as cautionary tales. "The Greek Novel in the Italian Renaissance: On the Margins of the Canon," MLA convention, December 1992.

2. Gordon Braden's phrase; see "Love and Fame: The Petrarchan Career," in *Pragmatism's Freud*, ed. Joseph H. Smith and William Kerrigan (Baltimore: Johns Hopkins University Press, 1986), p. 128.

3. In some ways the physical purity of Daphnis and Chloë—lovers whose sexuality is thwarted until marriage—is a precursor of the troubadour *asag* or test of Love. The would-be lover is allowed to gaze on the naked lady and even touch her but may not consummate his desire. "In the *asag*, passion was born, exalted, and tested, and it usually ended before the lovers reached sexual climax." See René Nelli, "Love's Reward," trans. Alyson Waters, in *Zone: Fragments for a History of the Human Body*, ed. Michel Feher, Ramona Naddoff, and Nadia Tazi (Cambridge, Mass.: MIT Press, 1989), 2:222.

4. Sara Sturm-Maddox, *Petrarch's Laurels* (Pittsburgh: University of Pittsburgh Press, 1992); Nancy Vickers, "Vital Signs: Petrarch and Popular Culture," *Romanic Review* 77 (1988): 184–95.

5. Jean-François Lyotard, *Discours, figure* (Paris: Klincksieck, 1971), p. 378; the translation is Bill Readings's, cited in *Introducing Lyotard* (London: Routledge, 1991), p. 26. I am indebted to Bill Readings for introducing me to Lyotard through his remarkably astute readings, readings which consistently place Lyotard in a literary context. In this passage, Lyotard refers to two anamorphic portraits: the first, analyzed by Stephen Greenblatt in *Renaissance Self-Fashioning* (Chicago: University of Chicago Press, 1980), pp. 17–27, is Holbein's *Ambassadors*; the second, discussed by Jurgis Baltrusaitis in *Anamorphoses, ou magie artificielle des effets merveilleux* (Paris: Olivier Perrin, 1969), pp. 91–116, is a portrait of Charles I, done in 1649 by an anonymous royalist sympathizer after Charles's death. In order to see the "good form" in the Charles portrait, the viewer needs a cylindrical mirror. Otherwise, like a television image where the vertical-horizontal button is nonfunctional, the king is a distorted crescent of a man.

6. See Baltrusaitis, *Anamorphoses, ou magie artificielle des effets merveilleux*, p. 22.

7. See Greenblatt's discussion in *Renaissance Self-Fashioning*, pp. 17–27.

8. Robert Coover, "Hyperfiction: Novels for the Computer," *New York Times Book Review*, August 29, 1993, p. 8.

9. Jonathan Goldberg, *Sodometries: Renaissance Texts, Modern Sexualities* (Stanford: Stanford University Press, 1992), p. 58. Future references are cited in the text.

10. Walter Benjamin, "The Work of Art in the Age of Mechanical Reproduction," in *Illuminations*, ed. Hannah Arendt, trans. Harry Zohn (New York: Schocken, 1986), p. 236.

11. Luce Irigaray, "The Gesture in Psychoanalysis," trans. Elizabeth Guild, in *Between Feminism and Psychoanalysis*, ed. Teresa Brennan (London: Routledge, 1989), pp. 132, 130.

12. *The Pastoral Loves of Daphnis and Chloë*, trans. George Moore (London: Folio Society, 1954), p. 17.

13. Irigaray, "The Gesture in Psychoanalysis," p. 133.

14. Jessica Benjamin, "A Desire of One's Own: Psychoanalytic Feminism and Intersubjective Space," in *Feminist Studies / Critical Studies*, ed. Teresa de Lauretis (Bloomington: Indiana University Press, 1986), p. 94.

15. Eve Sedgwick, *Between Men: English Literature and Male Homosocial Desire* (New York: Columbia University Press, 1985), p. 36.

16. Jean-François Lyotard, *The Postmodern Explained*, trans. Julian Pefanis and Morgan Thomas (Minneapolis: University of Minnesota Press, 1993), p. 80.

17. Joel Fineman, *Shakespeare's Perjured Eye: The Invention of Poetic Subjectivity in the Sonnets* (Berkeley and Los Angeles: University of California Press, 1986), p. 194.

18. *Petrarch's Lyric Poems*, ed. and trans. Robert Durling (Cambridge: Harvard University Press, 1976), p. 27. Future references are to this edition and will be cited in the text.

19. Braden, "Love and Fame: The Petrarchan Career," p. 128.

20. Vickers, "Vital Signs: Petrarch and Popular Culture," 187.

21. Gordon Braden, "Beyond Frustration: Petrarchan Laurels in the Seventeenth Century," *SEL* 26 (1986): 8.

22. L. P. Hartley's phrase, from *The Go-Between* (New York: Stein and Day, 1980), p. 3.

23. Sheila Fisher and Janet Halley, *Seeking the Woman in Late Medieval and Renaissance Writings* (Knoxville: University of Tennessee Press, 1990); Nancy Vickers, "Diana Described: Scattered Woman, Scattered Rhyme," *Critical Inquiry* 8 (1981–82): 65–79, and Marguerite Waller, "Academic Tootsie: The Denial of Difference and the Difference It Makes," *Diacritics* 7 (1987): 2–20, expanded version, "The Empire's New Clothes: Refashioning the Renaissance," in *Seeking the Woman*, pp. 160–83.

24. Ann Rosalind Jones, *The Currency of Eros: Women's Love Lyric in Europe, 1540–1620* (Bloomington: Indiana University Press, 1990); Constance Jordan, *Renaissance Feminism* (Ithaca: Cornell University Press, 1990); Barbara Lewalski, *Writing Women in Jacobean England* (Cambridge: Harvard University Press, 1992); Maureen Quilligan, "The Constant Subject: Instability and Female Author-

ity in Wroth's Urania Poems," in *Soliciting Interpretation: Literary Theory and Seventeenth-Century English Poetry*, ed. Elizabeth D. Harvey and Katharine Eisaman Maus (Chicago: University of Chicago Press, 1990), pp. 307–35. For the variety of interesting ways in which women's writing is being read over, see Elizabeth Hageman, "Recent Studies in Women Writers of the English Seventeenth Century," *ELR* 18 (1988): 138–67.

25. Jones, *The Currency of Eros*, p. 6.

26. Carol Thomas Neely, "Constructing the Subject: Feminist Practice and the New Renaissance Discourses," *ELR* 18 (1988): 15.

27. Rosalie Colie, as quoted in *The Resources of Kind: Genre Theory in the Renaissance*, ed. Barbara K. Lewalski (Berkeley and Los Angeles: University of California Press, 1973), p. 7.

28. Ibid., p. 7.

29. Jean-François Lyotard, *The Differend: Phrases in Dispute*, trans. G. Van den Abeele (Minneapolis: University of Minnesota Press, 1988), p. 70. Future references to this edition will be cited in the text.

30. Judith Butler, *Bodies That Matter: On the Discursive Limits of "Sex"* (New York and London: Routledge 1993), p. 19. Future references are cited in the text.

31. Judith Butler, *Gender Trouble* (London: Routledge, 1990), p. 142. Future references are cited in the text.

32. Judith Scherer Herz, "Excerpts from a Panel Discussion," in *Renaissance Discourses of Desire*, ed. Claude J. Summers and Ted-Larry Pebworth (Columbia: University of Missouri Press, 1993), p. 267.

33. Denise Riley, *"Am I That Name?" Feminism and the Category of "Women"* (Minneapolis: University of Minnesota Press, 1988), p. 98. Future references are cited in the text.

34. Jean-François Lyotard, *The Post-Modern Condition: A Report on Knowledge*, trans. Geoff Bennington and Brian Massumi, foreword by Fredric Jameson (Minneapolis: University of Minnesota Press, 1984), p. 81.

35. For a general survey of feminist criticism postulating the "woman's space," see Butler, *Gender Trouble*; Barbara Correll, "Notes on the Primary Text: Woman's Body and Representation in *Pumping Iron II: The Women* and 'Breast Giver,'" *Genre* 22 (1989): 287–308; Leslie Dunn, "Ophelia's Songs in *Hamlet*: Music, Madness, and the Feminine," presented at the MLA convention, December 1990; Ruth Salvaggio, "Theory and Space, Space and Woman," *Tulsa Studies in Women's Literature* 7 (1988): 261–82; Kaja Silverman, "'Histoire d'O': The Story of a Disciplined and Punished Body," *enclitic* 7 (1983): 63–81.

36. Silverman, "'Histoire d' O," pp. 63–81.

37. Dunn, "Ophelia's Songs in *Hamlet*," p. 6.

38. Salvaggio, "Theory and Space, Space and Woman," 275.

39. Colie, in *The Resources of Kind*, pp. 76–82.

40. Geraldine Heng, "A Woman Wants: The Lady, Gawain, and the Forms of Seduction," *Yale Journal of Criticism* 5 (1992): 121.

41. Ibid., p. 130.

42. Shoshana Felman, "Rereading Femininity," *Yale French Studies* 62 (1981): 32.

43. Ann Rosalind Jones calls such a critique "negotiation . . . or the process

through which readers respond in partial self-interested ways to the ideologies encoded into cultural forms." See "Imaginary Gardens with Real Frogs in Them: Feminist Euphoria and the Franco-American Divide, 1976–88," in *Changing Subjects: The Making of Feminist Literary Critics*, ed. Gayle Greene and Coppelia Kahn (New York and London: Routledge, 1993), p. 76.

44. In reading the lyric to account for the woman's space and the poet's ambivalence, the dynamic suggested here differs from the theories of recent critics who similarly trace the influence of Petrarch on subsequent poets: Roland Greene and Jane Hedley. Roland Greene, "Sir Philip Sidney's *Psalms:* The Sixteenth-Century Psalter and the Nature of the Lyric," *SEL* 30 (1990): 21; Greene amplifies these points in *Post-Petrarchism: Origins and Innovations of the Western Lyric Sequence* (Princeton: Princeton University Press, 1991); Jane Hedley, *Power in Verse: Metaphor and Metonymy in the Renaissance Lyric* (University Park: Pennsylvania State University Press, 1988), p. xi. Though they similarly view the lyric in terms of several auditory dimensions, neither Hedley nor Greene focuses on the woman as conscious subject.

45. Gayle Ormiston, "Foreword," in *Phenomenology, Jean-François Lyotard* (Albany: State University of New York Press, 1991), p. 18.

46. Colie, *The Resources of Kind*, p. 14.

47. *Introducing Lyotard*, p. 152.

48. James Baumlin, *John Donne and the Rhetoric of Renaissance Discourse* (Columbia: University of Missouri Press, 1991), p. 305. Future references are cited in the text.

49. "The Dream-Work Does Not Think," trans. Mary Lydon, *The Lyotard Reader*, ed. Andrew Benjamin (London: Basil Blackwell, 1989), pp. 23–24. Future references are cited in the text.

50. Judith Butler, "Imitation and Gender Insubordination," in *Inside Out: Lesbian Theories / Gay Theories*, ed. Diane Fuss (London: Routledge, 1991), pp. 26 and 27. Future references are cited in the text.

51. Readings, *Introducing Lyotard*, p. xxxii.

52. For recent discussions of the poem, see John Carey, *John Donne: Life, Mind, and Art* (New York: Oxford University Press, 1980), pp. 104–8 and 116–18; Antony Easthope, *Poetry and Phantasy* (Cambridge: Cambridge University Press, 1989), p. 56; William Empson, "Donne in the New Edition," *Critical Quarterly* 8 (1966): 274; William Empson, "There Is No Penance Due to Innocence," *New York Review of Books*, December 3, 1981, pp. 42–50; Thomas Greene, "The Poetics of Discovery: A Reading of Donne's 'Elegy 19,'" *Yale Journal of Criticism* 2 (1989): 129–43; Christopher Ricks, "Donne after Love," in *Literature and the Body: Selected Papers from the English Institute, 1986*, ed. Elaine Scarry (Baltimore: Johns Hopkins University Press, 1988), pp. 59–61. Mary Ann Radzinowicz points to yet another pun on cover: "Donne takes advantage of the double meaning of *covering*—that is of clothing and mating with the two prepositions used with it, covering of a man and covering *by* a man, to say 'if you take off your covers you will be well covered.'" See "The Politics of John Donne's Silences," *John Donne Journal* 7 (1988): 4.

53. Antony Easthope argues for the lady's verbal power even as he ignores her

libidinal impulses. First he says that the "Donne speaker is himself advanced to the role of confessional interlocutor whose imperatives seek to elicit truth from the woman" (*Poetry and Phantasy*, p. 56). He then maintains that [the speaker's] scopophilia "makes possible only a narcissistic phantasy which conforms to the ideological promotion of individual inwardness" (p. 59). Easthope first admits to the possibility of verbal cover (the poem is designed to get the woman to confess); however, he denies that possibility when he reasons that the man's verbal cover is designed to render the woman fantastic. She might undress in his dreams but she cannot confess in his life. She's only a visual object, not a speaking subject. Within the context of Easthope's reading (and that of most readers of the poem), the woman is reduced to Laura-Daphne, an other the poet doesn't really want to have.

54. Diane Fuss, *Essentially Speaking* (London: Routledge, 1989), p. xi.

55. Frank Lentricchia, *Ariel and the Police* (Madison: University of Wisconsin Press, 1987); see also Paul Smith, "A Conversation," in *Men in Feminism*, ed. Alice Jardine and Paul Smith (London: Routledge, 1989), p. 256: "A lot of my own energy around this question of men in feminism comes from my objection to being regarded as the subject of a history that's not necessarily mine, but is the history of a group into which I've been placed."

56. Laura Claridge and Elizabeth Longland, eds., "Introduction," *Out of Bounds: Male Writers and Gendered Criticism* (Amherst: University of Massachusetts Press, 1990), p. 10.

57. See Fuss, *Essentially Speaking*, and Jonathan Dollimore, *Sexual Dissidence* (Oxford: Clarendon Press, 1991), p. 26.

58. *The Poems of Sir Philip Sidney*, ed. William A. Ringler (Oxford: Clarendon Press, 1962), p. 165.

59. *The Poems of George Herbert*, ed. F. E. Hutchinson (Oxford: Clarendon Press, 1967), p. 51.

60. Patricia Fumerton, "Secret Arts: Elizabethan Miniatures and Sonnets," in *Representing the English Renaissance*, ed. Stephen Greenblatt (Berkeley and Los Angeles: University of California Press, 1988), p. 121.

61. Ibid., p. 126.

62. That shift from nature to art also bends the focus of Ann Rosalind Jones and Peter Stallybrass's claim that the "central rhetorical situation in *Astrophil and Stella* is that Astrophil speaks; Stella is the object of that speech. Whether he writes a solitary meditation, an epistle to Stella, or a defense to outsiders of his love, he controls the experience insofar as he articulates it" ("The Politics of *Astrophil and Stella*," *SEL* 24 [1984]: 54).

Here, the argument is that, since the woman may be inside already, the rhetorical situation is interchangeable. Writing becomes an imitation of someone writing and the someone who writes may be Stella herself. In looking inward, Astrophil might find not the wit of an already inscribed masculinist poetic but something that is thickened from the start by the fact that there is no clearly defined inner and therefore no absolutely certain other. Within an anamorphic frame, Stella writes the poem. Her Muse has the last word. The poet copies her writing self. He is her mirror image and imagist.

63. Greene, *Post-Petrarchism*, p. 1.

64. Mieke Bal, "Sexuality, Sin, and the Emergence of Female Character: A Reading of Genesis 1–3," in *The Female Body in Western Culture*, ed. Susan Rubin Suleiman (Cambridge: Harvard University Press, 1985), pp. 323, 336.

65. Ibid., p. 336.

66. Greene, "The Poetics of Discovery," pp. 129–43; Anne Ferry, *The Inward Language* (Chicago: University of Chicago Press, 1983).

67. Thomas Docherty, *John Donne, Undone* (London: Methuen, 1986), p. 62.

68. Citing Ferry, Bruce Smith argues that "Shakespeare manages to maintain the illusion of inwardness in four ways: by picking up on Sidney's clue and playing up the inadequacies of poetic rhetoric to tell the heart's secrets; by implying major narrative events that happen between sonnets, 'offstage,' as it were in an 'outward' public world somewhere else; by depicting the outward world as vicious and hostile; and by granting his beloved an inwardness as strongly compelled as the speaker's own." *Homosexual Desire in Shakespeare's England* (Chicago: University of Chicago Press, 1991), p. 238. Clarke Hulse similarly maintains that, after sonnet 34, Astrophil "resolves to address a double audience, an outer one of the court dummy wits and an inner audience consisting of Stella and himself." See "Stella's Wit: Penelope Rich as Reader of Sidney's Sonnets," in *Rewriting the Renaissance*, ed. Margaret W. Ferguson, Maureen Quilligan, and Nancy J. Vickers (Chicago: University of Chicago Press, 1986), p. 278.

69. Fumerton, "Secret Arts," p. 126.

70. Hélène Cixous, "The Laugh of the Medusa," trans. Keith Cohen and Paula Cohen, in *New French Feminisms*, ed. Elaine Marks and Isabelle de Courtivron (New York: Schoken, 1981), p. 258.

71. Julian Pefanis, *Heterology and the Postmodern: Bataille, Baudrillard, and Lyotard* (Durham: Duke University Press, 1991), p. 118.

72. Reed Way Dasenbrock, *Imitating the Italians: Wyatt, Spenser, Synge, Pound, Joyce* (Baltimore: Johns Hopkins University Press, 1991), p. 11.

73. Claudio Guillen, *Literature as System: Essays Towards the Theory of Literary History* (Princeton: Princeton University Press, 1971), p. 111.

74. Wallace Stevens, "An Ordinary Evening in New Haven," *Collected Poems* (New York: Knopf, 1954), p. 489.

75. Monique Wittig, "Homo Sum," in *The Straight Mind and Other Essays* (Boston: Beacon Press, 1992), p. 55.

76. Charles Altieri's phrase, *Painterly Abstraction in Modernist American Poetry* (Cambridge: Harvard University Press, 1989), p. 211.

77. Cixous, "The Laugh of the Medusa," p. 258.

78. Salvaggio, "Theory and Space, Space and Woman," 257.

79. Adrienne Rich, "Contradictions, Tracking Poems, 29," in *Your Native Land, Your Life* (New York: W. W. Norton, 1986), p. 111.

Inverting the Order: Laura as Eve to Petrarch's Adam

1. Mieke Bal, "Sexuality, Sin, and the Emergence of Female Character," in *The Female Body in Western Culture*, ed. Susan Rubin Suleiman (Cambridge: Harvard University Press, 1985), p. 336.

2. Giuseppe Mazzotta, "The *Canzoniere* and the Language of the Self," *Studies in Philology 75* (1978): 282.

3. "The Symposium," *The Dialogues of Plato*, trans. B. Jowett (New York: Random House, 1937), 1:316–19.

4. See especially, Patricia Parker, *Literary Fat Ladies: Rhetoric, Gender, Property* (London and New York: Methuen, 1987), pp. 178–283.

5. John Freccero, "The Fig Tree and the Laurel: Petrarch's Poetics," *Diacritics 5* (1975): 37. Of the mutuality of disintegration, Nancy Vickers writes: "Within the context of Petrarch's extended sequence, then, the lady is corporeally scattered; the lover emotionally scattered; and the relation between the two is, by extension, one of mirroring." "The Body Re-membered: Petrarchan Lyric and the Strategies of Description," in *Mimesis: From Mirror to Method, Augustine to Descartes*, ed. John D. Lyons and Stephen G. Nichols, Jr. (Hanover and London, 1982), p. 104.

6. Marianne Shapiro, *Hieroglyph of Time: The Petrarchan Sestina* (Minneapolis: University of Minnesota Press, 1980), pp. 71–72.

7. Expanding on Sara Sturm-Maddox's argument that "there is a deliberate ambiguity in the syntax of his expression of hope" ("The Poet-Persona in the *Canzoniere*," in *Francis Petrarch Six Centuries Later: A Symposium*, ed. Aldo Scaglione [Chapel Hill and Chicago: North Carolina Studies in the Romance Languages and Literatures Symposia, 3, and The Newberry Library, 1975], p. 193), Marguerite Waller adds, "It could be that he hopes his suffering will produce the anticipated effect in the reader or it could be that he hopes something about the *poetry itself* will evoke the reader's response." Waller maintains that the "style" may even "operate independently of, or at variance from, experience." *Petrarch's Poetics and Literary History* (Amherst: University of Massachusetts Press, 1980), p. 39. Both critics suggest that the suffering is a creation, an artifact which begs for its own response.

8. *Petrarch's Secret*, trans. William H. Draper (Westport, Conn: Hyperion Press, 1978), p. 124. Future references will be cited in the text.

9. John Freccero writes about the Augustinian connection between ends and beginnings: "The redemptive process is a tautology ending where it began." See "The Fig Tree and the Laurel," p. 35.

10. Durling's footnote helpfully alludes to Augustine's "allegorical interpretation of Genesis 1, according to which the separation of the dry land from the sea is taken to mean conversion of the passage to the next life (*Confessions* 13.17–18); here, 'the living earth' is Petrarch's soul, 'the waves' his flesh or 'principle of mutability.'" *Petrarch's Lyric Poems*, ed. and trans. Robert Durling (Cambridge: Harvard University Press, 1976), p. 394; future text citations are from this edition.

11. Durling assumes she is Diana. See his note, *Petrarch's Lyric Poems*, p. 396.

12. See Gertrude Jobes, *Dictionary of Mythology, Folklore, and Symbols* (New York: Scarecrow Press, 1961), 1:511.

13. Of 181 and 188, Sturm-Maddox writes, "The identification of the beloved as the 'adorno suo male et nostro' reveals that for both Daphne and Laura there is another feminine prototype, that of Eve, the first woman." *Petrarch's Metamorphoses: Text and Subtext in the Rime Sparse* (Columbia: University of Missouri Press, 1985), p. 114. Of multiplying Lauras, Thomas Bergin speaks of *four* Lauras:

"the desirable Laura-Daphne, the celestial Laura-Beatrice, the dangerous Laura Sophonisba, and Laura-qua-Laura, a young woman with whom the poet fell in love on an April day of 1327." *Petrarch* (New York: Twayne, 1970), pp. 162–63, 164. Giuseppe Mazzotta writes of two Lauras, one loved, the other hated: "The symmetrical coupling of contradictory experiences is, in one sense, the emblem of Petrarch's split, the steady play of attraction and repulsion for Laura that has come to be identified as the distinctive trait of his morality and of his voice." See "Petrarch's Song 126," in *Textual Analysis, Some Readers Reading*, ed. Mary Ann Caws (New York: MLA Publications, 1986), p. 125.

14. *The Poems of George Herbert*, ed. F. E. Hutchinson (Oxford: Clarendon Press, 1967), p. 189.

15. On Laura's changeableness, Leonard Barkan writes: "[Her] identification with the breeze makes her variable in herself and the cause of variation (*mi volve*) in others." *The Gods Made Flesh: Metamorphosis and the Pursuit of Paganism* (New Haven: Yale University Press, 1986), p. 207.

16. Mazzotta, "The *Canzoniere* and the Language of the Self," pp. 271–96; Vickers, "Diana Described," pp. 265–79.

17. Virginia Woolf, *A Room of One's Own* (New York: Harcourt Brace, 1957), p. 108.

Laura as Mercury to Petrarch's Battus

1. Giuseppe Mazzotta, "The *Canzoniere* and the Language of the Self," *Studies in Philology* 75 (1978): 271–96; Giuseppe Mazzotta, "Petrarch's Song 126," in *Textual Analysis: Some Readers Reading* (New York: Modern Language Association, 1986), pp. 121–31.

2. Timothy Bahti, "Petrarch and the Scene of Writing: A Reading of *Rime* CXXIX," *Yale Italian Studies* 1 (1980–81): 45–63.

3. Of the inside-outside dichotomy, Timothy Bahti writes, "There is a curious association of a face which *represents* the poet's 'inside,' his soul, and a face which the persona's 'inside' (his mind) *presents* or marks or traces." See Bahti, "Petrarch and the Scene of Writing," p. 47.

4. Barbara Hodgdon, "He Do Cressida in Different Voices," *ELR* 20 (1990): 26.

5. *The Metamorphoses*, trans. Mary Innes (New York: Viking Penguin, 1986), p. 69.

6. See Barbara Johnson's discussion of apostrophe in *A World of Difference* (Baltimore: Johns Hopkins University Press, 1987), pp. 187–88.

7. Mazzotta, "The *Canzoniere* and the Language of the Self," p. 296.

8. Kaja Silverman's phrase; see " 'Histoire d'O': The Story of a Disciplined and Punished Body," *enclitic* 7 (1983): 78.

9. Mazzotta, "The *Canzoniere* and the Language of the Self," p. 291.

10. Mazzotta, "Petrarch's Song 126," p. 130.

11. For a discussion of the remarkable change from affirmation to nullification in these lines, see Bahti, "Petrarch and the Scene of Writing," 49–50.

12. Ibid., p. 52.

13. *Rime Petrose* 3, *Petrarch's Lyric Poems*, p. 620.

14. Gordon Braden, "Beyond Frustration: Petrarchan Laurels in the Seventeenth Century," *SEL* 26 (1986):8.

Taking Bread: Wyatt's Revenge in the Lyrics, and Sustenance in the Psalms

Unless otherwise specified, citations from Wyatt's poetry are taken from *Sir Thomas Wyatt: The Complete Poems*, ed. R. A. Rebholz (New Haven: Yale University Press, 1978).

1. Alexandra Halasz, "Wyatt's David," *Texas Studies in Literature and Language* 30 (1988): 326. Future references are cited in the text.

2. Joel Fineman, *Shakespeare's Perjured Eye: The Invention of Poetic Subjectivity in the Sonnets* (Berkeley and Los Angeles: University of California Press, 1986), p. 194.

3. For a brief critical history of the identification of Wyatt's "inwardness," see Nancy Leonard, "The Speaker in Wyatt's Lyric Poetry," *HLQ* 41 (1977): 1–8; John Kerrigan, "Wyatt's Selfish Style," *Essays and Studies* 34 (1981): 1–18; Anne Ferry, *The "Inward" Language* (Chicago: University of Chicago Press, 1983); Stephen Greenblatt, *Renaissance Self-Fashioning* (Berkeley and Los Angeles: University of California Press, 1980); and Shormishtha Panja, "Ranging and Returning: The Mood-Voice Dichotomy in Wyatt," *ELR* 18 (1988): 347–68.

4. Commenting on Wyatt's privatization as revenge against an intrusive world, John Kerrigan writes: "A Wyatt poem is typically plain (advertising the sincerity of its self in a world that is otherwise) and extraordinarily opaque (reserving the self to itself)." "Wyatt's Selfish Style," p. 7.

5. Jonathan Crewe, *Trials of Authorship* (Berkeley and Los Angeles: University of California Press, 1990), p. 39.

6. David Rosen similarly argues, "When the singer puts down his lute, it is not because he has breathed his last, but because he has finally successfully dealt with and done his beloved." "Time, Identity, and Context in Wyatt's Verse," *SEL* 21 (1981): 17.

7. Donald Guss maintains that it is "the lady's falsity [that] makes it impossible to assail her with pitiful plaint. . . . Wyatt's personification of his sighs reflects his alienation from love and his sense that he has been imposed on." See "Wyatt's Petrarchism: An Instance of Creative Imitation in the Renaissance," *HLQ* 29 (1965): 12.

8. Crewe, *Trials of Authorship*, p. 34.

9. Anthony Low, "Wyatt's 'What Word is That,'" *ELN* 10 (1972): 89–90.

10. Of the positive, infusive, rather than exhaustive nature of the hermaphrodite, Lauren Silberman writes: "From our wider perspective, we can see Hermaphrodite as a biform sign in which arbitrary semiological difference plays against sexual difference. The 'he-she' hermaphrodite is neither genuinely androgynous nor genuinely a boundary figure; it is arbitrarily classed with 'she.'" See "The

Hermaphrodite and the Metamorphosis of Spenserian Allegory," *ELR* 17 (1987): 212.

11. Greenblatt, *Renaissance Self-Fashioning*, p. 21.

12. Panja, "Ranging and Returning: The Mood-Voice Dichotomy in Wyatt," p. 362.

13. Greenblatt, *Renaissance Self-Fashioning*, p. 23.

14. Marguerite Waller, "The Empire's New Clothes," in *Seeking the Woman in Late Medieval and Renaissance Writings*, ed. Sheila Fisher and Janet Halley (Knoxville: University of Tennessee Press, 1990), p. 178.

15. Commenting on David's success in the *Psalms*, Robert G. Twombley argues, "Wyatt seems to press a bargain with God, a contract establishing some sort of permanent and fixed relationship. In this Wyatt is being entirely original." "Wyatt's Paraphrase of the *Penitential Psalms*," *Texas Studies in Literature and Language* 12 (1970): 375.

16. Roland Greene, "Sir Philip Sidney's *Psalms:* The Sixteenth-Century Psalter and the Nature of the Lyric," *SEL* 30 (1990): 23.

17. Of the revisionism Lyotard reviles, Bill Readings writes: "Auschwitz is a name to which no concept should be applied, which can only be betrayed by becoming the object of a representation, a matter for cognition. This is the weight of Lyotard's analysis of Faurisson's critique of the historical reality of the sufferings of victims of Nazi gas chambers. The sufferers in the gas chambers are victims of the double bind imposed by a representable law: to have seen a gas chamber work is to be dead, unable to speak of the wrong one has suffered. The victim is one who has suffered a 'damage' accompanied by the loss of the means to prove the damage" (*The Differend*, p. 5). In this sense, the women David subsumes in his self-aggrandizement can no longer prove the damage.

"Liking This": Telling Wyatt's Feelings

1. Jonathan Crewe, *Trials of Authorship* (Berkeley and Los Angeles: University of California Press, 1990), pp. 23–47; Alexandra Halasz, "Wyatt's David," *Texas Studies in Literature and Language* 30 (1988): 320–44; Pamela Royston Macfie, "Sewing in Ottavia Rima: Wyatt's Assimilation and Critique of a Feminist Poetic," *Early Modern Papers* (1987): 25–37; Marguerite Waller, "The Empire's New Clothes: Refashioning the Renaissance," in *Seeking the Woman*, ed. Sheila Fisher and Janet Halley (Knoxville: University of Tennessee Press, 1990), pp. 160–73.

2. These questions are labeled (1) a connection between the sweeping discourses of power and the painstaking requirements of form; (2) a tension between narrator and David; (3) a competition between female art and male inscription; (4) a discrepancy between male supremacy and the "vanishing woman" by Crewe, Halasz, Macfie, and Waller respectively.

3. On the formation of this questioning of the fateful seeing and the seeing fate, see Norman O. Brown, "Metamorphoses II: Actaeon," *American Poetry Review* 1 (1972): 8.

4. Macfie, "Sewing in Ottavia Rima," 34–37.

5. Ibid., 34–35.

6. Donald Freedman easily makes the equation in his essay on "They flee from me": "What he is thinking of primarily is the contrast between the deceptive amenity of the women in the past and their unbridled 'ranging' in the present. He is dismayed to find that his skill as a hunter (poet-courtier-seducer) has not in truth changed their natures." "The Mind in the Poem: Wyatt's 'They flee from me,' " *SEL* 7 (1967): 7.

7. Leonard Barkan, "Diana and Actaeon: The Myth as Synthesis," *ELR* 10 (1970): 341.

8. Giordano Bruno, *The Heroic Frenzies*, trans. Paul Memmo (Chapel Hill: University of North Carolina Press, 1965), p. 125. See also Brown, "Metamorphoses 2: Actaeon," 40.

9. Gregory Nagy, *Greek Mythology and Poetics* (Ithaca: Cornell University Press, 1990), pp. 263 and 264.

10. Though he doesn't specifically apply what he says to Petrarch, Robert H. Deming elaborates loving well: "What, then, did the love lyricists believe their poetry to be? What are the relationships between loving and knowing that they established? To be sure, they discovered that love is merely the process of desiring something which one cannot have. To have what one desires will yield a pleasure and happiness which is static (or perhaps ecstatic) while the process of loving is dynamic." "Love and Knowledge in the Early Modern Lyric," *Texas Studies in Language and Literature* 16 (1975): 395–96. Petrarch embraces the dynamic of failure. The Wyatt of "The long love" is trapped in the stasis of failure.

11. On Actaeon's "victimized innocence" in Ovid, see Barkan, "Diana and Actaeon: The Myth as Synthesis," pp. 323–24.

12. Nancy Vickers, "Diana Described: Scattered Woman and Scattered Rhyme," *Critical Inquiry* 8 (1981–82): 270.

13. For a summary of the critical perspective see Waller, "The Empire's New Clothes," p. 181.

14. Greenblatt, *Renaissance Self-Fashioning*, p. 147.

15. Waller, "The Empire's New Clothes," p. 178.

16. Crewe, *Trials of Authorship*, p. 39.

17. Waller, "The Empire's New Clothes," p. 178.

18. *Collected Poems of Sir Thomas Wyatt*, ed. Kenneth Muir and Patricia Thomson (Liverpool: Liverpool University Press, 1969), p. 267; Rebholz, ed., *Sir Thomas Wyatt: The Complete Poems*; Waller, "The Empire's New Clothes," p. 172.

19. Crewe, *Trials of Authorship*, p. 39.

20. Waller, "The Empire's New Clothes," p. 174.

21. Ibid., p. 175.

22. About the maled-female, Jonathan Crewe writes: "Appropriating the unspeakable, nonvernacular language of the absolute as her warrant, the hind not only becomes the untouchable one, but constitutes herself in the rigorously subject-forming relation of bondage claiming to be the sole authentic subject of the poem: 'I am.' " *Trials of Authorship*, p. 42.

329

Small Change: Defections from Petrarchan and Spenserian Poetics

Unless otherwise specified, citations from Donne's poems are taken from *John Donne: Elegies and Songs and Sonnets*, ed. Helen Gardner (Oxford: Clarendon Press, 1965).

1. Patrick Crutwell, "The Love Poetry of John Donne: Pedantique Weedes or Fresh Invention?" in *Metaphysical Poetry*, ed. Malcolm Bradbury and David Palmer (Bloomington: Indiana University Press, 1977), p. 22.

2. Janel Mueller, "Women among the Metaphysicals: A Case, Mostly of Being Donne For," *Modern Philology* 87 (1989): 147.

3. Janet Halley, "Textual Intercourse: Ann Donne, John Donne, and the Sexual Politics of Textual Exchange," in *Seeking the Woman in Late Medieval and Renaissance Writings*, ed. Sheila Fisher and Janet Halley (Knoxville: University of Tennessee Press, 1990), p. 199.

4. Ann Rosalind Jones, "Imaginary Gardens with Real Frogs," in *Changing Subjects*, ed. Greene and Kahn (New York: Routledge, 1993), p. 76.

5. Ilona Bell, "The Role of the Lady in Donne's Songs and Sonnets," *SEL* 23 (1983): 116, 124.

6. Ilona Bell, "Under ye Rage of a Hott Sonn & Yr Eyes: John Donne's Love Letters to Ann More," in *The Eagle and the Dove: Reassessing John Donne*, ed. Claude Summers and Ted-Larry Pebworth (Columbia: University of Missouri Press, 1986), p. 27.

7. Marguerite Waller, "The Empire's New Clothes," in *Seeking the Woman*, ed. Fisher and Halley, p. 167.

8. Sheila Fisher and Janet E. Halley, "Introduction," in *Seeking the Woman*, ed. Fisher and Halley, pp. 13–14.

9. Annabel Patterson, for example, maintains that it is "one of the paradoxes of language that in the personal letters the spontaneity of self-expression meets certain conventions of privatization; and never more so than in the seventeenth century." See "Misinterpretable Donne: The Testimony of the Love Letters," *John Donne Journal* 1–2 (1982): 40–41.

10. Robert Lowell, "Epilogue," *Day by Day* (New York: Farrar, Straus and Giroux), p. 127.

11. Christopher Ricks, "Donne after Love," in *Literature and the Body: Selected Papers from the English Institute*, 1986, ed. Elaine Scarry (Baltimore: Johns Hopkins University Press, 1988), p. 33.

12. William Kerrigan, "What Was Donne Doing," *South Central Review* 4 (1987): 12. On the value of full sexual consummation for Donne's poetry, see also Kerrigan and Gordon Braden, *The Idea of the Renaissance* (Baltimore: Johns Hopkins University Press, 1989), pp. 175–178.

13. *The Sermons of John Donne*, vol. 6, ed. Evelyn M. Simpson and George R. Potter (Berkeley and Los Angeles: University of California Press, 1962), p. 170.

14. Miles Coverdale, *The Christen State of Matrimonye* (London: Nicholas Hyll for Abraham Vale, 1552), pp. 7–8. Punctuation and spelling are modernized. Similar views are expressed by Gervase Babington, *Certaine Plaine, briefe, and comfort-*

able notes vpon every chapter of Genesis (London: Thomas Charde, 1592), and John Rogers, *The Glasse of Godly Love* (London: New Shakespeare Society, 1876).

15. See Patricia Parker, *Literary Fat Ladies: Rhetoric, Gender, Property* (London and New York: Methuen, 1987), p. 179.

16. Thomas de Vio, *Commentarii in quinque Libros* (Paris, 1539), as translated and quoted by Ian MacLean in *The Renaissance Notion of Women* (Cambridge: Cambridge University Press, 1980), p. 9.

17. Edmund Spenser, *Poetical Works*, ed. J. C. Smith and E. de Selincourt (London: Oxford University Press, 1932), p. 381.

18. Rosalie Colie, *Paradoxia Epidemica: The Renaissance Tradition of Paradox* (Princeton: Princeton University Press, 1966). See her discussion on the reactions to Pascal's experiments, pp. 252–72.

19. Colie, *Paradoxia Epidemica*, pp. 256–72.

20. On infinity as a formless imperfection, see Joseph E. Grennan, "John Donne on the Growth and Infiniteness of Love," *John Donne Journal* 3 (1984): 34.

21. David A. Hedrich Hirsch reads these lines more positively: "Despite being shattered by love's plague-like decay, ['The Broken Heart'] possesses an integrity still potentially salvageable because 'nothing can to nothing fall.' " See "Donne's Atomies and Anatomies: Deconstructed Bodies and the Resurrection of Atomic Theory," *SEL* 31 (1991): 76.

22. James S. Baumlin argues that the failure of poetry to assuage the loss of absence is a theme for Donne. "Writing provides but a weak compensation and surely no antidote for absence, becoming a *pharmakon* or drug—or more precisely, a compulsive action that seeks to allay (though it never can cure) the anxiety of separation." See *John Donne and the Rhetorics of Renaissance Discourse* (Columbia: University of Missouri Press, 1991), p. 190.

23. Of the self-creation here, John Freccero sums up the critical consensus: "The idolatrous love for Laura, however self-abasing it may seem, has the effect of creating a thoroughly autonomous portrait of the poet laureate." See "The Fig Tree and the Laurel: Petrarch's Poetics," *Diacritics* 5 (1975): 38. See also Leonard Barkan, who writes of Petrarch's exaltation: "Petrarch at the nadir point of his experience declares that he is drawn out of his own *imago*, meaning that he is metamorphosed and poetically bankrupt; now, in the envoy, he tells us that he would not leave that original laurel for any *nova figura*." *The Gods Made Flesh: Metamorphosis and the Pursuit of Paganism* (New Haven: Yale University Press, 1986), p. 214.

24. Of the ascent, Albert J. Rivero writes, "There is no fall; the movement is upward; now the words which 'honour' his lady soar . . . Sexual love has been sublimated into a more acceptable form." See "Petrarch's 'Nel Dolce Tempo de la Prima Etade," *MLN* 94 (1979): 107.

25. William Empson writes of the difference between this poem and those in which Donne consoles the woman, "There is none of the Platonic pretence Donne keeps up elsewhere that their love is independent of being together; he can find no satisfaction in his hopelessness but to make as much of the actual situation of parting as possible." *Seven Types of Ambiguity* (New York: New Directions, 1968), p. 139.

26. Mieke Bal, "Sexuality, Sin, and the Emergence of Female Character," in *The Female Body in Western Culture*, ed. Susan Rubin Suleiman (Cambridge: Harvard University Press, 1985), p. 336.

27. Tilottama Rajan speaks of the poem as a commentary on the insufficiency of substitution: "As an attempt to restore the presence of the beloved [the poem] is aware of itself as growing from an experience of loss and absence and therefore as an enterprise whose compensatory nature only serves to heighten the realities that if fights off." "Nothing Sooner Broke, Donne's *Songs and Sonnets* as Self-Consuming Artifact," *ELH* 49 (1982): 816.

28. See Eve Sedgwick, *Between Men: English Literature and Male Homosocial Desire* (New York: Columbia University Press, 1985). Jonathan Goldberg similarly writes of Silvia's artificial being: "The song inserts Silvia within a poetic economy, Ovidian metamorphosis as her end. Poets have always affirmed that they confer immortality, as Sidney among others, might remind us. Silvia's excellence is textual; her 'being,' literally is figurative. No wonder then that she ends up in the forest, voiceless." *Voice Terminal Echo: Postmodernism and English Renaissance Texts* (New York and London: Methuen, 1986), p. 69.

Sylvia Transformed: Returning Donne's Gifts

1. Patricia Fumerton, "Exchanging Gifts: The Elizabethan Currency of Children and Poetry," *ELH* 53 (1986): 270.

2. Ovid, *The Art of Love*, trans. Rolfe Humphries (Bloomington: Indiana University Press, 1963), p. 20.

3. See *Petrarch's Lyric Poems*, trans. Robert Durling (Cambridge: University Press, 1976), p. 556. Future references are cited in the text.

4. Sir Thomas Wyatt, "They flee from me."

5. Gordon Braden and William Kerrigan refer to Ovid and Wyatt's "giving" ladies as exceptions to the "routine of sexual resistance inherent to Petrarchism." See *The Idea of the Renaissance* (Baltimore: Johns Hopkins University Press, 1989), p. 201.

6. Natalie Ziemon Davis's phrase. "Women on Top," in *Society and Culture in Early Modern France: Eight Essays* (Stanford: Stanford University Press, 1975), p. 128.

7. Janel Mueller, "Women among the Metaphysicals: A Case, Mostly of Being Donne For," *Modern Philosophy* 87 (1989): 126.

8. Christopher Ricks, "Donne after Love," in *Literature and the Body: Selected Papers from the English Institute*, 1986, ed. Elaine Scarry (Baltimore: Johns Hopkins University Press, 1988), p. 66.

9. Dwight Cathcart says of this mutual understanding: "One has the sense in any one poem of two persons with fine and fully developed intellects, whose interests lie around all the points of the compass and whose experience has been deep and productive. One understands that they know themselves and each other well and may speak elliptically and be understood." *Doubting Conscience: Donne and the Poetry of Moral Argument* (Ann Arbor: University of Michigan Press, 1975), p. 15.

10. James Baumlin, *John Donne and the Rhetorics of Renaissance Discourse* (Columbia: University of Missouri Press, 1991), p. 219.

11. See for example, Judah Stampfer, *John Donne and the Metaphysical Gesture* (New York: Funk and Wagnalls, 1970), p. 211.

12. On the links between "The Relique" and "The Funerall" see Cathcart, *Doubting Conscience*, p. 95 and Stampfer, *Donne and the Metaphysical Gesture*, p. 182.

13. J. B. Leishman does not see a split in the poem. He argues that the humility/bravery sections are continuous. Of the self-assessment, he maintains that the speaker uses the terms to express the double implications of the wreath: "The speaker claims, I shall at least have displayed humility in having attributed to it the power of a soul, and some pride in having buried some of her who would save none of me." *The Monarch of Wit* (London: Hutchinson and Co., 1965), p. 239.

14. *The Poems of Sir Philip Sidney*, p. 113.

15. Comparing this poem to others on the "love-dream" theme, Mario Praz says that "Donne's lady is so much of a flesh-and-blood presence that she can be invited to 'act the rest.'" See "Donne's Relation to the Poetry of His Time," in *John Donne: A Collection of Critical Essays*, ed. Helen Gardner (Englewood Cliffs, N.J.: Prentice-Hall, 1962), p. 65.

16. On the psychological benefits of delay, see William Kerrigan and Gordon Braden, *The Idea of the Renaissance* (Baltimore: Johns Hopkins University Press, 1989), pp. 204–10.

17. Ruth Salvaggio, "Theory and Space, Space and Woman," *Tulsa Studies in Women's Literature* 7 (1988): 275.

18. On the physical effect of the dream, see Arthur Marotti, *John Donne: Coterie Poet* (Madison: University of Wisconsin Press, 1986), p. 92.

19. Of the interspace, Pierre Legouis maintains, "The woman it seems remains seated and out of reach. So the man tries to lure her forward." *Donne, the Craftsman* (New York: Russell and Russell, 1962), p. 76. Ilona Bell also says that "the lady departs prematurely." See "The Role of the Lady in Donne's Songs and Sonnets," *SEL* 23 (1983): 126. Christopher Ricks too maintains, "The act of love may be to come. . . . It is so in 'The Dreame,' which, whatever it may say, prefers this being unsatisfied." See "Donne after Love," p. 58.

"A Pregnant Bank": Contracting and Abstracting the "You"

1. Barbara Johnson, "Les Fleurs du mal arme: Some Reflections on Intertextuality," in *Lyric Poetry: Beyond New Criticism*, ed. Chaviva Hosek and Patricia Parker (Ithaca: Cornell University Press, 1985), p. 280.

2. William Kerrigan, "What Was Donne Doing," *South Central Review* 4 (1987): 12.

3. Ibid., 7.

4. See, for example, Ilona Bell, "The Role of the Lady in Donne's Songs and Sonnets," *SEL* 23 (1983): 113–29; and Elaine Scarry, "But Yet the Body Is His Book," in *Literature and the Body: Essays on Populations and Persons* (Baltimore: Johns Hopkins University Press, 1988), pp. 70–105.

5. Scarry, "But Yet the Body Is His Booke," p. 82.

6. Albert Cook, "The Wilderness of Mirrors," *Kenyon Review* 8 (1986): 91.

7. Elaine Scarry suggests that Donne is also aware of another dimension: "Windows at the time Donne was alive, were often still made of oiled paper and muslin, in other words, of materials whose overt resemblance to the materials of letters or books allows him to play with the analogy in many ingenious directions." "But Yet the Body Is His Book," p. 81.

8. On the enclosures of Donne's naming, see ibid., p. 83, and Arthur Marotti, *John Donne: Coterie Poet* (Madison: University of Wisconsin Press, 1986), p. 150.

9. On the "fears that won't go away," see John Carey, *John Donne: Life, Mind, and Art* (New York: Oxford University Press, 1980), p. 196.

10. Scott W. Wilson describes another kind of reflection, arguing that Donne creates "a complex self-referential process engaging both the reader and the persona within a fictive framework which is at once a house of mirrors and an echo chamber." See "Process and Product: Reconstructing Donne's Personae," *SEL* 20 (1980): 94–95. The argument here about "Window" is that the process so involves the woman in its matrix of self-reference that she, and any sense that she might offer of a solidly realistic base, disappears. The poet is left only with a reflection of his own imagination—manic in its vision of paradise, depressive in its vision of sequence.

11. James Baumlin similarly writes: "Far from sustaining his own living voice, the engraved name becomes the poet's grave, a gruesome pun that has echoed throughout the poem from the beginning stanza." See *John Donne and the Rhetorics of Renaissance Discourse* (Columbia: University of Missouri Press, 1991), p. 183. Baumlin argues further that the poet deconstructs poetry: "The poem itself preach[es] the death of living speech, the death of the transcendental subject, the death of the author in writing," p. 184.

12. W. B. Yeats, "Whence had they come (Supernatural Songs)," *The Poems*, ed. Richard Finneran (New York: Macmillan, 1983), p. 287.

13. Helen Gardner, *John Donne: The Elegies and Songs and Sonnets*, p. 137. Gardner writes, "With characteristic sophistry, Donne confuses things that cannot exist without movement or 'change,' such as music, with eternity which is 'contrayr to Mutabilitie' being its term or end."

14. Donne, *Paradoxes and Problems*, ed. Helen Peters (Oxford: Clarendon Press, 1980), p. 48.

15. Ibid., p. 49.

16. Ibid.

17. Hélène Cixous, "The Laugh of the Medusa," trans. Keith Cohen and Paula Cohen, in *New French Feminisms*, ed. Elaine Marks and Isabelle de Courtivron (New York: Schoken, 1981), p. 258.

18. Thomas Docherty, *John Donne, Undone* (London: Methuen, 1986), p. 62.

19. Stanley Fish argues that the "beatitude [at the end] might mark an achieved coherence in a poem like Spenser's *Mutability Cantos* whose conclusion it resembles, but here it marks only the dislodgement of the centered self by the fragmentary ecphrastic discourse it presumed to control." See "Masculine Persuasive Force: Donne and Verbal Power," *Soliciting Interpretation: Essays in Seventeenth-Century Poetry*, ed. Elizabeth D. Harvey and Katharine Eisaman Maus (Chicago: University of Chicago Press, 1990), p. 231. Determined to demonstrate that the

woman has "long since been left behind" (p. 231) and that the poem illustrates both Donne's tendency "to push his fears into others" (p. 250) and then to re-produce a self that can never be its own, Fish ignores the possibility that the overcome Donne might be speaking as the woman. Moreover, Fish dismisses the beatitude he identifies. If it has no sayer, it emerges (by Fish's own reasoning) unsaid. The critical task in the analysis of "Change" is to account for—rather than to deny, as Fish does—the extraordinary concluding lines.

20. Luce Irigaray, "This Sex Which Is Not One," trans. Claudia Reeder, in *New French Feminisms*, ed. Elaine Marks and Isabelle de Courtivron (New York: Schocken, 1981), pp. 100–102.

21. Ibid., p. 116.

22. Ruth Salvaggio, "Theory and Space, Space and Woman," *Tulsa Studies in Women's Literature* 7 (1988): 278.

Appropriations of Female Power in "Damon the Mower" and "The Gallery"

Unless otherwise specified, citations from Marvell's poems are taken from *The Poems and Letters of Andrew Marvell*, 3d ed., ed. H. H. Margoliouth, rev. Pierre Legouis and E. E. Duncan-Jones (Oxford: Clarendon Press, 1971).

1. See Denise Riley, *"Am I That Name?" Feminism and the Category of "Women"* (Minneapolis: University of Minnesota Press, 1988), p. 98.

2. Richard Linche, *The Fountaine of Ancient Fiction* (London: Adam Islip, 1599), pp. CII–CIII.

3. Ibid., p. N.

4. Julian Pefanis, *Heterology and the Postmodern: Bataille, Baudrillard, and Lyotard* (Durham: Duke University Press, 1991), p. 118.

5. Paul Alpers, "Convening and Convention in Pastoral Poetry," *New Literary History* 14 (1983): 292–93.

6. For a discussion of the pun on scythe/sighs, see Donald Friedman, *Marvell's Pastoral Art* (Berkeley and Los Angeles: University of California Press, 1970), p. 133.

7. Elaine Hoffmann Baruch argues that, like Donne, Marvell may be saying " 'death thou shalt die.' If the mower can mow himself, then perhaps death can mow itself down too." But that logic ignores the constant mirroring which suggests that, like Time, death mimics eternity and survives by becoming part of a larger process. See "Theme and Countertheme in 'Damon the Mower,' " *Comparative Literature* 26 (1974): 259.

8. Harold Toliver maintains that the poem has a rhetorical intent: "And so Clora may be convinced and reformed. . . . The exaggerations of the earlier portraits have a dramatic and educational function to perform, namely, to show the cruel mistress to herself and to suggest a cure." *Marvell's Ironic Vision* (New Haven: Yale University Press, 1965), p. 174.

9. On the Italian origin of "The Gallery," see John Dixon Hunt, *Andrew Marvell: His Life and Writings* (Ithaca: Cornell University Press, 1978), p. 65. Specula-tions about the sources for Marvell's "Gallery" range from Rosalie Colie's links to Francis Quarles's emblems (*My Echoing Song: Andrew Marvell's Poetry of Crit-

icism (Princeton University Press, 1970), pp. 106–7; to Jean Hagstrum's references to "Rembrandt, Rubens, Caravaggio, and Occasionally the Bolognese Eclectics" in *The Sister Arts* (Chicago: University of Chicago Press, 1971), pp. 114–17; to Louis Martz's allusions to mannerist art in "Marvell and Herrick: The Masks of Mannerism," in *Approaches to Marvell: The York Tercentenary Lectures*, ed. C. A. Patrides (London: Routledge and Kegan Paul, 1978), pp. 205–6; to Phoebe Spinrad's references to George Wither's 1635 *Collection of Emblemes, Ancient and Modern;* see Spinrad, "Marvell's Gallery of Distorted Mirrors," *Interpretations* 3 (1983): 2.

In my estimation, Hunt comes closest to naming a source when he identifies "the tiny closet created by Vasari for Francesco de Medici in 1570; its walls are covered with bronzes and exquisite paintings, including portraits of women and allegorical and mythical subjects such as Marvell invokes for his picture of Clora. The rarefied claustrophobic little room into which Francesco could have shut himself away is the three-dimensional counterpart of Marvell's gallery, where he contemplates the several lodgings of his soul." See *Andrew Marvell: His Life and Writings*, p. 65. While the Florentine studio does contain mythological paintings (of, for example, Jason and Medea, Perseus and Andromeda), at its entrances are portraits of Cosimo I and Leonora di Toledo, stylized reminders of their artist's powerfully political patrons. See Alfredo Lensi, *Palazzo Vecchio* (Milan, 1929), pp. 245–69, and Luciano Berti, *Il Principe Dello Studiolo: Francesco I dei Medici e la Fine del Rinascimento Fiorentino* (Florence, 1967). Marvell's love gallery is, by contrast, deliberately unpolitical. It enthrones the artist. Since the studiolo was only open by invitation, it isn't altogether clear that Marvell could have gained entrance. He might only have heard about it. But the Uffizi gallery was open to the public and it is almost certain that Marvell saw Botticelli's *Birth of Venus*, and used it as the model for the rising goddess of stanza 5.

My suggestion about the polyptych is merely that Marvell might have been as interested in the connections among the paintings as in the individual tableaux and might have been as influenced by what he had remembered from Ghent as by what he might have seen in Italy. Certainly the Christian frame of the polyptych allows him the advantage of irony. My thanks to Professor Roberta J. M. Olson for her help in identifying the Italian sources.

10. Hélène Cixous, "The Laugh of the Medusa," trans. Keith Cohen and Paula Cohen, in *New French Feminisms*, ed. Elaine Marks and Isabelle de Courtivron (New York: Schocken, 1981), p. 263.

11. Spinrad, "Marvell's Gallery of Distorted Mirrors," 8.

12. Lotte Brand Philips, *The Ghent Altarpiece and the Art of Jan van Eyck* (Princeton: Princeton University Press, 1971), p. 200.

13. Erwin Panofsky, *Early Netherlandish Painting: Its Origins and Character* (Cambridge: Harvard University Press, 1966), p. 214–15.

Marvell's Nymph and the Revenge of Silence

1. Ann Rosalind Jones, *The Curency of Eros: Women's Love Lyric in Europe, 1540–1620* (Bloomington: Indiana University Press, 1990), p. 9.

2. Wendy Griswold, *Renaissance Revivals: City Comedy and Revenge Tragedy* (Chicago: University of Chicago Press, 1986), p. 65.

3. Jonathan Goldberg, *Voice Terminal Echo* (New York and London: Methuen, 1986), p. 14.

4. Geoffrey Hartman, " 'The Nymph Complaining for the Death of Her Fawn': A Brief Allegory," *Essays in Criticism* 18 (1968): 115.

5. Harry Berger, Jr., "Andrew Marvell: The Poem as Green World," *Forum for Modern Language Studies* 3 (1967): 297.

6. Carolyn Heilbrun, *Writing a Woman's Life* (New York: Norton, 1988), p. 15.

7. John Webster, *The Duchess of Malfi*, ed. Fred Millet (Northbrook, Ill.: AHM, 1953), p. 75.

8. Asking "what, in short, separates the Nymph from Emmeline Grangerford," John J. Teunissen and Evelyn J. Hinz conclude that "the secrets of its foundations lie in the fact that the Nymph is complaining not of . . . the death of her pet but the death of her offspring, her child. . . . The fawn motif is a projection, a homeopathic pain which the Nymph has invented to account for her grief" ("What Is the Nymph Complaining For?" *ELH* 45 [1978]: 412–13). Teunissen and Hinz call the deer a figure for the nymph's literal child. I see him as a figure for an adopted child, her substitute of art for nature.

9. Taking a completely opposite approach, Elaine Hoffman Baruch, "Marvell's 'Nymph': A Study of Feminine Consciousness," *Etudes Anglaises* 31 (1978): 152–60, argues that Marvell offers "a study of a feminine sensibility that sums up a host of Western stereotypes from the point of view of someone who believes them" (p. 159). For Baruch, the nymph remains victim of hunters and herself. Bypassing the Diana references, she maintains that the nymph is passively uncreative.

10. Most critics ignore the Diana-Agamemnon reference. Jonathan Goldberg, for example, asks: "Why *Diana?* As chaste nymph and as killer of the huntsman, Actaeon (h[e]artslain), Diana is the meeting place of nymph and hunter. Her name embodies transcendent purity and necessary slaughter, the coincidence of the h[e]art and the hunt, duplicitous repetition" (*Voice Terminal Echo, Postmodernism and English Renaissance Texts* [New York and London: Methuen], p. 34). Carolyn Asp, "Marvell's Nymph: Unravished Bride of Quietness," *Papers on Language and Literature* 14 (1978): 402, speaks of two Dianas but not by linking either of them with specific mortals: "She is associated with the earth as huntress and with the sky through her symbol the moon. She is patroness of both chastity and fertility, and ironically, of the hunter as well as of the hunted beast. She is the divine model of *concordia discors.*"

11. Patricia Fumerton, "Secret Arts: Elizabethan Miniatures and Sonnets," in *Representing the English Renaissance*, ed. Stephen Greenblatt (Berkeley and Los Angeles: University of California Press), p. 126.

12. *Shakespeare's Ovid: The Metamorphoses*, ed. W. H. D. Rouse (New York: Norton, 1961), p. 67.

13. Joannes Secundus, "The First Kiss," *Poems*, trans. F. X. Mathews (Kingston, R.I.: Winecellar Press, 1984), unpaginated. For the influence of Secundus on Marvell, see Clifford Endres, *Joannes Secundus: The Latin Love Elegy in the Renaissance* (Hamden, Conn.: Archon Books, 1981), pp. 31 and 34.

14. Kenneth Cool, "The Petrarchan Landscape as Palimpsest," *Journal of Medieval and Renaissance Studies* 11 (1981): 94.

15. Gordon Braden, "Beyond Frustration: Petrarchan Laurels in the Seventeenth Century," *SEL* 26 (1986): 8.

16. William Shakespeare, *The Sonnets*, ed. Douglas Bush and Alfred Harbage (Baltimore: Penguin, 1961), p. 87.

17. Hartman, "'The Nymph Complaining,'" p. 125.

18. Hartman comments, referring also to "Nymph" and "Coy Mistress," on Marvell's *hastening* lovers. "'The Nymph Complaining,'" p. 123.

A-mazing and A-musing: After the Garden in "Appleton House"

1. Ruth Salvaggio's definition of female space; "Theory and Space, Space and Woman," *Tulsa Studies in Women's Literature* 7 (1988): 273.

2. William Kerrigan, "What Was Donne Doing?" *South Central Review* 4 (1987): 12.

3. Monique Wittig, "Homo Sum," in *The Straight Mind and Other Essays* (Boston: Beacon Press, 1992), p. 49.

4. Ibid., p. 50.

5. Ibid., p. 53.

6. Ibid., p. 55.

7. For the origin and translation of this list, see Ian MacLean, *The Renaissance Notion of Woman* (Cambridge: Cambridge University Press, 1980), pp. 2–3. Wittig incorporates the list in her essay "Homo Sum," pp. 49–50.

8. See Charles Molesworth, "Property and Virtue: The Genre of the Country House Poem," *Genre* 1 (1968): 141–57, and Rosalie Colie, *My Echoing Song: Andrew Marvell's Poetry of Criticism* (Princeton: Princeton University Press, 1970), pp. 282–83.

9. Jim Swan, "'Betwixt Two Labyrinths': Andrew Marvell's Rational Amphibian," *Texas Studies in Literature and Language* 17 (1975): 566.

10. Harry Berger, Jr., "Marvell's 'Upon Appleton House': An Interpretation," *Southern Review* 1 (1965): 7.

11. Charles Molesworth, "Marvell's 'Upon Appleton House': The Persona as Historian, Philosopher, and Priest," *SEL* 13 (1973): 149–62.

12. Harold Skulsky, "'Upon Appleton House': Marvell's Comedy of Discourse," *ELH* 52 (1985): 617.

13. Jim Swan writes about the connection between family history and poetic quest: "In many ways the poem is an attempt to work through the pain of separation and death implied in the experience of family continuity, particularly as it is envisioned in the midst of a breakdown in the continuity of the body politic." "'Betwixt Two Labyrinths': Andrew Marvell's Rational Amphibian," 552.

14. *Discours, figure* (Paris: Klincksieck, 1971) p. 378, in *Introducing Lyotard*, trans. Bill Readings (London: Routledge, 1991), p. 26.

15. Colie plays with the biblical reduction: "Only if the fundamental reference is inverted and all grass becomes flesh, does the rail's significance, so much greater than the creature itself, begin to emerge." *My Echoing Song*, p. 260.

16. Harolid Toliver calls the women "clearly more dangerous in their heterosexuality than the subtle nuns who tempt the 'Virgin Thwates.'" *Marvell's Ironic Vision* (New Haven: Yale University Press, 1965), pp. 166–67.

17. Wittig, "Homo Sum," p. 55.

18. Jane Hedley, *Power in Verse: Metaphor and Metonymy in the Renaissance Lyric* (University Park: Pennsylvania State University Press, 1988), pp. 1–13.

19. Leslie Dunn, "Ophelia's Songs in *Hamlet*: Music, Madness, and the Feminine," presented at the MLA convention, December 1990, p. 6.

20. Rosalie Colie writes, "It is unclear whether he contrives to capture any of the fish. He fishes childishly: his lures are Toyes." *My Echoing Song*, p. 246.

21. Lynn Enterline sees this marginalization as "self-reflexive and self-destructive," arguing that, in "Appleton House," Marvell "tries as he did in 'The Garden,' to dissolve the boundary between the speaking subject and the 'objects' of his figurative landscape." See "The Mirror and the Snake: The Case of Marvell's Unfortunate Lover," *Critical Quarterly* 29 (1987): 105. But Enterline does view the intrusion of Maria as antipoetic: "Thus the vertiginous, unanchored transformation in the poem blurring the distinction between within and without, between the observing and the observed *and* the self-reflexive lament of the I, both cease when femininity comes on the scene." "The Mirror and the Snake," p. 107.

22. Robert Cummings, "The Forest Sequence in Marvell's 'Upon Appleton House,'" *Huntington Library Quarterly* 47 (1984): 183.

23. Ruth Salvaggio, "Theory and Space, Space and Woman," p. 278.

Musing Afterward

1. For a discussion of the river as microcosm, see Leonard Barkan, *Nature's Work of Art: The Human Body as Image of the World* (New Haven: Yale University Press, 1975), p. 250.

2. Charles Altieri's phrase in *Painterly Abstraction in Modernist American Poetry* (Cambridge: Cambridge University Press, 1989), p. 211.

3. Mary Jo Salter, "A Poem of One's Own," *The New Republic*, March 4, 1991, p. 31.

4. Thomas Greene, "The Poetics of Discovery: A Reading of Donne's 'Elegy 19,'" *Yale Journal of Criticism* 2 (1989): 132.

5. Leslie Donn, "Ophelia's Songs in *Hamlet*: Music, Madness, and the Feminine," presented at the MLA convention, December 1990, p. 6.

6. Wallace Stevens, *Opus Posthumous* (New York: Knopf, 1957), p. 85.

7. Jessica Benjamin, "A Desire of One's Own: Psychoanalytic Feminism and Intersubjective Space," in *Feminist Studies / Critical Studies*, ed. Teresa de Lauretis (Bloomington: Indiana University Press, 1986), p. 98.

8. Kazimir Malevich, as quoted in exhibit flyer for *Kazimir Malevich*, Metropolitan Museum of Art, February 12 through March 24, 1991, unpaginated.

9. Monique Wittig, "Homo Sum," in *The Straight Mind and Other Essays* (Boston: Beacon Press, 1992), p. 55.

10. John Bowitt, "Kazimir Malevich and the Energy of Language," in *Kazimir*

Malevich, ed. Jeanne D'Andrea (Los Angeles: The Armand Hammer Museum of Art, 1990), p. 180.

11. "Kazimir Malevich and the Energy of Language," p. 186.

12. Exhibit flyer for *Kazimir Malevich*.

13. Barbara Correll, "Notes on the Primary Text: Woman's Body and Representation in *Pumping Iron II* and 'Breast Giver,'" *Genre* 22 (1989): 287.

14. Lyotard, *The Post-Modern Condition: A Report on Knowledge*, trans. Geoff Bennington and Brian Massumi (Minneapolis: University of Minnesota Press, 1984), p. 81.

15. Correll, "Notes on the Primary Text," 307.

16. Hélène Cixous, "The Laugh of the Medusa," trans. Keith Cohen and Paula Cohen, in *New French Feminisms*, ed. Elaine Marks and Isabelle de Courtivron (New York: Schoken, 1981), p. 258.

17. Adrienne Rich, "Turning," *Time's Power* (New York: Norton, 1988), p. 54.

18. David Kalstone, *Five Temperaments: Elizabeth Bishop, Robert Lowell, James Merrill, Adrienne Rich, John Ashbery* (New York: Oxford, 1977), p. 6.

19. Ibid., p. 7.

20. Adrienne Rich, "When We Dead Awaken," in *On Lies, Secrets, and Silence: Selected Prose, 1966–1978* (New York: Norton, 1979), p. 39.

21. Kalstone, *Five Temperaments*, p. 8.

22. Janet Malcolm, "Annals of Biography," *New Yorker*, August 23 and 30, 1993, p. 84.

23. Adrienne Rich, *Atlas of a Difficult World* (New York: Norton, 1991), p. 29.

24. Dale B. J. Randall maintains that there is a "strong possibility" that "the right reading" of the last line of "Coy Mistress" is "grates," a reading that goes back, through Tennyson, to William Popple, Marvell's nephew and editor. See "An Old Crux and a New Reading of 'To His Coy Mistress,'" in *On the Celebrated and Neglected Poems of Andrew Marvell*, ed. Claude J. Summers and Ted-Larry Pebworth (Columbia: University of Missouri Press, 1992), p. 48.

INDEX

Adam-Eve, 12, 41–60, 66, 118, 158–61,
  193–98, 249–50, 252, 286
Alighieri, Dante, *Rime petrose*, 84
Alpers, Paul, 231
Altieri, Charles, 324 n.76, 339 n.2
Aristotle, 281–82
Asp, Carolyn, 337 n.10

Babington, Gervase, 330 n.14
Bahti, Timothy, 61, 67–68, 83,
  326 nn.3, 11
Bal, Mieke, 29–30, 41, 42, 48, 172, 181
Baltrusaitis, Jurgis, 319 nn.5, 19
Barkan, Leonard, 126, 326 n.15,
  329 n.11, 331 n.23, 339 n.1
Baruch, Elaine Hoffmann, 335 n.7,
  337 n.9
Baumlin, James, 21, 35, 36, 183,
  331 n.22, 334 n.11
Beckett, Samuel, *Krapp's Last Tape*,
  263
Bell, Ilona, 149–52, 157, 333 nn. 4, 19
Benjamin, Jessica, 8–9, 313
Benjamin, Walter, 5, 6
Bennington, Geoff, 321 n.34, 340 n.14
Berger, Harry, Jr., 261, 275, 283
Bergin, Thomas, 325 n.13
Berti, Luciano, 336 n.9
Bible: Genesis 1, 44, 154, 155, 160, 213,
  214, 218, 284–85, 293; Genesis 2, 12,
  29–30, 41, 42, 44, 51–53, 69, 119,
  154, 158, 181, 193–94, 213, 215, 243,
  249, 285, 286, 293, 308; Genesis 3, 51,
  66, 158, 243, 286, 293, 308; Isaiah,
  65, 101, 102; Revelations 4, 218
Bordone, Paris, *A Pair of Lovers*, 1–9,
  60, 154, 315

Borges, Jorge Luis, "The Revenge of the
  Mirror People," 33–34, 230
Bowitt, John, 339 n.10
Braden, Gordon, 11, 270, 319 n.2,
  320 n.21, 327 n.14, 332 n.5, 333 n.16
Brown, Norman O., 328 n.3
Bruno, Giordano, 126–27
Butler, Judith, 63, 185, 241, 282, 303;
  Bodies That Matter, 15–16, 27, 28,
  35, 37–38, 55, 62, 66, 74, 127, 152,
  195, 267; *Gender Trouble*, 15–16, 18–
  20, 27, 37, 60, 73, 299, 315, 321 n.35;
  "Imitation and Gender Insubordina-
  tion," 23, 26–27, 30, 32–33, 313

Carey, John, 322 n.52, 334 n.9
Carroll, Lewis, 292
Cathcart, Dwight, 332 n.9, 333 n.12
Chaucer, Geoffrey, *The Canterbury
  Tales*, 101
Cixous, Hélène, 33, 34, 92, 214, 242,
  324 n.77
Claridge, Laura, 25
Cohen, Keith, 340 n.16
Cohen, Paula, 340 n.16
Colie, Rosalie, 15, 17, 20, 165, 335 n.9,
  338 nn. 8, 15, 339 n.20
Cook, Albert, 204
Cool, Kenneth, 270
Coover, Robert, 5
Correll, Barbara, 315, 321 n.35,
  340 n.13
Coverdale, Miles, 158–62, 170, 171
Crewe, Jonathan, 96, 106, 123, 137,
  138, 145, 328 n.2, 329 n.22
Crutwell, Patrick, 330 n.1
Cummings, Robert, 299

Dasenbrock, Reed Way, 34, 93
Davis, Natalie Ziemon, 332 n.6
de Man, Paul, 149
Deming, Robert H., 329 n.10
Docherty, Thomas, 31–32, 35, 334 n.18
Doctorow, E. L., *Ragtime*, 304, 311
Dollimore, Jonathan, 26
Donne, Ann, 150
Donne, John
  poetry: "Broken Heart, The," 36,
    132, 152–58, 162–67, 174–79, 181,
    190, 204, 233, 240; "Dreame, The,"
    36, 60, 179–82, 191–202, 221, 310,
    312, 313; "Elegy: Change," 29, 36,
    37, 152, 200–203, 212–23, 255–56,
    258–60, 277–79, 282, 302, 303, 307–9,
    310, 312, 315, 318; "Elegy: To his
    Mistris Going to Bed," 1, 10, 24–25;
    "Extasie, The," 155, 201, 221; "Fu-
    nerall, The," 152, 180–82, 186–93,
    197, 198, 233, 257; "Jeat Ring Sent,
    A," 152, 180–87, 191–94, 198, 275;
    "Relique, The," 188; "A Valediction:
    Forbidding Mourning," 204; "A
    Valediction: Of My Name in the
    Window," 201–13, 219–21; "A Vale-
    diction: Of Weeping," 36, 152, 153,
    156–58, 167, 168, 170–79, 181, 221
  prose: "Christmas Day Sermon,
    1624, The," 154–55, 158–60, 162,
    218; "Why doe Woemen delight so
    much in Feathers," 213–14
Draper, William H., 325 n.8
Dunn, Leslie, 297–98, 312, 321 nn.35,
  37
Durling, Robert, 11, 325 nn.10, 11,
  332 n.3

Easthope, Anthony, 322 nn.52, 53
Eliot, T. S., "The Love Song of J. Alfred
  Prufrock," 146
Ellman, Mary, 262
Empson, William, 322 n.52, 331 n.25
Enterline, Lynn, 339 n.21
Eyck, Jan van, *The Ghent Altar-Piece*,
  241, 247–54

Felman, Shoshana, 321 n.42
Ferry, Anne, 30, 32, 33, 113, 327 n.3
Fineman, Joel, 10, 327 n.2
Fish, Stanley, 334 n.19

Fisher, Sheila, 14, 330 n.8
Franco, Veronica, 14, 256
Freccero, John, 325 nn.5, 9, 331 n.23
Freedman, Donald, 329 n.6
Freud, Sigmund, 7
Friedman, Donald, 335 n.6
Fumerton, Patricia, 28, 33, 180, 265
Fuss, Diane, 26, 323 n.54

Gardner, Helen, 213
Gogh, Vincent van, 22–23, 33, 278, 313
Goldberg, Jonathan, 16, 19, 36, 41, 152,
  260, 261, 275, 320 n.9, 332 n.28,
  337 n.10
Greenblatt, Stephen, 110, 137, 319 n.5,
  327 n.3
Greene, Roland, 29, 111, 322 n.44,
  328 n.16
Greene, Thomas, 30–33, 312, 322 n.52
Grennan, Joseph E., 331 n.20
Griswold, Wendy, 258
Guillen, Claudio, 35
Guss, Donald, 327 n.7

Hageman, Elizabeth, 321 n.24
Hagstrum, Jean, 336 n.9
Halasz, Alexandra, 93, 95, 110, 111,
  122, 123, 328 n.2
Halley, Janet, 14, 149–52
Hartley, L. P., 320 n.22
Hartman, Geoffrey, 260, 275, 338 n.18
Hedley, Jane, 297, 322 n.44
Heilbrun, Carolyn, 262
Heng, Geraldine, 18, 26
Herbert, George: "Love III," 51;
  "Prayer," 28
Herz, Judith Scherer, 16
Hinz, Evelyn J., 337 n.8
Hirsch, David A. Hedrich, 331 n.21
Hodgdon, Barbara, 63
Holbein, Hans, *The Ambassadors*, 4–5,
  61, 284
Hughes, Olwyn, 149
Hulse, Clark, 324 n.68
Humphries, Rolfe, 332 n.2
Hunt, John Dixon, 335–36 n.9

Ibsen, Henrik, *When We Dead
  Awaken*, 64
Innes, Mary, 326 n.5
Irigaray, Luce, 7, 8, 222, 223

Irving, John, *The World According to Garp*, 263

Jobes, Gertrude, 325 n.12
Johnson, Barbara, 201, 326 n.6
Jones, Ann Rosalind, 14, 150, 256, 321 n.43, 323 n.62
Jordan, Constance, 14
Jowett, B., 325 n.3

Kalstone, David, 315
Kerrigan, John, 327 nn.3, 4
Kerrigan, William, 153, 202–3, 280, 332 n.5, 333 n.16

Labé, Louise, 14, 256
Langland, Elizabeth, 25
Legouis, Pierre, 333 n.19
Leishman, J. B., 333 n.13
Lensi, Alfredo, 336 n.9
Lentricchia, Frank, 25
Leonard, Nancy, 327 n.3
Lewalski, Barbara, 14
Linche, Richard, *The Fountaine of Ancient Fiction*, 228–32, 235
Longus, *Daphnis and Chloë*, 1, 3, 5, 7, 9, 25
Low, Anthony, 106
Lowell, Robert, "Epilogue," *Day by Day*, 151, 226
Lydon, Mary, 322 n.49
Lyotard, Jean-François, 6, 19, 26, 32–34, 125, 303, 313; *The Differend: Phrases in Dispute*, 15–17, 19, 21–22, 33, 61, 138, 146, 154, 298, 328 n.17; *Discours, figure*, 4, 284; "Dream-Work Does Not Think, The," 22, 28, 30, 35, 55, 61, 81, 151, 240, 305, 313, 318; *Post-Modern Condition, The*, 17, 340 n.14; *Postmodern Explained, The*, 10

Macfie, Pamela Royston, 123, 124, 328 n.2
MacLean, Ian, 338 n.7
Malcolm, Janet, 149, 150–51, 316
Malevich, Kazimir, 313–14
Marotti, Arthur, 333 n.18, 334 n.8
Martz, Louis, 336 n.9
Marvell, Andrew: "Damon the Mower," 36, 227, 231–41, 252–55; "Gallery, The," 36, 227, 228, 230, 239–55, 280, 287; "Garden, The," 108, 246, 259, 262, 279–81, 299, 307, 308; "Nymph complaining for the death of her Faun, The," 36, 227, 255–78, 309, 312, 313, 318; "On a Drop of Dew," 276, 300; "To His Coy Mistress," 258–59, 262, 276, 307; "Upon Appleton House," 11, 36, 37, 227, 228, 259, 277–303, 305–8, 312, 315, 318; "Upon the Death of Lord Hastings," 255, 257–59
Marx, Groucho, 218
Massumi, Brian, 321 n.34, 340 n.14
Mathews, F. X., 337 n.13
Mazzotta, Giuseppe, 41, 58, 61, 67–68, 77, 79, 326 n.13
Middleton, John, *The Changeling*, 186
Milton, John, *Samson Agonistes*, 95; *Paradise Lost*, 194
Molesworth, Charles, 283, 338 n.8
Moore, George, 320 n.12
Mueller, Janel, 149, 181
Muir, Kenneth, 138

Nagy, Gregory, 127
Neely, Carol Thomas, 15, 154
Nelli, René, 319 n.3
Newton, Esther, 27

Olson, Roberta J. M., 336 n.9
Ormiston, Gayle, 20
Ovid: *Amores*, 180; *Metamorphoses*: Actaeon-Diana, 63, 65, 123, 125–27, 132, 136–40, 257–65, 271, 274, 306; Apollo-Daphne, 10, 11, 12, 14, 24, 66, 85, 220, 306–8; Battus-Mercury, 12–14, 63–65; Diana-Agamemnon, 257, 264, 271–77; Narcissus, 139, 235, 306

Panja, Shormishtha, 110, 327 n.3
Panofsky, Erwin, 336 n.13
Parker, Patricia, 159, 325 n.4
Patterson, Annabel, 330 n.9
Pausanias, 127
Pefanis, Julian, 33, 230
Petrarch, Francis: *Africa*: 20; *Rime sparse* 1: 142, 157, 257, 261; *Rime sparse* 19: 114–16; *Rime sparse* 23: 9, 12–14, 23, 37, 60–70, 75, 81, 82,

Petrarch, Francis (*cont.*)
85–88, 90, 311–13, 317, 318; *Rime sparse* 105: 12, 14, 23, 60, 61, 69–77, 80–81, 85–87, 89, 90, 163; *Rime sparse* 106: 23, 14, 70, 87, 88; *Rime sparse* 125: 9, 12, 60, 61, 68–70, 75–78, 80, 81, 85–87, 89; *Rime sparse* 126: 9, 12, 60, 68–70, 75, 76, 78–81, 83, 85–87, 89, 90; *Rime sparse* 127: 9, 12, 60, 61, 68–70, 75, 76, 79–82, 85–87, 89, 90; *Rime sparse* 129: 9, 12, 60, 61, 68–70, 75, 76, 80–90, 153, 156–57, 167–70, 176; *Rime sparse* 135: 107; *Rime sparse* 140: 133–34; *Rime sparse* 153: 104; *Rime sparse* 181: 9, 12, 43, 50–54, 56, 58–60; *Rime sparse* 188: 9, 12, 43, 50, 51, 54–56, 58–60; *Rime sparse* 189: 112–14; *Rime sparse* 190: 133, 138–40; *Rime sparse* 191: 140; *Rime sparse* 237: 9, 12, 43–51, 53, 58–61, 283; *Rime sparse* 265: 100, 102, 264, 276; *Rime sparse* 354: 9, 12, 43, 50, 51, 56–60; *Rime sparse* 359: 69, 88, 180, 190; *Secretum, The*, 43–45, 154
Philips, Lotte Brand, 248
Picasso, Pablo, *Ma Jolie*, 97
Plath, Sylvia, 149
Plato, 41, 214, 281; *The Symposium*, 41–42
Poe, Edgar Allan, "The Raven," 203
Praz, Mario, 333 n.15

Quarles, Francis, 335 n.9
Quilligan, Maureen, 14

Radzinowicz, Mary Ann, 322 n.52
Rajan, Tilottama, 332 n.27
Randall, Dale B. J., 340 n.24
Readings, Bill, 23, 319 n.5, 328 n.17, 338 n.14
Rebholz, R. A., 138
Rich, Adrienne, 324 n.79; "Contradictions Tracking Poems," 29, 38; "She," 315–18
Ricks, Christopher, 153, 181, 322 n.52, 333 n.19
Riley, Denise, 16–17, 35–36, 152, 335 n.1
Rivero, Albert J., 331 n.24
Rogers, John, 331 n.14

Rose, Jacqueline, 149
Rosen, David, 327 n.6

Salter, Mary Jo, 311–12
Salvaggio, Ruth, 223, 321 nn. 35, 38, 324 n.78, 333 n.17, 338 n.1, 339 n.23
Santayana, George, 209
Scarry, Elaine, 203, 333 n.4, 334 n.7
Secundus, Joannes, "The First Kiss," 268–69
Sedgwick, Eve, 9, 178
Shakespeare, William: *Antony and Cleopatra*, 130–31, 132; *Hamlet*, 21, 32, 33, 255, 258–59; *King Lear*, 258; *Merchant of Venice*, 101; *Midsummer Night's Dream, A*, 13–14, 229; *Much Ado About Nothing*, 79, 304, 314; *Richard II*, 4, 237; *Romeo and Juliet*, 88, 171, 264–65; "Sonnet 65," 272–73; "Sonnet 116," 183; "Sonnet 129," 215; "Sonnet 130," 158–59; *Twelfth Night*, 126, 127; *Two Gentlemen of Verona*, 148, 178–79, 182, 257, 310; *Winter's Tale, The*, 166–67, 260, 262–63
Shapiro, Marianne, 42–43
Sidney, Philip: "Astrophil and Stella 1," 27–29, 32, 34; "Astrophil and Stella 38," 192; "Ye gote-herd gods," 190
Silberman, Lauren, 327 n.10
Silverman, Kaja, 321 nn. 35, 36, 326 n.8
Skulsky, Harold, 283
Smith, Bruce, 324 n.68
Smith, Paul, 25
Spenser, Edmund, *The Faerie Queene*, 157, 160–64, 167, 219, 291
Spinrad, Phoebe, 246, 336 n.9
Stallybrass, Peter, 323 n.62
Stampfer, Judah, 333 nn. 11, 12
Stevens, Wallace, 36, 40, 309–11; "An Ordinary Evening in New Haven," 36; "Desire & the Object," 313; "Rock, The," 39, 310; "So-and-So Reclining on Her Couch," 311; "To an Old Philosopher in Rome," 309
Strand, Mark, 305, 307
Sturm-Maddox, Sara, 4, 325 nn.7, 13
Swan, Jim, 283, 338 n.13

Teunissen, John J., 337 n.8
Thomson, Patricia, 138
Titian, *The Death of Actaeon*, 127
Toliver, Harold, 335 n.8, 339 n.16
Twombley, Robert G., 328 n.15

Van den Abeele, G., 321 n.29
Van Eyck, Jan. *See* Eyck, Jan van
Van Gogh. *See* Gogh, Vincent van
Velázquez, Diego de, *Las Meninas*, 175
Vickers, Nancy, 4, 11, 14, 58, 137,
    325 n.5

Waller, Marguerite, 14, 110–11, 123,
    137–39, 151, 325 n.7, 328 n.2
Ward, James O., 319 n.1
Waters, Alyson, 319 n.3
Webster, John, *The Duchess of Malfi*,
    260, 262–64
White, Hayden, 35
Wilson, Scott W., 334 n.10
Wittig, Monique, 37, 281, 282, 313,
    339 n.17
Woolf, Virginia, 59

Wyatt, Sir Thomas: "Go, burning
    sighs," 95, 104–6, 146, 232; "Long
    love, The," 36, 123, 125, 133–36,
    145, 270; "My galley charg'd with
    forgetfulness," 112–13; "My lute
    awake," 95–100, 257; *Penitential
    Psalms, The*, 36, 93–95, 109–23, 125,
    132; "Process of time," 95, 100–104,
    108, 146, 232, 276–77; "She sat and
    sewed," 123–25, 132, 144, 145;
    "Some fowls there be," 114–16;
    "They flee from me," 36, 60, 93–95,
    103, 109, 123, 125, 128–34, 136, 144–
    46, 177, 180, 193, 313, 315; "What
    word is that," 106–7; "When first
    mine eyes," 95, 98–100; "Whoso list
    to hunt," 29, 36, 37, 123, 125, 133,
    136–46, 152–54, 177, 255–56, 258,
    276, 278, 282, 302, 307, 308, 310, 312,
    318; "Will ye see what wonders,"
    95, 107–9, 312

Yeats, W. B., "Supernatural Songs,"
    212

About the Author

Barbara L. Estrin is Professor of English
and Department Chair at Stonehill College.
She is the author of *The Raven and the Lark:
Lost Children in Literature of the English
Renaissance* and numerous articles on a
variety of topics ranging from Renaissance
poetry and drama to contemporary
fiction and poetry.

Library of Congress Cataloging-in-Publication Data

Estrin, Barbara L., 1942–
Laura : uncovering gender and genre in Wyatt, Donne, and
Marvell / Barbara L. Estrin.
p.   cm. — (Post-contemporary interventions)
Includes bibliographical references and index.
ISBN 0-8223-1500-9 (alk. paper). — ISBN 0-8223-1499-1 (pbk. : alk. paper)
1. English poetry—Early modern, 1500–1700—History and criticism.
2. Love poetry, English—Men authors—History and criticism.
3. Women and literature—England—History—16th century.   4. Women
and literature—England—History—17th century.   5. Wyatt, Thomas,
Sir, 1503?–1542—Characters—Women.   6. Marvell, Andrew, 1621–1678—
Characters—Women.   7. Donne, John, 1572–1631—Characters—Women.
8. English poetry—Italian influences.   9. Sex role in literature.
10. Literary form.   I. Title.   II. Series.
PR535.L7E88   1994
811'.309354—dc20   94-13794   CIP